Familiar Perversions

Familiar Perversions

The Racial, Sexual, and Economic Politics of LGBT Families

LIZ MONTEGARY

Rutgers University Press

New Brunswick, Camden, and Newark, New Jersey, and London

Library of Congress Cataloging-in-Publication Data

Names: Montegary, Liz, author.
Title: Familiar perversions : the racial, sexual, and economic politics of LGBT families /
Liz Montegary.
Description: New Brunswick : Rutgers University Press, [2018] | Includes bibliographical
references and index.
Identifiers: LCCN 2017055196 | ISBN 9780813591360 (cloth : alk. paper) |
ISBN 9780813591353 (pbk. : alk. paper)
Subjects: LCSH: Gay parents—United States. | Sexual minorities' families—United
States. | Families—United States. | Family policy—United States. | Equality—United States. |
Gay rights—United States.
Classification: LCC HQ75.28.U6 M66 2018 | DDC 306.874086/64—dc23
LC record available at https://lccn.loc.gov/2017055196

A British Cataloging-in-Publication record for this book is available from the British Library.

An earlier and much shorter version of chapter 1 appeared as "'Like Nowhere Else': Imagining Provincetown for the Lesbian and Gay Family," in *Tourism Imaginaries at the Disciplinary Crossroads: Place, Practice, Media*, edited by Maria Gravari-Barbas and Nelson Graburn,
180–194 (Farnham: Ashgate, 2016). Reprinted with permission.

A shorter version of chapter 2 was published as "Cruising to Equality: Tourism, U.S.
Homonationalism, and the Lesbian and Gay Family Market," *WSQ: At Sea* 45, no. 1/2 (2017).
Reprinted with permission.

∞ The paper used in this publication meets the requirements of the American National
Standard for Information Sciences—Permanence of Paper for Printed Library Materials,
ANSI Z39.48-1992.

www.rutgersuniversitypress.org

Manufactured in the United States of America

For Nanny Scoop

Contents

Familiar Perversions

Introduction

••••••••••••••••••••••

Familiar Perversions

This is a book about lesbian, gay, bisexual, and transgender (LGBT) families; national politics; sexuality; capitalism; and race in the United States. It is about the ways activists, marketing experts, and government officials talk about and advocate for families described as LGBT, and it is about the kinds of claims parents and children from these families make on the state, the marketplace, and the general public in the name of social justice and "family equality." A relatively new cultural formation, the LGBT family emerged as a concept in the late 1990s out of a long history of lesbian and gay parenting activism.[1] The term is meant to signal family formations in which one or more lesbian-, gay-, bisexual-, or transgender-identified adult is parenting a child but is often used to refer specifically to committed same-sex couples living together and raising children who legally belong to them. Over the past few decades, LGBT families have gradually become more visible within U.S. political and popular culture.

In 2009, President Barack Obama assumed office and pledged to "do more to support and strengthen LGBT families," and he kicked off his first term by inviting children with lesbian or gay parents to participate in the annual Easter Egg Roll (Family Equality Council 2009b; Bellantoni 2009). In 2012, the White House concluded its first ever LGBT conference series with a special event on the health and safety issues facing parents and their children. In 2014, at the inaugural gala dinner of the American Military Partners Association, a senior Pentagon official applauded the contributions of lesbian and gay military families and explained how the Department of Defense planned to make its family readiness programs more inclusive (Lyle 2014). Today, Hallmark

1

offers a gay-friendly line of Mother's and Father's Day cards (White 2014; Wong 2014); major corporations, including Chevy, Nabisco, and Coca-Cola, have aired commercials featuring same-sex couples and their children;[2] and popular television shows like *Modern Family*, *The Fosters*, and *Transparent* revolve around the lives of gay, lesbian, and transgender parents, respectively. Most recently and perhaps most significantly, when the Supreme Court issued its landmark decision legalizing same-sex marriage, concern for the emotional and financial well-being of lesbian and gay families was a centerpiece of the decision. What was once an impossibility—the juxtaposition of "LGBT" and "family" as anything more than an oxymoron—is now a fairly commonplace sight.

Familiar Perversions tells the story of how we arrived at this moment. What has made possible the destabilization of long-standing perceptions of homosexuality as the antithesis to the family and a threat to life more broadly? How, in such a short span of time, have we gone from queers dying in the streets at the height of the AIDS crisis to queers raising children and buying family homes in the age of marriage equality?[3] How did the LGBT family become a legible and increasingly legitimate cultural formation? In this book, I trace a loosely chronological path through the recent history of LGBT family advocacy work, moving across the distinct yet overlapping arenas of lesbian and gay community-building projects, popular and consumer culture, national-level policy debates and legislative decisions, and (financial) health promotion initiatives. Put another way, I offer an account of the rise of the LGBT family.

But make no mistake: this book is not an uncritical celebration of the recognition now afforded to LGBT families of a particular stripe. I do not interpret the growing visibility of middle-class LGBT households headed by married white couples as evidence that homophobia has receded and given way to a postgay era in which civil rights and full equality have finally been achieved. Rather, I take as my starting point the fact that the struggle to align queerness with reproductive and national futurity takes place amid expanded forms of state violence and exacerbated economic inequalities. The integration of a select class of lesbian and gay families into the national imaginary has occurred alongside and in relation to the continued dismantling of the welfare state; the ongoing Islamophobic wars on terror; the perpetuation of national and global health insecurities; the intensified policing of poor, nonwhite, and immigrant communities; and the expansion of racial profiling, mass incarceration, and detention and deportation efforts.

By situating the recent successes of LGBT family politics within this broader context, *Familiar Perversions* contributes to a more capacious understanding of how, at the turn of the twenty-first century, the expansion of rights for same-sex couples and protections for lesbian- and gay-identified individuals has accompanied the intensification of racial and economic violence. How do we account for the fact that the alignment of queerness with marriage, parenthood, and family life has neither interrupted the capitalist state's methods of social control nor significantly transformed the sexual and racial borders of U.S. citizenship? How do we make sense of the ways in which the gradual incorporation of certain LGBT families into the imagined nation has only consolidated economic disparities and exacerbated racialized vulnerabilities?

Queer Cultural Studies and LGBT Families

Despite the extensive body of work on "reproductive futurity" and the state of queer politics in the United States,[4] the LGBT family has received remarkably little attention within recent queer studies analyses of U.S. lesbian and gay rights organizing.[5] This is not, however, to suggest there is a dearth of scholarly work on LGBT-identified parents and their children. In fact, there is a substantial body of scholarship that has contributed to the transformation of the LGBT family into a respectable social formation. Psychologists and sociologists have been studying lesbian and gay family life for the past three decades with a vested interest in gathering evidence of positive parenting outcomes in same-sex-headed households and debunking perceptions of homosexuals as unfit for parenthood.[6] Qualitative social scientists have, in turn, offered ethnographic accounts of how LGBT-identified parents and their children negotiate the traditional terms of kinship to consolidate their own familial relations.[7]

While this research focuses on the psychological and interpersonal dynamics of LGBT families in the hopes of making these alternative kinship arrangements visible as normal, healthy, and distinctly (post)modern family forms, there is also a related set of scholarship concerned directly with the politics and politicization of LGBT families in the United States. *Familiar Perversions* is indebted to this small but incredibly rich body of work, which documents the ways in which LGBT-identified parents and their children have tried to resist and rework heteropatriarchal familial standards in their everyday lives and as a part of broader social movements.[8] Additionally, this book is informed by the work of legal scholars and political theorists whose astute and visionary analyses of how lesbian and gay families function within public policy and the law have clarified my thinking on the relationship between queer politics and family life.[9] Placing this body of work in conversation with queer of color critique and other recent queer studies scholarship, I take a closer look at the last twenty years of national-level LGBT family advocacy in order to ask what these cultural practices reveal about the politics of race, sexuality, and the family in the contemporary United States.

By placing parents and their children at the center of my analysis of mainstream LGBT rights organizing, *Familiar Perversions* offers new insights into the recent reconfiguration of lesbian and gay political agendas and the uneven yet persistent attempt to reconcile a certain brand of queerness with domesticity and reproductivity. In many ways, I see this book as picking up where the cultural anthropologist Kath Weston left off in her now canonical *Families We Choose* (1991). Writing about the late 1980s, a moment when lesbians and gay men were starting to become parents in more visible and intentional ways, she concluded her book by asking what this new embrace of parenthood and family life might mean for the future of queer politics, especially in the face of what appeared to be a rising conservative family values movement. *Familiar Perversions* sets out to understand why, and with what ramifications, Weston's concerns have proved to be well-founded. Why have the most well-resourced LGBT organizations abandoned queer efforts to transform the meaning of family and started seeking, instead, recognition for same-sex kinship formations according to normative familial standards? What accounts for the recent successes enjoyed by the family equality movement and other assimilatory LGBT advocacy projects? And most pressingly, what have been the unintended effects of achieving ostensibly more inclusive versions of marriage law and family-centric public policy?

Adopting a cultural studies approach to the examination of LGBT family politics (a method that both departs from and builds on the classic style of ethnographic inquiry exemplified in Weston's work[10]), I try to answer these questions by assembling an extensive archive of primary materials dealing with, working against, or gesturing toward the LGBT family. This archive spans a range of textual sources, such as legal documents, marketing data, activist publications, government reports, public policy studies, and news media accounts, and includes my participant observation research in LGBT family-building seminars, at family-centric community events, and even aboard Rosie O'Donnell's gay family cruise. Using these materials as my starting point, I aim to make sense of the ascendancy of the LGBT family by mapping the broader field of U.S. sexual politics at the turn of the twenty-first century—specifically, by tracking shifts in public opinion about same-sex relations, by charting changes in commonsensical perceptions of what the LGBT community wants and needs, by tracing the contours of debates among activists and within the broader public sphere about the proper relationship between queerness and the family, and by illuminating the ableist imagery and racialized economic logics that have historically organized and continue to organize such debates.

Moving beyond a strictly discursive mode of analysis, *Familiar Perversions* offers a model for doing queer cultural studies by engaging in the radical work of contextualization.[11] This is not to suggest that struggles over the meaning of same-sex desire and the representation of LGBT families are insignificant. In contrast, I understand discursive practices as a subtler mode of social control that operates alongside and often in tandem with more explicit forms of repression and domination. As the once widespread belief in homosexuality's inherent incompatibility with family life has begun to give way to the increasingly prevalent perception of LGBT-identified people as uniformly longing for marriage and parenthood, new criteria for evaluating same-sex sexual relations and for distinguishing between respectable and disreputable LGBT social formations have started to emerge. What the contextual moves of cultural studies bring to this discursive examination is a wider frame of analysis capable of accounting for the embeddedness of these new criteria in existing relations of power and their entanglement with various forms of state violence. This book situates the emergence of these newly configured modes of sexual control in relation to broader social, political, and economic contexts and with respect to the longer history of (homo)sexuality in the United States.

In the chapters that follow, I argue that the successes of the family equality movement are best understood as contingent on and constitutive of the reconfiguration of U.S. state formation, the remapping of racialized national borders, and the neoliberal reworking of the global economy. Bringing together the insights of Marxism, poststructuralist thought, and feminist and queer theory, I tease out the precise ways in which ostensibly progressive sexual politics have been mobilized to bolster the "scattered hegemonies" of patriarchal nationalisms, white supremacist capitalist structures, and normative standards of health, normalcy, and dis/ability.[12] My hope in writing this book is not simply to outline the limits and dangers of family equality advocacy but, in doing so, to offer a nuanced analysis of the racialized management of sex, perversity, and the family today. Without a clear understanding of the historical and contemporary contexts shaping the field of U.S. sexual politics, it will be impossible to build more transformative movements for racial, sexual, and economic justice. *Familiar Perversions* is thus my contribution to the ongoing work of imagining and reimagining LGBT family politics.

Family Equality Advocacy

Family equality advocacy is a rather new cultural phenomenon. To make such a claim, however, is not to erase the more than one-hundred-year history of homosexual parenting in the United States. Even though mainstream news media outlets and even the lesbian and gay press often treat parenting as a relatively new LGBT issue—a product of the "gayby boom" of the late 1980s and 1990s—people engaging in or fantasizing about engaging in same-sex erotic activities have been raising children since long before the invention of homosexuality as a concept in the late nineteenth century. Furthermore, lesbian and gay activists have been devising alternative kinship formations, advocating for racial and reproductive justice, and fighting for custodial rights and better health care for themselves and their children since the formation of a vibrant homosexual rights movement in the mid–twentieth century. What sets the twenty-first century apart from these earlier instantiations of familial politics, I argue, is the distilling of what had once been broad-based movements, defined by strategic alliances and a diversity of tactics, into a narrow identity politic centered on privatized and increasingly financialized forms of domesticity. Rather than working in solidarity with racially and economically marginalized families struggling in the face of welfare cuts, fewer public housing and education options, and less access to medical and mental health services, LGBT family advocates have, over the past two decades, focused almost exclusively on securing marriage, adoption, and other domestic rights for LGBT parents who are consistently portrayed as white, comfortably middle class, and uniformly able-bodied and able-minded.

Recent queer studies scholarship provides a useful framework for making sense of how, why, and with what effect calls for rights and recognition have supplanted an investment in coalition building and a politics of redistribution.[13] By situating the shifting priorities of activist movements with respect to broader social, political, and economic changes, this work collectively moves beyond simply diagnosing the complicities of contemporary LGBT rights activism. Instead, these cultural studies–informed projects illustrate the importance of studying how political arguments take shape in the public sphere and why advocacy strategies gain traction at particular historical conjunctures.[14] Building on this body of scholarship, each of the chapters in this book zeroes in on a different moment in the recent history of family-centric LGBT politics in order to contextualize the emergence and evolution of family equality advocacy and to explore the limits and possibilities of specific tactics and strategies. In the remainder of this section, I set the stage for the detailed analytical work that will follow by offering a more general critique of assimilatory rights-based agendas and the effects of organizing U.S.-based LGBT family politics around (neo)liberal inclusionary logics.

To begin, the mainstream lesbian and gay movement's adoption of pragmatic platforms focusing almost exclusively on incremental change and institutional inclusion must be understood in relation to the rearrangement of U.S. sexual politics under neoliberalism. What we have witnessed over the past few decades is the rerouting of lesbian and gay advocacy agendas through the neoliberal ideals of privatization and personal responsibility. The rise of what Lisa Duggan terms "homonormativity" has initiated a lesbian and gay rights movement that "does not contest dominant heteronormative assumptions and institutions but upholds and sustains them, while promising the possibility of a demobilized gay constituency and a privatized, depoliticized gay culture anchored in domesticity and consumption" (2003, 50). The resulting reinvigoration of respectability politics hinges on an imagined lesbian or gay subject who shows the utmost of respect for marriage and family life. In the process, new norms have emerged for distinguishing between deserving and undeserving queer subjects—that is, between individuals who are recognized as healthy and productive members of society and thus deserving of rights-based legal protections and those who are marked as dangerous or otherwise suspicious and thus undeserving of access to full and robust forms of citizenship. These new norms are organized, in large part, around new standards for same-sex relations. For LGBT-identified individuals who forge relationships closely aligned with the white middle-class ideal of the nuclear family, entrance into the rights and privileges of U.S. citizenship, albeit to varying extents, becomes a possibility. At the same time, these new standards instigate the further stigmatization of queers who cannot or who will not organize their lives around monogamy, long-term commitment, and privatized forms of domesticity. To borrow the words of Roderick Ferguson, white homonormative subjects gain access to a limited set of privileges at the expense of communities marginalized by raced, classed, and gendered regulations that deem them the "cultural antitheses of a stable and healthy social order" (2006, 65).

The place of parents and parenting activism within this reconfigured realm of sexual politics is, as the rest of this book will show, somewhat strange. While the lesbian or gay parent is often assumed to unambiguously occupy the position of homonormative subject par excellence, the persistence of anxieties about the relationship between queers and children and the myopic focus on individual identity-based rights (which cannot always address the needs of an entire family) have relegated parenting issues to the margins of mainstream organizing efforts. That said, family equality advocacy has most certainly played a role in the production of new norms for queerness and new standards for same-sex intimacies. To assuage deep-rooted concerns about allowing homosexuals in close proximity to children, advocates have relied on the expertise of supportive pediatricians, psychiatrists, psychologists, and other social science researchers to affirm the capacity of same-sex couples for parenthood and to assure all parties involved that the sexual identity of parents has no bearing on child-rearing outcomes.

To this end, family equality advocates have made a concerted effort to increase the visibility of respectable LGBT families. In some cases, advocates have pointed to the willingness of prospective parents to foster or adopt "hard-to-place" children—a category that, in the United States, refers to older children, children of color, and children with disabilities—as a way of marking LGBT families as particularly valuable. According to this narrative, the desire of same-sex couples to become parents is so strong that they exhibit a limitless degree of generosity and will eagerly take on the costs of caring for children with "special needs."[15] It is, however, an even more common practice for advocates to hold up happy, healthy, and heterosexual children who have been born into two-parent LGBT families via assisted reproductive technologies as material evidence of the capacity for same-sex couples to achieve normal familial life. This distorted image of LGBT parents as fairly wealthy, predominantly white, and intentionally planning families—an image bolstered by activist campaigns, marketing reports, and public policy debates—obscures the lived realities of a much wider range of families who might be described as LGBT.

Analyses of recent demographic data offer a more accurate depiction of the raced and classed experiences of LGBT-identified adults caring for children. Using findings from the 2000 census, legal scholars Gary J. Gates and Adam P. Romero conclude that African American and Latina women in same-sex couples were "more than twice as likely as their white counterparts to be rais-ing a child" and that African American and Latino men in same-sex couples were "four times as likely to be raising children as their white male counter-parts" (Gates and Romero 2009, 232). Their analyses also revealed that, con-trary to the popular assumption that LGBT families reside in northern urban centers, child rearing among LGBT-identified adults in the United States is "most common in Southern, Mountain West, and Midwest regions" (Gates 2013, 1): same-sex couples "who live in more socially and politically conser-vative areas are more likely than their counterparts living in more liberal areas to have children" (Gates and Romero 2009, 234).[16] Demographic data from the last five years confirm these racial and geographical trends and iden-tify the economic disparities continuing to inflict LGBT families. Same-sex couples raising children across racial and ethnic groups and regardless of their gender have lower median annual incomes: "Married or partnered LGBT individuals living in two-adult households with children are twice as likely as comparable non-LGBT individuals to report household incomes near the poverty threshold" (Gates 2013, 5). While Gates and Romero's data, based on reported age and stated relationships, suggest the prevalence of LGBT parent-ing arrangements resulting from children from previous relationships (2009, 235–236) or as extensions of multigenerational family ties (Rodríguez 2014, 40), even the most incisive analyses of census findings are unable to uncover the intricate and often improvised ways people build families, develop networks of care, and narrate their most intimate and important relationships. Children can, as Juana María Rodríguez reminds us, end up in LGBT-headed house-holds "through informal adoption within family and social networks" or as a result of "unplanned pregnancies and child rearing through casual (hetero)-sexual hookups" (2014, 40). Moreover, not all LGBT-identified people par-ent in pairs, not all parenting arrangements are confined to single households, and not all people who take on parenting roles as part of LGBT families, such as exes, lovers, friends, donors, surrogates, and birth parents, serve as full-time caretakers.

Family equality advocates and LGBT rights organizers are, by and large, not mobilizing in the service of these families and have, in the recent past, failed to adequately address the diverse array of queer family forms in the United

States. Instead, mainstream efforts tend to prioritize the interests of racially and economically privileged LGBT families and often base their calls for legal rights and state protections on gaining recognition as families according to hegemonic relational norms. In other words, they deploy the two-parent familial household as a route to political and cultural forms of citizenship, thus leaving the primacy of marital family formations intact and dominant relations of power unchallenged. The promise of a personally responsible lesbian and gay citizenry has coincided with a recoding of key terms from the history of progressive-left social movements: demands for "equality," for instance, have been disarticulated from racial and economic justice and the availability of material resources and are now about gaining "narrow, formal access to a few conservatizing institutions" (Duggan 2003, 65). While such efforts may improve the lives of families who are privileged enough to experience access to marriage and the marketplace as life-affirming gestures, the achievement of "family equality" in the form of increased visibility and individual rights does little to alleviate the precarity of families, queer or not, struggling in the face of a privatized economy and "a leaner, meaner government" (10). In fact, the desire for inclusion that drives what David Eng (2010) describes as "queer liberalism" depends on a disavowal of the racism organizing the liberal nation-state and the global economy. It is only possible to embrace the fantasy of legal equality as the most efficient (if not the only) path to sexual freedom if one refuses to acknowledge the ways in which rights-based projects expand and strengthen the structures of institutionalized violence that ensure the continuation of the United States as a settler state and an imperial force. Under the conditions of U.S. neoliberalism, Chandan Reddy (2011) argues, the pursuit of queer emancipation via juridical recognition is necessarily predicated on state violences enacted domestically and globally.

By seeking the benefits and protections afforded by the institution of U.S. citizenship,[17] LGBT family advocates have only further legitimated the mechanisms through which the state wages wars, militarizes its borders, imprisons large swaths of the population, and channels resources away from families and communities whose intimate social lives are deemed unruly and thus un-American. The forms of recognition now being extended to a limited class of LGBT families are the consequence of what Jasbir Puar calls "homonationalism"—that is, the convergence of historical and geopolitical forces that has created the conditions for a "shift in the production of nation-states from the insistence on heteronormativity to the increasing inclusion of homonormativity" (2013, 26).[18] In the United States, over the course of the late twentieth century and at an accelerated pace since the turn of the twenty-first, biopolitical practices of population control have begun to relocate select forms of queerness from "the side of death" to "the side of life" (35). The emergence of state projects and cultural practices designed to make homonormative citizen-subjects live serves as an alibi for the United States: the nation-state can then hold itself up as an exceptionally tolerant and sexually progressive democracy while still engaging in the violent work of sexual subjugation and imperial domination at home and abroad. Populations deemed racially, erotically, culturally, religiously, or economically perverse remain vulnerable to an increasingly brutal regime of U.S. state violence.

Building on Puar's theorization of homonationalism, *Familiar Perversions* joins other recent queer studies projects in offering a detailed account of the distinct yet overlapping modes of sexualized social control that either actively pursue the expulsion, subordination, or destruction of the racial or colonial other or, just as cruelly, abandon those populations to a perpetual state of dying.[19] While much of this work takes as its starting point the figures that have been marked for death via neoliberal forms of state and nonstate power, this book pivots attention to a figure that is increasingly being marked for life and, in doing so, offers new insights into contemporary modes of population control. By placing the LGBT family at the center of my analysis of the selective incorporation of queerness into U.S. national culture, I bring into focus the ways in which the work of sexual regulation currently requires not the squelching of same-sex desires but rather the routing of those desires through privatized marital family forms. The management of sexuality today, I argue, occurs not according to a hierarchical binary opposition between heterosexuality and homosexuality but through the subtler and strategic deployment of long-standing racialized relational norms.

The Familial Management of Perversity

In order to fully understand the rise of the LGBT family and the emergence of newly revised forms of social and sexual control, it is necessary to situate these developments in relation to the longer history of sexuality, familialism, and capitalism in the United States. To this end, the remainder of this introduction provides the historical context necessary to understand the stakes involved when LGBT households gain access to marriage and recognition as families. Within Western liberal democracies, the family exists neither as a natural or prepolitical formation nor as a private realm disconnected from the public sphere; rather, the family is best understood as an instrument of state power and a political-economic mechanism. As a cultural institution intended to organize individual desires around an investment in personal responsibility and reproductive futurity, the marital family serves the interests of capital, the U.S. settler state, and its imperial ambitions. More specifically, the family has historically functioned as a tool for policing, containing, and controlling ways of life deemed unnatural or abnormal. Looking back at the late nineteenth century, I begin by showing how earlier forms of racial and colonial domination gave way to what we might think of as the familial management of racialized perversities—that is, the casting of black, indigenous, and other non-Western European lives as perverse and the coercive imposition of nuclear family norms upon these populations. This section considers the emergence of racial knowledges and racialized modes of social control in relation to the establishment of monogamous couplehood and the single-family household as the national ideal and a structuring logic of U.S. empire.

The legacies of conquest and enslavement on which the United States is founded have a sexual politics. On the one hand, to make such a claim is to mark the sexual and reproductive violence central to these systems of domination.[20] On the other hand, an analysis of the sexualized dimensions of colonialism and slavery reveals how the dehumanization of indigenous and black bodies occurred in part through a refusal to recognize non-European practices of kinship and intimacy as legitimate social or familial forms. During the sixteenth and seventeenth centuries, religious authorities justified the colonization of the Americas by constructing Native men as feminized and prone to sodomy and demonizing indigenous kinship networks as violations against Christian patriarchal traditions.[21] This projection of an ungodly perversity onto indigeneity served as an excuse for theft and murder and enabled the undermining of Native sovereignty. Within the project of settlement, indigenous cultural patterns were dismissed as uncivilized and denied recognition as legitimate bases for geopolitical organization.[22] In a similar yet distinct manner, chattel slavery in the United States depended upon the equation of blackness with perversity and primitivity and the refusal to acknowledge black kinship formations and social attachments. Perceived as inhabiting wildly eroticized and grotesquely gendered or genderless bodies, men and women of African descent were imagined as dangerously hypersexual and thus incapable of marriage and nuclear family formation.[23] Although some enslaved people organized their intimate lives around the principles of conjugality, slave codes denied black couples access to civil marriage, and slave owners often sold and traded their "property" with no regard for the social bonds forged among the people they owned.[24] Under the parallel systems of colonialism and slavery, the willful misrecognition of indigenous and black relationality enabled the exclusion of these populations from the very category of humanity.

Following the abolition of slavery and the rapid growth of the U.S. market economy, racial and colonial domination took new forms over the course of the late nineteenth century. The marital family ideal played a central role within this reconfigured landscape of power. During this period, the extension of citizenship rights to African Americans instigated a crisis in the racial borders of the nation that was exacerbated by the state's increasing need for exploitable land, labor, and resources. It became harder to sustain the fantasy of a homogenously Anglo-American nation as the United States expanded its territorial borders into the Pacific and the Caribbean and with the influx of Chinese laborers in the West and of Southern and Eastern European immigrants in northeastern industrial cities. The ideological struggle to maintain white dominance and settler-imperial rule under these conditions instigated a rethinking of racial difference and a preoccupation with the biology of race. Fueled by intensifying anxieties over the black-white color line and informed by well-established discourses of xenophobia, Orientalism, and white supremacy, this scientific body of thought tended to affirm existing social hierarchies and, in effect, naturalized the systemic inequalities sustaining the expanding national economy.

This racial science took shape alongside the formulation of gendered bodily norms, the emergence of sexualized discourses of disability and degeneracy, and the consolidation of conjugal domesticity as the national ideal. As such, medicalized racial knowledges often sutured racial difference to social and sexual deviance. In the frantic effort to establish whiteness as a stable and superior class of personhood, populations falling outside of this newly congealing category were constructed as degenerative threats not only because they were said to inhabit unevolved and inherently unhealthy bodies but also because they were seen as possessing social tendencies perversely at odds with marital family life. Amid growing concerns about race and the nation, several states passed antimiscegenation laws banning interracial marriage during the late nineteenth century. Such legislation sought to protect white supremacy by preserving the purity of white patriarchal bloodlines and by ensuring that white wealth remained in the hands of white men.[25] That said, the state's concerns about marital relations and domestic respectability were not focused entirely on white property owners. This period was also marked by efforts to legislate the intimate lives of the newly racialized laboring classes. Earlier modes of racial and colonial domination had interpreted improper or illegible forms of sociality as grounds for exclusion from citizenship and humanity itself. During this time, however, juridical methods of control were being developed in response to what was perceived as the increasing permeability of U.S. national borders. Specifically, the state devised strategies for normalizing the unruly nature of nonwhite social relations by making conformity to the nuclear family a condition for entrance into the nation. Within this framework, domination occurred through the legal enforcement of gender, sexual, and relational norms that mandated privatized family formations and rendered supposedly perverse ways of life unsustainable. The marital family was a key technology for mediating the racial remapping of the nation and assimilating racial difference to the demands of the capitalist state.

Take, for example, the postemancipation extension of marriage rights to newly freed black people in the South.[26] For couples who had lived as husbands and wives under slavery, the transformation of their informal marriages into state-sanctioned partnerships seemed to mark their ascendency into citizenship and was celebrated as such among abolitionists. For those who did not organize their intimate lives around the norms of monogamy and long-term partnership, however, the revision of marriage laws had a much different effect. The sudden availability of marriage left black people engaging in other kinds of erotic arrangements in violation of laws against adultery and fornication and thus susceptible to arrest, disenfranchisement, and thanks to the Thirteenth Amendment, functional re-enslavement. But more than just punitive in its criminalizing effects, marriage equality was regulatory by design. Nineteenth-century social reformers viewed marriage as a technology of domestication that promised to civilize savage tendencies and to remake black bodies into respectable citizens. Moreover, the imposition of marital family norms advanced the economic goal of privatizing the costs of reproducing a cheap labor force. By ensuring black men were legally responsible for black women and children, the state absolved itself from any ethical or financial obligation to care for the formerly enslaved. Ushering black people into civil marriages was a strategy for managing the supposed perversity of blackness and ensuring black social and sexual life would not interfere with the accumulation of white wealth.

The marital family also figured prominently in efforts to contain indigenous populations during the late nineteenth century. As administrative strategies displaced physical violence as the primary mode of colonization, the U.S. federal government began extending citizenship to Native Americans. This inclusionary gesture obscured the status of Native people as citizens of colonized nations and instead tried to fold them into the U.S. national imaginary as a racial minority that could be internally managed.[27] To this end, the state developed gendered and sexualized methods of control designed to dismantle tribal cultures and collective land holdings while simultaneously assimilating indigenous peoples into U.S. citizenship and capitalist culture. The Dawes Act of 1887 is an excellent example of how the enforcement of white familial norms facilitated the ongoing work of settler colonial dispossession. Known as the General Allotment Act, this law divided selected reservation lands, allocated parcels to Native American men who were to assume roles as patriarchs of single-family households, and granted citizenship and property rights to those deemed "competent" according to federal standards. The coercive conferral of U.S. citizenship on indigenous adults mandated participation in marriage, heterocouplehood, and the system of private property ownership.[28] At the same time, the federal government was also targeting its ideological efforts at Native youth through the establishment of off-reservation Indian boarding schools. More than just drawing children away from tribal identification and indigenous spiritual practices, these Christian-based schools aimed to prepare students for life in allotment households and low-wage employment by offering gender-specific lessons in the virtues of piety, domesticity, and menial labor.[29] Like the Dawes Act, Indian boarding schools undermined Native women's authority, condemned polygamous arrangements, and discouraged perversely communal styles of living. In addition to disrupting indigenous genealogical traditions and chipping away at Native sovereignty, such efforts enabled the colonizing state to manage indigeneity by forcefully organizing indigenous social relations in the service of the industrializing economy.

During this same period, as the nation grew more reliant on immigrant labor and expanded its territorial boundaries overseas, familialism became a key strategy in the state's efforts to manage the non-Western European populations seeking entry into the continental United States and residing in places now under U.S. imperial rule. Since assuming control over immigration in the late nineteenth century, the federal government has prioritized the arrival of families as units and facilitated the reunification of families who did not immigrate together. Policies of this kind may have been framed as reflecting the state's benevolent commitment to preserving family ties, but the privileging of marital and filial relationships has also served the economic interests of the nation. By embedding new arrivals within heteropatriarchal family formations, U.S. immigration policy aimed to domesticate a laboring class believed to lack sexual mores and a work ethic and, in doing so, to privatize the costs of maintaining an easily exploitable workforce.[30] Put into place at the height of exclusionary anti-Asian border control efforts,[31] family-centric policies tended to favor European immigrants, including Southern and Eastern Europeans who were beginning to be racially recoded as white.[32] In contrast, Chinese laborers were regularly exempted from family reunification provisions based on the presumed deviance of Asian intimacies and the racialized construction of "Chineseness" as lacking the capacity for free will, romantic love, and domestic respectability.[33] Early immigration law deployed familial norms as a way of regulating labor and preserving the supremacy of whiteness. Yet at the same moment when the federal government was developing immigration policies designed to hold "foreign" racial threats at a distance from the national body, U.S. imperial projects were pulling other non-European forms of racial difference into close proximity with the American citizenry. In 1898, the United States illegally annexed Hawaii and acquired Guam, Puerto Rico, and the Philippines through the Spanish-American War. As the U.S. empire expanded its reach, the imperial outposts established abroad called upon the colonial administrative techniques and racialized modes of control that had been devised at home. As such, the United States thrust marital family norms upon its newest colonial subjects and enforced moral codes organized around hard work, self-discipline, and patriarchal responsibility.[34] Within the overlapping contexts of immigration policy and imperial governance, the demand for decency doubled as a demand for the docility on which U.S. national interests depended.

By the end of the nineteenth century, marriage and the single-family household had not just been institutionalized as the official national ideal but were being wielded as a key instrument of state power for managing racialized populations and establishing U.S. dominance in the emerging global capitalist economy. Heteropatriarchal family norms were deployed to regulate the intimate lives of people marked as degenerate and to coercively rearrange their perverse socialities into formations more conducive to capital and the state. Not surprisingly, with intimacy under heightened scrutiny, irregular erotic activities and nonprocreative sexual behaviors started to attract special attention and professional concern. It is thus within the context of the state's enforcement of white supremacist relational norms that theories of sexuality—and of same-sex desire in particular—start to take shape. *Familiar Perversions* opens with a look back at this period not only to expose the marital family as a regulatory institution but also to situate the invention of homosexuality with respect to the racist, sexist, and ableist operations of U.S. imperial power.

Homosexuality's Reproductive Pasts and Futures

With the turn of the twentieth century, medical and psychiatric experts in North America and Western Europe began trying to make sense of sexual desire on its own terms. In the process, the concept of perversity took on a more precise meaning in scientific discourses and political culture—no longer circulating solely as a general marker for ways of life deemed "unnatural" but now functioning as a scientific tool for diagnosing "sexual abnormalities." In an attempt to gain control over the unruly and increasingly expansive realm of sexual perversity, doctors and sexologists developed an extensive vocabulary for classifying erotic practices and took part in the taxonomic creation of what Michel Foucault describes as a "family of perverts" (1990, 40). Experts agonized over the causes and effects of myriad sexual perversions, including fetishism, voyeurism, exhibitionism, and bestiality, but it was homosexuality that emerged as the quintessential form of perversity. Posing a danger far greater than nonprocreativity alone, homosexuality represented a mode of intimacy at ideological odds with the relational norms on which Western liberal democracies were coming to depend.

Anxieties regarding family life were already at a high in the United States during this period. Industrial forms of capital may have required the marital family and its gendered division of labor,[35] but the wage-labor system had unhinged individual survival from familial attachments and made it possible for people to sustain adult lives outside the bounds of marriage and parent-hood (D'Emilio 1993). Within this newly configured political-economic con-text, homosexuality emerged as a grave threat to a social and sexual order that had been destabilized by the remapping of the nation's racial borders. This section considers the history of homosexuality—and the corollary develop-ment of regulatory apparatuses for managing homosexual desire—in relation to this perceived assault on the marital family's status as the most natural and desirable way of life. This crisis in the family dovetailed with broader concerns about the reproductive health of the national body and the racial purity and domestic respectability of the emerging white middle class. My purpose in retelling homosexuality's history is twofold. First (and perhaps predictably), I want to illuminate the ways in which homosexuality emerged as a discur-sive formation defined against the family. At the same time, however, I refuse to read homosexuality's relationship to domesticity and reproductivity as strictly oppositional or even antagonistic; instead, I offer a historical account that insists on a more nuanced understanding of the relationship between same-sex desire and modern family life and that effectively foreshadows the late twentieth-century incorporation of a privileged kind of queerness into the national imaginary.

During the late nineteenth century, as U.S.-based experts developed a "sci-ence of sex" in dialogue with the racial sciences, the study of homosexuality took on a uniquely American form with respect to familial and national futurity. Efforts to establish scientific standards for "sexual normalcy" were animated by anxieties over the shifting borders of U.S. citizenship and con-cerns about the supposedly debilitating effects of poverty, urbanization, and racial and ethnic mixing. Within this framework, homosexuality emerged as yet another form of hereditary degeneracy threatening the sanctity of the national body and endangering the progress of Western civilization. In *Queer-ing the Color Line* (2000), Siobhan Somerville documents the ways in which "both sympathetic and hostile accounts of homosexuality were steeped in assumptions that had driven previous scientific studies of race" (17).[36] The physiological abnormalities attributed to black, indigenous, and other non-Western European bodies, especially those classified as female, had frequently been interpreted as signs of an atavistic propensity for unnatural and non-procreative erotic behavior. Medical experts involved in early sexuality studies often deployed these same anthropometric logics in their attempt to under-stand sexual perversions and thus searched for anatomical markers that would visibly distinguish the animalism of "sex inverts" from normal, fully evolved people. The belief that manifestations of perversity stemmed from an inher-ited lack of restraint was only bolstered by the perception that same-sex erotic practices were concentrated among the morally suspect lower classes and nonwhite populations. The specter of homosexuality served as a prescient warning against the dangers of unfit parentage and untamed reproductive capacities.

In the early twentieth century, as hereditarian theories of perversion took hold, medical professionals and the public officials they influenced called upon disability imagery to produce homosexuals as morally weak, physically unwell, and mentally unstable and thus "proper subjects for discrimination" (Baynton 2001, 34). Whereas sexological interpretations of homosexuality as a congenital abnormality inspired movements against the criminalization of sodomy in Western Europe, the pathologization of perversity generated little sympathy for the homosexual living in the United States. In *An American Obsession* (1999), Jennifer Terry shows how discourses of U.S. individualism and self-improvement enabled experts to blame those who "exhibited an unwillingness or inability" to constrain their erotic desires for their failure to overcome their biological deficits (10). As such, homosexuality was easily integrated into a "eugenics-crime paradigm" (Ordover 2003, 77). Doctors dealing with socially and economically marginalized communities were apt to declare homosexuals (criminally) insane, to incarcerate them in asylums, and, in some cases, to surgically sterilize them. While a number of physicians experimented with castration and hysterectomies as both punitive and therapeutic responses to persistently perverse behavior, the eugenic impulses underlying such efforts must not be discounted (Largent 2011). According to prevailing theories of degeneration, the homosexual's depleted line of descent would produce children who, if not sick or sterile from birth, would at least have the proclivity for criminal or pathological behaviors later in life. While the perversity of this figure may have hinged on its construction as decidedly nonprocreative, homoerotic tendencies were neither believed to be a sign of reproductive incapacity nor thought to foreclose the possibility of engaging in "normal" procreative sexual activities. Medicolegal efforts to contain homosexuals—through sterilization, incarceration, or institutionalization—must also be understood as attempts to quell the perverse genetic potential they were thought to embody. In other words, the relationship between homosexuality and reproductivity was not mutually exclusive: while a penchant for nonprocreative sexual practices was held up as a sign of the homosexual body's degeneracy, the homosexual body was a source of concern precisely because of its procreative potential.

Over the course of the twentieth century, however, new theories of sexuality began to yield new strategies for managing same-sex eroticisms in the United States. As state officials and medical professionals witnessed a stark increase in the number of cases of homosexuality among seemingly respectable citizens, psychological and sociological understandings of sexuality grew in popularity. Authorities began to ask if and how social factors might affect the sexual development of individuals. At the heart of these newly developing theories lay deep-seated anxieties about the ways in which modernization and urbanization were eroding the race, class, and gender distinctions on which civilized social and sexual order depended. The city, as a chaotic site of proximity and promiscuity, was perceived to facilitate the congregation of "defectives" from the United States and abroad, leading to the formation of elaborate homosexual subcultures in working-class neighborhoods.[37] According to these logics—and the anti-immigrant and antimiscegenation sentiments undergirding them—the sexualized socialities erupting in urban spaces were responsible for compromising the moral integrity of people who would, under "normal" conditions, have aspired toward white middle-class family life. Experts, never allowing social scientific explanations of homosexuality to entirely supplant hereditarian theories, continued to associate perversion primarily with racially and economically stigmatized populations. As homophobic rhetoric coincided with racism, classism, and nativism, the presence of homoerotic tendencies among the middle and upper classes was read as "a kind of dangerous infection caused by contact with bad environments made worse by rising rates of bad breeding" (Terry 1999, 116–117).

Within this social scientific context, not all homosexuals were created equally perverse. While fears of degeneracy justified the continued use of state and medical violence to contain homosexual bodies residing on the margins of society, experts who adopted psychobiological explanations of desire started devising treatment plans designed to rehabilitate perverts from more privileged backgrounds. Interpreting white middle-class expressions of homosexuality as signs of "sexual maladjustment," some psychiatrists, psychologists, and social engineers believed they could help patients overcome their deviant urges if they encouraged them to conform to social conventions and to form proper relationships. In addition to promoting hard work and practices of self-discipline, some experts urged maladjusted adults to ignore their homoerotic inclinations and to embrace marriage, parenthood, and domesticity. This selective incorporation of homosexuality into reproductive life brings into focus the ways in which the pervert could, under certain circumstances, be put to work for the nation-state. At a moment when public figures were panicking about the nation's shifting racial demographics, the attempted recuperation of normative femininity and masculinity served the larger eugenic project of encouraging white middle-class adults to have children as a way of combatting the threat of "race suicide."[38] Proper family life was imagined capable of rendering homoerotic desires impotent (if not impossible) and to set would-be-homosexuals on straighter and, from the perspective of the nation-state, more profitable paths. Even if marriage and parenthood failed to fully extinguish perverse longings, the social and legal obligations associated with these arrangements were assumed to be enough to prevent those tendencies from instigating and sustaining homosocialities at odds with the demands of capital.

By highlighting these early twentieth-century efforts to bring white middle-class manifestations of homosexuality into the familial and national fold, I am pushing back against a simplistic historical understanding of homosexuality as the conceptual antithesis to the marital family. My goal in doing so is to bring into focus what we might consider the prehistory of homonormativity.[39] The raced and classed practice of distinguishing between deserving and undeserving queer subjects has a history that stretches back not just a few decades but almost to the discursive inception of homosexuality as a category. As such, this book approaches contemporary family equality advocacy as part of a longer history in which the management of sexuality takes place via the reconciliation of racially and economically privileged forms of perversity with domesticity and reproductivity.

The Pervert and the Child

That said, *Familiar Perversions* is also attentive to the ways in which LGBT claims on parenthood continue to be haunted by persisting fears about the dangers homosexuals present to children. During the early twentieth century, the function of the family within the larger project of (homo)sexual regulation was not only curative but also preventative, especially when it came to the question of childhood sexual development. Concerns about the uncertainty of the nation's sexual future had begun to coalesce around the figure of the child. Backlashes against the successes of the women's suffrage movement had left the U.S. public less convinced of white middle-class women's innocence and vulnerability. In response, state officials and their civil society partners turned their attention to the health and safety of white middle-class children and, specifically, to the dangers that sexual depravity created for their well-being. Much was believed to be at stake in the affective development of the child. Following industrial capitalism's transformation of the home into a site for reproducing heteropatriarchal relations and able-bodied subjects (McRuer 2006, 90–93), children came to signify more than an heir to or an extension of their father's property and were now seen as future workers, citizens-in-formation, and the next generation of parents.[40] In this section, I show how growing concerns about the psychosexual health of children set the stage for transforming disquietude over the ideological threat that homosexuality posed to familial and national futurity into widespread panic over the material threat that actual homosexuals allegedly posed to individual children.

In the 1920s, the ascendency of psychological theories of sexuality fueled anxieties over childhood as parenting experts warned that sexual development always involved perverse twists and turns. Normativity was never guaranteed, not even for the child growing up in the whitest and wealthiest of homes. Within this theoretical framework, desire existed as an unruly psychic force that, in the absence of proper guidance or if let loose in the wrong social environment, could easily derail the formation of (hetero)sexually mature subjects.[41] Women, in their roles as wives and mothers, were tasked with the labor of guarding their families against illness, disease, and sexual pathology and, in the process, were subject to greater degrees of scrutiny by state and medical authorities concerned with newly established childhood norms.[42] As more centralized and statistically driven approaches to family welfare emerged during this period, the systematic targeting of "unfit" parents left poor families—especially in black, indigenous, and immigrant communities—vulnerable to government intervention (Cravens 1993). Yet even as white middle-class domesticity was held up as the primary bulwark against psychic and physical infection, there was an acknowledgement that the home could never be fully secured and the child would always be at risk. To borrow Tim Dean's playful synopsis of Freud's theory of infantile sexuality, "We cannot protect kids from perverts, because we cannot effectively insulate any child from [themselves]" (2006, 827). Thus the respectable parent's role in preserving reproductive futurity was not necessarily to obliterate all nonreproductive tendencies but rather to manage perverse desires and minimize their adverse effects.

Over the course of the 1930s, abstract concerns about the perverse potential lying within the child began to manifest as fears of actual perverts lusting after real children. The implementation and enforcement of sex offender laws during this period only bolstered the perception of the homosexual as a predatory figure looking to destroy the family.[43] This recasting of perversity as a threat emerging from outside the home—a recasting dependent on the assumption not only that perverts were always adults but also that the parent and the pervert were mutually exclusive categories—served, in part, to reconsolidate the white supremacist fantasy of the healthy and heteronormative home that theories of infantile sexuality and psychosexual development had destabilized. At the same time, the panic that seemed to suddenly erupt around the homosexual subcultures that authorities had largely ignored in previous decades was also a direct response to the social and economic instabilities engendered by the Great Depression.[44] As anxieties over excessive consumer desires coincided with apprehensions about illicit erotic inclinations, the homosexual emerged as an easy scapegoat for dealing with a perceived crisis in morality and the family. Across the country, city and state officials outlawed same-sex sexual practices, making no distinction between consensual and nonconsensual acts, and criminalized less overtly erotic practices, like cross-dressing and congregating in public. Sensationalist media coverage of "sex crimes" ignored the injustices of sex offender laws and focused instead on incidents of rape, assault, and child molestation. As a result, homosexuality was sutured to physical and sexual violence. Children were thought to be particularly vulnerable to such deviance precisely because the homosexual was imagined as trapped in an arrested state of development and obsessively drawn to undeveloped and easily dominated bodies (Terry 1999, 322). While the attachment of same-sex eroticism to child sexual predation was a common rhetorical practice when it came to the policing of sex among socially and economically marginalized communities,[45] the hysteria that broke out over homosexuality during this period sparked newly configured suspicions about the danger that sex perverts, regardless of their race, nationality, or class background, posed to family welfare and public safety.

When the United States entered World War II, however, anxieties around homosexuality and sex crimes subsided in noticeable ways. The war's destabilization of the nuclear family undercut efforts to normalize gender and sexual relations and rendered the project of distinguishing perverts from patriots even less definitive. In *Sexual Politics, Sexual Communities* (1983), John D'Emilio argues that the mobilization of U.S. families during the war disrupted the aspirationally white and middle-class path to sexual maturity that had been established with the rise of industrial capitalism. Young people who took jobs in the defense industry and filled vacancies in the civilian labor force were able to avoid or at least delay marriage and as such enjoyed a period of independence outside their family homes. Within these "nonfamilial [and] often sex-segregated environments," they were able to explore a multitude of sexual possibilities (23). In a similar vein, the military created conditions equally conducive to homoerotic exploration and the cultivation of perverse attachments (Bérubé 1990). In short, the disorganization of American family life during World War II opened unfamiliar space for the collective formation of lesbian and gay identities. In the wake of the war, as more visible and vibrant subcultural communities emerged around these shared identities, authorities blamed mass military and industrial mobilizations for unhinging individuals from the bonds of the family and leaving them susceptible to what were interpreted as antisocial influences. Common narrations of lesbian and gay community building located same-sex eroticism outside the family and thus upheld the belief that postwar efforts to restore order to domestic life would curb public expressions of homosexual desire.

In the hopes of fortifying the nation against the menace of Communism, authorities made a concerted effort to revive normative familial life and, in doing so, reignited existing and often overtly racialized fears of perversity. Early Cold War panic led to the demonization of anyone who engaged in social or political practices, such as "race agitation" and "sexual deviancy," that bucked dominant notions of respectability and railed against the supremacy of white domesticity (Mogul et al. 2011, 38–39). In particular, homosexuals emerged as a major "security threat" and became the target for systemic persecution, leading to the expulsion of many men and women from their jobs with government agencies and in the private sector (Johnson 2004). The sex pervert, already perceived as an inherently suspect and susceptible figure, was thought to have a propensity for radicalism and un-American sentiments and was thought to be highly vulnerable to seduction and/or extortion by enemy agents. To suppress this treasonous potential, the state called upon the family to preserve the mental and moral hygiene of the citizenry: in addition to tasking mothers with the work of raising patriotic and properly gendered children who would value family life and capitalist freedoms, public officials also instructed parents to keep watch for Communist infiltrators who were not above preying upon vulnerable youth.[46] As the Cold War intensified family-centric child protectionist sentiments, anti-Communist hysteria fueled and was fueled by enduring fears of a diseased and disordered homosexual underworld. The predatory nature of homosexuals was no longer interpreted as a strictly erotic compulsion but was read as indicative of a coordinated recruitment effort. In a rhetorical move that conflated sexual perversion with political subversion while also invoking the homosexual's presumed incapacity for reproduction, homosexuals were accused of trying to grow their ranks by luring unsuspecting youth away from their families and inducting them into a clandestinely perverse way of life.[47] Within this political-economic context, the construction of the sex pervert as a dangerous force trying to penetrate the family from the outside had the desired effect of locating perversity at a safe distance from the home.

By the mid–twentieth century, the homosexual had been consolidated as a dangerous figure believed to threaten the sanctity of childhood and the futurity of white domesticity. It was through—and in negotiation with—these discursive terms that a U.S.-based homosexual emancipation movement took shape. The early Cold War era's "lavender scare" may have ushered in a period of state repression and violence directed against anyone perceived to be homosexual, but this hostility also created the conditions of possibility for the politicization of homosexuality and the cultivation of a new political identity based on a shared experience of sexual stigma and a complicated relationship, in both theory and practice, to middle-class family life. Rallying around the category of homosexual meant occupying a discursive position that was pitted against the child within the national imaginary. Thus from the earliest days of homophile, lesbian, and gay organizing, activists, regardless of where they stood on the issue of homosexual parenting, have been forced to engage—whether to refute, to accept, to embrace, or to reimagine—queerness's antithetical relationship to reproductive futurity. In the chapters that follow, I focus specifically on how lesbian and gay parenting activists navigated this discursive terrain during the late twentieth and early twenty-first centuries. *Familiar Perversions* offers a detailed analysis of the complex, ongoing, and always fraught negotiations that have allowed the LGBT family to cohere as a respectable social formation.

Chapter Overview

Chapter 1, "Anxiety," situates the rise of family equality advocacy within a longer tradition of lesbian and gay parenting activism in the United States. Picking up where the introduction leaves off, this chapter begins by examining the contested place of parenthood within the homophile movement of the 1950s and 1960s and then turns to the activist strategies deployed by lesbian and gay parents who struggled to maintain custody of their children after coming out in the 1970s and 1980s. While these early activist efforts often involved direct challenges to normative notions of kinship and, at times, sought to deregulate gender, sexuality, and intimacy, the national parenting movement that emerged out of this history focused primarily on constructing lesbian- and gay-headed households as aligned with prevalent familial norms. Over the course of the 1990s, the formalization of lesbian and gay family activism and the eventual formation of a national nonprofit organization reflected the broader trend within social justice organizing away from coalitional work in the name of redistributive justice and toward identity-based and increasingly professionalized calls for rights and recognition.

Tracking the reconfiguration of U.S. sexual politics in relation to the implementation of neoliberal economic agendas and governing strategies, this chapter approaches family equality rhetoric as a particular iteration of homonormativity and describes the ways parents started incorporating discourses of personal responsibility and privatized notions of citizenship into their advocacy work. The project of reconciling queerness with domesticity and reproductivity, when carried out by and on behalf of families, required a careful negotiation of lingering anxieties—anxieties often held by parents themselves—about how prolonged exposure to homosexuality and, worse, homophobia might negatively impact the children of lesbians and gay men. In the hopes of providing their children with a network of support, parenting advocates began organizing family-centric lesbian and gay pride events, such as the annual Family Week celebration in Provincetown. Ironically, as the mainstream lesbian and gay movement retreated from its earlier attachments to queer public culture, community-building activities were becoming a central component of family equality advocacy. By showing how children are thought to both enrich and endanger—and to be both enriched and endangered by—the space of a gay resort destination like P'town, this chapter explores the ways in which parents manage the threat that queer community events pose to the construction of lesbian and gay family life as a private zone cordoned off from public sexual cultures and thus perfectly suitable for raising the next generation of properly desiring subjects.

Chapter 2, "Visibility," examines lesbian mom icon Rosie O'Donnell's attempt to capitalize on the popularity of these family-centric pride events by starting a vacation company catering exclusively to lesbian and gay parents and their children. Turning a critical eye on the cruise packages she offered during the first decade of the twenty-first century, I consider the political function of community-building activities forged under the sign of family equality. Far from striving to cultivate feelings of collectivity or interdependence, such efforts are better understood as assembling a critical mass of individual family units who engage publicly in wholesome leisure activities and, in doing so, serve as visual evidence of the fitness of lesbians and gay men for parenthood and, by extension, citizenship.

Central to this chapter is an investigation into the politics of visibility that underwrites this celebrity-backed tourist venture and family equality advocacy more broadly. The first half of the chapter situates the launch of O'Donnell's company in 2003 with respect to the U.S.-led war on terror (which was, at this point, at its height) and the George W. Bush administration's aggressively heteronormative brand of patriotism. While government officials were proposing constitutional amendments against same-sex marriage and trying to limit the rights of lesbian and gay adults to foster or adopt children, O'Donnell was offering families a chance to escape state-sponsored homophobia and to enjoy a sense of validation and national belonging via cosmopolitan mobility and transnational practices of consumption. By drawing media attention to lesbian and gay families spending U.S. dollars in the global marketplace, she hoped to combat negative perceptions of same-sex desires and relations by crafting an image of lesbian and gay couples as respectable consumers and responsible caregivers.

In the second half of this chapter, I draw upon my participant observation aboard the company's 2009 cruise to Alaska, and I explore the significant changes that were taking place at this time in terms of O'Donnell's business and within the broader field of U.S. sexual politics. Although the novelty of her cruises had worn off by the time my ship set sail, I discovered that an investment in visibility politics continued to structure the lesbian and gay family cruise experience, but with an Obama-era twist. The recent presidential election had ushered in an unprecedented degree of optimism concerning the future of LGBT family politics, as the new administration subscribed to a version of U.S. exceptionalism that understood national excellence as increasingly tied to the expansion of state protections for LGBT populations. According to the family equality advocates aboard my ship, same-sex couples and their children were going to have to assume a great deal of responsibility for mustering the public support that would empower the president to advance a sexually progressive agenda: they would need to seek out opportunities in their local communities where they could share their personal stories and render themselves visible as American families deserving of legal rights and state recognition.

Chapter 3, "Equality," looks specifically at the involvement of LGBT families in the freedom to marry movement. To show how the legalization of same-sex marriage in the United States became a family affair, I trace the history of marriage equality activism through the deployment of the figural child and unravel the ways in which LGBT claims on parenthood both enabled and impeded calls for same-sex marriage rights. This chapter then turns a critical eye on the Supreme Court's landmark decisions—*United States v. Windsor* in 2013 and *Obergefell v. Hodges* in 2015—and offers a detailed analysis of the majority and dissenting opinions as well as the amicus briefs filed both for and against marriage equality. What interests me most in relation to these cases is how both proponents and opponents of same-sex marriage rights mobilized actual children from LGBT families in their campaigns. Whereas family equality advocates invited young children and teenagers to explain the devastating economic and emotional effects marriage inequality had on their otherwise happy and healthy lives, conservative forces found grown children who would share their personal experiences with the horrors of homosexual and transsexual parenting in the hopes of thwarting the "gay agenda." Reading the homophobic child alongside its homonormative counterpart, I illustrate how a critical engagement with the inflammatory arguments against family equality can sharpen our analyses of the state's strategic incorporation of same-sex intimacies organized around racist, ableist, and capitalist relational norms. At the core of the decision to extend legal and financial protections to the children of LGBT families, in the form of marital rights for their parents, lies an investment in white supremacist logics of private property.

This chapter concludes by pushing back against the LGBT family movement's tendency to hold LGBT parents (who are almost exclusively represented as raising straight children) at a rhetorical distance from LGBT youth (who are often presumed to be raised by straight parents). Following an examination of how, after securing access to marriage, family equality advocates reinvested in making uncritical demands for expanded fostering and adoption rights, I ask what LGBT family politics might look like if organizers decentered the desires of relatively privileged prospective parents and prioritized instead the needs of queer and trans youth entangled in the foster care system. Refusing to idealize privatized domestic settings, a queer family politics can insist on the value of supporting youth in care and their families of origin by providing them with the material resources needed to build broader and decidedly queerer networks of care.

Chapter 4, "Vitality," opens with the question begged by the family equality movement's contention that same-sex marriage rights would afford LGBT families increased economic security. To what extent has marriage equality actually enhanced the financial health of LGBT parents and their children? Before tackling this question, I step back to account for the ways in which lesbian and gay activist agendas were rerouted through neoliberal logics of financialization and discourses of risk management during the late twentieth and early twenty-first centuries. In the process, the individualizing rhetoric of financial security effectively displaced collective demands for economic justice. Within the context of family equality advocacy, access to marital rights and other identity-based protections gained value not as strategies for facilitating a more equitable distribution of material resources but as means for removing the discriminatory barriers that prevented current and prospective LGBT-identified parents from efficiently building their families, managing their household budgets, and maximizing their future health and wealth potential.

Not surprisingly, then, in the wake of the *Obergefell* decision, the wealthiest of LGBT-identified parents began working with financial planners to determine if and how to deploy marriage as yet another financial mechanism capable of shielding their family's wealth from federal tax obligations. For the disproportionate number of LGBT families living near or below the poverty line, however, the freedom to marry tended to have little positive effect on their precarious economic conditions. The availability of marriage did not translate into access to basic necessities like food or shelter, and a change in marital status, for many couples, threatened to interfere with their eligibility for state-sponsored health care programs and other social safety net services. In this chapter, as I tease out the uneven effects of marriage equality on same-sex couples raising children in the United States, I situate the legalization of same-sex marriage with respect to the Obama administration's broader efforts to address the persisting disparities in LGBT health and the widespread problem of LGBT poverty. While the federal government's LGBT health promotion initiatives were advancing a rather progressive version of LGBT family politics that departed, in ways, from a family equality agenda, the Department of Health and Human Services was at the same time working to develop LGBT-inclusive "healthy marriage and relationship education" programs for "low-income" adults and "at-risk" youth. This chapter closes by exploring how such efforts are ultimately designed to impose relational norms upon marginalized populations and thus mark a continuation of the state's long-established practice of wielding the marital family ideal as a coercive tool for managing perverse relationalities.

In the conclusion, I put forth a vision for a queer family politics organized not around the rhetoric of equality and freedom but around a commitment to advancing racial, sexual, and economic justice. Calling upon the alternative genealogies of lesbian and gay parenting I highlight in chapter 1—and expanding the proposal I outline in chapter 3 for forging intergenerational solidarities between queer parents and queer youth—*Familiar Perversions* concludes by imagining a broad-based movement focused on both the immediate goal of making more resources available to more familial forms and the queer world-making work of cultivating perversely unfamiliar forms of family life.

On the one hand, a more transformative approach to family politics must, as queer feminists have long argued, prioritize building alliances between LGBT-specific political projects and other movements challenging white, abled, and middle-class relational norms. By collectively demanding public policies designed around a flexible definition of *family* premised upon self-determination and mutual dependencies (as opposed to legal and blood ties), coalitional movements can strive to destabilize the primacy of the marital family form as a way of facilitating the downward distribution of wealth and other life chances. On the other hand, a queer family politics must also mobilize the reproductive potential of queerness. I propose that intergenerational encounters—such as those between parents and children or between adult allies and youth organizers—are opportunities for fostering erotic variety, gender variance, and creative intimacies and, in the process, broadening the horizon of sexual and ethical possibilities for the next generation. Pushing back against the ways in which neoliberal logics can limit our imaginative capacities regarding the future of queer families and politics, I suggest devising strategies for encouraging desire formations and social attachments that are incongruous with—and potentially disruptive to—the models of subjectivity and relationality undergirding the white supremacist, capitalist nation-state. In other words, a queer family politics reaches toward a more just future by working to secure the material resources and discursive spaces needed to inspire and sustain more perverse modes of desiring and doing family.

1

Anxiety

• • • • • • • • • • • • • • • • • • • •

The History of Lesbian and
Gay Parenting Activism

In July 2015, more than five hundred LGBT families descended upon Provincetown, Massachusetts, to celebrate the twentieth anniversary of Family Week.[1] The annual event, hosted by the national nonprofits Family Equality Council and COLAGE (the group formerly known as Children of Lesbians and Gays Everywhere), advertises itself as the largest formal gathering of LGBT-identified parents and their children in the United States. What began as a small backyard barbecue has since exploded into seven days of corporate-sponsored activities designed to help families "build community" and "get empowered on today's issues" (Family Equality Council, "Family Week," n.d.). The 2015 lineup, sponsored by Tylenol, General Motors, and ABC Family's *The Fosters*,[2] consisted of a wide range of social events, support groups, and educational workshops—including a variety show, a children's movie night, a beach party for teens, a mixer for single parents, a happy hour for parents of color, a gathering for families with disabled members, a panel about trans parenting and genderqueer families, and a "State of the Movement" address featuring the Council's top leaders. Held just one month after the Supreme Court's ruling in favor of marriage equality, the twentieth anniversary was a particularly joyous occasion for the Council and its members, as the organization had been at the forefront of the freedom to marry movement since the inception of Family Week. The Council encouraged families to celebrate "how far [they've] come" while also cautioning against complacency and reminding them that "much remain[ed] to secure [their] true legal and lived equality."[3] At the very end of the week, the Council and COLAGE gathered everyone together for the culminating event, the Family Pride Parade. Together, parents and children marched down Commercial Street, the main drag of the famous gay resort town, waving handmade signs reading, "Two Moms Are the Best," "I Heart My Two Dads," and "All You Need Is Love."

Given the Council's professed goal of "changing attitudes and policies" by showing the American public that LGBT-identified parents are "just like any other community of parents" (Family Equality Council, "About Us," n.d.), it is perhaps surprising to find its main event, Family Week, staged in a town with a reputation as a site for sexual exploration and homoerotic hedonism. The decision to march children down a street home to tea parties and erotica shops, not far from the popular cruising site affectionately known as the "Dick Dock," hardly seems conducive to the organization's official mission. What, I ask, has made it possible for the Council to host its child-centric community-building event in a place once described by local law enforcement officials as "a hotbed of public sex for randy exhibitionists" (Jordan 2008)? In what ways has this annual tradition both helped and hindered efforts to establish the fitness of lesbians and gay men for parenthood and to align same-sex desires and relations with the nationalist ideals of domesticity and reproductivity? What convergence of historical, sociocultural, and political-economic forces enables LGBT-identified parents to take their children to a place like P'town while still claiming that there is nothing out of the ordinary about LGBT family life? I begin this chapter with the annual Family Week celebration as a way of opening a larger set of questions about how activists have managed the anxieties that surround the relationship of parents and children to public sexual cultures and lesbian and gay politics over the course of the late twentieth and early twenty-first centuries. The setting of Family Week, especially when considered within a wider historical frame, reveals the uneasy place of lesbian and gay parents within the broader field of U.S. sexual politics and brings into focus the precise ways in which family equality advocacy negotiates the terms of national belonging and U.S. settler citizenship under late capitalism.

Located on the easternmost tip of Cape Cod, P'town boasts a long history as a travel destination for people looking to escape the repressive conditions of everyday life, a history that local tourism boards often trace back to the arrival of the Pilgrims. Town officials pride themselves on the fact that the Pilgrims first landed in what would later become Provincetown and signed the Mayflower Compact in the harbor before proceeding to Plymouth. Popular histories of the resort town, such as the narratives in local guidebooks and on display at the Provincetown Museum, offer a sanitized account of colonialism devoid of European violence and Native resistance. Jumping from the

Mayflower's landing to the establishment of a Yankee whaling village in the nineteenth century, these historical accounts gloss over the displacement, dispossession, and enslavement of the indigenous people who hunted and fished at the end of the Cape; instead, they focus on the circuits of immigrant labor that gave way to the town's vibrant Portuguese fishing community (and that bolster perceptions of the United States as a nation welcoming of diversity). In the early twentieth century, as the end of the whaling industry wreaked havoc on the town's economy, Provincetown joined other New England towns in promoting itself as an idyllic and quintessentially American vacation destination. To this end, local officials erected a 250-foot granite obelisk that marked the "birthplace" of U.S. democracy and, in effect, naturalized settlement as the foundation for modern freedoms.[4]

Despite attempts by town officials to repackage the fishing village as a vestige of "colonial America," the town's expanding art colony played a more influential role than the Pilgrim Monument in shaping Provincetown's tourist future. The eclectic lifestyles of the artists and writers who convened in the town, coupled with the eroticized commodification of the local Portuguese communities, attracted a wide range of travelers in search of (homo)erotic subcultural experiences. By the end of the twentieth century, the vitality of the local economy depended heavily on the consumption practices of an emerging and predominantly white lesbian and gay niche market.[5] Tourism promoters mobilized Pilgrim mythology to sell the resort town as the perfect destination for people wishing to escape persecution of all kinds—religious, sexual, or otherwise.[6] As such, during the golden age of lesbian and gay travel in the 1990s, the local tourist imaginary was organized around a gay subject who, freed from the bonds of marriage and parenthood and enabled by the lifestylization offerings of consumer capitalism, ran wild along the streets and shores of P'town.[7] A trip to the Cape was a chance to claim one's settler legacy and enjoy an erotic freedom imagined as the direct descendant of a romanticized American democratic tradition.

In 2015, Scott Davenport, who cofounded Family Week with his now ex-husband Tim Fisher, reflected on that period in P'town history in a *Huffington Post* story about the twentieth anniversary of the annual celebration. In the beginning, Davenport explains, lesbian and gay families were forced to brave a P'town overrun with "dance boys from Boston" (Shapiro 2015). Over the past two decades, however, the organizers of Family Week have worked both to carve out space for parents within the resort town and the broader LGBT imaginary and to demand recognition for a domesticated lesbian and gay subject who values privacy and conjugality over anonymous sexual encounters. The annual celebration, according to Davenport's account, has been instrumental in converting P'town from a sexual playground for adults into a space with actual playgrounds for children. He goes on to suggest that visibility events like these have been key to challenging negative representations of LGBT lifestyles and transforming public attitudes about same-sex relationships. The author of the *Huffington Post* article, following Davenport's lead, likens the parents who attended the first Family Weeks to the "pioneering . . . religious dissidents" who arrived on the *Mayflower*. Crediting their bravery with paving the way for the success of the marriage equality movement, the article conjures the image of the Pilgrim not as a symbol of unregulated sexual freedom, as the tourism boards have done, but rather as a domesticating force tasked with the work of taming unruly desires and improper social and sexual formations. The inadvertent gesture to the colonial project of imposing marital family norms on indigenous kinship structures (which I discuss in the introduction) illuminates the racial and civilizational resonances underpinning Davenport's respectability politics and his desire to distance lesbian and gay parents from "that party-boy stereotype." At the same time, however, this simplified and largely fictionalized narrative about how Family Week single-handedly changed gay culture and "the course of gay history" obscures the political-economic conditions structuring P'town, lesbian and gay activism, and U.S. public culture at the turn of the twenty-first century.

My primary goal in this chapter is to push back against the tendency, exemplified by Davenport, for family equality advocates to craft reductive historical narratives in which parents emerge as the heroes of the LGBT rights movement. According to such accounts, the same-sex couples who overcame homophobic resistance, fulfilled their parental desires, and demanded visibility as families during the 1990s are believed to be largely responsible for convincing the rest of the country that lesbians and gay men are respectable Americans deserving of state recognition and legal protections. In contrast, this chapter tells a more nuanced and deeply historicized story about the emergence of LGBT family politics. In the process, I debunk perceptions of parenthood as having had an invariably normalizing effect on queer cultures and of parenting activism as having always already been wedded to an assimilatory politics. LGBT parents are not a new phenomenon, and parenthood has never had a single meaning within LGBT communities. By showing how same-sex family-building practices have been mobilized in the service of and in solidarity with various political projects, I identify alternative genealogies of queer parenting activism in the United States. Without an understanding of the dynamic place of parenthood within the history of homophile, lesbian, and gay movements, it is impossible to fully understand how and with what effect LGBT family politics coalesced around a rights and recognition platform.

To this end, I situate the annual Family Week celebration within a much longer trajectory of U.S.-based lesbian and gay parenting activism. Turning my attention to midcentury homosexual rights organizing, I begin by tracing the different discursive strategies that actual and aspiring parents deployed in negotiating the construction of homosexuality as ideologically at odds with modern family life. Along the way, I track the move from debating whether homosexuals could or should parent during the 1950s and 1960s to collectively demanding the right to parent as open homosexuals—and making such demands alongside other communities marginalized by narrow white supremacist definitions of parental fitness—during the 1970s. I then take a closer look at the "gayby boom" to explore the political ramifications of a sudden increase in the visibility of lesbian and gay parents and a growing preoccupation with lesbian mothers who conceived via artificial insemination. In addition to asking how the rise of a conservative family values movement during the 1980s and 1990s contributed to the shift among parenting activists from reimagining kinship relations to seeking recognition as traditional American families, I illuminate the broader cultural, political, and economic factors that thwarted the cultivation of intersectional analyses and coalition-building projects during this period and that facilitated the ascendency of an inclusionary rights-based agenda organized through white middle-class relational norms and an affective investment in nuclear family life.

By contextualizing the shifting terrain of lesbian and gay parenting activism with respect to histories of settler colonialism, (neo)liberal racial and sexual politics, and the reconfigured logics of social movement building in the post–civil rights era, I account for why a family equality framework emerges as the dominant mode of LGBT family politics at the end of the twentieth century. After sketching out this history, I return to the scene of Family Week to examine both the anxiety-ridden incorporation of parenthood into lesbian and gay culture and the complex processes of negotiation involved in reconciling queerness—especially procreative forms of queerness—with familial and national futurity. Upon considering the unexpected and potentially disruptive effects of immersing children within the increasingly commodified yet still eroticized atmosphere of P'town, I explore the conflicts that have taken place between the parents and children who attend Family Week each year and the childless gay elite with more permanent property-based ties to the area. The colonial New England tourist landscape of Provincetown brings into focus the tensions organizing the broader field of homonormativity and, in doing so, clarifies the strategies through which LGBT families have tried to fold themselves into the capitalist project of reproducing the U.S. imperial social and sexual order.

The (Im)Possibility of Parenting

In the United States, the origins of a national lesbian and gay movement can be traced to the period immediately following World War II. As I explained in the introduction, the Cold War era produced the homosexual as a danger-ously predatory figure with a propensity for pedophilia, Communism, and other "un-American" activities. The ensuing "lavender scare" resulted in con-certed efforts on the part of the U.S. government and local police forces to sur-veil and suppress homosexual subcultural life, but this intensification of state violence and repression also prompted the formation of an overtly politicized homosexual identity and a vibrant homosexual rights movement. While ear-lier efforts to mobilize homosexuals in the United States, such as the creation of the Society for Human Rights in 1924, had proven unsustainable, the post-war period was much more conducive to the work of movement building. The destabilization of national sexual norms—along with the expansion of port cities following the demobilization of lesbian and gay troops (Bérubé 1990) and the development of communication and transportation technologies, which facilitated transnational exchanges with European homophile groups (Churchill 2008)—made possible the emergence of a U.S.-based movement that could be sustained at a national level. This is not, however, to suggest that a uniform coherence existed across the movement: homophile activists in dif-ferent parts of the country may have shared the goal of homosexual emanci-pation, but they had different ideas on what that would look like and how it would be achieved. Among homophiles, there was much debate over the issue of homosexual marriage and parenthood and the broader question of the proper relationship between homosexuals and youth. Early activists devised various strategies for negotiating the discursive construction of homosexuality as the antithesis of the child and, in the process, attached different meanings to the practice, both real and imagined, of homosexual parenting.

Historians often trace the beginnings of U.S. lesbian and gay activism to the formation of the Mattachine Society in Los Angeles in 1951 (D'Emilio 1983; Duberman 1993; Stein 2000). Founded by five white men who were variously involved in leftist politics and the Communist Party, the Matta-chine Society advocated a Marxist style of criticism that refused to inter-pret homosexuality as a personal pathology and that identified racism and capitalism as sources of antihomosexual sentiment. Early homophile activ-ists sought to diagnose the ways in which deeply embedded social and eco-nomic relations—namely, the nuclear heterosexual family—systemically oppressed homosexuals as a cultural minority. Organizing the Society around a Communist-inspired structure of secret cells, the founders set out to pro-vide a protected space apart from family life where men and, in some instances, women could cultivate a distinctly homosexual ethic.

One of the most well-known founders, Harry Hay, believed activists could make a case for the value of the homosexual minority by emphasizing the fact that, since they were free from the obligations of traditional family life, homosexuals could provide social services and fulfill community needs for busy American families. Notably, Hay's vision for homosexual emancipation "ground[ed] modern sexual minority identities and politics in the appropriation of Native culture" (Morgensen 2011, 48). He sought to naturalize homosexuality by citing European sexological writing on the apparent celebration of gender-transitivity and same-sex desire within "primitive" societies, and he held up Western anthropological accounts of the berdache—a childless Native American male who dressed in feminized ways, had sexual contact with other males, and was revered for the carework they performed in their community—as justification for granting homosexual rights to U.S. citizens in the mid–twentieth century.[8] This treatment of Native peoples as only existing in the past and of Native histories and traditions as available for discovery, possession, and mobilization serves as a stark reminder of how leftist critiques of structural oppression often remain contained within the logics of settler colonialism. Yet even as Hay's analysis of U.S. sexual politics stopped short of recognizing familialism as an instrument of colonization in the Americas, his refusal to accept the family as the sole arbiter of morality did open space for insisting on the ethical value of social formations forged beyond the narrow confines of heteropatriarchal family life.

Shortly after its inception, the Mattachine Society moved away from its explicitly Marxist origins, abandoned its secret cell model, and incorporated as a nonprofit organization. In what was, in part, a strategic attempt to dissociate homophile activism from the twinned specters of Communism and pedophilia (Meeker 2001), the Society replaced its materialist cultural critiques of heterosexuality and the family with an ostensibly accommodationist approach to social change. Official Mattachine rhetoric encouraged members to present themselves as valuable, responsible, and gender-conforming citizens as a way of distinguishing themselves from truly dangerous sexual deviants. According to the organization's public documents, respectable homosexuals valued normative family life: they were capable of containing their perversity and had no interest in corrupting the next generation. To this end, the Society officially banned people under the age of twenty-one from joining the organization and publicly condemned any intimate associations between members and youth (Sears 2006). The most visible actors in the homophile movement thus promised a homosexual who kept away from children and who posed no threat to the future of white domesticity.

As the movement grew during the late 1950s and 1960s, activists tended to maintain an uncritical distance from family life. When debates drifted toward the issue of whether homosexuals should demand the right to parent or even to marry, homophile organizations handled the family with care. In *Radical Relations*, Daniel Rivers (2013) documents the fraught discussions that took place among activists concerning the homosexual's relationship to domesticity and children in particular. In 1964, the Miami-based Atheneum Society surveyed several organizations about their official views on key issues, specifically asking if they "believe[d] homosexuals should be allowed the legal bonds of matrimony" and whether "these 'families' should be allowed to adopt children" (quoted in Rivers 2013, 47). The Philadelphia-based Janus Society emphatically declared marriage rights extraneous to the homophile struggle and firmly opposed the extension of adoptive rights to homosexuals. Atheneum concurred, fearing that such "wild and radical" notions would alienate the general public and compromise efforts to achieve the more immediate goals of securing the right to associate in public and ending antihomosexual harassment and discrimination (48). In a similar vein, the newly formed San Francisco–based Society for Individual Rights argued that until homosexuality was decriminalized, concerns about marriage and parenting were moot. The Toronto-based Gay Publishing Company and San Francisco's chapter of the Mattachine Society were more willing to entertain the notion of homosexual family life. Yet while they were in favor of granting legal recognition to same-sex relationships, their support for adoption rights was contingent on getting assurance from experts that homosexual parents would not inadvertently "convert" their presumably heterosexual children (48). Anxieties over the threat homosexuals posed to the sexual development of children reflected the ways in which efforts to locate the perverse outside the home shaped homosexual emancipation efforts. Rather than insisting on the inherent perversity of desire, activists participated in a rhetorical framing that reduced perversity to homosexuality, implanted this form of perversion in an adult body, and then agonized over the child's proximity to a visible embodiment of perversity.

This is not to say that the homophile movement adopted a uniformly accommodationist stance on if and how homosexuals should interact with children. Behind the scenes, the Mattachine Society's relationship to young people was far more ambiguous than its official publications suggest. Despite the public performance of social conformity, the organization provided social services to a wide range of "sexual variants," including people who crossdressed or identified as transsexuals, people who participated in "sadomasochism" and other forms of power play, and people who engaged in pederastic practices (Meeker 2001, 91). In fact, several of the organization's leaders had fond memories of being inducted into gay erotic and political life through relationships with older men. Hay, for example, was only seventeen years old in 1929 when he learned all about homosexual politics and "all the positions a homosexual boy needs to know" from a thirtysomething-year-old who had been involved, sexually, with the Society for Human Rights (Sears 2006, 115). Other Mattachine members, even if they stopped short of condoning pederasty or promoting adult-youth relationships, questioned the ethics of neglecting adolescents and developed educational outreach programs designed to guide homosexual youth into adult gay life (Meeker 2001, 98–99).

At times, the fostering of homoeroticism among young people extended beyond the question of a political agenda and coincided with calls for a homosexual style of parenting. In 1961, ONE Inc., which was founded a year after the Mattachine Society and known for its edgier and more combatant style of organizing, published a provocative (and potentially satirical) piece in its monthly magazine. James R. Steuart's article "Homosexual Procreation" outlined a blueprint for a world in which lesbians and gay men would collectively raise children in a pro-homosexual environment encouraging of non-monogamous same-sex relationships (quoted in Rivers 2013, 48–49). While his insistence that lesbians only be inseminated with the sperm of gay men with high IQs reveals the troubling eugenic impulses guiding his utopic longings, Steuart's willingness to imagine a regenerative form of homosexuality is noteworthy for how it departed from ongoing debates about the fitness of homosexuals for parenthood. Not unlike homophile efforts to mentor homosexual youth into homosexual adulthood, this alternative vision for parenting rejected the assumption that heterosexuality was the only desirable outcome for childhood development and instead sought to channel the perverse desires traversing family life toward a collective lesbian or gay identity.

For lesbian activists, the question of parenting emerged not as a hypothetical scenario but as a rather pressing issue. The Daughters of Bilitis, the women-centered homophile organization founded in 1955 by four couples (which included two women with children), sought to address the particularities of the lesbian experience. During this period, far more lesbians than homosexual men were living with children. While many were caring for children from previous marriages—women were more likely than men to maintain custody of their children, especially if they kept their sexuality secret, and even if they moved in with their partners, two women living together raised fewer suspicions than two men—others were raising children conceived while engaging in heterosexual sex for money, pleasure, or both. It was not uncommon, as Rivers documents, for lesbian mothers to live in interracial bohemian neighborhoods and raise children within working-class butch/femme communities (2013, 34–42).

This was not, however, the version of lesbianism at the heart of the Daughters of Bilitis's efforts to "promot[e] an educational program on the subject of sex variants, and for sex variants" (quoted in Gallo 2006, 7). Started initially as a social club for women in San Francisco looking for an alternative to the bar scene where police harassment was the norm, the group eventually grew into a national organization officially committed to empowering professional lesbians "of good moral character" and advancing the "integration of the homosexual into society" (4, 11). In addition to supporting the production of accurate and affirming knowledge about homosexuality, the Daughters of Bilitis advocated for legislative reform and homosexual rights. During the early

years, individual members, who tended to be white and middle class, sometimes resented the ways in which public sex practices fueled antihomosexual
sentiments among state officials, but the organization remained committed to
the homophile project of challenging the police brutality and unfair sex laws
endangering the lives of their male counterparts and other marginalized sexual
minorities.[9]

From the start, the Daughters of Bilitis adopted a "staunchly feminist orientation," focusing on the intersections of sexism and heterosexism and attuned
to the specific needs of lesbian women (Gallo 2006, 27). Because mothers
were always a part of the organization—a 1958 survey of members indicated
that nearly 15 percent of the more than 150 respondents were raising children
(Rivers 2013, 49)—family and parenting issues were regular themes in local
chapter programming. Just a year after forming, the organization was already
running discussion sessions titled "Raising Children in a 'Deviant' Relationship." In the hopes of assuaging the fears of lesbian mothers who worried their
children would become homosexuals, the organizers invited child psychiatry
experts who would assure members that, as long as they were loving parents,
they would not damage or endanger their children's social and sexual development (50). Over the next decade, as lesbian mothers from across the country
wrote to the Daughters of Bilitis asking for advice and expressing their appreciation for the organization's existence, the leaders began collecting these letters as a way of recording the collective experience of lesbian motherhood
and ideally aiding future research on the subject (51). In the late 1960s, the
New York City chapter dedicated several "Gab 'n' Java" sessions to the topic of
homosexual parenting. While the women in attendance were similarly anxious
about the potential effects of their lesbianism on their children, these discussion groups did not revolve around the testimony of medical or psychiatric
authorities but were instead opportunities for women to share their experiences and to learn from each other (51). With the rise of the women's liberation movement and demands for feminist analysis and self-definition, more
members of the Daughters of Bilitis were willing to value their own "expertise"
rather than feeling beholden to the outside expert's perspective on lesbian life
(Gallo 2006, 134). These efforts marked the beginning of the more militant
forms of lesbian and gay parenting activism that would come to define the following decade.

The Right to Parent

As liberationist approaches to homosexual activism began to transform accommodationist strategies, direct action in the name of parental rights became
more possible during the 1970s. Lesbian and gay activists, enraged by unrelent-
ing police violence and inspired by the protest culture of antiracist and antiwar

movements, began calling for more combative styles of organizing and started more forcefully challenging the pathologization of same-sex desire. Following the successful removal of homosexuality from the American Psychiatric Association's list of "mental disorders" in 1973, lesbian- and gay-identified parents were empowered to fight to retain custody of—or at least maintain contact with—their children from previous heterosexual relationships. The right to parent thus emerged as a central organizing principle within certain circles of lesbian and gay activism. Importantly, however, the notion of parental rights during this period held broader meaning when compared to how the concept circulates within family equality advocacy today. While calls for the right to parent—or perhaps more accurately, the right to continue parenting after coming out—were often specifically about securing custodial rights and parental recognition from the state, lesbian mothers and gay fathers were also working in solidarity with racial, economic, and reproductive justice movements. As such, they often pursued a notion of parental rights that mobilized radical democratic traditions and thus exceeded a liberal legal framework. In the battle for the right to parent during the 1970s and early 1980s, lesbian and gay activists combined pragmatic courtroom strategies with intersectional feminist critiques and toggled between investments in redistributive politics and attachments to respectability projects.

In her historical account of family law and sexual politics in the early 1970s, Nancy Polikoff shows how the era's shifting "sexual mores" and changing attitudes around divorce and single motherhood enabled attorneys to ask courts to "disregard a parent's sexual orientation unless it was shown to have an adverse impact o[n] the child" (1999, 39). Family law practitioners relied on clinical experts whose research could provide evidence demonstrating the capacity of lesbians and gay men to raise well-adjusted heterosexual children. Taking shape at precisely the moment gay liberation gave rise to a "militant gay liberalism" (Hanhardt 2013, 83–84), this pragmatic legal approach countered claims about the homosexual's unfitness for parenthood with a version of lesbian and gay parenthood compatible with the norms of healthy family life. During this period, judges in several states awarded custody or visitation rights to openly identified lesbians and, in a few instances, gay men, and a Colorado appeals court even ruled in favor of a "transsexual" man whose children had been removed from his home after transitioning (Polikoff 1999, 40). While the increased visibility of same-sex relationships cast suspicion on "strange" domestic arrangements and involuntarily outed parents who might have opted against fighting for parental rights as lesbians or gay men, others saw the courtroom as a key site for advancing a lesbian and gay agenda. They envisioned battles for custody and visitation as a way of pushing back against the state's narrow conceptualization of the family. The indeterminacy of family law, as Kimberly Richman (2010) argues, opened space for redefining parenthood and reconfiguring the legal terrain during the 1970s. On an individual level, however, lesbians, gay men, and transgender parents were subject to the whims of individual judges and remained in vulnerable positions. Not surprisingly, given the eugenicist logics undergirding public debates about homosexual parenting and legal strategies organized around parental fitness, the cases that garnered the most attention and sympathy involved white, middle-class, and normatively gendered women who were separated from their biological children. Yet despite the court's stated "maternal preference" and unstated race and class biases, social and economic privilege did not always translate into victories for lesbian mothers.[10] It was not uncommon for judges, even as they conceded to the individual homosexual's legal right to parent, to attempt to protect children from a threat greater than a single improperly desiring body: homosexual social formations. As such, parents who were awarded custody or visitation were often prohibited from living with their partners, associating with known homosexuals, or engaging in lesbian and gay activism (Polikoff 1999, 40).

In an effort to support mothers navigating this treacherous legal terrain, activists established informal networks for sharing resources and, when necessary, for helping women and children go into hiding during contentious custody battles. This collective labor laid the groundwork for the development of more formalized lesbian mother groups during the 1970s. According to Rivers, while most of these grassroots organizations saw custody as a pressing concern for lesbians and maintained legal defense funds to assist mothers in need, the women leading these groups saw the struggle for parental rights as extending beyond the realm of legal recognition and as tied to a broader feminist movement for racial and economic justice. Driving much of this work was a critique of the state's use of the family as a regulatory relational norm for distinguishing between populations deserving of support and those deemed a threat to child welfare and national prosperity. The Bay Area–based Lesbian Mothers Union, the Seattle-based Lesbian Mothers' National Defense Fund, and the New York City–based Dykes and Tykes group were all founded by lesbian activists who had come to understand the politics of motherhood through their earlier involvement in welfare advocacy, homophile organizing, the civil rights movement, feminist health care activism, and antiwar and anti-imperialism protests (Rivers 2013, 96–98). Never limiting their agenda to a single-issue identity politic, these organizations developed sophisticated analyses of the interlocking systems of oppression that make mothering outside of the white patriarchal family such a precarious enterprise. By foregrounding intersectional approaches that linked motherhood to women's health and economic justice issues, these activists tried to advocate for the depathologization of homosexuality without demonizing others—especially other mothers—living at the margins of respectability.

Take, for example, the coalition-building work of Dykes and Tykes. In addition to calling for the removal of homophobic family court judges, Dykes and Tykes collaborated with antiracist reproductive justice organizations to fight for free abortions and against sterilization abuses (98–99). Similarly, the Lesbian Mothers' National Defense Fund railed against the racist, ableist, and classist logics that inform governmental policies concerning family life and viewed the denial of custodial rights to lesbian mothers as connected to the state's systemic efforts to remove children from poor mothers, disabled mothers, Native mothers, and non-Native mothers of color (101–102).[11] When the two organizations held coordinated Mother's Day rallies on opposite coasts in 1978, they invited speakers, including Audre Lorde (who did a poetry reading at the New York City event), to situate the struggle for parental rights within a larger antiracist redistributive political project. By demanding a more equitable distribution of wealth, resources, and social services, lesbian mother activists saw the fight for the right to parent as involving a broad-based movement dedicated to securing the material support women needed to care for their children, to sustain their households, and to make meaningful decisions about their bodies and their relationships. Yet even as these solidarity projects recognized Native women as highly vulnerable to racialized forms of population control, lesbian mother activists tended to demand changes in state policy without necessarily challenging the legitimacy of the U.S. colonial government. Accepting the nation as self-evident, these coalitional efforts reinforced the authority of the increasingly multicultural settler state and thus remained incommensurable with broader struggles for indigenous sovereignty.[12]

During the 1970s and 1980s, a number of gay father organizations cropped up in urban areas across the United States. As Rivers documents, these groups served an integral function for gay fathers in search of erotic and political community. In the early 1970s, as men struggled to reconcile their position as parents with the "antifamily ethos" of the liberationist movement (Stacey 1996, 109), a feminist politics of gay fatherhood emerged. In Detroit, San Francisco, and New York City, men involved in countercultural activist projects challenged the supremacy of the marital family and the gendered division of labor on which middle-class domesticity depends. Informed by intersectional anticapitalist critiques of marriage and motherhood, they called for and, in some cases, participated in nonnuclear collectives and communal child-rearing arrangements that they believed could give way to a new social order (Rivers 2013, 114–120). Like their lesbian mother counterparts, early gay father organizations engaged in coalition-building practices that were, in many ways, in line with post-Stonewall activism. At the same time, however, activists focusing on parenting during this period often felt alienated by the antifamily sentiments of the lesbian and gay movement: white gay liberationists often denounced the family as the most oppressively heterosexualizing social institution, and white lesbian feminists frequently regarded all forms of domestic and reproductive life as inherently misogynistic and homophobic. For parents who were marginalized not only by mainstream society but also by the countercultural circles that were supposed to sustain them, parenting groups served an important community-building purpose, and the political import of this affective work must not be discounted.

Over the course of the late 1970s and early 1980s, many of these gay father groups morphed into more formal organizations and adopted a more explicitly assimilatory politics of respectability. Such changes were due, in part, to the influx of white professionals into these groups: as more men found it possible to come out without completely sacrificing their race, class, and gender privilege, new members of these groups joined not in the hopes of revolutionizing the family but in search of legal resources and social support as they ended or negotiated marriages with children. Many of these men were noncustodial fathers who were invested in maintaining good relations with their wives or ex-wives in order to secure access to their children. This demographic shift begins to account for the emphasis gay father groups started placing on inclusionary strategies, but this animation of respectability politics was also a response to the backlash taking place against lesbians and gay men during this period. After several cities passed ordinances preventing sexuality-based discrimination in housing and employment, right-wing opponents sought to reverse civil rights gains by reviving the myth of the homosexual as a pedophilic recruiter. In 1977, when Anita Bryant launched her Miami-based "Save Our Children" campaign—which successfully led to Florida instituting the first ban on adoption by lesbians and gay men in the United States—she inspired local movements across the country that fought to replace legal protections for lesbians and gay men with statutes that would bar "perverts" from having contact with children. These antigay efforts galvanized the growing professional class of gay fathers who believed that an increase in their visibility as aspirationally white middle-class family men would provide the best rebuttal to the claim that homosexuals endangered the well-being of children. In the wake of Bryant's campaign, groups like Gay Fathers of Los Angeles, the Gay Fathers Forum of New York, and San Francisco Bay Area Gay Fathers saw their participation in pride parades as an antidote to the younger, hedonistic, and overtly eroticized aspects of lesbian and gay culture that they thought fueled the Right's homophobic attacks (Rivers 2013, 121–127). This new wave of gay father activism shifted away from solidarity organizing in the name of economic justice and toward an identity politic organized around calls for parental civil rights. This is not, however, to suggest that these father groups did not function as or were somehow disconnected from public sexual cultures.

In the early 1980s, with the onset of the AIDS crisis, the priorities of many local gay father organizations shifted out of necessity. While the exact toll the epidemic took on parenting communities is largely undocumented, Rivers, based on the oral histories he collected, estimates that between 70 and 90 percent of the members of the gay father groups in Los Angeles and San Francisco died from AIDS-related illnesses during the 1980s (2013, 135). As members scrambled to respond to the devastating effects of the epidemic, these groups held sessions on how to handle material concerns like wills and health insurance and how to deal with emotions ranging from fear to grief to a desire for "unsafe" sex, and their newsletters became key sites for sharing information about transmission and prevention and for memorializing the lives of fathers who died of complications from AIDS (134). One of the founders of Bay Area Gay Fathers—who, as the owner of the Sutro Bath House, was also fighting against repressive public health measures during this period—recalls healthy members becoming caretakers for those who were dying (134). For parents, the networks of care that lesbians and gay men developed at the height of the epidemic intersected with communal forms of child rearing. At the same time, the public's persisting concerns about homosexuality's disease-like communicability were now manifesting as panic over the always already HIV-positive gay man who posed an immediate threat to the health and safety of all families, including his own. Aware of how this climate of fear was affecting children, the Gay Fathers Forum of New York started an "AIDS and Action" group for teenagers with gay dads and scheduled public discussions about how AIDS-related anxieties were interfering with men's relationships with their children and their children's mothers (135).

During this period, however, while local groups were working to support families grappling with homosexuality's repathologization, a national gay father movement was taking shape around the goal of normalizing gay men as able-bodied and able-minded parents. The formation of the Gay Fathers Coalition International in 1979, the umbrella organization that would eventually become Family Equality Council, kick-started a coordinated nationwide effort to increase the visibility of gay men committed to fatherhood and familial futurity. To borrow Robert McRuer's language, rather than cultivating a queer family politics indebted to AIDS activism, feminist health movements, and "cultures of disability" more broadly, the national lesbian and gay parenting movement was built around a "cult of ability," where healthy homosexuals promised to raise even healthier children (2006, 86).

The Gayby Boom

During the 1970s, conversations about lesbian and gay parenting, within activist circles and beyond, revolved largely around the experiences of men and women who were struggling to maintain parental rights over the children they had before coming out. Over the course of the 1980s, however, public debates about sexuality and family life changed as an increasing number of open lesbians and gay men decided to bear, raise, adopt, foster, coparent, or somehow incorporate children into the kinship networks they were creating. Unlike their homophile-era counterparts, people who came of age in the wake of lesbian and gay pride were less likely to think of themselves as pathologically perverse or to regard their desires and relations as inherently dangerous to children. As such, more lesbians and gay men were willing to devise creative legal, technological, and community-based solutions to what was now perceived as the logistical problem of having children without engaging in reproductive sex with a primary partner.[13] Activist organizations began hosting workshops and conferences on building families and raising children outside of procreative marriages, and stories about the "gayby boom" started appearing in the lesbian and gay press as well as mainstream news media outlets. The majority of lesbians and gay men who were parents during this period were raising adopted children or children from previous heterosexual relationships, but within the national imaginary, the face of gay parenting belonged to the lesbian mother who conceived through donor insemination. While the panic around HIV/ AIDS may have reignited deep-seated fears about perversity and promiscuity and revived gay masculinity's association with disease and death, the growing interest in procreative forms of homosexuality, and lesbianism in particular, sparked a new host of anxieties about the state of family life in the United States. The shift taking place within lesbian and gay communities—from fighting for the right to continue parenting the children they had before coming out to insisting on the right to form families as openly lesbian or gay adults—must be understood with respect to the coinciding rise of a conservative family values movement forged in response to a perceived crisis in the American family.

In *Families We Choose*, Kath Weston (1991) identifies this period as a pivotal moment for queer politics in the United States. While she situates the spike in planned lesbian pregnancies in relation to the pronatalist sentiment of the 1980s, she is careful not to dismiss gay parenting as a "homosexual adjunct" to a larger national trend (168). Instead, Weston explores the ways in which the desire for parenthood "developed and [was] meaningfully interpreted" within broader conversations about the politics of kinship (168). According to her ethnographic research, as sexism, racism, and classism fractured the fantasy of a coherent lesbian and gay community united under the disco anthem "We Are Family," lesbians and gay men began to deploy the language of kinship in describing the smaller-scale and more intimate relationships on which their survival depended. As a consequence, many of Weston's informants who were living in the Bay Area during the mid- and late 1980s were less likely to see the coming-out process as necessitating one's "exile" from kinship or denouncement of the idea of family. Instead, they talked about forming "chosen families" that could provide an escape from or a supplement to their "families of origin." This critical engagement with kinship marked a significant departure from the skepticism with which some gay and feminist activists regarded family life, a skepticism that threatened to alienate people with children, poor and working-class people, Native peoples, and non-Native people of color. An antifamily ethos could not account for why some lesbians and gay men might want to preserve their cultural or political attachments to families and communities who were homophobic or why others might see parenthood not as a heterosexual imperative but as a way of fighting back against histories of genocidal violence and reaching toward more just futures. As such, Weston wondered if the preoccupation with lesbian pregnancy and gay parenting might disrupt the unmarked whiteness of the growing lesbian and gay movement by instigating dialogue about the racial and sexual politics of family life.

Moreover, Weston saw transformative potential in the diverse networks of care that lesbians and gay men were building together as the height of the AIDS crisis coincided with the early years of the "gayby boom." These alternative family formations, established not just out of necessity but, at times, as part of larger ethical commitments, often spanned multiple households, thus refusing the privatized model of domesticity. Family, within these contexts, revolved around a shared sense of belonging and responsibility rather than an investment in a single romantic partnership. The donor insemination agreements and coparenting arrangements made between lesbians and gay men—like the kinship bonds forged among exes, lovers, and friends working together to care for those dying of AIDS-related illnesses—valued political alliances and nonerotic intimacies as legitimate components of family life. Becoming a parent did not necessitate a retreat from collective life into the privacy of the home; rather, intentional family-building practices, as exhausting and as complicated as they were, could function as ways of fulfilling decolonial desires, sustaining racial and ethnic communities, and expanding queer cultural formations. In *Waiting in the Wings* (1997), for instance, Cherríe Moraga looks back on her decision to have a child in an "era of dying" (32) and reflects on the process of "making queer familia" (119) with her white femme lover and her gay Chicano "comadre" (who started out as a donor and ended up as a kind of a father to her son). As she chronicles the deaths of her friends who had lived on the margins of respectability—men of color, some of whom identified as gay, who had contracted HIV and women of color, many of whom identified as lesbians, who had developed cancer—she wonders if there might have been a "queer balance" to the "birthing and dying" that marked this period (62). The radical potential of lesbian and gay parenting, as Weston explicitly argues and Moraga's narrative suggests, lay in the hope of raising children who might imagine lives not already scripted by white middle-class familial norms. Yet despite Weston's account of the efforts to dislodge the primacy of conjugal domesticity and the nuclear family, she was concerned that mounting right-wing pressures would divert activist energies away from reconceptualizing the relationship between family life and public culture and toward the more conservative project of securing marriage rights for committed couples. She presciently closes *Families We Choose* by cautioning against a movement that would "privileg[e] certain forms of family while delegitimating others" (1991, 209).

As we now know, Weston's fears were not unfounded: the rightward shift of U.S. public culture during the late twentieth century had profound effects on lesbian and gay organizing and social justice activism more broadly. In the early 1980s, the rise of the Moral Majority and the election of Ronald Reagan unleashed a powerful backlash against the radicalism, antifamilialism, and "cultures of downward redistribution" associated with the social and economic justice movements of the 1960s and 1970s (Duggan 2003, xvii). Leaders of the New Christian Right mobilized their conservative base by manufacturing a moral panic around the disintegration of the American family. They pointed to falling birth rates; rising divorce rates; and increasing rates of single mothers, unmarried domestic partners, and step- and blended families as evidence of the crisis. By refusing to recognize these demographic trends as a common occurrence across deindustrializing nations during this period, the Right absolved itself from addressing the ways in which newly configured economic conditions rendered the nuclear family ideal an even less achievable—let alone sustainable—formation for already marginalized communities (Stacey 1996, 43). Ignoring the devastating effects that deregulatory reforms and the financialization of capital were having on everyday lives, the Right identified changes in familial patterns as the cause (rather than the effect) of growing poverty rates.

According to this logic—which mobilized 1960s research on the social and structural causes of urban poverty for explicitly conservative ends[14]— unmarried nonwhite parents, especially single black mothers receiving public assistance, were failing to protect their children from crime, violence, drug use, and unemployment and were therefore responsible for the tragic deterioration of their communities. The moralizing tone of such assessments thinly masked the racism and, specifically, the antiblackness of the political-economic agenda underlying the Right's profamily cultural project. Coding their pathologization of black sociality—and black female sexuality in particular—by talking about the "culture of dependency" plaguing urban black communities, conservative leaders mobilized enduring perceptions of black bodies as primitively perverse and morally unsound (as discussed in the introduction)—and more recent diagnoses of the breakdown of the black family (as exemplified by *The Moynihan Report* [1965][15])—to justify the implementation of what would come to be known as neoliberal reforms—namely, the dismantling of the already weak U.S. welfare state and the dramatic expansion of policing and punishment systems.[16] Within this landscape, conjugal domesticity, held up as the linchpin of social order, was presented as the only way to stop intergenerational poverty and to preserve the health and safety of American society.

Given the overwhelmingly heteronormative character of this white supremacist family values movement,[17] it is not surprising that the Right was also waging war on what was frequently referred to as the "homosexual lifestyle" during this period. On the heels of Anita Bryant's pedophilic hysteria and in the midst of the HIV/AIDS panic, little rhetorical work was needed to stoke fears about the homosexual's assault on national morality and domestic health. At times, the construction of homosexuality as antithetical to the family rendered lesbian- and gay-identified parents invisible within national sexual politics debates. In the 1986 *Bowers v. Hardwick* decision, for instance, the Supreme Court upheld the constitutionality of state sodomy laws by refusing to extend the right to privacy to men who had sex with men, arguing that such a privilege was reserved for consensual sexual conduct related to "family, marriage, or procreation," activities with which homosexuality had "no [demonstrated] connection." By positioning the homosexual outside of and at odds with family life while also ensuring the continued criminalization of sodomy, *Bowers* left actual and aspiring lesbian and gay parents legally vulnerable within a profamily climate growing increasingly hostile to deviations from white domestic norms.

Consequently, when lesbians and gay men asserted their desire to form families, the state was ready and willing to push back. Take, for example, the limits placed on the rights of lesbians and gay men to foster or adopt children through government-funded child welfare programs: in 1985, Massachusetts declared heterosexual families the ideal choice for placing foster children; in 1987, New Hampshire officially banned lesbian and gay adults from fostering or adopting children; and in 1988, Reagan's federal task force on adoption issued recommendations against allowing homosexuals to become adoptive parents (Rivers 2013, 184). Additionally, due to the growing visibility of lesbian mothers conceiving through artificial insemination, resistance to gay parenting was also bound up with backlashes against feminist health activist efforts to achieve more autonomy over reproductive processes. The grassroots distribution of insemination resources on low-tech, at-home alternatives to expensive and often exclusionary clinical procedures denaturalized reproduction while challenging the masculinist authority of medical professionals. As a threat to the Right's investment in naturalizing the supremacy of whiteness and the heteropatriarchal order of things, anxieties over pregnant lesbians during the 1990s dovetailed with racialized concerns about unmarried parents and the rise of fatherless families.

This became even clearer as advisers to the Bush administration pushed "family values" as a central issue during the 1992 presidential race. In the lead-up to the election, George H. W. Bush repeatedly expressed his dismay over the decline of the American family. But it was the vice president who offered the most memorable performance of Republican moral panic. In a speech before the elite Commonwealth Club of San Francisco, Dan Quayle condemned the fictional television character Murphy Brown for her decision to have a child outside of marriage.[18] Delivered just two weeks after the Rodney King protests, his speech traced the roots of the Los Angeles "riots" to the "breakdown of family structure" and called for more "law and order" to address the "poverty of values" infecting inner cities. According to the vice president, the "lawless social anarchy" that the nation had just witnessed stemmed from the growing number of "never married mothers" held back by a "welfare ethos" that enabled "permanent dependence," and he demanded reforms to the family welfare and criminal justice systems that would promote "education," "hard work," "personal responsibility," and "dignified independence." In the final moments of his speech, he stepped away from his "urban agenda" to take aim at prime-time television's assault on family values: he was appalled to see the program *Murphy Brown* glorifying single motherhood by "mocking the importance of fathers" and "calling it just another 'lifestyle choice.'" Making no explicit mention of lesbians or gay men, Quayle's use of the language of "lifestyle" conjured up the image of the homosexual. Within the context of his speech and U.S. national culture, his comments gestured toward the Right's concerns about the antifamily nature of homosexuality and the dangers associated with what was perceived as the sudden surge in lesbian and gay parenting.

From Parents to Families

The vice president's branding of single straight motherhood as a "lifestyle choice" was also significant in that it served as a clear reminder that not all practicing heterosexuals could escape the mark of perversity. Heteronormativity deems the sexual choices of any figure desiring outside the bounds of white middle-class domesticity as morally suspect, an affront to civilized life, and unworthy of citizenship status. In her brilliant analysis of the racial and sexual stigmatization of "punks, bulldaggers, and welfare queens," Cathy Cohen illuminates the ways in which intersectional critiques can "identify those spaces of shared or similar oppression and resistance that [might] provide a basis for radical coalition work" (1997, 453).[19] During the early 1990s, as the Republican Party was ramping up its war on nonnormative family structures, the emerging national lesbian and gay family movement could have built on its historical ties to antipoverty activism and women of color organizing to resist the familial standards that limited their collective capacity to become parents and to gain recognition as such. This is not, however, the direction that lesbian and gay parenting activism took at the end of the twentieth century. As U.S. political culture drifted further rightward, social justice workers had access to even fewer resources and, in the face of these constraints, often chose to focus on narrow problems that were legible to a wide audience, that could be solved via legal mechanisms, and that would as such be attractive to private funders.[20] Under these conditions, broad-based mobilizations in the United States fractured into smaller, less disruptive single-group or single-issue projects: "identity politics, in the contemporary sense of the rights-claiming focus of balkanized groups organized to pressure the legal and electoral systems for inclusion and redress, appeared out of the field of disintegrating social movements" (Duggan 2003, xviii). It is this convergence of cultural, political, and economic forces that curtailed the emergence of a lesbian and gay family movement predicated on a coalitional analysis of American familialism and that facilitated instead a movement organized around a desire for recognition as American families. Operating at the margins of the larger lesbian and gay movement, parenting activists followed the lead of the most well-resourced organizations and sought access to citizenship via an increasingly assimilatory rights-based agenda.

In 1992, when lesbian and gay parenting advocates issued an official statement in response to the Right's defense of traditional American values, they focused strictly on the homophobic exclusions of same-sex intimacies from the category of family without calling into question the very concepts of "tradition" and "Americanness." The Gay and Lesbian Parents Coalition International (GLPCI), which had changed its name from the Gay Fathers Coalition International six years before, weighed in on these national debates after President Bush took specific aim at homosexual parenting. One month after Quayle's *Murphy Brown* speech, in an interview with the *New York Times* about his first term and future goals, the president was invited to clarify his family values platform. When asked if he thought it was wrong for lesbians and gay men to have children, he explained that he "can't accept as normal life style people of the same sex being parents" because he believed that "the best shot that a kid has is to have a mother and father" (*New York Times* 1992). A week later, when the GLPCI convened in Indianapolis for their annual conference, the organization crafted an official response to Bush's comments. Taking a stance against the Right's narrow conception of proper familial forms, the leaders argued that the American family had "evolved" and was better understood as "individuals who love and care for one another, whatever their biological connections, marital status or sexual orientation" (Gay and Lesbian Parents Coalition International 1992). At the close of the weekend-long event, the newly elected executive board held a press conference, where they insisted that the "most important ingredient" for bringing up happy and healthy children was not marriage or heterosexuality but unconditional parental love (*Weekly Observer* 1992, 5).

Additionally, the GLPCI collected signatures from parents and children at the conference and later released an open letter to the president about lesbian and gay family values. The letter began by arguing that the Republican Party's homophobic remarks indicated a lack of familiarity with the "over four million lesbian mothers and gay fathers" that, according to very liberal estimates, were "raising eight to ten million children" in the United States.[21] According to the GLPCI (1992), lesbian and gay parents shared Bush and Quayle's concerns about the state of the American family, but they failed to see how "more rhetoric about . . . what is 'normal'" would improve the situation: if the government were actually invested in "strengthening the family," then public officials would turn their attention to issues like "the economy, affordable health care, child care, an education system that works for all children, and non-discrimination in [the] legal system." Notably, even as the GLPCI reframed the crisis in the family in a way that reflected its historical ties to broad-based economic justice movements, the organization broke from those radical roots when, in the following paragraph, the parents and children who signed the letter demanded recognition as "the American family." This embrace of an imagined U.S. national culture is indicative of the race and class privilege and settler and citizenship status that was coming to characterize the national parenting rights movement even in its nascency. Lesbians and gay men, the GLPCI argued, are uniformly dedicated to teaching their children traditional values like "telling the truth, working hard, doing homework, and being good neighbors and citizens." Like all loving parents, the letter explains, they worry about "how to pay for a college education," "whether or not [their kids] watch too much television," and "keeping them away from drugs and alcohol." By deploying the same rhetoric mobilized by Bush and Quayle to demonize black family life, the GLPCI strategically distanced its constituents from the "broken families" supposedly responsible for urban chaos and the demise of American society. More than just an attempt to increase the visibility of lesbian- and gay-headed households, the letter sought to construct lesbian and gay parents as respectable, future-oriented citizens motivated by familial and national attachments and invested in instilling capitalist values in their children.

The GLPCI's uncritical claims on citizenship were consistent with the assimilatory trends that were coming to define social justice activism during this period and that facilitated what Urvashi Vaid (1995) has described as the "mainstreaming of gay and lesbian liberation." In the early 1990s, the emergence of a professional gay middle class—a population consisting predominantly of white, upwardly mobile, and normatively gendered men who had gained a reputation as powerful organizers through their AIDS activism—caught the attention of strategists working for marketing firms and political campaigns. Unlike the Republican leaders who were advancing an unapologetically homophobic agenda, the Democratic Party was trying to figure out how to take advantage of the electoral value attached to this newly forming niche market. While some of the targeted lesbian and gay voters were, of course, parents who had been previously married or who had started families as "gayby boomers," it was their money, not their parental status, that Bill Clinton's campaign found politically attractive. Unable to guarantee increased funding for AIDS research and unwilling to take on the cause of lesbian and gay family politics, the Democratic Party courted individual donors and political action committees with the rather modest campaign promise of expanded antidiscrimination legislation. Far from offering any sort of substantive political-economic change, Clinton's willingness to entertain a lesbian and gay civil rights bill was, at best, a pledge to remove the barriers that prevented the already privileged from realizing their full entrepreneurial potential in a competitive neoliberal marketplace. By reimagining the concept of civil rights in ways that disavowed the antiracist and anti-imperialist legacies of earlier movements, the rhetoric of lesbian and gay equality was put to work in the service of neoliberalism's consolidation of wealth and upward distribution of resources (Vaid 1995; Duggan 2003). In the end, the election of Clinton led to neither the repeal of the military's exclusionary policy[22] nor the implementation of federal employment nondiscrimination laws. Still, the 1992 presidential race had a lasting effect on lesbian and gay organizing in the United States: upon recognizing the apparent viability of a rights-focused agenda, movement leaders and philanthropic foundations diverted the limited resources available for lesbian and gay activism toward inclusionary projects organized around litigation, lobbying, and legislation.

Over the course of the 1990s, as activists negotiated the Clinton administration's secular brand of family values, calls for marriage and adoption rights joined and, to a degree, supplanted demands for military access, nondiscrimination protections, and hate crimes legislation as the top priorities for lesbian and gay organizations in the United States. In 1996, when the president responded to growing concerns over the prospect of same-sex marriage by signing into law the Defense of Marriage Act (DOMA), he, as I will discuss in chapter 3, galvanized the freedom to marry movement. Consistent with the anti-intersectional trends defining lesbian and gay activism during this period, neither the major national organizations nor the burgeoning family movement prioritized the cultivation of solidarity alliances with other communities impacted by Clinton's oppressive family-centric policies. The same year that DOMA passed, the president also approved two other pieces of legislation that "mandated middle-class marital heterosexuality as the official norm and penalized anyone who was unable or unwilling to conform" (Luibhéid

2002, 28): the Personal Responsibility and Work Opportunity Reconciliation Act (also known as the Welfare Reform Act), which limited cash assistance for the poor and favored marriage promotion and low-wage employment as the solution to poverty,[23] and the Illegal Immigration Reform and Immigrant Responsibility Act, which raised the income requirements for people trying to sponsor relatives for immigration via family reunification policies. Passed within a few weeks of one another, these three acts brought into sharp focus the capitalist state's reliance on the marital family as a tool for managing racially and sexually perverse populations. As such, this historical juncture might have served as a rallying point for forging "transformational coalitional politics among marginalized subjects" and "develop[ing] political analyses and political strategies effective in confronting the linked yet varied sites of power in this country" (Cohen 1997, 482). Instead, lesbian and gay activists, answering to the gay moneyed elite, adhered to the rules of contemporary identity politics and pursued access to marriage as a singular issue tied to a singular identity group. Posing no challenge to the regulatory mechanisms of heteronormativity, lesbian and gay rights projects demanded rights and recognition for same-sex couples who organized their intimate lives around white supremacist relational norms.

In doing so, the mainstream movement professed a collective desire that was no longer directed toward the cultivation of queer public culture but was now oriented toward the kind of privatized family life on which the neoliberal state depends.[24] The figure of the lesbian or gay parent occupied an ambiguous position within this newly configured field of lesbian and gay activism. Symbolically, parents held out the promise of advancing a domesticated agenda by rendering lesbian and gay social formations familial and, by extension, legible. Parental rights—narrowly defined through a liberal legal framework and largely focused on adoption rights—thus emerged as a key issue for lesbian and gay rights organizations. Despite the growing consensus among legal experts and social scientists regarding the fitness of lesbians and gay men for parenthood, the 1990s was a volatile period for prospective and current parents: the much-publicized Sharon Bottoms case encapsulated the persisting precarity of lesbian- and gay-identified parents in the arena of custody battles,[25] and the restrictions on fostering and adoption rights proposed in seven states and passed in two illuminated the anxieties that continued to surround the presence of children in lesbian and gay households. The major U.S.-based lesbian and gay organizations responded directly to these attacks and prioritized the removal of discriminatory barriers that interfered with the right to be a parent, but the pragmatic focus on individual identity-based rights often failed to address the needs of lesbians and gay men raising children in an age of heightened visibility and vulnerability. Efforts to gain symbolic entrance to citizenship via marriage and parenthood at some point in the hopefully near future did little to assuage the concerns of parents worried about how the stigma associated with same-sex desires and relations affected their children's emotional and economic well-being in the immediate present. Ironically, as lesbian and gay activist power consolidated around the rhetorical project of domesticating queerness, the GLPCI was left to grapple with the material realities and political complexities of lesbian and gay family life on the underfunded margins of the mainstream movement.

Community Building for Children

The invention of the annual Family Week celebration in Provincetown was one of the strategies GLPCI developed to address the particular needs of families who were dealing with a general public still hostile to the very notion of lesbian and gay parenting. According to Family Week's official origin story, Davenport, a successful corporate consultant, and Fisher, the then president of GLPCI, stumbled upon the idea of hosting a mass gathering for lesbian and gay families while vacationing in Provincetown with their son and daughter in 1995. After spending a week on the beach meeting other lesbian and gay couples with children, Fisher and Davenport invited about fifteen families back to their rental house for a barbecue. The informal event was such an emotionally rewarding experience for the children in attendance that they decided they needed to find a way to re-create the scene for even more families. "It was a magical event," Davenport recalls, "at which children of gay parents—many of whom didn't know other families like theirs—suddenly felt less alone" (Family Equality Council, "Family Week FAQs," n.d.). He and Fisher understood the importance of building community for lesbian and gay parents, but they had not anticipated how crucial lesbian and gay social networks might be for their children. At precisely the moment when the mainstream movement was working to privatize lesbian and gay politics and identities, parenting activists were suggesting that the health and happiness of domesticated lesbian and gay lives might depend on the continuation of vibrant lesbian and gay public cultures. Since its inception, the Family Week tradition has, perhaps unwittingly, worked both for and against ongoing efforts to showcase the fitness of lesbians and gay men for parenthood and to reconcile same-sex desires and relations with domesticity, reproductivity, and national futurity.

Although the official narration of Family Week's inception suggests that Fisher and Davenport were the first to have this epiphany about the importance of lesbian and gay networks for childhood development, community-building events for lesbian and gay families were, in fact, quite common during this period. By the mid-1990s, one of the primary concerns facing parenting advocates, as evidenced by news stories in the mainstream media (Gross 1991; Goleman 1992; Chira 1993) and the lesbian and gay press (Gallagher 1995;

Sundquist 1995), was the ways in which homophobia negatively impacted the social and psychic lives of children being raised by same-sex couples. Marking a significant break from earlier fears about how *homosexuality* might disrupt the sexual and emotional development of children, parenting groups were now obsessing over the ways in which *homophobia* plagued the everyday lives of their children. Reports revealed that young teens often endured teasing from their classmates or felt stigmatized by their parents' sexual identities. Some children, in the hopes of avoiding such harassment, stayed closeted about their families at school and never invited friends to their homes, which then led them to feel cut off from their peers. Feelings of isolation were also common among children who were open about their parents' identities and who were connected with local lesbian and gay communities because, even within those settings, they did not always encounter other children with lesbian and gay parents. With these experiences in mind, parents and advocates started organizing camps, barbecues, and conferences as a way of helping children from lesbian and gay families connect with one another. In fact, the GLPCI's annual conference had, since 1989, included specific programming for children, and had, since 1991, doubled as the annual conference for its autonomous youth-centered program called Just for Us. Family Week may have ended up as the largest of these family-centric events, but at the time, it was neither the first nor the only of its kind.

Over the next decade, as Family Week grew in size and scale,[26] the annual swarming of lesbian and gay families to Provincetown attracted ever more media attention (Kiritsy 2002; Howey 2003; Bernstein 2007). As such, Fisher and Davenport's child-centric community-building event was soon doubling as a visibility project serving the interests of a family movement increasingly preoccupied with marital rights and relationship recognition. By pouring its limited resources into an event that attracted predominantly white two-parent families who were physically able and financially capable of vacationing on Cape Cod, the GLPCI was, in many ways, advancing the mainstream movement's agenda of aligning same-sex intimacies with respectability and reproductivity and marking lesbian and gay couples as deserving of state recognition and legal protections. At the same time, however, the very premise of Family Week interrupted the privatization of lesbian and gay life by insisting on the continued importance of public culture. Putting forth a model of parenting at odds with the (neo)liberal fantasy that all our emotional needs can be met within the confines of nuclear family life, the GLPCI's investment in community threatened to undermine its ongoing efforts to affirm the fitness of lesbians and gay men as parents. Family Week presumes the inadequacy of lesbian and gay households for the task of raising well-adjusted children and, in spite of persisting anxieties regarding the child's proximity to queerness, suggests that the health and happiness of some children actually depends on their access to lesbian and gay social formations. In a striking reversal of earlier fears of homosexual subcultures that were allegedly out to molest, convert, or simply destroy the child, the organizers of Family Week were advocating for the immersion of children into lesbian and gay culture.

The staging of the annual event in P'town, a gay tourist resort known for its sexualized public culture and queer cultural productions, only makes Family Week seem even more at odds with the GLPCI's agenda. Given the organization's investment in casting lesbian and gay families as "just like" any other middle-class American family, Fisher and Davenport's decision to hold the event on beaches where nudity and sex acts were not uncommon and in the streets where drugs, alcohol, sex toys, and assless chaps flowed freely is somewhat surprising. But the founders of Family Week tell the origin story in ways that emphasize the location's reputation as the most beautiful gay-friendly summer destination in the United States, a place where families would "not have to explain who [they] are" and would be "able to totally relax" (*Queer Spawn* 2005). Ignoring the ways in which some queer families try to resist the "politics of sexual shame" and to liberate youth from "a prescribed notion of what it means to be a sexual, alive, [and] loving person" (Epstein 2005, 13), the appeal of P'town, according to the organizers' official accounts, has nothing to do with the fact that parents might want access to erotic subcultural activities or might want to introduce their children to a creatively sex-positive environment. Yet even if all the families who sign up for Family Week attend with only the most wholesome of expectations, I cannot help but wonder about the unintended effects involved in exposing young people to public expressions of gender and sexual variety. Is it possible that P'town, not exactly a "normal" site for a family vacation, might nurture children's tendencies toward perverse fantasies and embodiments?

Take, for example, Tristan Taormino's memories of P'town. The feminist sex educator, known for her best-selling guides to anal sex and open relationships, locates some of her most formative experiences during a summer in the mid-1980s, when she lived with her gay father on the tip of the Cape. In her contribution to *Out of the Ordinary*, a collection of essays by children who grew up with gay, lesbian, or transgender parents, Taormino recalls working as a fifteen-year-old in a leather shop in P'town and spending her free time at lesbian potluck dinners and five o'clock tea dances at the famous Boatslip bar (2000, 18). She traces her "power femme" identity and her penchant for "daddy play" back to the time she spent with her father, his cross-dressing friends, and his community of lovers (20). With this story in mind, Fisher and Davenport's attempt to offer the children of lesbian and gay families a broader sense of community might be interpreted as also providing them with the chance to think more inventively about gender and sexuality in a setting capable of opening up new possibilities for their erotic futures.

While I am not trying to equate Taormino's largely unsupervised summer-long foray into queer life with the experiences of children participating in structured Family Week activities, I think it is worth considering how inviting children to imagine themselves as part of lesbian and gay communities might affect the formation of their desires and identities. If, as Freud (2000) theorizes, all children possess a polymorphously perverse potential, then improperly staged familial scenes coupled with access to lesbian, gay, and queer cultural formations would surely derail the developmental journey that, even in ideal circumstances, can only ever arrive at an approximation of sexual normalcy. But even without taking up a psychoanalytic framework, a social constructionist perspective on sexual development opens space for considering the unique erotic grammars that parents and communities imprint upon children from a very young age. Different family and social settings, while not necessarily capable of altering psychic forces or physiological sensations, might enable children to develop more creative ways of interpreting and acting on their desires and to become fluent in multiple gender and sexual languages over the course of their lifetimes.[27]

The short film *Queer Spawn* (2005), which focuses on the lives of children from lesbian and gay families in the United States, gestures toward this potentiality. Filmmaker Anna Boluda follows one of her subjects to the tenth-anniversary celebration of Family Week in 2005 and, while there, interviews several teenagers and young adults raised by lesbian or gay parents and invites them to talk about their own sexual identities. One twenty-four-year-old woman explains that both she and her mother identify as "queer" and, using language common at events like Family Week, describes herself as "second generation."[28] She then clarifies that she identified "very strongly as straight" until she got to college and finally realized that she was just "protecting [her] family" and trying to prove that "queers can make straight kids." Another woman, an eighteen-year-old who had been attending Family Week since she was twelve, admits to spending a good portion of her childhood devastated that she would never "really truly" belong to the broader community if she were not also gay: she now accepts her straightness, but she "remember[s] sort of thinking to [her]self, 'Well, maybe I could be a lesbian. Maybe that would work out.'" In the end, these narratives treat sexual orientation as an innate and unchanging aspect of a person's personality. At the same time, they also reveal how contact with lesbian, gay, and queer social life—contact that can incite a will to defend or even belong to an imagined community—can shape the ways in which children experience desire at various points in their lives.

The effects of living and vacationing in such close proximity to lesbian, gay, and queer socialities are not limited to the realm of the erotic and might impact children's political identities and orientations as well. In the closing moments of the film *Queer Spawn*, a final voice-over clarifies that, while decades of social science research show sexual orientation to be irrelevant with respect to parental outcomes, studies have found "one difference" about the children of lesbian and gay parents: "they are more tolerant." Given the overrepresentation of white and economically privileged adults and children in the research on "same-sex parenting," I am hesitant to interpret evidence of "tolerance" as anything more than a sign of a weak multiculturalist ethic, but I am willing to entertain how a familiarity with the cultural practices and productions of places like P'town might afford children from lesbian and gay families a certain savviness when it comes to responding to gender ambiguity or navigating alternative modes of social and sexual behavior. As Juana María Rodríguez suggests, following Sara Ahmed's theorization of race, inheritance, and familial bonds, proximity offers a useful framework for understanding the "acquired skills that come to us through lived exposure to certain people, social conditions, and surroundings" (2014, 45). In some cases, however, more than just inheriting a particular way of seeing and gesturing, children might experience their firsthand encounters with homophobia and their front-row seats to queer artistic and activist responses as formative politicizing events.

The collection *Out of the Ordinary* includes several essays by grown children from lesbian and gay families who describe their involvement in the lesbian, gay, bisexual, transgender, and queer (LGBTQ) community organizing during their teens and early adulthood: several of the contributors discuss their role in forming gay-straight alliances in their high schools while others, many of whom lost parents, parental figures, or family friends to AIDS-related illnesses, reflect on starting HIV/AIDS activist movements on their college campuses (Howey and Samuels 2000). In his contribution to the collection, Stefan Lynch, the lifelong activist responsible for coining the term "queer spawn," recalls in grave detail the specter of antigay violence that loomed large during his childhood in Canada. He also fondly remembers helping his dad (who was involved in the Gay Fathers of Toronto, one of the organizations that founded GLPCI) plaster the city with stickers that read, "No More Shit! Gays Bash Back!" (2000, 65). Years later, in the early 1990s, after losing his father and his father's partner to AIDS complications, Lynch longed to once again be a part of a vibrant activist community and, armed with the inheritance left to him, decided to start a group for kids of queers. Shortly after, he linked up with the leaders of Just for Us, the GLPCI's newly formed youth program, and over the next few years, played an instrumental role in establishing the national organization Children of Lesbian and Gays Everywhere (which has, since 1995, gone exclusively by its acronym COLAGE and has adopted a more bisexual- and transgender-inclusive mission).

In 1999, GLPCI and COLAGE replaced their annual joint conference with Family Week, and P'town has since become a key site for recruiting new COLAGErs. In addition to providing children from lesbian and gay families with an extensive social support network, COLAGE has also worked to empower youth to engage in LGBTQ identity politics and to advocate for safer schools and relationship recognition from a variety of positions, including as "second genners," as straight-identified allies, or like Lynch, as "erotically straight and culturally queer" activists (Woog 1999, 72). Even as COLAGE has remained closely tied to its parent organization, its leaders, a predominantly white group in the early years, often took a more progressive approach to visibility projects, an approach indicative of a broader engagement with antiracist trans and queer movements. For instance, when they weighed in on the same-sex marriage debates with their youth-produced film *In My Shoes* (2005), COLAGE included representations of trans parents, featured racially diverse and not-so-neatly planned families, and raised questions about immigration (albeit in relation to a binational couple, thus ignoring the needs of LGBTQ immigrants not partnered with U.S. citizens and obscuring the particular insecurities facing undocumented immigrants). Now, while I am certainly not looking to celebrate Family Week or even COLAGE as radicalizing forces for the next generation, I read these essays and films as reminders of the ways in which families and family-centric organizing are not inherently repressive sites but can function as productive spaces for transforming desires, inspiring cultural critiques, and constructing politicized subjects. The unintended effects of an event like Family Week—which emerged out of a national parenting movement striving for recognition as normal American families—include the generation of alternative ways of being, desiring, and relating and of more imaginative frameworks for organizing social lives and political movements.

Raising Respectable Citizen-Consumers

That said, Family Week has officially advanced a more conservative set of goals: to provide families with the chance to meet other LGBT-identified parents and their children and to learn more about the "issues" facing LGBT families across the country (Family Equality Council, "Family Week," n.d.). Shortly after the invention of Family Week, the GLPCI underwent significant operational and organizational adjustments and changed its name, in 1999, to Family Pride Coalition and then, in 2007, to Family Equality Council. While the name changes have been explained, respectively, as a way of becoming more inclusive of bisexual- and transgender-identified parents and signaling their expanded commitment to advocating for changes in family law and public policy, these rebranding efforts—which I interpret as reflective of the movement's shift from demanding broadly conceived parental rights to seeking legal recognition as American families—have coincided with the adoption of a top-down corporate-style of management. In addition to abandoning its tradition of holding an annual conference, the organization also hired its first paid executive director and began producing bigger and better corporate-sponsored Family Weeks and developing similar but smaller-scale regional events around the country. Whereas the annual conference had historically served as an opportunity for members to determine the umbrella group's policy positions and to elect the organization's next board (Haider-Markel 1997, 131), Family Week and its offshoots have taken the form of fun and relaxing vacations. Breaking from a tradition of grassroots mobilizing, Family Equality Council adopted a service provision model of organizing that prioritized not survival services for the most vulnerable LGBT families but an educational leisure service for families already enjoying a notable degree of privilege. In many ways, the corporatized expansion of Family Week underlines the ways in which the Council has incorporated the same neoliberal organizing logics that now govern larger mainstream organizations. At the same time, however, a closer look at the annual celebration—and the uneasiness surrounding the staging of a child-friendly gay event in a high-end gay resort town—reveals a clash between competing norms of queerness within the realm of U.S. homonormativity. Because the desires of lesbian and gay parents exist in tension with those of the childless gay moneyed elite, the Council must navigate a discursive terrain in which purchasing power has come to represent the most efficient path to full citizenship.

Today, Family Equality Council works closely with COLAGE to plan Family Week schedules that feature educational sessions and empowerment workshops for parents and children struggling against pervasive forms of homophobia and, to a lesser extent, transphobia in their everyday lives. The programming reflects the Council's recent hiring of professional advocates trained in nonprofit management and its growing reliance on funding from corporate partners and corporatized philanthropic organizations.[29] Take, for example, the "State of the Movement" session at the twentieth-anniversary celebration. At this event, the Council's executive director, senior legislative counsel, and director of public policy provided the parents and children in attendance with a list of the issues families will continue to face in the wake of marriage equality and a detailed account of what the organization was doing to advocate for relevant changes in law and policy. Within this framework, professional movement leaders are tasked with identifying needs, setting the agenda, and leading reform efforts, and the work of base building takes place predominantly through the collection of donations and membership dues. This is not, however, to suggest that the organization wields nearly as much political power as other major lesbian and gay rights organizations in the United States. The Council operates on a budget a fraction the size of that of the Human Rights Campaign (HRC)—a fact made readily apparent during Family Week when comparing the HRC's permanent storefront on Commercial Street to the garage-like space the Council rents a few blocks away as an event registration hub during the annual celebration. I also do not want to discount the importance of Family Week for the many parents and children who wait all year to reconnect with the communities they have built during their summers in P'town. I do, however, want to flag the ways in which the annual celebration is designed less as a vehicle for politicization and mass mobilization and more as a week-long opportunity for capturing videos and photographs of responsible and respectable families that, once uploaded to the Council's website, will ideally garner sympathy and support in the form of monetary contributions.

In an interview published on the *Huffington Post* about the twentieth anniversary of Family Week, Davenport expresses a great deal of pride over the role he believes the annual celebration has played in transforming not just the perception of lesbian and gay people but also the look of lesbian and gay places (Shapiro 2015). Reflecting on the past two decades, he fashions a narrative that, in crediting parents with turning Commercial Street into a more appropriate family vacation destination, echoes and repackages the laments of longtime P'town fans who blame the arrival of strollers and baby carriers for dulling the town's sexual edge. Aside from discounting the possibility that some might find the prospect of engaging in sexual acts in the vicinity of children thrilling, his reductive interpretation of the resort town's recent history fails to account for a more powerful political and economic force at work: the influx of white gay capital into P'town. If crackdowns on public sex on the docks and unlicensed drag performances on the street have rendered P'town a more family-friendly tourist site, this change must be understood with respect to the real estate boom fueled by wealthy gay men during the 1990s who deployed their rapidly expanding purchasing power to acquire residential properties that they reserved for personal summer and weekend use and rarely rented out to the public (Faiman-Silva 2004; Krahulik 2005). The accompanying conversion of guesthouses into single-occupancy homes and repurposing of the wharves into premium condos have left P'town less amenable to the vibrant sexual cultures long associated with the town: in addition to decreasing the number of affordable short- and long-term rentals needed to sustain a community of artists, writers, and travelers, these architectural changes have also encroached upon the spaces that have historically served as sites for anonymous sex and erotic forms of queer sociality (Colman 2005).

The sense of a shrinking public sphere has been exacerbated by the heightening of police presence in nude sunbathing areas and popular cruising locations. While debates about how to handle the issue of sex in public are not new and have dominated local Provincetown politics for the better part of the twentieth century, the early twenty-first century has been marked by a noticeable decline in tolerance for nudity, street culture, and sexual transgressions and a dramatic increase in arrests and citations for public indecency and disorderly conduct (Cayleff 2007). These crackdowns have, in many cases, been waged in the name of protecting innocent children from exposure to sex—news coverage of law enforcement efforts often referenced incidences involving families who were whale watching or exploring the dunes when they stumbled upon groups of naked men engaged in a host of sexual acts (Bragg 2008; Jordan 2008)—but it is hardly fair to solely blame parents, of any sexual identity, for the backlash against sexual publics and the enforced privatization of gay sex. It is crucial to recognize the ways in which white gay capital has been entangled with the town's reinvigorated efforts to "clean up" the gay scene. This is not to suggest that the accumulation of wealth necessarily entails a dissipation or normalization of desire but rather to draw attention to the ways in which concerns about private property value can displace investments in public sexual cultures. In other words, if P'town now feels like a space where queerness is more harshly regulated, this is likely symptomatic not of the "gayby boom" but of the gay elite's participation in ongoing gentrification processes.

Further, there are many ways in which these changes have made P'town less conducive to family life. For starters, skyrocketing real estate prices have had devastating effects on the town's year-round population and have driven working-class white and Portuguese families out of town and up or off the Cape (Krahulik 2005, 198–200). As a result of these twenty-first-century displacements, Provincetown High School, the building where Family Week now holds most of its workshops, was forced to shut down in 2010 due to low student enrollment (Oakes and Tobin 2010). Additionally, the housing takeover by a gay moneyed elite has also coincided with shifts within the travel industry. In an attempt to remain competitive in a saturated lesbian and gay tourism market, Provincetown has tried to remake itself into a less exclusively gay destination where the main attraction is not a sexualized public culture but alternative artistic and cultural productions. Yet even as many business owners have, over the past few years, lifted their "no children allowed" policies to accommodate what has been interpreted as a more "suburban" crowd, the town's boutique guesthouses, upscale restaurants, and art galleries are designed for travelers, gay or straight, with "sophisticated" tastes and plenty of disposable income (Desroches 2006). Generally speaking, P'town is an expensive destination for a family vacation, especially for lesbian and bisexual mothers and trans parents who are statistically more likely to be working with a tighter budget. Family Week may advertise itself as for "all families" (Family Equality Council, "Family Week FAQs," n.d.), but the event, by nature of its location, caters specifically to families who are not only able to handle the costs of vacationing on Cape Cod at the height of the summer season but also willing and able to navigate a predominantly white resort town largely inhospitable to people with mobility disabilities. In an attempt to make Family Week more financially accessible, the Council has a sliding-scale option for the event's registration fees and, as of 2015, offers extra funding through the competitive Fisher-Davenport Scholarship Fund. Additionally, COLAGE includes a number of tips on its website for making Family Week a more affordable experience, such as staying at hostels in nearby Truro or taking advantage of the campgrounds in the area (COLAGE, "Tips for Making Family Week," n.d.).

It is this need for money-saving recommendations that seems to be the source of much of the anxiety surrounding Family Week's impact on Provincetown. In 2008, when the Council changed the dates of Family Week to a more popular week of the summer, members of the Provincetown Business Guild, a nonprofit organization dedicated to promoting the town as a premier LGBT travel destination, expressed its frustrations with the annual family celebration. Notably, their main gripe was not about a perceived loss of eroticism due to the presence of children but rather about the measurable loss of profits that accompanied the arrival of lesbian and gay families. While a story about the backlash against Family Week on the *Provincetown Banner* website elicited several comments from readers enraged about the war that parents seemed to be waging on the town's sexual culture,[30] the business owners interviewed for the article were far more concerned about the harmful effects that the influx of families had on sales at bars, restaurants, guesthouses, and high-end retail shops. The figure of the child, according to this formulation, threatens a gay culture defined not by promiscuous encounters but by conspicuous consumption. While these attacks on Family Week might have been an occasion for the organizers to push back against the myth of gay affluence and to bring questions of economic justice to the fore, the Council bypassed a critique of elitist forms of queer culture and instead aligned LGBT families with consumer citizenship and reproductive futurity. Jennifer Chrisler, the Council's executive director at the time, sympathized with local businesses and emphasized the "value" that Family Week brings to P'town year after year. The Provincetown Chamber of Commerce confirmed that toy stores, ice cream shops, whale-watching tours, and the Pilgrim Monument do, in fact, enjoy an increase in business when children are present, but Chrisler also reminded the owners of other businesses that Family Week should be understood as an investment that promises future returns since the annual celebration functions as "a great introduction to Provincetown for a whole new generation" (Sowers 2008). Children who vacation in P'town, she suggests, grow up to become adults who vacation in P'town.

Acknowledging the family as a site of desire production, the Council refracts the possibility of a "second generation" through the tourism industry and emphasizes the role parents play in shaping consumer desires. The child in this scenario represents a future filled not with more queers but with more consumers—specifically, consumers motivated by nostalgia for the commodified settler and sexual fantasies organizing Provincetown. Over the past two decades, the Council's efforts to make LGBT families visible as consuming units have doubled as an attempt to mark these parents as respectable citizens. Advancing an agenda far removed from the redistributive efforts of the lesbian feminist mothers and radical gay fathers who were organizing in the 1970s, the Council encourages participation in market mechanisms—mechanisms founded upon ongoing processes of colonization, racial subjugation, and ever-expanding systems of displacement and dispossession—as a way of becoming legible and legitimate. Staged within a tourist landscape where settlement is naturalized and commemorated as the foundation of national democratic traditions, what Family Week offers is not a freedom from sexual or kinship regulation; rather, attendees are afforded the freedom to consume as Americans or, more accurately, to enact their Americanness through consumption. Long-standing fears of a reproductive queerness capable of taking down Western civilization, while alive and well within certain right-wing circles, are almost hard to recall when LGBT families are climbing to the top of the Pilgrim Monument and buying their way, quite literally, into the imperial national imaginary. For LGBT-identified parents who spend money not to participate in perverse sexual cultures but to better the lives of their children, a family vacation in P'town can become a route to full and robust citizenship.

2

Visibility

● ●

Local Communities,
Transnational Economies,
and the Exceptionally
American Family

In June 2003, Rosie O'Donnell, the former talk show host and newly out "queen of nice," announced plans for the first cruise designed exclusively for lesbian and gay parents and their children. Inspired in part by the annual Family Week celebration in P'town, her then partner and former Nickelodeon executive, Kelli Carpenter, had teamed up with gay travel expert Gregg Kaminsky. Together, they formed R Family Vacations, chartered a ship through a leading cruise line, and were taking reservations for a Caribbean trip the following summer. In addition to using O'Donnell's celebrity connections to secure top-notch talent for the nightly entertainment, Carpenter and Kaminsky also invited Family Pride Coalition (the organizers of Family Week) to provide educational programming aboard the ship. Billing it as a "gay cruise with 'family values,'" they pitched their child-friendly adventure at sea as uniquely designed for the newly "exploding" lesbian and gay family market (Salvato 2004). Early news coverage of R Family Vacations wondered if the company would be able to improve public perceptions of lesbian and gay parenting within a national climate that was quite hostile to same-sex relations. Launched at the height of the war on terror, the company was taking shape in the face of an aggressively heteronormative and Islamophobic brand of U.S. patriotism. One reporter, reflecting on the newfound visibility that this celebrity-backed venture was affording lesbian and gay families, optimistically speculated that O'Donnell might be "cruis[ing] to equal rights" (Stockwell 2006).

Taking R Family Vacations as its starting point, this chapter examines how performances of parenthood converged with post-9/11 practices of consumption to remake lesbians and gay men into respectable and, importantly, valuable citizens. One of my primary goals in this chapter is to contextualize the formation of O'Donnell's company with respect to the longer history of identity-based consumption and lesbian and gay identity politics in the United States. While commercial activities and touristic styles of consumption have played a central role in the consolidation of middle-class lesbian and gay identity across the twentieth century, the hailing of lesbian and gay consumers specifically as parents marked a new phase within the marketization of LGBT identities and politics. The family vacation, as I began to argue in the previous chapter, can serve as an effective vehicle for resignifying lesbian and gay modes of consumption by distancing them from frivolously perverse activities and aligning them, instead, with family- and future-oriented practices.

Parenthood, by the turn of the twenty-first century, had been imbued with a new significance in the United States. In her analysis of post-Reaganite and post-Clintonite national culture, Lauren Berlant tracks the emergence of what she describes as the "intimate public sphere" and the arrival of new standards for citizenship (1997, 4). To become a valued citizen within this newly configured political context requires a record not of civic acts that invest in a public good but instead of personal acts, "especially acts originating in or directed toward the family sphere" (5). Building on Berlant's formulation, scholars like Ann Anagnost, David Eng, and Alison Shonkwiler have illuminated the ways in which parenting has become "a newly intensified domain" for producing U.S. citizens (Anagnost 2000, 391). For white, abled, and middle-class adults in the age of neoliberalism, "the possession of a child, whether biological or adopted, has . . . become the sign of guarantee both for family and for full and robust citizenship, for being a fully realized political, economic, and social subject in American life" (Eng 2010, 101). By providing parents with the opportunity to publicly perform "maturity and social acceptability" in both material and affective terms, R Family Vacations sought to inscribe lesbian and gay families within U.S. familial ideology through their legibility as consuming units (Shonkwiler 2008, 549–550). In short, the cruise company drew attention to child-centric marketplace activities that could render lesbian and gay adults fit for parenthood and, by extension, citizenship.

At the heart of O'Donnell's foray into lesbian and gay tourism was an investment in the politics of visibility. While the lesbian and gay travel industry has, since its formalized inception in the early 1990s, held out the promise of seeing and being seen by the world, I am not simply referring to the implicit ways in which R Family Vacations was hoping to capitalize on a fantasy revolving around the supposedly transformative effects of spending "pink dollars" across the globe.[1] What I find even more noteworthy is the fact that, thanks to O'Donnell's celebrity status and popular culture connections, the company publicized the development of a lesbian and gay family vacation industry and, in the process, drew extensive media attention to the family-oriented leisure practices of lesbian and gay consumers within the transnational marketplace.

Additionally, O'Donnell granted HBO permission to create a documentary about her 2004 inaugural journey that, while also functioning as a ninety-minute commercial for her vacation company, crafted a positively glowing representation of lesbian and gay American families. As I discuss later, her decision to collaborate on a documentary was motivated, in large part, by her desire to combat homophobic perceptions of same-sex couples and lesbian and gay parenting. Willfully engaging in what Berlant describes as "a kind of vicious yet sentimental cultural politics," O'Donnell sought to intervene in the "mass-mediated space of opinion" and the ongoing battle over which "images and faces" would represent normal and healthy family life in the United States (1997, 3–4). The film follows a few select families over the course of the week-long cruise in order to tell a much larger story about the exceptional nature of lesbian and gay parents, with a specific focus on white parents who build their families by fostering to adopt children of color. Through a close reading of the HBO documentary, I show how the film's portrayal of white parents managing their children's racial difference serves the multicultural nationalist project undergirding calls for lesbian and gay equality during the war on terror. Along the way, I pay particular attention to how discourses of U.S. exceptionalism were mobilized to produce a select class of lesbian and gay parents as exceptionally deserving of legal rights and protections.

After the inaugural cruise, R Family Vacations began organizing smaller land-based vacation packages while also continuing to charter entire ships once or twice a year. In July 2009, I boarded the company's ninth (and what would turn out to be its final) full charter cruise and, for the sake of research, set sail to Alaska. Drawing upon my participant observation research aboard the ship and the interview I conducted with Kaminsky while on the cruise, the second half of this chapter explores the changes that took place in the lesbian and gay travel industry and within the realm of LGBT family advocacy following the election of Barack Obama and in response to what was perceived as the changing landscape of U.S. sexual politics. While the R Family cruise I took departed with virtually no fanfare and attracted, to my knowledge, no media attention, questions of visibility still figured centrally on the decks of the ship and in the broader context of family equality politics.

Over the course of the week, what I discovered as I attended the educational workshops hosted by Family Equality Council (which had recently changed its name from Family Pride Coalition) was the national LGBT family movement's investment in a subtler and smaller-scale version of visibility politics. The facilitators of the workshops were optimistic about the future of LGBT rights given the recent changes within the federal government, but they were also adamant in their insistence that individual families needed to appreciate the ways in which the casual conversations they had in their everyday lives could affect the larger project of rendering LGBT family life legible, respectable, and worthy of state recognition. According to the facilitators, families—narrowly envisioned as two-parent middle-class households—could move us closer to equality if they took more responsibility for how they were seen in their local communities and if they were more intentional in the stories they were telling about themselves on a day-to-day basis. This chapter concludes by illustrating how the Council enacted what Anagnost describes as the intimate public sphere's "ironic reversal of feminist strategy" by "making the political personal" and emphasizing interpersonal exchanges as a key strategy in advancing a family equality agenda increasingly organized around the fight for same-sex marriage rights (2000, 395).

Tourism and the Politicization of Consumption

In the early days of R Family Vacations, when the cofounders would give interviews about their business venture, they often recited the story of their fairy-tale beginning. The details vary between retellings, but the gist is always the same. When Kaminsky was still working for the gay tour operator Atlantis Events, he invited O'Donnell to perform on one of his cruises after a last-minute cancelation (Mersmann 2004). O'Donnell, who was still hosting her daytime talk show and not publicly identifying as a lesbian, decided to help and embarked on her first all-gay vacation. Moved by the sense of community she experienced, she asked Kaminsky if he thought they could organize cruises specifically for lesbian and gay families (Salvato 2004). Over the next few years, O'Donnell went public with her sexuality, began advocating for lesbian and gay parents, and became involved in efforts to overturn Florida's homophobic foster and adoption policies (Stockwell 2006). In fact, she only agreed to grant Diane Sawyer an exclusive interview about her personal life and her "coming out" if she could talk about Florida's ban on lesbian and gay adoptions and if *Primetime Thursday* would do an investigative piece on the state's discriminatory policy (Williams 2002). She then attended the annual Family Week celebration in Provincetown, Massachusetts, with Carpenter and their children. Upon seeing how excited her son was to be around other children with two mothers, she decided that they had no choice but to start running cruises for families (Bernstein 2007). R Family Vacations thus capitalizes on the historical importance of travel for lesbian and gay community formation while simultaneously recasting these potentially suspect modes of consumption as linked to a form of same-sex desire organized around white, middle-class ideals of domesticity.

In her narration of the company's origins, O'Donnell admits to having had high hopes for R Family Vacations. With Carpenter's marketing expertise, Kaminsky's experience in the cruising industry, and her money and fame, she figured there was no way they could fail. At the same time, she claims that turning a profit was never her motive. In one interview, O'Donnell and Carpenter recall one of their first conversations about the possibility of starting a cruise company:

ROSIE: What's the best ship you can get?
KELLI: The *Norwegian Dawn* is a $3 million ship. You don't rent ships for $3 million.
ROSIE: Kelli, we have $3 million. Why can't we rent a $3 million ship?
KELLI: Chances are we might not even break even the first year.
ROSIE: That's ok. We don't have to break even. In fact, if we lost it, that would be ok. (Brunner 2005)[2]

The important thing, according to O'Donnell, was to provide families with the chance to finally "experience being cherished and being treated with dignity and respect" (*PlanetOut* 2006). So she chartered what she claimed was the best ship on the seas, Norwegian Cruise Line's *Norwegian Dawn*, and began taking reservations for a Caribbean cruise scheduled for July 2004. The ship would leave from New York City for a week at sea, and the itinerary included two ports of call in Florida—Cape Canaveral and Key West—and stops in Nassau, Bahamas, and Great Stirrup Cay (a private island owned by the cruise line). Family Pride Coalition was tasked with providing educational programming: in addition to running workshops on parenting issues and seminars on adoption and assisted reproductive technologies, the Coalition would also facilitate discussions for children about their experiences growing up with lesbian and gay parents (Salvato 2004). Yet as much as O'Donnell wanted to provide families with practical information and emotional support, she was also invested in securing high-class entertainment for her passengers. In the months leading up to their departure, as Carpenter and Kaminsky took care of the logistical side of things, O'Donnell focused on the talent. She hired Schoolhouse Rock Live! to perform for the kids; she locked in stand-up performances from well-known comedians, including fellow lesbian mom Judy Gold; and she recruited a cadre of Broadway stars to perform musical numbers each night of the trip. Booking a cabin on O'Donnell's cruise would grant families access to a magical experience where, perhaps for the first time in their lives, they would be surrounded by other people like them.[3] As Kaminsky told *Passport Magazine*, R Family Vacations was setting out to create a "whole new world" designed for lesbian and gay families (Mersmann 2004).

The decision to cater to the family may have marked a new phase in the lesbian and gay travel industry, but there was nothing particularly novel about marketing vacation packages as a way of escaping heteronormativity and finding a sense of community. While the celebration of travel as a mode of self-discovery or, more accurately, self-making has been a basic theme of Western modernity (MacCannell 1999), touristic styles of consumption have played a pivotal role in the consolidation of middle-class lesbian and gay subjectivities in the United States (Montegary 2011). Since the early twentieth century, participation in the erotic subcultures emerging out of bars, bathhouses, and bookstores has facilitated the formation of alternative sexual identities.[4] The search for community via commercial venues prompted patterns of domestic travel through resort towns, like Provincetown and Key West, and major metropolitan centers, including Chicago, New York, Los Angeles, and San Francisco (Waitt and Markwell 2006, 58–65). For people with the necessary financial and cultural resources and for whom international tourism was legally and physically possible, the desire to escape oppressive social contexts at home inspired travel abroad, not only to Western European cities with vibrant homosexual rights movements (54–58), but also to non-Western locations shrouded in colonial fantasies of unrestrained homoeroticism—namely, in North Africa, Latin America, and the Mediterranean (41–54). With the rise of mass tourism in the wake of World War II, individual sexual odysseys gave way to organized group tours. The "grandfather of gay tourism," Hanns Ebensten, is credited with running the first trips for men in the 1950s (Puar 2002a, 104). Over the course of the 1960s and 1970s, as the gay liberation movement enabled more people to claim a gay identity, a distinct travel sector targeting this newly visible population took shape (Waitt and Markwell 2006, 66–70). While the proliferation of gay-themed guidebooks and gay-owned guesthouses enabled travelers to plan their own itineraries, the growth of gay travel companies following Ebensten's lead provided tourists with the option of "traveling as gay" or, specifically, as part of a gay community (Puar 2002a, 108–109).

Cruise ships proved a successful venue for hosting community-building vacations. Since the advent of the industry in the late nineteenth century and the popularization of cruising in the 1980s (Dickinson and Vladimir 2008), cruise operators have enticed passengers with the promise of seeing the world from "well-protected zones of comfort and consumption" (Weaver 2011, 683). The perceived safety of the cruise ship was especially appealing for lesbian and gay tourists who wanted to be "out and about" but were concerned about encountering homophobic violence. In 1985, when the travel company RSVP Vacations chartered a ship for the first all-gay cruise, it introduced a concept that would become central to lesbian and gay tourism. Over the next twenty years, the largest U.S.-based tour operators would offer specialized cruise products. For instance, the lesbian-feminist-record-label-turned-vacation-company Olivia Travel featured packages for a clientele largely made up of lesbian couples, whereas Atlantis Events, Kaminsky's former employer, catered to younger gay men looking for a week-long party and the chance to cruise for sex at sea (Hughes 2006, 99). By the time R Family Vacations arrived on the scene, mainstream cruise lines were courting lesbian and gay travel companies to tap what was now recognized as a highly profitable sector. Questions of personal and national security had become increasingly pressing for travelers as concerns about terrorism intensified worldwide, but cruise operators were responding to such fears by advertising their packages as safer alternatives to vacations organized around air travel.[5] In 2003, Community Marketing Inc., a firm specializing in the lesbian and gay market, estimated that lesbian and gay tourism represented a $54 billion industry in the United States alone and found that lesbians and gay men booked cruises at a higher rate than their straight counterparts (Hughes 2006, 46, 98–99). Casting lesbian and gay travelers as craving communal experiences on the high seas, the tourism industry viewed the lesbian and gay cruise as a lucrative enterprise.

R Family Vacations sought to build on this tradition, but with a twist. By turning the lesbian and gay cruise into a child-friendly product, they were hoping to cultivate a new market: lesbian and gay travelers looking to flee, not from their families of origin, but with the families they were building. Industry experts had already been speculating about the profitability of lesbian and gay parenthood when R Family Vacations launched and were curious to see what kind of money could be made by targeting this niche within a niche (Alterio 2004).[6] In the early 1990s, interest in lesbian and gay consumers was fueled by the image of gay men as dual-income couples with no kids (DINKs) who were inherently more cosmopolitan than their straight counterparts and who were therefore more willing to spend their impressive amounts of disposable income on high-end travel opportunities (Badgett 2001, 112; Puar 2002b, 937–938). A decade later, reaching out to travelers within this niche who had children, R Family Vacations increased the visibility of lesbians as consumers, producing a maternal image that departed from earlier and occasional efforts to market "lifestyle lesbianism" as chic and trendy (Clark 1991).

While Kaminsky occasionally discussed his efforts to generate a consumer demand and a corresponding market—"That's what R Family is trying to do," he once explained, "to create what the next phase is for us as gay people" (Mersmann 2004)—R Family Vacations tended to frame the company as responding to an already existing need among parents and their children. At times, Kaminsky would reflect on his past with Atlantis to craft a narrative about what he saw as the natural evolution of lesbian and gay culture. Whereas the travel industry once had to satisfy the desires of tourists looking for "end-less partying," lesbians and gay men were now far more interested in having "kids," "a great relationship," and "a life that is about friendship and fun and health" (Mersmann 2004). Put simply, he painted R Family Vacations as ful-filling the collective wishes of a market overlooked in the world of commercial tourism. Adding a personal touch to Kaminsky's industry narrative, Carpenter often emphasized how being a parent herself means she is attuned to the "vaca-tion needs" of this sector and understands how important it is for children to "see other families that are like theirs" (Salvato 2004). Marketing themselves as the first travel provider to acknowledge a maturing lesbian and gay population, Carpenter and Kaminsky pitched their product as a social service designed to rescue parents and children from isolation and to build a community of lesbian and gay families. In many ways, R Family Vacations is the logical extension of the corporatized nonprofit model that produces the annual Family Week cele-bration: moving lesbian and gay family advocacy work beyond a reliance on corporate sponsorship and corporate decision-making models, Carpenter and Kaminsky set out to build an actual for-profit corporation organized around Family Pride Coalition's style of service provision.

To make complete sense of the emergence of R Family Vacations, however, demands a consideration of the interplay between lesbian and gay identity politics and identity-based consumption during the early twenty-first century. As advertisers and marketers began more aggressively courting the lesbian and gay market over the course of the 1990s, group-based commercial activities, like leisure travel and the consumption of other lifestyle products, took on new meaning with respect to identitarian politics forged in the name of rights and recognition.[7] Lesbian and gay identity, within this framework, was imag-ined to be consolidated around a shared set of desires—a set of desires that had increasingly less to do with same-sex eroticism and that was instead defined by common political interests and consumer wants. This entanglement of mar-ketplace activity and rights-based activism not only transformed the private act of consumption into a mode of political participation and community building[8] but also turned the recognition of lesbians and gay men as consum-ers into a key component of the struggle for full citizenship.[9] By extending such recognition to lesbian- and gay-identified parents, R Family Vacations sought to capitalize on the presumed desire for consumer citizenship. As Car-penter explained, they were offering "something special" to families who had "spent years feeling ostracized . . . [and] like people haven't embraced [them]" (Brunner 2005). Within this context, the opportunity to spend money on a Caribbean cruise could be experienced not only as a way of finding respite from the heterosexism of everyday American life but, just as importantly, as an unprecedented form of validation to be enjoyed in lieu of and, ideally, as a precursor to state recognition and legal protections.

Notably, O'Donnell was offering lesbian and gay parents the right to consume at precisely the moment the war on terror was imbuing family-oriented modes of consumption with a new level of patriotic significance. Domestic activities and family life have figured prominently within U.S. political culture throughout the history of U.S. imperialism (Kaplan 1998), but in the wake of September 11, the animation of the family within homeland security debates was marked by the state's disavowal of its ability to protect all American families. Neoliberal ideals of privatization and responsibilization reassigned the work of security to the private sphere and encouraged the management of insecurities through familial and often feminized practices of consumption (Grewal 2006; Cowen and Gilbert 2008). At a moment when concerns about personal safety and national security were believed to be best handled via individualized market solutions (Brown 2006, 704), O'Donnell invited lesbian and gay parents to take personal responsibility for the well-being of their children by investing in a week-long escape from the hostility their families endured in the form of homophobic policies and politicians. Bringing together discourses of patriotism, parental obligation, consumer citizenship, and lesbian and gay identity politics, R Family Vacations developed a product attuned to the personal and political anxieties of a newly identified niche market.

In effect, R Family Vacations was transforming the meanings associated with lesbian and gay modes of travel and consumption. While this discursive shift served the pragmatic purpose of cultivating a market capable of sustaining Carpenter and Kaminsky's venture beyond year one, O'Donnell, in her new role as parenting advocate, recognized the political potential of an endeavor that distanced respectable lesbians and gay men, rhetorically and geographically, from unruly forms of queerness. The rapid expansion of the lesbian and gay tourism industry had depended on a distorted image of gay men (and to a lesser extent, lesbians) as uniformly affluent, predominantly white, inherently cosmopolitan, and thanks to their lack of children, armed with impressive amounts of disposable income (Gluckman and Reed 1997; Badgett 2001). In contrast, R Family Vacations offers a lesbian and gay subject even more compatible with middle-class norms—a subject who, as Shonkwiler observes, is constituted "within the larger production of the American family in market terms" (2008, 540). By rendering these alternative forms of travel familial and thus familiar, their new company countered perceptions of lesbians and gay men as marshalling unlimited financial resources to support deviant lifestyles.

In 2003, even as the decriminalization of sodomy at the federal level[10] and the legalization of same-sex marriage in Massachusetts extended a measure of legitimacy to domesticated lesbian and gay relationships, the intensification of the U.S.-led war on terror was fueling a combatively heteronormative and family-centric brand of nationalism. The following year, in the months before the inaugural journey, the backlash against this limited expansion of rights, in the form of President George W. Bush's endorsement of a federal marriage amendment and the Eleventh Circuit's decision to uphold Florida's ban on lesbian and gay adoption, illuminated persisting fears about the dangers same-sex desire presented to children and the future of the nation. When HBO approached O'Donnell about making a documentary based on her inaugural cruise, she heard them offering a chance to assuage anxieties surrounding lesbian and gay parenting. As she told the *New York Times*, O'Donnell hoped the film would give people "a chance to see what they're afraid of" and, in the process, debunk the illusion that gays are "all about sex" (Lee 2006). By increasing the visibility of a privileged class of lesbians and gay men who consume not in pursuit of hedonistic pleasures but for the sake of their children's well-being, the documentary could align same-sex relations with marital family desires. Moreover, as the president's counterterrorist efforts instituted a white Christian citizen ideal rooted in unwavering support for neoliberal discourses of security and freedom, R Family Vacations would construct lesbian and gay parents as wholesomely patriotic Americans deserving of inclusion within an increasingly nativist national imaginary.

Exceptionally American Families

The film *All Aboard! Rosie's Family Cruise* (2006) opens in the New York Harbor with five hundred families boarding the *Norwegian Dawn* in July 2004. As the ship sets sail, the camera captures the faces of two white lesbian mothers who are overcome by the profound happiness they have experienced since arriving on the ship. One of the women, despite having only boarded a few moments ago, confirms that Rosie has succeeded in her quest to provide parents and children with a safe space. As she surveys the deck, she declares, "This is nobody judging you." The other woman, wiping a tear from her eye, declares that she "has never felt so free." The utterance of these words on a boat racing toward international waters might initially suggest that, for lesbians and gay men, freedom is only possible outside the United States. But these opening scenes are set against the New York City skyline, just three years after the World Trade Center attacks, and are imbued with a palpable degree of nationalist sentimentality. The Statue of Liberty appears in several shots of families enjoying the sail-away party (and repeatedly throughout the film thanks to the picture of the monument emblazoned on the hull of the ship), aligning the lesbian and gay family escape with a specifically American and, as I clarified in chapter 1, distinctly imperial mode of consumer citizenship.

Since the making of the lesbian and gay market has historically depended upon the linking of consumption with the promise of national belonging,[11] the launch of this family-centric cruise company at the height of the U.S.-led war on terror invites deeper analysis of this dynamic in the early twenty-first century. Recalling President Bush's mandate to continue traveling and consuming in the wake of 9/11, tourism had taken on a particularly patriotic meaning at this moment. Although the travel industry suffered a sharp decline in the weeks after the September 11 attacks, government officials and corporate leaders called upon U.S. citizens to resume their daily activities. Tourism was cast as a matter of national security: to cancel vacations and not spend U.S. dollars was tantamount to "letting the terrorists win" (Puar 2006, 78–79). Passengers were thus not only meeting their parental obligation to enhance their children's safety and happiness but also fulfilling their national duty to spend U.S. dollars at home and abroad. While motivated by frustrations with the homophobia of political leaders, R Family Vacations, far from an un-American enterprise, reminded lesbian and gay families why they should feel proud to be Americans. Without mention of the wars in Iraq and Afghanistan, *All Aboard!* celebrates the singularity and superiority of American values while simultaneously issuing a warning to the United States concerning its homophobic policies. In other words, the documentary reworks narratives of U.S. exceptionalism to tell a story about the unwavering patriotism of lesbian and gay families and, even more interestingly, to hinge the future of national excellence on the expansion of lesbian and gay rights.

The film employs discourses of multiculturalism to construct the United States as a nation with an exceptional capacity for inclusivity. When a group of reporters greets R Family at their first port of call in Cape Canaveral, O'Donnell tells the press that, "in [her] opinion," the world she has created aboard the ship is "what America is really about." Her passengers enjoy a better version of the country, a future where racial equality (imagined by O'Donnell as having already been achieved) gives way to an appreciation of same-sex love and intimacy. In a postcruise interview, O'Donnell recalls getting "all choked up seeing the beautiful multicultural Benetton rainbow of families" vacationing together (Brunner 2005). This overt aestheticization of racial and ethnic difference reflects the weak multicultural politics of a family equality movement that contains, reinscribes, and "deracinate[s] culture of any meaningful difference" (Eng 2010, 110). While O'Donnell's vague claims about the diversity of R Family passengers reveals little about the racial demographics of her cruise, the families featured in *All Aboard!* who are likely being coded as multicultural consist, almost uniformly, of white parents and their nonwhite children. Take, for example, the first family introduced in the film: a pair of white dads from New Jersey who fostered and eventually adopted two boys and, after learning these children had siblings in care, adopted another boy and two girls. Though the racial identities of the children are not explicitly addressed in the documentary, the five children range in skin tone from ambiguously white to dark brown and exemplify the "rainbow family" driving the narrative of the film and central to O'Donnell's advocacy work. Evidence of a deep and undeniable desire for parenthood, signaled by a willingness to take in the neediest of children regardless of their race or ethnicity, is meant to bolster lesbian and gay calls for domestic rights. As such, when O'Donnell speaks before a cheering crowd during their stop in Key West, she can make the argument that ending Florida's ban on lesbian and gay adoption would solve the state's crisis in foster care. The value of the multicultural gay family may have been unappreciated on land, but at sea, R Family Vacations aims to make visible the exceptional nature of lesbian and gay parents.

Without any consideration of the racism and classism structuring the U.S. child and family welfare system, O'Donnell pits aspiring lesbian and gay parents against what she has elsewhere described as "failed heterosexual families that weren't able to care for kids" and, in doing so, tries to construct her passengers as model citizens deserving of full parental rights (Stockwell 2006). To grasp the state of child welfare in the United States today requires a critical consideration of how centrally the policing of family life—and, specifically, the denial of parental rights—has historically figured in the processes of settlement, enslavement, and imperial expansion and the (neo) liberal management of racialized and sexualized populations. The history of the U.S. government's capacity to disrupt and restructure the familial lives of vulnerable populations spans "from the forcible removal of children from Native American reservations and their placement in Indian schools, to the more recent boat lifts and air lifts of Cuban and Vietnamese 'orphans' after the rise of Fidel Castro's revolutionary government (1960–1962) and the fall of Saigon (1975)" (Eng 2010, 103). Since the 1970s, when the implementation of antidiscriminatory measures made domestic welfare services more widely available to African American women and to a growing number of migrant women from Asia, Latin America, and the Caribbean, the U.S. family welfare system has been recast as a child protection agency. No longer envisioned as a social service system designed to help impoverished families, child welfare now functions as an explicitly regulatory project tasked with investigating allegations of abuse and neglect and removing children from homes deemed unsafe and unhealthy.[12]

As Dorothy Roberts (2002) has meticulously documented, the punitive function and overt antiblackness of family welfare have only expanded as the continued demonization of black motherhood and fatherhood has coincided with the pathologization and criminalization of poverty. Following the passage of the Adoption and Safe Families Act (ASFA) in 1997, the federal government began instituting policies that systematically deprioritize family reunification and that instead encourage states to expedite the process of terminating parental rights. By "freeing" children in the foster system for adoption, family welfare agencies can transfer financial responsibility for the health and well-being of children in care to adoptive parents deemed fit according to white middle-class standards of able-bodied/able-minded domesticity. Calls for lesbian- and gay-inclusive policies that would increase the number of permanent placement options unwittingly work in synchrony with the state's practice of removing children from poor families, especially from black mothers and disabled parents. Whereas earlier lesbian mother activism was forged in solidarity with antiracist and antipoverty feminist movements that challenged hegemonic definitions of parental fitness, O'Donnell's brand of foster and adoption advocacy takes shape in a political landscape organized around a narrowly conceived identity politics and a myopic emphasis on institutional access. The singular focus on securing LGBT-identified adults the right to become foster parents detracts attention from the ways in which the welfare system's investment in rigid gender, sexual, and relational norms leaves poor lesbians, queer mothers, and gender-nonconforming parents at a heightened risk for losing their children. In the context of *All Aboard!*, the story about LGBT parents and the foster care system becomes a narrative of salvation starring comfortably middle-class lesbian and gay citizens who are ready, willing, and able to save the "unwanted" children of America.

In addition to obscuring the national and transnational structures of economic inequality organizing the removal of children from their families of origin, sentimental rescue narratives also mask the multitude of factors that might contribute to an aspiring parent's decision to pursue the foster-to-adopt route. Interestingly, the HBO documentary includes footage from an informational workshop on adoption hosted aboard the ship. This brief scene gestures toward the ways in which questions of money can influence parenting decisions and, as such, threatens to undercut the film's construction of lesbian and gay parents as possessing a limitless supply of generosity and a "colorblind" desire to nurture children. The camera captures the workshop's facilitator as he matter-of-factly explains to a room filled with R Family passengers that "adoption is very expensive today." Upon breaking the news that "your average foreign adoption will run you between $25,000 and $35,000," he gives hope to prospective parents lacking this kind of capital by outlining other options that might be available to lesbians and gay men "depending on what [they] want and what [they] are willing to accept."[13] If, for instance, they are open to adopting "an African American child" or "a child where the birth mother has a drug history," then, the facilitator suggests, they will likely be able to avoid exorbitant fees, excessive wait periods, and elaborate gatekeeping mechanisms.[14] By revealing how a willingness to foster "hard-to-place" children can double as a time- and cost-saving strategy for aspiring parents, the heroic act of adoption takes on the air of an exercise in smart shopping and consumer savviness, and family-building practices are exposed as reproducing the market valuation of human lives according to racial hierarchies and normative measures of health and dis/ability.[15]

This scene is also noteworthy as it contains *All Aboard!*'s only explicit reference to transnational adoption, a reference that, by stressing the expenses associated with such practices and alluding to the ways in which infants "are entangled in transnational flows of human capital" (Eng 2010, 94), further threatens to undermine the film's efforts to tell a story about lesbian and gay adults selflessly rescuing children in need of families. While white parents with children who read as Asian occasionally appear on screen when the camera pans the decks of the ship, the documentary does not showcase any families formed via transnational adoption and thus glosses over the significant number of LGBT families created through these mechanisms.[16] This oversight is likely due, at least in part, to the film's attempt to craft a narrative in the service of O'Donnell's celebrity activism against U.S. policies barring lesbians and gay men from becoming foster parents. *All Aboard!* advances a domestically contained family equality agenda that, taking shape amid a war-fueled revival of U.S. patriotism, attempts to turn the gesture of saving the nation's most vulnerable citizens into a lesbian and gay citizen-making project. That said, the film's depiction of an adoption seminar staged on a luxury cruise ship sailing through international waters quite literally situates LGBT family-building processes within global circuits of mobility and exchange. The documentary neither offers a critique of the uneven distribution of wealth and resources that make the work of child care impossible for so many families and nations across the globe nor considers the local displacements and transnational migrations involving children that make possible the multicultural families who are shown enjoying a privileged form of leisure mobility aboard O'Donnell's cruise. *All Aboard!* celebrates middle-class patterns of travel and consumption—specifically, in the form of the family vacation—as markers of the enriched domestic setting that lesbians and gay men can offer American children who have ended up without a proper familial home.

En route to the Bahamas, O'Donnell, Carpenter, and Kaminsky learn that two churches are planning to protest their arrival in Nassau. R Family Vacations circulates a memo letting passengers know about the situation and assuring them these actions are not representative of the entire nation. While this was not the first time a Caribbean island had tried to prevent lesbian and gay cruise goers from coming ashore—a few years earlier, the Cayman Islands denied docking privileges to an Atlantis-chartered ship while Kaminsky was still working for the company[17]—O'Donnell is shocked to hear that people are willing to protest families. On the night before their arrival, she tells the camera that "nothing would make [her] happier than to see these amazing families walking out with their head [sic] held high, with their hands on their children . . . and saying liberty and justice for all." The next day, as passengers disembark, protestors greet them at the dock, waving signs reading, "If You're Gay, Stay Away," and shouting at them to take their "filth and amorality" off the island. The film intersperses footage of the demonstration with shots of R Family children looking scared and, more interestingly, of other Bahamians expressing their disapproval of the protest. As one man puts it, "I say let them all come in. We are a tourist nation."

By highlighting the Bahamian economy's dependence on foreign money, *All Aboard!* casts the protest as an irrational rejection of Western capital while depicting the tourist practices of R Family Vacations in a benevolent light. Exercising the imagined right to cosmopolitan travel is transformed into a humanitarian gesture. Such a framing, however, obscures the coercive role the United States has played, often via military force, in restructuring the global economy and transforming "developing" nations into places where Western-ers can play and profit.[18] The expansion of the cruise industry in particular has had devastating effects on local tourist markets: put simply, cruises have made it possible for travelers to consume the Caribbean without actually contribut-ing to Caribbean economies. Although the region is the most popular sailing destination and was controlling nearly half the worldwide cruising capacity in the early 2000s (Pattullo 2010, 402), much of the profits generated by these arrivals were channeled back into non-Caribbean-owned companies (Sheller 2004, 17). Island nations "struggle[d] to keep their 'product' (shops, services, facilities, and friendly people) up to international standards," while cruise lines remained at liberty to cut destinations from itineraries without warning or, as Norwegian Cruise Line has done, to purchase uninhabited land to "create their own version of paradise" (Sheller 2004, 17; Pattullo 2010, 409). Further, thanks to the flags-of-convenience system, the *Norwegian Dawn* is registered under the ensign of the Bahamas, which means the companies chartering this ship technically operate in a place exempt from U.S. tax codes and labor laws (Klein 2017; Terry 2017). Contrary to the narrative constructed by the film, R Family's encounter with the Bahamas begins long before docking in Nassau. In many ways, the experience of freedom that O'Donnell attempts to manu-facture for her passengers depends on the systemic unfreedoms of the Global South. The families featured in the documentary find pleasure and purpose through a transnational marketplace marked by inequality and exploitation and maintained by the United States in its self-appointed role as the global security state.

In the absence of this political-economic context, *All Aboard!* is able to frame the multicultural gay family marching past protestors and into local shops as a triumph of modern American love over primitive forms of hostility and intolerance. The camera pays close attention to the New Jersey dads when they arrive in Nassau, following them as they walk past the demonstration and comfort their younger daughter, who is upset by the shouting. After stopping in a jewelry store and discussing the rings they will use in the wedding ceremony they have planned for their last day at sea, they head into another shop, where they hire a Bahamian woman to braid their older daughter's hair. As the woman works silently in the background, performing the racialized and feminized affective labor on which Caribbean tourist economies (and American LGBT families) depend, one of the dads reflects on the pedagogical value of exposing his children to the protest: his kids have heard about "prejudice" before, and now they have firsthand experience with it. The film's narrow focus on anti-LGBT discrimination ends up suggesting, quite unbelievably, that these children of color have never encountered racial "prejudice" or felt the effects of white supremacy while growing up in the United States. This strange insistence on an image of America as devoid of intolerance was not an uncommon reaction to the protests: shortly after the cruise, Kaminsky told *Passport Magazine* about a white lesbian couple, the mothers of two African American children, who defiantly told the protestors that their children already know "what love looks like," and now they see "what hate looks like" (Brunner 2005).

When abstracted from the colonial legacies informing Bahamian nationalist discourses of respectability, media coverage of this encounter cannot recognize these Christian, middle-class relational norms as the product of British imperial interventions and is unable to acknowledge the Western familial ideals that often govern postcolonial citizenship practices (Alexander 1994, 11–15). Instead, the protestors are, at best, pitied for their uncivilized prejudices and, at worst, dehumanized as the embodiment of hatred. In both instances, white parents portray the Bahamas as the foil for the United States and, in the process, deploy antiblack racism to school their children of color in lessons of U.S. exceptionalism. As they perform the labor of raising respectable American citizens, the parents in question engage in a process that is arguably more about shoring up their own position as citizens and that is complicated by the fact that their children are not racially identified with them. While *All Aboard!* obscures the ways in which parents, even as they can bestow a potentially more privileged class and citizenship status upon their adopted children, can never pass along their racial privilege, the documentary begins to capture how full and robust citizenship can be "*socially* effected from child to parent" and thus relies on the affective and ideological labor of children, including transracial and transnational adoptees (Eng 2010, 101, emphasis in original). Far from posing a threat to national futurity, lesbian and gay parents are seen reproducing patriotic attachments by instilling American pride in a new and increasingly diverse generation.[19] These enlightened parental figures, the film argues, are not the proper subjects for discrimination. Ultimately, *All Aboard!*

treats the homophobic vestiges encountered in the Bahamas as something barbaric and seemingly eternal while approaching the heterosexism embedded in U.S. legal code as a problem that can and will be remedied through democratic processes. Sailing in and out of international waters, R Family Vacations maps the boundaries between progress and primitivism. The multicultural gay family, an agent of homonationalism,[20] produces the United States as a site of freedom and diversity defined against the oppressive monoculturalism thwarting the development of an island tourist nation.

Back in their stateroom, as the *Norwegian Dawn* leaves the Bahamas behind, the camera captures the New Jersey dads getting their children ready for bed on the eve of their wedding. The next day, they head to the chapel, where the Metropolitan Community Church minister who has been officiating "holy unions" all week is waiting to pronounce them life partners. She opens the ceremony by acknowledging the setting: "This is a timeless moment. And I think it's wonderful that we're at sea because the sea is timeless in a way we can hardly understand." This language, while not uncommon by way of nautical imagery and not at all strange at a wedding, feels quite out of place given the film's construction of the scene as a gesture toward a not-so-distant future. If *All Aboard!* opens by framing O'Donnell's cruise as a chance for families to escape to an America-to-come, the film concludes by urging viewers to see this future as imminent, because to do otherwise, to allow further delay in granting domestic rights to lesbian and gay citizens, would be un-American. The encounter with the Bahamian protestors serves as a reminder of the alignment of homophobia with a lack of civilization within the imagined geographies of the war on terror. At a moment when the president was promising to defend the world from the violently repressive regimes of terrorist-harboring Islamic nations in the Middle East, the film gestures toward the ways in which the United States' production of itself as the quintessential modern democracy was coming to depend on its willingness to identify respectable lesbians and gay men as worthy of state recognition. In the end, *All Aboard!* presents these white Christian dads and their "rainbow" family as productive figures for mediating the contradictory idealization of the United States as "a properly multicultural heteronormative but nevertheless gay-friendly, tolerant, and sexually liberated society" (Puar 2006, 68).

Changing Tides

Five years after O'Donnell's first trip, I cobbled together a gay family for myself and embarked on R Family Vacations's Alaska cruise. My then girlfriend and I met my grandmother and one of my sisters in Seattle, and the four of us boarded the *Norwegian Dawn*'s sister ship, the *Norwegian Star*. Our itinerary included ports of call at Ketchikan, Juneau, and Skagway in Alaska; a journey through the Alaskan portion of the Inside Passage; and a final stop in Prince Rupert Island, Canada. My goal in turning to participant observation was to gain a more intimate sense of the discursive space of O'Donnell's cruises. Over the course of the week, I took detailed field notes tracking the rhetorical structuring of the entertainment, the community-building activities, and the educational workshops hosted by Family Equality Council. What I came to appreciate during my time on the cruise were the ways in which the end of the first decade of the twenty-first century was marking a significant shift at the level of national political culture and, specifically, sexual politics in the United States. Moreover, the optimism surrounding what was perceived as a move toward a more LGBT-inclusive way of American life was having a noticeable impact on the lesbian and gay travel industry and its entanglement with the family equality movement.

During our first few moments on the ship, our experience was, in many ways, identical to the one advertised in *All Aboard!* After checking out the tiny, windowless "stateroom" we would be calling home for the week, we headed up to the Oasis Poolside, where a banner commanding us to "Create. Dream. Evolve." greeted us for the sail-away party. As we enjoyed our first round of overpriced drinks, a version of Sister Sledge's gay anthem blared through the ship's sound system, and a line of performers danced by waving letters that spelled out "We R Family." I spotted the white woman featured in the film who had paid her tailor to turn a pride flag into a pair of shorts and who was now pairing those shorts with a set of rainbow pom-poms and identifying as the unofficial R Family cheerleader. As the deck filled with families, a quick survey of the crowd revealed a gender and racial makeup similar to what was depicted in the documentary. There were considerably more lesbian than gay families on the cruise, the parents heading to Alaska were overwhelmingly white, and the few faces of color among the passengers belonged primarily to children.[21] What I also observed—and what I suspect had been conspicuously left out of frame in *All Aboard!*—were the many nonwhite people performing labor aboard the ship. In addition to the racial diversity of Norwegian Cruise Line's employees (who were required to wear nametags bearing the flags from their countries of origin, which tended to be in South Asia and Central America), several gay fathers and some of the celebrities onboard were cruising with their nannies of color.

By the time we climbed into our bunks that first night, however, I had begun to realize that this year's journey was very different from the maiden voyage. For starters, this trip seemed to lack the sense of urgency that had fueled the launch of the company. Several of the passengers had been on multiple (if not all) of O'Donnell's cruises, so the sail-away party had become an almost routine event for them. Furthermore, as I observed over the next few days, the election of Obama had left many passengers—the families, the entertainers, and the workshop leaders—feeling quite hopeful about the place of lesbian and gay parenting within the national landscape. President Obama had ushered in an era of exceptionalist patriotism that, while still capable of sustaining ground wars and counterterrorist operations, broke from Bush's perception of the United States as the exception to, and thus exempt from, international law. He had run on a campaign platform that, breaking from the hostile heterosexism of the previous administration, promised to advance the LGBT equality agenda by expanding rights and protections for LGBT-identified citizens. In addition to pledging to bolster AIDS-prevention efforts, enact hate crimes and employment nondiscrimination legislation, repeal the military's "Don't Ask, Don't Tell" policy and the federal Defense of Marriage Act (DOMA), and reform the immigration system to make family reunification possible for binational same-sex couples,[22] he also responded to a letter of inquiry from Family Equality Council with a strong statement declaring his support for strengthening families in all their diverse forms, expanding family and medical leave protections, and creating more inclusive family and adoption laws.[23] Although many R Family passengers expressed their frustration with how slowly Obama was acting on his campaign promises—and were especially dismayed by his administration's decision to allow the Department of Justice to defend DOMA in a U.S. District Court just a few weeks before we set sail—there seemed to be a consensus aboard the ship that this White House had the best interests of LGBT families in mind. By resuscitating a "morally exemplary, multicultural, and multilateral" brand of U.S. exceptionalism (Pease 2014), the new administration held out hope for the future of lesbian and gay politics and the inevitability of family and marriage equality. Yet at the same time, this optimism was offset by an almost mutinous atmosphere aboard our cruise.

Bad news had spread quickly across the decks of the ship: O'Donnell and Carpenter had broken up, and O'Donnell, who had never missed an R Family vacation, was not coming with us to Alaska. When chatting with more seasoned passengers, I was repeatedly warned that this trip was going to pale in comparison. While these predictions were based, in part, on the belief that O'Donnell's celebrity presence was the key to creating a feeling of community on the ship, most of the people I spoke with had an even bigger concern about our trip. It was well known at this point that O'Donnell's personal wealth had been instrumental in keeping R Family afloat for the past five years (Kaminer 2008). This year, however, when Carpenter and Kaminsky failed to book enough cabins to cover the cost of chartering the entire ship, O'Donnell did not lay out the money needed to guarantee the *Norwegian Star* as an R Family–only space. Instead, Norwegian Cruise Line ran a promotion for their regular customers offering discounted staterooms on our cruise. (According to the assistant cruise director, who ran the afternoon karaoke sessions, approximately 1,700 passengers had reserved cabins through R Family Vacations and approximately 800 additional passengers took advantage of NCL's last-minute special.) For many passengers, this unannounced change in policy violated Carpenter and Kaminsky's promise to provide parents and children with a secure environment where they would be surrounded exclusively by other lesbian and gay families. As far as they were concerned, the presence of non–R Family passengers, even if they did not compromise the immediate safety of their families, would diminish the experience they had come to expect aboard O'Donnell's cruises.

Among the R Family passengers, however, not everyone was traveling as part of nuclear, child-centric family units. While the majority were same-sex couples with children, I encountered a host of other social formations vacationing with R Family on my trip. Newly single Carpenter, for instance, appeared to be cruising with a circle of friends who I read as other single lesbian professionals. On my zip-lining excursion, I met a group of four truck drivers, two lesbians, one gay man, and one straight man (none of whom were parents), who were traveling together as friends. They booked cabins on the R Family cruise after learning that their favorite gay satellite radio stars, Derek Hartley and Romaine Patterson of *DNR*, would be broadcasting live from the ship all week. A few nights later, I found myself sitting next to a group of forty-something-year-old gay men, all of whom identified as bears, in the Stardust Theatre as we waited for the nightly entertainment to begin. One of the men had won an R Family vacation package in a raffle and convinced his friends to join him on his journey. For them, the appeal of Kaminsky and Carpenter's product was not the child-friendly aspect but rather the sexually flexible space that refused to abide by the ageist and fatphobic bodily norms associated with most all-male gay cruises. This group of men was not alone in finding R Family Vacations an affirming space: in anticipation of the regular presence of this community on the cruise, the company organized a series of mixers, dinners, and cocktail hours for passengers identifying as bears, which were advertised in the daily newsletters that circulated across the ship.

Over the course of the week, my family and I (save my grandmother, who often found her way to the casino) spent most of our evenings with a small contingent of white gay men in their thirties from New York City. Thanks to their friends who were working as performers on the ship, they were on their second employee-discounted R Family cruise. I hit it off with one of the men on our first night when we discovered, quite unexpectedly, that we graduated from the same high school in the suburbs of central New Jersey. I was somewhat surprised to learn that he and his travel companions were also lamenting the ways in which our Alaska cruise failed to measure up to their vacation experience from the previous year. One of the biggest problems with the 2009 trip, as far as they were concerned, was the itinerary. For starters, the Seattle departure, in contrast to leaving from New York Harbor, required a cross-country flight and thus limited their ability to bring along the copious amounts of recreational drugs that had been an integral part of their inaugural journey. Additionally, the cold, dreary, and often rainy weather we experienced on our northwestern-bound cruise limited our opportunities not just for daytime communal activities but also, more disturbingly for my informants, for late-night encounters on the outdoor decks. According to them, the hot tubs had been a prime spot for being cruised by dads who were looking for some fun after putting their kids to bed.[24] Kaminsky and Carpenter may have been successful in discursively distancing their company from the unruly forms of queerness associated with a place like P'town, but the promiscuously lived realities of gay middle-class domestic life had no trouble infiltrating the lived space of an R Family vacation. Sex and drugs aside, however, my cruise friends confessed that they too felt that the loss of O'Donnell had marred their vacationing experience. In addition to blaming her break from the company for the lack of actual Broadway talent on this year's cruise, they saw her absence as contributing to what they also described as a diminished sense of community aboard the ship.

As the person running our trip, Kaminsky offered a very different spin on the recent changes. On our third day at sea, after spending the morning in Juneau, we were invited to the Spinaker Lounge for a Q&A session titled "Ask Gregg." While this event was billed as a chance to learn about the R Family 2010 vacation lineup, several people jumped at the opportunity to ask Kaminsky about O'Donnell's absence and about the changes for this year's trip. He acknowledged that, while he and Carpenter were grateful for O'Donnell's past generosity, they were both invested in developing a sustainable business model that would ensure they could keep offering vacation packages long into the future. O'Donnell's "philosophies [and] feelings" would always be central to their enterprise, but the goal was now to find less risky ways of serving their clientele. Never directly responding to concerns about the non–R Family passengers onboard, Kaminsky did his best to turn our attention to R Family's new product: the group cruise. For 2010, R Family was planning three different cruise packages: the "Ultimate Hawaii Spring Break Cruise" in March, the "R First-Ever European Cruise" in June, and the "R Family Vacations Summer Reunion" in August. Rather than chartering entire ships, Kaminsky and Carpenter would assemble groups of three hundred to four hundred passengers who would sail on much larger cruises to what they were framing as even better locations. The development of this new product, he explained, was not just a cost-saving move for the company but also a response to industry shifts. As cruise lines phased out smaller boats in favor of larger vessels, niche companies like R Family Vacations were embracing the group cruise model and retaining their identities by arranging private dining and entertainment experiences for their passengers.

In addition to responding to trends in the world of cruising, the reorganization of R Family Vacations was also aligning the company's business model with that of other travel providers who were working to tap this niche within a niche. While O'Donnell was often credited with honing what had been the industry's vague interest in lesbian and gay families, the tour operators and event planners who followed her lead had taken a more conservative approach to cultivating this emerging market. Shortly after her inaugural journey, the company Cruise One developed a group cruise package for lesbian and gay families who wanted to vacation together but who were comfortable doing so on a "straight cruise." Domestic lesbian and gay tour operators began expanding their repertoires to offer trips for travelers with children: Alyson Adventures established a separate division focused on child-friendly vacation options, and Olivia Travel began offering family-focused resort packages for their clientele. In a similar vein, annual pride celebrations, which often function as tourist events, began designating areas for children and incorporating family-centered activities. In 2007, for instance, a women's event promoter in South Florida tried building on the immense popularity of the annual "Gay Days" celebration at Disney World by developing separate "Gay Day Family" programming. These ventures may have relied on the same convergence of identity-based consumption and lesbian and gay American pride that fueled the formation of R Family Vacations, but they were rather modest enterprises when compared to O'Donnell's insistence on a full ship charter. To be clear, the financial trouble Kaminsky and Carpenter were experiencing was not a sign that the lesbian and gay family market was an unprofitable niche. In fact, the year before I boarded the Alaska cruise, a Los Angeles–based gay travel expert predicted that family vacations would be the "biggest change in [gay travel trends] in the next 10 years" (Wetherbe 2008). Success on this front would, however, require a more strategic cultivation of a market that was not nearly robust enough to sustain O'Donnell's grand vision of manufacturing a floating utopia for lesbian and gay parents and their children.

When Kaminsky and I met over coffee the day after the "Ask Gregg" event, I pressed him on the ways in which group cruises seemed to undermine R Family's original political investment in carving out a special space for lesbian and gay families. Surprised and somewhat confused by my perception of their company as an activist venture, he insisted that R Family was never about politics and had always been about leisure. He suggested that if I were interested in vacations involving volunteer work, I should probably look into lesbian vacation packages because a product like that—a product he was clearly reading as feminized—would be more appealing to their clientele. As for the state of lesbian and gay politics, Kaminsky was quite optimistic: marriage equality, he assured me, was "just a matter of time." Distancing his work from the realm of activism, he explained that his job was to figure out a way to continue producing quality vacations for parents and children. The precise configuration of those trips was inconsequential, and an exclusively lesbian and gay environment was not essential. After assuring me that the group cruise model would enable R Family passengers to enjoy the same sense of community the company had always offered, he reminded me that because their clientele was a "very blendable" group, they would have no trouble vacationing on a larger, more inclusive ship. While his reference to the "blendability" of R Family passengers gestured both to the familial form of queerness he associated with LGBT parenthood and to the fact that LGBT families were themselves often a blend of straight and nonstraight people, his confidence in the desirability of group cruise packages likely reflected his knowledge of recent trends within the lesbian and gay travel industry. The *15th Annual Gay and Lesbian Tourism Report*, released by Community Marketing Inc. the year after I spoke with Kaminsky, highlighted the ongoing shift away from a demand for "all-gay" vacation options and toward a preference for travel in a "gay-friendly mix" (2010, 6). The tourism industry was now offering lesbian and gay consumers a form of validation that had less to do with celebrating their lifestyle differences and was increasingly about recognizing their sameness and familiarity.[25] Moving away from their original efforts to capitalize on the fantasy of escape, R Family Vacations was holding out the promise of inclusion and assimilation.

Making Families Familiar

At the same time, even as Kaminsky was confident about the future of LGBT rights and adamant about the apolitical nature of his vacation packages, he admitted that R Family Vacations was still invested in its partnership with Family Equality Council and in inviting the organization to run seminars and workshops aboard its cruises. With so many LGBT families together in a single location, Kaminsky noted, how could they not provide space for parents and children to talk about the struggles they faced in their day-to-day lives? On our trip to Alaska, in addition to including informational seminars on family-building options (specifically, one seminar on private adoptions and two on advanced reproductive technologies), the Council's programming featured educational workshops on specific parenting topics (such as "13 Is the New 18," "Managing Gender Issues in Our Families," and "Talking to Your Children about Being in an LGBT Family") and broader political matters (like "Is Obama OUR President?," "Our Families and the Medical Community," and "Beyond Marriage Equality: What Matters Most to LGBT Families?"). The programming, I observed, reflected the top-down style of organizing that, as I discussed in the previous chapter, the Council had adopted along with its corporatized nonprofit model. Rather than creating opportunities for consciousness raising or even agenda setting, the educational workshops identified the most pressing LGBT family issues, updated passengers on what the organization's leaders were doing to advance family equality, and encouraged them to become official members of the Council (which would build their membership base in terms of numbers as well as through annual dues).

What I discovered over course of the week, however, were the subtler ways in which the workshops were designed to mobilize passengers in the service of what Jennifer Chrisler, the executive director of the Council at the time, had recently described as "family-centered approaches to grassroots organizing" (Family Equality Council 2009a). Chrisler, like Kaminsky, was optimistic about what the election of Obama meant for same-sex couples and their children, but she also believed that the success of the family equality movement depended on changing public perceptions of LGBT-headed households. To this end, the workshops she offered aboard the ship sought to enlist parents and children in a very localized visibility project: LGBT families, she suggested, should not be afraid to turn casual exchanges in their everyday lives into opportunities to promote positive images of their LGBT family and to educate people on their daily struggles. By providing families with a framework for talking about themselves and telling their stories, the workshops aimed to shape how parents saw the families they built, perceived their political needs, understood their personal responsibility for their children's well-being, and demanded recognition as deserving citizens of their local communities.

Take, for example, the workshop titled "Talking to Your Children about Being in an LGBT Family." Held on our first full day at sea, this event was one of the most well-attended parenting workshops of the entire week, with more than sixty parents filling the small auditorium reserved for educational programming. Chrisler, who was on the cruise and running most of the Council's programs, teamed up with Kim Bergman, a member of the Council's advisory board and the co-owner of Growing Generations (a Los Angeles–based surrogacy agency initially launched to serve the needs of aspiring gay fathers). Together, they ran the hour-long workshop, which consisted of brief presentations from each of the facilitators followed by an open discussion where audience members were encouraged to ask follow-up questions.[26] According to the official description distributed to R Family passengers, this event was designed to "support parents in responding to their children's questions (spoken and unspoken)" about "where they come from" and about "negative images and messages [concerning LGBT families] encountered in schools and in the media."[27]

Yet despite the Council's framing of the event as emerging out of a concern for the struggles children face when navigating a social world that renders their families illegible or, worse, illegitimate, the actual workshop seemed designed to alleviate the fear, guilt, and shame that was assumed to burden lesbian and gay parents. Both Bergman and Chrisler opened their respective presentations by validating lesbian and gay family formations, alluding to the robust body of social scientific data affirming that lesbian and gay adults achieve just as good (if not better) parental outcomes than their straight counterparts,[28] and then offered suggestions for how parents can help their children make sense of their origin stories and narrate their familial attachments in meaningful ways. Further, although the event was advertised as dealing broadly with LGBT family issues, the workshop focused exclusively on lesbian- and gay-identified parents, dedicated more time to children created through advanced reproductive technologies, and presumed a homogenously white and nondisabled family. In contrast, the community-building activities organized by R Family Vacations did acknowledge the significant number of LGBT families raising children with disabilities and constituted through transracial and transnational adoptions. The company planned meet-ups for families with "special needs" children and a short class on "African American hair care" as part of their social programming aboard the ship. The official rhetoric of the Council's educational series may have emphasized its investment in supporting "a diversity of family constellations,"[29] but the conversations staged in their workshops over the course of the week almost uniformly cordoned off questions of race and dis/ability, thus privileging the sexuality of parents over other identity or community attachments and prioritizing homophobia as the greatest concern facing LGBT families.

In the "Talking to Your Children" workshop, Bergman and Chrisler focused on instructing parents on how to rewrite the heteronormative script for family life by disrupting the reductive equation of blood ties with parental legitimacy. Bergman, for instance, encouraged parents to teach their children that every person is made with "four ingredients"—a sperm, an egg, a womb, and a home—and to emphasize that the only "ingredient" that matters is the home because that is where a person can find their family. In a similar fashion, Chrisler pushed audience members to abandon outdated notions of parenthood that hinge on biological connections and to instead embrace an understanding of parenting based on what parents do and defined by the care and love they give their children. Together, the facilitators invited parents not only to take pride in the families they have built but, importantly, to take ownership over how they and their children make sense of their family lives. I was initially excited by the ways in which these efforts to denaturalize reproduction and parenthood might have opened space for destabilizing other biologically essentialist beliefs (namely, around sex and gender), but I quickly realized that these lessons in rescripting served a very different purpose within the context of the Council's family equality agenda.

One of the pieces of cautionary advice that Chrisler bestowed upon lesbian mothers who conceived children with donated sperm was the importance of distinguishing a "donor" from a "dad." While she stopped short of explic- itly advising parents against the conflation of these terms, she did stress the ways in which this rhetorical move could confuse their children and their broader communities. I interpreted her comments as strongly recommend- ing that lesbians shore up their legibility and legitimacy as mothers by always describing donors, known or anonymous, in nonfamilial terms. Similarly, when asked during the discussion period about the Donor Sibling Registry, an online platform designed to connect children who were conceived via the same anonymous donors,[30] both Bergman and Chrisler were adamant in their position that children who share a donor are most certainly not "siblings" and that parents should discourage this kind of talk if they truly believe "love makes a family." At the core of the workshop lay a deep discomfort with and real skepticism toward the very possibility of a family formation that might span multiple households or that might allow for more than two parents. In an attempt to mitigate the potentially perverse effects of using donors or other reproductive technologies (while not even acknowledging the possibility of intentionally queer desires for polyamorous or polymorphous family forms), the Council provided a discursive framework through which parents could render their creative familial arrangements intelligible according to domi- nant logics that expect the borders of a family to coincide with a privatized household network of care. By setting the parameters for how parents should name and narrate their most intimate relationships, the workshop, far from offering an expansive form of parental support, instructed the audience in the narrow formula for LGBT family life that undergirded the Council's advo- cacy agenda.

To be sure, the value of these lessons in self-representation from a family equality standpoint was not lost on the Council. Bergman and Chrisler were careful to remind the audience that, in addition to instilling a sense a pride in children about belonging to an LGBT family, parents should also be forth- coming about the fact that they will inevitably encounter people who will not approve of or who might simply not understand their familial configu- ration. Conversations with teachers, trips to the doctor's office, or a family night out at a restaurant, they lamented, can involve invasive questions and hurtful comments and, even when dealing with well-meaning people, would almost always require parents and children to explain how they are all related. Given the amount of affective labor LGBT families must perform to make themselves visible in their day-to-day lives, it was, as far as the facilita- tors were concerned, essential that parents and children not only develop a language for describing their relationships but actually become quite comfort- able with the process of talking about their families with strangers. Bergman and Chrisler acknowledged how unfair it was that LGBT families must sac- rifice their privacy and bear the burden of educating their communities about family diversity, but they also urged parents to recognize the ways in which this kind of work advanced the Council's larger mission of "changing hearts and minds."[31] By insisting that other people read them as families, parents and children were challenging commonsensical notions of who could be a parent and what counts as a family. Precisely because she believed these day-to-day exchanges held such enormous potential, Chrisler encouraged families to seek out opportunities to talk about who they are and how they came to be rather than only doing so in response to the hostility or confusion of others.

Over the course of the week, during the other Council-led workshops held on the ship, Chrisler suggested strategies for how parents might more effectively mobilize their stories. Posting pictures of and updates about your partner and your children on Facebook, she argued, could be a powerful way of establishing yourself as a family and making yourself visible as such within your community.[32] More pointedly, at the "Is Obama OUR President?" workshop, she asked parents to view the line at the grocery store and the sidelines of a soccer game as perfect settings for striking up conversations about some of the most urgent issues facing LGBT families. A story about the teasing a child has undergone because of their parents' sexual identities might inspire other parents to talk to their own children about tolerance and family diversity. Likewise, by casually mentioning the negative impact marriage inequality has on one's ability to access family health care plans, parents could help the people around them see how laws supposedly designed to support family values end up harming some of the families in their community. This emphasis on interpersonal exchanges reveals a great deal about the privatized and family-centric form of grassroots activism that the Council was cultivating within an increasingly intimate public sphere. If, as Berlant suggests, U.S. national culture is now envisioned as consisting of "simultaneously lived private worlds" (1997, 5), then it would follow that attempts to change public perceptions of LGBT families would have to take place through ordinary exchanges between individual people. Rather than focusing on assembling a critical mass and making collective demands on a publicly accountable government, the Council approached the everyday work of social change as a private matter to be handled by and among families.[33]

This is not, however, to detract from the Council's efforts to convince parents and children to advocate for themselves in more overtly politicized ways. While Chrisler was careful to acknowledge how little free time busy families have, she reminded parents that it was possible to turn advocacy work into an activity for the whole family. Visiting a Congress member or attending a march or demonstration, she argued, could be a "fun" family outing as well as an important "civics lesson." Additionally, Chrisler suggested organizing "playdates with a purpose," where your children would entertain their friends while you educated their friends' parents about upcoming elections and key

LGBT family issues. She offered as a model the families in California who, just the year before, had deployed this strategy in the ultimately unsuccessful state-level fight against Proposition 8, the hotly debated ballot measure that eliminated same-sex marriage rights for Californians. Stressing the importance of intensifying these interpersonal interventions, she encouraged passengers to take similar kinds of action in their own communities, such as hosting a "pot-luck" for LGBT families and then inviting a local politician to join them to learn more about who they are and what they need. According to the Council's logic, a personalized story about the effects of anti-LGBT discrimination relayed in the privacy of one's own home could be incredibly effective in persuading fellow voters as well as elected representatives to adopt more sympathetic views of LGBT families and to become more supportive of inclusive laws and public policies. Such suggestions, however, presume an LGBT family who enjoys a degree of class privilege that affords them the time, space, and money to orchestrate social events of this kind and lives in a comfortably middle-class community surrounded by parents who have the resources to be as equally and intimately engaged.

As I listened to Chrisler's workshops over the course of the week, her recommendations for how parents and children could become more involved in family equality advocacy read to me as directly informed by an initiative she had spearheaded a few years before when the organization was still operating as Family Pride Coalition. In October 2005, the Coalition launched the "Real Families, Real Facts" public awareness project to "combat" the "vitriolic misinformation campaign being waged by the radical right": by "arm[ing]" parents with "credible social science research, reliable facts and [their] own stories," the Coalition hoped to "fundamentally shift the way [LGBT] families [were] talked about and treated in the media, in [their] communities, and by [their] politicians" (Family Pride Coalition n.d., 1, 5).[34] One of the cornerstones of this project was the OUTSpoken Families initiative, which trained a nation-wide speakers bureau of more than two hundred families who were tasked with responding to media inquiries and seeking out public speaking engagements at their schools, in their places of worship, and at local community events. A close reading of the 153-page "OUTSpoken Families Speaker's Toolkit" brings into focus the strategic logics that guided the public awareness campaign and that were underlying the workshops I attended on the cruise. Even as Chrisler never mentioned the speakers bureau or encouraged the staging of formal public appearances, her storytelling advice for R Family passengers reflected the Council's continued investment in helping parents and children hone their personal narratives (embellished as necessary) into "cohesive, persuasive messages" that would "move and inform" listeners about the need for more LGBT-inclusive schools, health care policies, and marriage and adoption laws (2, 21). The key to crafting a convincing narrative, according to the "Speaker's Toolkit," was remembering that "it's not about gay or straight, it's about FAMILY": parents "must share with the community-at-large [their] experiences of simply being parents—caring and looking out for [their] children" (23).

In other words, to become effective family equality advocates, lesbian and gay parents needed to take advantage of the ways in which their status as parents rendered their homosexuality more palatable and their critiques of homophobia less alienating. Rather than appearing to advance the sexualized agenda of a fringe special-interest group, parents who make demands on behalf of their children's health and safety can be seen as advancing a domesticated lesbian and gay rights agenda concerned with the security and stability of individual families. The Council's assumption that the possession of children grants lesbians and gay men full access to mainstream parenting culture, however, is premised on a lesbian or gay subject imbued with a great deal of race, class, bodily, and relationship privilege. Queer people who do not adhere to the white able-bodied, middle-class, and gender-conforming norms of monogamous homocouplehood find it much harder, if not impossible, to cross the "imaginary border from pleasure-seeking perverts to sanitized sexless adult guardians" (Rodríguez 2014, 53). In fact, as Juana María Rodríguez observes, for the most marginalized queers, parenthood can have the effect of marking them as "more, rather than less, perverse" (53). The Council was presuming a lesbian or gay parent who would embrace the cultural mandate of parental self-sacrifice, renouncing their individual longings and aspirations and finding happiness and satisfaction in the act of assuming personal responsibility for their children's well-being.

As Chrisler repeatedly reminded us on the cruise, lesbian and gay parents identify as "parents first" and "lesbian or gay second." Presenting this claim as a universal truth of LGBT family life, she not only foreclosed the possibility of parents privileging or even maintaining other meaningful identity attachments but also demanded a distancing from queer public culture, including and especially modes of queer life organized around sexual desire and erotic pleasure. The Council's rhetorical positioning of "parent" before "lesbian or gay" signaled a form of LGBT sociality and a style of LGBT advocacy driven by love (not sex), forged in the name of the child, and oriented toward familial and national futurity. Despite the ways in which R Family Vacations advertised its cruises as a community-building enterprise, the educational programming aboard our Alaska trip fostered a sense not of collectivity among and across families but of an atomized community consisting of individual families. By imagining the desires of passengers, leisure-wise and politically speaking, as arranged around a nuclear two-parent family model, the Council's family-centered approach to grassroots activism depended upon a lesbian and gay subject who pledged allegiance to their identity as a parent over and above any broader communal attachments.

Sailing beyond Same-Sex Marriage?

Parents were not, however, the only people on whom the Council's family equality agenda depended. As storytelling became an increasingly central tactic in the project of privatizing and desexualizing sexual identities and rights agendas, LGBT family advocates began to recognize the usefulness of incorporating children's voices in their organizing strategy. The "Speaker's Toolkit," for instance, reminded parents that children can be "incredibly effective public speakers" and invited them to consider turning their speaking engagements into family affairs (65). In addition to advising parents on how to stage events to maximize the impact of their children's contributions (i.e., let children speak first to "warm up the audience" and then parents can fill in "any gaps" and reinforce the family's larger message [72]), the toolkit also provided guidelines for building age-appropriate "talking points" for different audiences and activity worksheets to help parents assist children in sharpening their stories into clear and concise narratives (65–71). While the workshops I attended on the ship did not focus on how to groom children for advocacy work, my trip to Alaska did provide me with a firsthand look at just how persuasive children could be in reorienting same-sex relations and calls for LGBT rights around familial desires for marriage and domesticity.

The most popular Council-led educational workshop of the week was by far the "Youth Panel," which had become a staple R Family Vacations event since the inaugural cruise (as seen in the film *All Aboard!*). This kind of workshop has a longer history that stretches back to the youth-centered programming that was developed at early GLPCI conferences in the late 1980s and early 1990s in the hopes of providing children with space to support one another in navigating a homophobic world while being raised by homosexual parents. While the youth panel I witnessed on my cruise was still framed as an event organized with the needs of children in mind and designed to acknowledge the work they do to advocate for their families in their everyday lives,[35] it became clear to me, as adults in the audience took the microphone to ask questions of the panelists, that this event, like the "Talking to Your Children" workshop, doubled as a mechanism for assuaging the anxieties that continued to plague lesbians and gay men about how their sexual identities and relationship statuses might affect the well-being of children. Unofficially tasked with the affective labor of managing parents' lingering insecurities, all the speakers on the panel delivered impassioned accounts of their unambiguously happy and healthy home lives. After observing just how skilled children were at putting current and aspiring parents at ease, I quickly realized why the Council was encouraging its members to put their children on stage and why, as I will discuss in the next chapter, the voices of children became such a valuable commodity in the freedom to marry movement.

On the day of the "Youth Panel," more than four hundred people gathered in the Spinnaker Lounge to hear the panelists talk about their families and answer questions about growing up in lesbian or gay families. The panel consisted of fifteen teenagers—ranging in age from eleven to fifteen, predominantly from the greater New York City area, all but one reading as white—who had been on nearly every R Family Vacations cruise. After the panelists introduced themselves and described their family's origin stories, they then fielded questions about the best and worst parts of being the children of lesbians and gay men. While I do not know what, if any, formal public speaking training the participants received, I was struck by the ways in which the panelists collectively participated in the same kind of exceptionalizing rhetoric that permeated the parent-focused workshops I attended. Yet even as they unanimously agreed that their parents were not just as good as but were, in many ways, even better than straight parents, they justified their claims in slightly different ways.

For instance, one girl claimed that she was more self-aware and more open-minded than the majority of her peers. Another boy, in contrast, emphasized the fact that, because he grew up with only moms and several sisters, he understood women better than most of the boys his age who were also trying to date girls. While I was not particularly surprised by the culminating argument that lesbian and gay parents raised exceptionally tolerant yet exceptionally straight children, I had not expected to hear the panelists focusing on the superiority of their parents' relationships in comparison to heterosexual marriages. One panelist claimed that, unlike husbands and wives who have trouble communicating with each other, his lesbian mothers never fought, and another pointed out that her dads had a more stable and loving partnership than many of their classmates' straight parents who had been married multiple times. When a member of the audience asked a question related to Proposition 8 and the question of same-sex marriage rights, the teens continued to advocate on behalf of their parents by voicing their enthusiastic support for marriage equality. One of the teens succinctly explained, "To be against gay marriage is to be against me and my family." Another panelist was nearly brought to tears as she explained that she wanted her moms to get married "so, so, so badly"; she even promised that, if they died before the legalization of same-sex marriage, she would get their ashes married. Without clarifying exactly why access to marriage was so important to them and to LGBT families in general, the youth panel could have easily been spun as evidence of the universal desirability of marital family forms and of the cruelty involved in denying innocent children access to the comforts of a proper domestic life.

The panelists' palpable enthusiasm for marriage equality reflected a deeper structure of feeling that was dominating the ship, the work of family equality advocacy, and the mainstream lesbian and gay rights movement in the United States. By the time I boarded the Alaska cruise, same-sex marriage had emerged as the single most pressing issue for an imagined LGBT community. Even as the Council's official agenda, according to the flyer advertising their onboard educational programming, included a broader commitment to "ensur[ing] LGBT family inclusion in health care reform, immigration policy, paid sick leave and a host of other family policy priorities," the fight for marriage equality had achieved a new position of primacy within the organization. During each of the educational workshops I attended on the ship, the Q&A sessions would almost always return to the topic of same-sex marriage rights. Although these conversations rarely delved into the details of what the ability to marry would mean for most LGBT families, the general consensus was that marriage equality represented the quickest and easiest solution to securing parental rights and relationship recognition. Moreover, I got the sense that marriage was believed to be a magic bullet that would bestow on families an unprecedented degree of respectability that would somehow undo the homophobic structures that have historically marked same-sex couples deviant and lesbian and gay parenting dangerous.

That said, it is important to clarify that the marriage agenda did not go uncontested on our ship. Terry Boggis, the then director of Center Kids at the New York City LGBT Center, was on our cruise and was running some of the Council's educational workshops. I recognized Boggis as a founding board member of the progressive New York City–based organization Queers for Economic Justice and as one of the original authors of the 2006 statement titled *Beyond Same-Sex Marriage: A New Strategic Vision for All Our Families and Relationships*. In an attempt to intervene on what they saw as the rapidly shrinking field of sexual politics in the United States, a group of twenty-two activists, scholars, and researchers, including Nancy Polikoff, Lisa Duggan, and other key figures who have informed this book, cautioned U.S.-based lesbian and gay advocates against a narrowly formulated marriage agenda and called instead for a broader movement uniting the struggles for social and economic justice. The battle for marriage rights, the original authors and signatories argued, should be a part of a "larger effort to strengthen the stability and security of diverse households and families": rather than privileging relationships that abide by the rules of privatized domestic life, a more just approach to queer movement-building would demand "freedom from state regulation of our sexual lives and gender choices, identities and expression," "legal recognition for a wide range of relationships . . . regardless of kinship or conjugal status," and "access for all, regardless of marital or citizenship status, to vital government support programs" (Beyond Marriage 2006).

On our last day at sea, Boggis ran the Council's final educational workshop, "Beyond Marriage Equality: What Matters Most to LGBT Families?" Given the sweeping support for a marriage-focused family agenda, I was eager to see how passengers would respond to what I suspected would be Boggis's attempt to highlight an alternative set of priorities for the national-level LGBT family movement. After opening her workshop by conceding to the widely held belief aboard the ship that the legalization of same-sex marriage was inevitable and would occur in the relatively near future, she asked us to imagine what would happen the day after lesbians and gay men were granted the right to marry their partners. Marriage, she warned, was no panacea. Pushing back against the assumption that marriage equality would eliminate or at least disempower the deep-seated homophobia organizing U.S. political and popular culture, she suggested that prejudice against LGBT-identified parents would likely persist and the teasing and bullying of LGBT youth and children from LGBT families would probably continue. Then in a nonconfrontational and seemingly off-the-cuff way, Boggis spent approximately ten minutes outlining a number of other challenges facing nonheteronormative family formations.[36]

In addition to drawing connections between LGBT family politics and disability justice activism by critiquing the use of reproductive technologies to deselect certain genetic traits,[37] she challenged the equation of adoption with rescue by highlighting the violence of a child and family welfare system that forcibly removes children from poor mothers, especially poor mothers of color, and she reminded us of the historical fact that this oppressive state practice has had a disproportionate effect on lesbians and other women who cannot or will not conform to white middle-class gender, sexual, and bodily norms. Finally, she invited the approximately twenty passengers in attendance to consider the ways in which all youth in the United States were impacted by the aggressive privatization of public education; the rapid expansion of policing, juvenile detention, and the prison-industrial complex; and the racist, classist, and (hetero)sexist practices of military recruitment that were sustaining the ongoing war on terror. In short, Boggis called for a progressive family politics that would respond directly to the militarized processes of neoliberalization affecting the lives of queer and nonqueer families alike.

Perhaps predictably, her efforts to intervene on the ship's structure of political feeling were not enough to derail the audience's preoccupation with marriage. The remainder of the workshop, which was framed as an open discussion, revolved almost entirely around DOMA and Proposition 8. While Boggis's unsuccessful attempt to interrupt the Council's family equality rhetoric may, at first glance, seem insignificant, her refusal to disengage from relatively well-resourced rights projects and her willingness to outline an alternative model for practicing politics deserve further consideration. For starters, Boggis's presence on an R Family cruise reminds us that the ascendency of LGBT equality agendas and same-sex marriage advocacy did not take place uncontested. Queer feminist organizers like Boggis have consistently resisted the organization of LGBT movements around consumer-based models of visibility and privatized notions of domesticity. Calling upon the legacies of earlier lesbian mother activism, they have strived to think more creatively and more intersectionally about what it means to organize as parents and to politicize queer family life. Like the *Beyond Same-Sex Marriage* statement, Boggis's workshop reinforced the importance of imagining otherwise aloud—by publicly questioning the terms of mainstream political debates and then putting forth more expansive frameworks for envisioning LGBT family politics.

3

Equality

●●●●●●●●●●●●●●●●●●●●●●

Same-Sex Marriage and
the Precarity and Perversity
of Children

On October 9, 2009, M. J. Kaufman and Katie Miles published their single-post blog *Queer Kids of Queer Parents against Gay Marriage!*, which offered a scathing critique of the "liberal gay agenda" and outlined an alternative vision for a radical family politics.[1] As "young queer people raised in queer families and communities," they felt obliged to weigh in on the ongoing debates about "gay marriage" since the campaign for marriage equality was, increasingly, being waged in their name. Kaufman and Miles were particularly perturbed by the ways in which LGBT rights advocates and sympathetic news outlets were framing the legalization of same-sex marriage as the only way to bestow a sense of security and legitimacy upon children growing up in LGBT families.

Given the ways in which the figure of the child organizes the realm of U.S. politics and must, as Lee Edelman observes, appear as the "fantasmatic beneficiary of every political intervention" (2004, 3), it is hardly surprising that debates about marriage, an institution discursively entangled with the projects of procreation and child rearing, coalesced around the question of lesbian and gay parenting. Defenders of "traditional man-woman marriage" argued that lifting marriage bans would amount to condoning unhealthy parenting practices and was thus at odds with the state's obligation to protect the well-being of the child by promoting an ideal family structure. In response, marriage equality activists pushed back against conservative deployments of the figural child by trying to reorient marriage debates around the interests of actual children being raised by same-sex couples. For these children, activists argued, homophobic laws and discriminatory policies presented a far greater danger than exposure to the homosexual lifestyle. In short, marriage equality activists offered up a version of queer relationality compatible with "reproductive futurism" and an LGBT rights agenda firmly located on the side of those "fighting for the children" (Edelman 2004, 2).

Specifically, Kaufman and Miles took issue with the marriage equality campaign's construction of the LGBT family as a desexualized and, even worse, depoliticized formation. They were "sick[ened]" by the images that activists were circulating of "big, happy, gay families" with parents "pushing kids on swings" and "making their kids' lunches." These sanitized representations, they argued, sought to render lesbian and gay parenthood familiar to an imagined heterosexual public and, in the process, obscured the ways in which queer family lives, like all family lives, are "tangled, messy, and beautiful." Moreover, Kaufman and Miles were troubled by how these images celebrated marriage equality as signaling the decline of loud, sexy, and angry queer public cultures and the rise of privatized and domesticated gay households: "The message is clear. Instead of dancing, instead of having casual sex, instead of rioting, all of the 'responsible' gays have gone and had children. And now that they've had children, they won't be bothering you at all anymore. There's an implicit promise that once gays get their rights, they'll disappear again. Once they can be at home with the kids, there's no reason for them to be political, after all!" Challenging the presumption that parenthood necessitates an end to perversity or politicization, they talk about the ways in which their "many queer biological and chosen parents" managed to "raise kids and raise hell at the same time." Their parents instilled in them an appreciation for queerness and, importantly, queer politics. Kaufman and Miles describe childhoods in which they never aspired to be "like everyone else" and always felt "incredibly safe" and "taken care of" by parents who lacked the right *and* the desire to marry. They were schooled in the activist traditions "that began with Stonewall and other fierce queer revolts and that continued through the AIDS crisis," and they learned the "awesomely radical history" of queers "building families . . . in highly political, inventive, and non-traditional ways." In short, they grew up to understand family as an elastic and expansive concept: the *Queer Kids of Queer Parents* blog emerged from their steadfast commitment to resisting the privileging of "long-term monogamous partnerships" above all other familial configurations and working against "the idea that any relationship based on love should have to register with the state."

In many ways, Kaufman and Miles offered themselves up as living proof of the regenerative potential of queerness, a queerness capable of breeding an affinity for both perversity and collectivity and, even more frightening for both liberals and conservatives, an aversion to capital and the nation-state. Raised with a strong sense of collective responsibility, they feel ethically obliged to pursue "economic justice for all" and as such will not settle for "formal rights" when what is needed is "real restructuring" and "wealth redistribution." By diverting money and energy away from efforts addressing the concerns of racially and economically marginalized communities, they argue, the marriage equality movement further exacerbates the precarity of families, queer or not, struggling to survive in the face of "welfare cuts, fewer after school programs, less public housing, worse medical care, not enough social workers, failing schools, [and] the economic crisis in general." They urge queer movements to center the needs of families abandoned by the state for failing or refusing to arrange their lives around marital relations (i.e., single mothers trying to access welfare benefits, extended family members attempting to gain custody of their relatives' children, and friends wishing to serve as each other's legal representatives) and families for whom the state represents a source of perpetual violence (i.e., immigrant families denied legal recognition and threatened with deportation and working-class families of color targeted for incarceration and military recruitment). For Kaufman and Miles, a radical family politics would prioritize building "networks of accountability and dependence" located "outside the bounds of the government" and structured around the needs of families enduring the worst conditions. In their vision for a more just future, queers would stop donating to major LGBT rights organizations and would instead pool their wealth and resources to create community-based "emergency fund[s]" available for families "fac[ing] foreclosure, need[ing] expensive medical care or find[ing] themselves in any other economic emergency."

The critiques waged by Kaufman and Miles were, for many queer scholars and activists, quite familiar. While their specific focus on the politics of queer parenting and their call for a community-based approach to sustaining a wide array of familial formations marked a unique intervention, their insistence upon a queer politics rooted in a commitment to racial and economic justice (as opposed to an investment in rights and recognition) was in line with the *Beyond Same-Sex Marriage* statement and the broader body of critical work emerging in response to the marriage equality movement.[2] What really sets their contribution apart from their fellow queer critics is the fact that they lodged their complaints from the vantage point of children with queer parents and that they did so at precisely the moment when children from LGBT families began playing an active role in the fight to legalize same-sex marriage.

Earlier that year, activists started inviting children raised by lesbian and gay couples to participate in state-level campaigns and to publicly voice their support for marriage equality. Activists featured them in publicity materials, arranged for them to testify before state legislatures, and even named them as coplaintiffs in lawsuits against the government. The children sent to the front-lines of the marriage debates—who tended to be the white, straight-identified children of lesbian mothers conceived via artificial insemination—almost uni-formly told the same story: after providing a few anecdotes to establish how similar their families were to their heteronormative counterparts, they then explained how their parents' marital status caused them much sadness and left them with a profound sense of insecurity. Marriage inequality was the only thing standing in the way of a safe and happy childhood for them. Over the next few years, the mobilization of this newly politicized subject—the child from the LGBT family—proved a successful strategy for marriage rights activ-ists. But as the *Queer Kids of Queer Parents* blog suggests, there was no way for proponents of marriage equality to control who would speak from this sub-ject position and what they would say. Conservative defenders of traditional marriage soon recognized the political value of this position and deployed a corps of grown children to speak out against marriage equality based on their firsthand experiences with the perils of homosexual and transsexual parenting. Consequently, when the Supreme Court prepared to hear cases on the consti-tutionality of federal- and state-level bans on same-sex marriage (in 2013 and 2015, respectively), the justices received amicus briefs on behalf of two differ-ent groups of children from LGBT families—one group in favor of marriage equality and the other vehemently opposing the gay marriage agenda.

In this chapter, I take a closer look at the ways in which the child from the LGBT family circulates within debates about marriage prior to, within the context of, and in the aftermath of the Supreme Court's landmark decisions. This chapter begins by looking backward in the hopes of answering and, in the process, reframing the question that opens the *Queer Kids of Queer Par-ents* blog: "What happened to us? Where have our communities gone? Did gays really sell out that easily"? While I am invested in troubling mainstream accounts that narrate the history of LGBT advocacy as a story of continuous progress and improvement, my goal is not to create a counternarrative that suggests a steady decline or deradicalization of queer politics in the United States. Rather, this chapter traces the uneven and oft-contested shifts that have taken place within LGBT and queer activism over the past few decades as a way of complicating our understanding of the move away from support-ing familial diversity and toward an embrace of marital family formations. To this end, I start by tracking the discursive place of the child, parenthood, and familial life across the history of the freedom to marry movement. Next, I analyze the race, class, and gender politics governing the mobilization of chil-dren from LGBT families in the service of marriage equality and guiding the construction of their parents as responsible caregivers and respectable citizens deserving of legal protections. I then turn to the amicus briefs filed on behalf of the conservative adult children of LGBT-identified parents to show how their defense of traditional marriage puts an unexpectedly productive pressure on national-level LGBT rights organizing and suggests new avenues for a queer family agenda.

Finally, this chapter looks forward to thinking not just after but beyond marriage and to imagine trajectories for a movement looking to reinvest in queerness and community. In doing so, I envision a queer movement designed to prioritize the needs of the parents and children most viciously affected by what Kaufman and Miles describe as the "structural, social, and economic forces that break families apart and take people away from their loved ones." What, for instance, might a queer family politics look like if the children at the center of the movement were not the privileged white children to whom the state has historically catered but rather the trans and queer youth currently entangled in the U.S. foster care system? How might a movement oriented around the interests of the most vulnerable children move us closer to the "not-yet" José Esteban Muñoz dared to long for, a future where trans and queer youth of color get to grow up and grow together (2009, 96)?

From Family Diversity to Marriage Rights

To begin, it is first necessary to understand how the right to marry became *the* central issue for U.S.-based lesbian and gay activists and, for mainstream parenting advocates, synonymous with family equality. Andrew Sullivan's libertarian vision for the gay movement is often credited with inaugurating the crusade for same-sex marriage rights in the United States. In August 1989, his now infamous "(conservative) case for gay marriage" appeared in the *New Republic*. Framed as a critical response to the New York Court of Appeals's decision a few weeks earlier in favor of Miguel Braschi—a decision that affirmed Braschi's right to stay in his partner's apartment after his death from AIDS-related complications and that, in effect, broadened the definition of "family" governing rent-control laws in New York City[3]—Sullivan's essay outlined a road map for lesbian and gay politics that was at glaring odds with the coalitional efforts of AIDS activists and family diversity advocates during this period (Sullivan 1989). Whereas many lesbian and gay activists celebrated Braschi's victory as an important step toward rewriting public policy in ways that would not predicate relationship recognition on marital status, Sullivan was apprehensive about the prospect of unhinging legal and economic benefits from the institution of marriage. Sullivan's sympathy for the Right's fiscal concerns about loosening restrictions on access to "already stretched entitlements" set his call for marriage rights apart from the economic justice agenda driving lesbian and gay efforts to make more resources available to a more diverse array of family formations. The bulk of his "case," however, revolved around his contention that the legalization of marriage would "coax gays into traditional values" and, in doing so, would foster "emotional stability, economic security, and the healthy rearing of the next generation."

According to Sullivan (1989), since the "fast-maturing gay community" was already moving beyond a "need to rebel" and professing a collective "desire to belong," it would be in the state's best interest to promote this "healthy social trend" by "institutionalizing gay marriage." In addition to pitching the expansion of marriage rights as a "public health measure" capable of curbing the promiscuous sexual behavior he blames for the AIDS crisis, Sullivan also gestured toward the possibility of gay men becoming foster or adoptive parents and suggested that same-sex marriage could "help nurture [their] children." (Predictably, the lesbian baby boom that was already under way makes no appearance in the essay Sullivan titles "Here Comes the Groom.") Ultimately, he pinned his hope for the future on the effects marriage would have on the lives of "young gay people": by providing youth with a "tangible goal" and respectable "role models," marriage would enable the next generation to avoid "laps[ing] into short-term relationships and insecurity" and to strive instead for the stability of lifelong monogamous commitments. Sullivan concluded his essay by speculating that because marriage would render gay relationships legible to the straight world, conferring the right to marry upon same-sex couples promised to "bridge the gulf . . . between gays and their parents" and, even more important, to "heal the gay-straight rift" dividing U.S. public culture. Looking back on his "stigmaphobic" argument (Warner 1999), Sullivan's essay seems to anticipate (if not initiate) the emergence of a mainstream lesbian and gay movement that would distance itself from any hint of illness, disability, or abnormality more broadly (McRuer 2006, 86).

While many lesbian and gay activists at the time had little sympathy for the conservatism at the heart of Sullivan's call for the right to marry, some legal experts and movement leaders were beginning to discuss the viability and desirability of a campaign for same-sex marriage rights. The contours of these early debates are often said to be best encapsulated in a pair of essays written by the executive director, Tom Stoddard, and the legal director, Paula Ettelbrick, of the Lambda Legal Defense and Education Fund. Published in the fall 1989 issue of *Out/Look: National Lesbian and Gay Quarterly*, both essays open with critiques of marriage's embeddedness in a heteropatriarchal system of property ownership, but they draw very different conclusions about the place marriage rights should occupy within the U.S. lesbian and gay movement.

Stoddard, for instance, believed that "the gay rights movement should aggressively seek full legal recognition for same-sex marriages" and hoped for a near future in which "the issue [would] rise to the top of the agenda of every gay organization" (1998, 476, 478). The end of his essay gestures toward the ways in which same-sex couples might "transform" the institution of marriage into "something new" and "divest[ed] . . . of the sexist trappings of the past" (479), but his argument in favor of prioritizing the right to marry rested on what he described as a "practical explanation" (476). It was, he argued, simply unfair to deny lesbians and gay men access to the legal and economic advantages afforded through marriage, such as tax breaks, survivor benefits, and the opportunity to sponsor noncitizen partners for entry into the United States (476). A few months before his exchange with Ettelbrick, in an article for the *Minneapolis Star-Tribune*, Stoddard grounded his pragmatic call for marriage rights in a particular example. He turned to the Sharon Kowalski incident—in which custody was granted, for more than a decade, to the parents and not the lover of a Minnesota woman who had experienced a disabling accident[4]—to illuminate the "monstrous injustice" of depriving same-sex couples the right to marry (1989, 11A). While his *Out/Look* essay neither mentions Kowalski by name nor addresses questions of medical proxy, hospital visitation, or custodial arrangements, he does emphasize the ways in which marriage might, to borrow Robert McRuer's language, "work *for*" illness and disability by enabling more lesbians and gay men to share their health care plans with their partners (2006, 85, emphasis in original). In the final moments of his essay, Stoddard admits to having little interest in ever getting married himself and clarifies that the issue at hand is "not the desirability of marriage, but rather the desirability of the *right* to marry" (1998, 478, emphasis in original). Since he could not envision a future in which marriage would be abolished or its primacy in U.S. legal code usurped, Stoddard saw a fight for marital rights as the most effective way of challenging the "subsidiary status" of same-sex couples and establishing lesbian and gay relationships as "significant" and "valuable" (478).

In contrast, Ettelbrick found the prospect of building a movement around the right to marry personally and politically "terrif[ying]" (1998, 483). To pursue the legalization of same-sex marriage, she contended, would be to "undermine" the distinctly feminist efforts of lesbian and gay activists who have been struggling to create a society that "respects and encourages choice of relationships and family diversity" (482). While she acknowledges that, for more privileged lesbians and gay men, marriage might represent a "principle of freedom and equality" and the "ultimate affirmation of identity" (483), Ettelbrick takes issue with the fact that the extension of marital rights to same-sex couples "would do nothing to correct the power imbalances between those who are married (whether gay or straight) and those who are not" (482). Alluding to the Kowalski incident, Ettelbrick pushes back against the suggestion that marriage would spare lesbians and gay men the pain of being kept from their partners in the midst of medical emergencies by pointing out that unmarried same-sex couples would remain illegible as families and thus vulnerable to the same discriminatory practices (484). Moreover, she notes that securing the right to marry would allow the select lesbians and gay men who have jobs with health insurance to extend coverage to their partners without addressing the "systemic abuses in a society that does not provide decent health care to all of its citizens" (484). Finally, her intersectional analysis of sexualized forms of oppression calls into question marriage's "relevance" within broader "struggles for survival": "what good is the affirmation of our relationships (that is, marital relationships)," she asks, "if we are rejected as women, black, or working class" (483)? For Ettelbrick, being queer—and organizing as such—means "pushing the parameters of sex, sexuality, and family" with the aim of "radically reordering" dominant conceptions of familial life (482, 485). The goal of lesbian and gay liberation, she argues, is to demand "societal and legal recognition of all kinds of family relationships," from the two gay men who are coparenting with a lesbian couple to the unmarried elderly partners who are cohabiting for companionship and economic convenience (484).

Seeking common ground between these different political and philosophical perspectives, Lambda Legal developed the "Family Bill of Rights" to clarify its position on marriage and family law (Polikoff 2008, 59). The document outlined a "blueprint" for more just public policy that, while supporting the rights of lesbian and gay couples to marry, proposed a legal framework in which family recognition was *not* contingent on marriage.[5] Ironically, this visionary statement was drafted by their new staff attorney Evan Wolfson, who would later become one of the most well-known advocates for "marriage equality" in the United States. Wolfson had written a 140-page thesis on the constitutionality of same-sex marriage rights as a Harvard Law student in 1983 and, by the time he arrived at Lambda Legal in 1989, was already known in some circles for his commitment to pursuing the marriage issue. Consequently, in 1991, when three same-sex couples decided to sue the state of Hawaii over the Health Department's refusal to issue them marriage licenses, local activists reached out to Wolfson in the hopes that he would represent the plaintiffs. While Wolfson's supervisors permitted him to help from behind the scenes and to write an amicus brief on behalf of the couples, Lambda Legal, like the other major U.S.-based lesbian and gay legal organizations, had no interest in taking a lead on this case. These organizations were reluctant to invest their limited resources in a cause that not only was divisive among lesbian and gay rights advocates but also seemed unlikely to yield any immediate victories (Polikoff 2008, 90).

Things drastically changed in 1993, however, when the Hawaii Supreme Court decided in favor of the plaintiffs' appeal and called into question the lower court's dismissal of their suit. The ruling remanded the case back the First Circuit Court and required the state's attorney general to demonstrate how prohibiting same-sex marriages, a potential violation of laws prohibiting sex discrimination, served "compelling state interests." This unexpected turn of events prompted Lambda Legal leaders to allow Wolfson to sign on as cocounsel for the plaintiffs and to name him director of the organization's newly established Marriage Project. As he prepared for the Hawaii trial, Wolfson also launched the National Freedom to Marry Coalition, which sought to unite lesbian and gay organizations across the country in a nationwide fight for marriage rights.

Freedom to Marry

One of the founding members of Wolfson's national network was the Gay and Lesbian Parents Coalition International (which would later become Family Equality Council). The GLPCI took particular interest in the battle for marriage rights as the Hawaii case began to coalesce around questions of parenting.[6] In 1994, when the Hawaii legislature responded to the court's decision by amending the state's marriage statute to define the institution as between one man and one woman, they justified these restrictions by linking the right to marry to procreation and child rearing and by framing marriage as a mechanism for protecting family life. Armed with this justification and anticipating the opposition's counterargument regarding the number of lesbian and gay couples already raising children, the state's attorneys were left to defend the ban on same-sex marriage as promoting heterosexual parenting as the ideal family formation and thus serving the best interests of children and society as a whole. In September 1996, when the case returned to the First Circuit Court, the nine-day nonjury trial resulted in an extended public debate about lesbian and gay parenting. Although the GLPCI weighed in on the case with an op-ed from the organization's vice president[7]—and despite the fact that one of the couples who filed the original lawsuit was raising a child—the trial had little interest in the experiences of actual families and was far more concerned with testimonies from medical doctors and social scientists regarding the fitness of lesbians and gay men as parents.

Three months later, the court issued its ruling in favor of the plaintiffs on the basis of the state's failure to prove that same-sex marriages would harm the general public. While the judge conceded that children benefit from "being raised by their mother and father in an intact and relatively stress free home," he was convinced by the evidence, presented by the plaintiffs as well as the defendant, that a person's sexual orientation had no bearing on the quality of their parenting and that a "nurturing relationship" was the "single most important factor in the development of a happy, healthy, and well-adjusted child" (*Baehr v. Miike* 1996). One of the defense's expert witnesses, when pressed, agreed with the opposition's contention that lesbian and gay parents are "doing a good job" and that "the kids are turning out just fine." Contrary to the defendant's assertion that the legalization of same-sex marriage would condone parenting arrangements that significantly and negatively impacted the development of children, the court found that it was marriage *in*equality that threatened the child: by denying same-sex couples the "protections and benefits that come with or become available as a result of marriage," the state was actually compromising the well-being of children growing up in lesbian and gay families. Although this early bid for marriage equality was eventually thwarted—before the state supreme court could hear the defendant's appeal, voters in Hawaii granted lawmakers the power to define marriage and rendered the newly revised marriage statute immune to judicial review—the unexpected success of the case galvanized both lesbian and gay parenting activists and right-wing defenders of traditional family values.

In September 1996, as the First Circuit Court in Hawaii finished hearing expert witness testimonies on lesbian and gay parenting, the national backlash against the push for the right to marry culminated in President Bill Clinton's signing of the Defense of Marriage Act. DOMA, as the law came to be known, defined marriage, for federal purposes, as "a legal union between one man and one woman" and granted states the right to not recognize same-sex marriages legally performed in other states. In the report that outlined the governmental interests undergirding the proposed legislation, the House Judiciary Committee argued that marriage is not, as Andrew Sullivan claimed in the prepared statement he submitted to the congressional hearing, simply about "meet[ing] the person we truly love" but is, in fact, a unique partnership that serves the "function and purpose of begetting" (U.S. Congress 1996). Relying on a combination of scriptural allusions and conservative social science research, the House report celebrated the "irreplaceable" role of marriage in guaranteeing "generational continuity." The refusal to even acknowledge the possibility of lesbians and gay men raising children enabled the congressional committee to revive long-standing perceptions of homosexuality as an inherently sterile and antisocial way of life. Within this context, DOMA promised to "preserve scarce government resources" by preventing greedy adults from taking unfair advantage of tax breaks and other marital benefits designed to protect parents and children.

While the rhetoric of defending marriage worked in synchrony with Clinton's punitive welfare and immigration reforms, which passed a few weeks before and after DOMA, respectively, to (re)establish the marital family as the national ideal, the House report explicitly described the law as signaling the government's "moral disapproval of homosexuality" and, even more tellingly, its investment in "promoting heterosexuality." According to the congressional committee, increasing social acceptance for homosexual relationships was causing confusion for children and encouraging homoerotic experimentation among teenagers. Without settling on a particular theory of sexual orientation or desire formation, the report asserted, via an article by a Harvard psychology professor, that "there is good reason to think that a very substantial number of people are born with the potential to live either gay or straight lives."[8] As such, in the interest of ensuring a reproductive national body, the state must maintain the "preferred societal status" of "traditional marriage" as a way of "encourag[ing]" heterosexual desire. Put another way, the House Judiciary Committee viewed heterosexuality as so fragile that the mere prospect of same-sex marriage threatened to derail normative sexual development and to inflame the perverse potential lurking inside many, if not all, children.

As the marriage equality movement took shape over the next two decades, LGBT rights activists did not base their case for same-sex marriage on Congress's denaturalization of the heterosexual lifestyle. Instead, they centered discourses of fairness and equality. This was how, in 2001, Wolfson convinced the Evelyn and Walter Haas Jr. Fund to award him a $2.5 million grant—what was at the time the largest foundation award ever invested in U.S.-based lesbian and gay activism—to support his freedom to marry efforts. When the Haas Fund, a San Francisco–based philanthropic organization founded by the heir of the Levi Strauss fortune, decided to start prioritizing lesbian and gay rights projects, the organization approached Wolfson for advice on how to most effectively pursue an edgier grant-making agenda. Seizing the opportunity, Wolfson made a pitch for the importance of marriage rights and, according to the Haas Fund's vice president of programs, "electrified" the organization's leaders with his case for funding a national marriage movement (Garafoli 2015). The legalization of same-sex marriage, Wolfson argued, would not only give lesbian and gay couples access to more than one thousand rights and protections but would also facilitate greater social acceptance and the eventual achievement of full legal equality.[9]

With the Haas Fund's financial backing, Wolfson was able to leave Lambda Legal, to incorporate Freedom to Marry as a nonprofit organization, and to dedicate his full attention to winning public support for marriage equality. In 2004, when activists working to secure the right to marry faced a major setback—voters reelected President George W. Bush, who supported a federal marriage amendment and, in eleven states, passed ballot initiatives banning same-sex marriages—Wolfson worked with the Haas Fund to form the Civil Marriage Collaborative, a group of major funding organizations, including the Ford and Gill Foundations, that publicly committed to financially supporting marriage rights campaigns on a state-by-state basis. While the passage of DOMA had created a discursive context in which activists found it increasingly difficult to retain a critical or even skeptical position on marriage (lest they be misheard as siding with the homophobic Right), Wolfson's efforts to make more grant money available for marriage equality projects made alternative visions for lesbian and gay politics even harder to sustain. The Civil Marriage Collaborative incentivized agendas that aligned with Freedom to Marry's strategic plan and, in the process, rendered organizations pursuing different and potentially more transformative goals unfundable. Private funding streams sustained a national marriage movement orchestrated not by mass mobilizations and grassroots organizing but by a network of professionalized leaders building careers within the lesbian and gay sector of the nonprofit industrial complex.[10]

Over the course of the 2000s, while legal advocates who were trying to secure marriage rights via courtroom litigation often relied on the growing visibility of lesbian and gay parents to mark same-sex couples as deserving of recognition[11]—this strategy proved successful in Massachusetts in 2003[12] and. in California and Connecticut in 2008[13]—the marriage movement's media advocacy and public awareness campaigns tended to avoid sentimental invocations of parenthood in the interest of distancing lesbians and gay men from children. Instead, these educational efforts frequently focused on enumerating the multiple ways in which discriminatory marriage policies relegated law-abiding citizens to a second-class status. The limits of this strategy became clear in 2008 during the hotly contested and impressively funded battle over California's Proposition 8. Although public polling in the lead-up to the election consistently showed proponents of same-sex marriage rights in a comfortable lead, the ballot proposition to amend California's constitution ended up passing, and the new definition of marriage nullified the state court's recent decision in favor of marriage equality. Reflecting on the final days before the election, some LGBT rights activists have attributed this upset to the opponent's convincing portrayal of homosexual marriage as a corruptive force that would infect heterosexual family life and pervert innocent children (Fleischer 2010). Take, for example, the "Princes" television ad that began airing a few weeks before the election. Funded by the National Organization for Marriage (NOM), the group that was founded the year before specifically to get Prop 8 on the ballot, the ad featured a young girl running into her kitchen holding the LGBT-friendly children's book *King and King* (2001) and excitedly announcing to her mother, "Guess what I learned in school today? I learned how a prince married a prince, and I can marry a princess!" This spot, which ran in both English and Spanish and was the most frequently aired ad on either side of the campaign, flamed fears that the legalization of same-sex marriage would result in parents losing control over their children's moral and sexual compasses.

Faced with the realization that incendiary claims about the child's susceptibility to queerness continued to hold sway over certain constituencies, marriage equality advocates began to reevaluate their tactical approaches and to finally develop a formal and centralized strategy. Freedom to Marry started collecting all the available data on public opinion about same-sex marriage and, in 2010, formed a secret partnership, which they called the Marriage Research Consortium, in order to develop new messaging protocol.[14] Working closely with organizations like Third Way and the Movement Advancement Project, Freedom to Marry determined that a more effective marriage campaign would move away from pragmatic calls for fairness and equality and would instead emphasize the ways in which lesbian and gay couples, like their heterosexual counterparts, desire stability and lifelong commitment. According to *Moving Marriage Forward*, the message-training document that emerged out of this research, activists needed to "speak to the heart" when addressing "non-gay individuals" and to explain "why marriage matters" by sharing personal stories about the familial lives of same-sex couples (Freedom to Marry 2010, 3–5). The document, attempting to reconcile marriage equality with reproductive futurity, instructed organizations to stress that lesbians and gay men view marriage as a unique bond that "says 'we're family' in a way that no other word can" (5). In addition to encouraging activists to invite older lesbians and gay men in long-term relationships to speak out for marriage rights, Freedom to Marry also suggested "tak[ing] advantage of opportunities to introduce families in which same-sex couples are raising children" in order to show others "how similar such a family's lives are to their own" (7). While family equality activists had, until this point, often felt sidelined within the mainstream marriage movement—in the wake of the Prop 8 defeat, for example, the executive director of the California-based Our Family Coalition reflected on how LGBT parents and their children were "very explicitly excluded" from public debates about marriage (Palevsky 2010)—the voices of parenting advocates and, even more interestingly, children from LGBT families took on a new role under this revised messaging strategy.

Voices of Children

Even before Freedom to Marry released its research-based guidelines for advancing marriage equality, LGBT rights activists had already begun to move beyond making claims on behalf of the figural child and to experiment instead with mobilizing actual children with lesbian and gay parents. On April 3, 2009, the Iowa Supreme Court ruled in favor of the six white couples who, working closely with Lambda Legal, had sued the state for denying them marriage licenses (*Varnum v. Brien* 2009). In many ways, this case resembled the successful courtroom bid for marriage equality in Massachusetts a few years earlier. Like Gay and Lesbian Advocates and Defenders (the Boston-based organization that handled the Massachusetts case), Lambda Legal represented several plaintiffs who were raising or who planned to raise children and framed the suit as seeking protection not just for the adults in question but for the families they were building.

What sets the Iowa case apart from its predecessor, however, is the fact that, shortly after filing the original lawsuit in 2006, Lambda Legal amended its claim to include the children of the couples as "minor plaintiffs." In addition to adding the newborn white son of the youngest lesbian pair involved in the case, Lambda Legal also named the four- and eight-year-old white daughters of Jen and Dawn BarbouRoske as coplaintiffs. One of the gay couples named in the suit, Jason Morgan and Chuck Swaggerty, were licensed foster parents who, by the time the case reached the state supreme court, had adopted two young black boys who were biological brothers. Although these children were never added to the lawsuit, Lambda Legal did include a picture of the new dads and their sons on their web page along with a brief bio of the family (Lambda Legal n.d.). When the court finally issued its affirmative ruling and the six families suddenly found themselves in the national spotlight, it was not, however, Morgan and Swaggerty's multicultural gay family that emerged as the face of Iowan marriage equality. This job was left to the BarbouRoskes: their family was named the *Iowa City Press-Citizen*'s 2009 "Persons of the Year," and, thanks to a well-circulated Associated Press photograph, their oldest daughter, McKinley, appeared in newspapers across the country. Taken the moment Lambda Legal leaders announced the court's decision to the plaintiffs, the photo captures the eleven-year-old leaping out of her seat with her hands triumphantly thrown into the air. Five months later, McKinley catapulted into a more visible role within the national marriage movement when she spoke out on Capitol Hill in favor of a legislative attempt to repeal DOMA (O'Leary 2010).

While it is possible to attribute McKinley's rise to fame to the fact that she was the oldest of the minor plaintiffs and that her parents were already locally known for running a monthly potluck for LGBT families, I do not think it is a coincidence that the most talked about child from the Iowa case was the white daughter of two white lesbians. The mainstream media's and the marriage movement's affinity toward McKinley reflected a trend repeated in several different states. McKinley was conceived via artificial insemination (a detail widely circulated in news stories and court documents) and bears a striking resemblance to Jen, her birth mother. Given the regularity with which news outlets have reported on lesbian artificial insemination since the "gayby boom" of the 1980s and 1990s, the BarbouRoskes provide the general public with a familiar story of LGBT family building in which a woman seems to fulfill her presumably natural desire to birth a child. Although McKinley is not biologically related to her mother Dawn or to her younger sister, who her parents fostered and later adopted, the entire family reads as white and, as such, as a visually coherent family.

It is also worth noting that neither of her midwestern parents do gender in a way that unsettles the binary norms of sexual difference organizing U.S. public culture and national LGBT organizing—neither veers toward a perversely masculine presentation nor edges on a performance of femininity that might be construed, via heteronormative conventions, as eroticized. In fact, the white lesbian mother's status as a desexualized figure is what makes families like the BarbouRoskes so valuable for the marriage equality movement. Despite the market for lesbian porn among straight men consumers, actual lesbian couples are often viewed as nonsexual: within a phallocentric imaginary, lesbian desire remains unthinkable and lesbian sex an impossibility. The illegibility of lesbian sexuality, especially when routed through suburban, middle-class family formations, keeps the specter of pedophilia at bay in a way that simply cannot happen for gay fathers. As the family equality movement worked to mobilize the children of LGBT families, the white children invited to participate in activist efforts came, almost uniformly, from similarly constructed families. Consider, for starters, the two middle schoolers who appeared before the legislatures in their home states of Vermont and New Jersey to speak out about the inadequacy of civil union laws and the need for marriage equality.

On March 18, 2009, twelve-year-old Evann Orleck-Jetter testified at the Vermont State House on behalf of her family and "families like [hers]" (*Democracy Now!* 2009). The Joint Senate and House Judiciary Committees were holding public hearings on proposed legislation that, if passed, would legalize same-sex marriages and put an end to what many LGBT rights activists viewed as the state's "separate but not equal" civil union policy. Notably, when Evann stepped up to the microphone that day, it was not the first time she had appeared before the joint committees. Nine years earlier, Evann and her younger brother were sitting on the laps of their mothers, Alexis Jetter and Annelise Orleck, as they testified before the legislature in support of the original civil union bill.[15] While neither Jetter nor Orleck was particularly concerned about securing a "stamp of approval" from the state, they did want to gain recognition as a family for the sake of their children. Their decision to speak out in favor of civil unions, even as they believed this framework to be an inadequate substitution for full marriage, was their way of "be[ing] political as mothers" (Yu 2000).[16] In her testimony years later, Jetter and Orleck's daughter echoed their concerns about the ways in which marriage inequality "hurts" the children of lesbians and gay men by making them feel "invisible" and like no one "accept[s]" or "honor[s]" their families ("Testimony" 2009).

At the same time, Evann situated her call for the "freedom to marry" within a larger civil rights framework and, in a move not uncommon among marriage activists, crafted a historical narrative in which expanded LGBT rights marked the next logical step for a nation that had already achieved racial equality: "Although black boys and white boys and black girls and white girls can play together now, we still don't accept that two people of the same gender can be together, married with kids of their own." Treating racism and homophobia as analogous modes of discrimination that need to be sequentially overcome via legal remedies—a rhetorical move that, as Kaufman and Miles (2009) argue, "erases queer people of color and makes light of the structural racism that the civil rights movement fought against"—Evann mobilized the words of Martin Luther King Jr. to argue that the only thing keeping the state of Vermont from reaching the "promised land" was its homophobic marriage laws. A few weeks later, when the legislature passed the proposed bill (and then overrode the governor's attempt to veto it), Evann quickly assumed a hero status within progressive circles. Although she was not the only young person to speak at the State House during those hearings, it was her testimony that gained national news coverage. The day after marriage was legalized in Vermont, Evann appeared on *Democracy Now!*, where Amy Goodman credited her impassioned plea for marriage equality with "moving [many legislators] to support the bill" (2009). Later in the year, her testimony was anthologized in the second edition of Howard Zinn and Anthony Arnove's *Voices of a People's History of the United States* (2009).

On December 7, 2009, ten-year-old Kasey Nicholson-McFadden testified at the New Jersey State House in support of a bill that would have done away with civil unions and legalized same-sex marriages. Like Evann and her brother, Kasey and his sister were the products of lesbian family planning—in these cases, each of the mothers in each family took a turn getting pregnant via artificial insemination using the same donor, resulting in racially homogenous families where the children share phenotypic similarities with at least one of their parents—and were the children of marriage equality activists. In 2002, Kasey's mothers, Karen and Marcye Nicholson-McFadden, had signed on as plaintiffs in the Lambda Legal–backed lawsuit that eventually led to the implementation of a civil union law in New Jersey. Seven years later, Kasey joined his parents at the Senate Judiciary Committee's hearings to speak out about how the illegibility of civil unions accords an inferior status to same-sex couples. "It doesn't bother me to tell kids my parents are gay," he explained. "It does bother me to say they aren't married. It makes me feel that our family is less than their family" (Wildman 2010a).

Although his testimony was unable to convince the legislature to pass the marriage equality bill, Kasey emerged as a local celebrity in the fight for the freedom to marry. The organization Garden State Equality included him in their educational materials. His school picture and a photograph of his family appeared alongside a long quote attributed to both of his mothers that elaborated on his alleged distress over his parents' relationship status: "When the kids at his elementary school talk about their families, they say, 'Oh you have two moms, are they married?' Kasey tries to explain what a civil union is. His classmates don't get it and he comes home distraught. It's a stigma no child should have to bear."[17] In 2010, when Lambda Legal filed another suit against the state of New Jersey, Karen and Marcye once again signed on, but this time, Kasey and their daughter joined them as "minor plaintiffs." Three years later, when the Superior Court ruled in favor of marriage equality and Governor Chris Christie agreed not to appeal the decision, Kasey, at this point a young high school student, appeared in the Associated Press's coverage of the news celebrating the victory with his family (Mulvihill and Zezima 2013).

In addition to relying on young white children to soften calls for marriage rights made in the name of fairness and equality, local organizers also recognized the value of mobilizing older children with lesbian mothers—namely, white adolescent boys—to speak out in defense of their families. On April 22, 2009, fourteen-year-old Sam Putnam-Ripley of Portland, Maine, testified at a public hearing on same-sex marriage held at the Augusta Civic Center. The Joint Committee on the Judiciary spent an entire day listening to both supporters and opponents of a proposed bill that sought to end discrimination in the state's administration of civil marriages. Sam's testimony, a political action conceived in the privacy of his family's kitchen, was almost immediately uploaded to YouTube and became a huge hit among local marriage equality activists (Wildman 2010b). He opened by assuring the legislature that his life was "pretty typical" (and pretty heterosexual) in spite of having a mother in a lesbian relationship: "I play football and baseball for my school, I'm an honor student, I like girls, and I enjoy hanging out with my friends."[18] The hardest thing for him was that, despite the fact that his mother's partner, Michelle, had helped raise him and his brothers for the past five years, his doctors, his teachers, and his friends' parents refused to see her as his "stepmom." The legalization of same-sex marriage, Sam reasoned, would help "kids all over the state" by making their families legible to their communities.

Two weeks later, after the House and the Senate approved the proposed legislation, the governor signed the bill into law and codified marriage as a union between two people regardless of sex. The next day, before any of the families Sam had hoped to represent could breathe a sigh of relief, opponents of marriage equality launched a campaign to repeal the law through voter referendum. Backed by NOM, the newly formed Stand for Marriage Maine (S4MM) coalition successfully petitioned to include a question on the November ballot that asked voters if they wanted to reject the new law that permitted same-sex couples to marry. As the coalition worked to persuade the public to vote "Yes" on what came to be known as "Maine Question 1," NOM provided S4MM with nearly $2 million in funding from undisclosed sources, thus enabling organizers to hire the same public relations firm that handled the Yes on 8 efforts in California and produced the "Princes" ad the year before (Hurwitz 2013).

To counter these efforts, the No on 1/Protect Maine Equality campaign asked Sam and his family to do a television spot in support of same-sex marriage rights. The resulting advertisement interspersed footage of Sam's testimony with a shot of him sitting between his mom and stepmom in a wooded backyard and explaining to the Maine public that voting "No" would help change the perception that families like his were somehow "lesser."[19] Although the structure of his family departs from the narratives of lesbian family planning showcased in the preceding examples, the image of Sam, flanked by his white mother and stepmother, aligned with the broader movement's preference for white nuclear families. In the end, Sam's work with the No on 1 campaign was unable to stop the NOM-funded push for a "people's veto," but his efforts, in retrospect, highlight the increasingly central role children were playing within the marriage equality movement.

The soft-focused ad in which Sam appeared was modeled off a successful 2007 television spot that aired in Massachusetts shortly before the state legislature considered a marriage protection amendment, which, if placed on the ballot and approved, would have undone the court's 2003 decision in favor of same-sex marriage. Mass Equality's ad featured Peter Hams, the son of the lesbian mothers known for being the first same-sex couple to obtain a Massachusetts marriage license. After praising his "hockey moms" for being such supportive parents and, in effect, situating his family within the white New England imaginary, Peter explains how "amazing" it was to watch his mothers marry and how "devastating" it would be to see those rights taken away.[20] In many ways, Peter comes off as rather boyish in the ad, talking about his parents taking him to school and practice and relying heavily on the filler "you know" as he speaks. Like Kasey and Sam, he easily occupies the privileged position of the fragile white boy child, the unmarked figure around whom policy debates often revolve and the subject frequently cast as embodying national futurity and thus deserving of state protections.[21] At the same time, however, Peter's scruffy face and muscular body read as much older; he was, in fact, twenty-seven when he shot this commercial. Never appearing on screen with his mothers, he achieves a degree of autonomy and adulthood that propels him into the position of defending his family from an intolerant public. With Peter, the child in need of protection doubled as the protector of his vulnerable parents.

The most stunning example of a white boy child assuming the role of surrogate patriarch for a lesbian household emerged out of Iowa two years after the court had already ordered the state to legalize same-sex marriages. When the House of Representatives announced plans for a public hearing on a proposal for amending the constitution to define marriage as between a man and a woman, the LGBT rights organization One Iowa and their legal partner, Lambda Legal, reached out to the college-aged son of lesbian mothers who had written an op-ed on marriage equality for the *Des Moines Register* back in 2009.[22] On January 31, 2011, nineteen-year-old Zach Wahls stood before the

Iowa House dressed in a suit and tie and offered his life story, delivered in the cadence of a practiced debater, as a rebuttal to the proposed marriage amendment. On the one hand, he took great pains to establish the ordinariness of his white, Christian, and middle-class family: they eat dinner, attend church, and take vacations together, just like "any other Iowa family."[23] On the other hand, Zach was careful to distinguish himself as an extraordinary young man, holding up his many accomplishments as evidence of his mothers' more-than-adequate parenting skills: as he tells the chairman of the hearings, "I scored in the ninety-ninth percentile on the ACT, I'm actually an Eagle Scout, [and] I own and operate my own small business."

Zach then clarifies that his endorsement of marriage equality is about securing symbolic recognition for families like his and not about demanding extra handouts from the state. While he admits that his birth mother's multiple sclerosis diagnosis has been difficult for his entire family, he makes no attempt to frame marriage as enabling her access to health care, ensuring medical decision-making powers for her partner, or otherwise working in favor of illness or disability. Instead, he assures the audience that his family does not "expect anyone to solve [their] problems" and that they will continue to "fight [their] own battles." Marriage equality, according to Zach, was a way of recognizing his mothers as respectable Iowans who deserve the "right to marry the person [they] love." Denying his parents and other gay couples access to marriage was, as far as he was concerned, the same as declaring them "second-class citizens."

The Outspoken Generation

Shortly after stepping away from the microphone, Zach's testimony was uploaded to YouTube, and he became an instant internet celebrity: his three-minute performance reached 1.5 million views within two weeks and was later named the most viewed political video of 2011 (Bolcer 2011). Over the next few years, Zach, who identifies as "straight . . . in every sense of the word,"[24] built himself a career as an LGBT rights advocate: he founded the organization Scouts for Equality to fight homophobia within the Boy Scouts of America; he secured a book contract for his autobiographical defense of LGBT families called *My Two Moms: Lessons of Love, Strength, and What Makes a Family* (Wahls 2012); and after teaming up with the Obama administration's LGBT outreach coordinators, he spoke at the 2012 Democratic National Convention and began campaigning for the president at pride events across the country. Additionally, in April 2012, just as his book was being released, Zach linked up with Family Equality Council to cochair their new youth advocacy initiative. He worked alongside Ella Robinson, the white daughter of the Episcopal priest who, in 2003, became the first openly gay bishop in a major Christian denomination, to help launch the Outspoken Generation program. This initiative sought to encourage "young adult children of LGBT parents" (who were at least sixteen years old) to stand up for their families by "speaking publicly at community events across the country, in front of local, state, and national legislative bodies, and directly to the media" (Majors 2012).

Building on the organization's tradition of providing children with opportunities to share their experiences in open forums (as discussed in the previous chapter), the Council was now asking youth to mobilize their stories for the express purpose of intervening on policy debates and transforming public opinion. In the press release announcing this new program, the Council emphasized the importance of the Outspoken Generation in light of the recent discovery that NOM was planning to recruit children of LGBT-identified parents to publicly criticize their own families. A few weeks earlier, a federal judge unsealed confidential NOM documents that had been disclosed when the organization challenged the constitutionality of Maine's campaign finance laws in an attempt to protect the anonymity of its donors and refute accusations of illegal and unethical activity during the state's 2009 battle over Question 1. In the planning document titled *National Strategy for Winning the Marriage Battle*, NOM outlined its plan to cultivate "a worldwide community of [expert witnesses] to credential [their] concerns . . . around gay marriage" and to hire an "outreach coordinator" to locate children of same-sex couples willing to go on record as "victims" of the marriage equality movement (2009, 21, 24–25). The Outspoken Generation, the Council argued, was the perfect answer to a coordinated effort designed to "demonize" LGBT-identified parents: as far as executive director Jennifer Chrisler was concerned, "Who better to refute the myths and lies of hate groups like NOM than [the LGBT community's] own grown up children" (Majors 2012)?

Over the next few years, the Outspoken Generation received widespread coverage in mainstream news media outlets, including NPR, PerezHilton.com, the *Huffington Post*, and Katie Couric's daytime talk show. Zach and Ella, as the cochairs of the program, provided the Council with mature, gender-conforming, and straight-identifying spokespeople well positioned to address a presumably white and heterosexual voting public. From the vantage point of early adulthood—Zach was now in his early twenties, and Ella was in her early thirties—they could defend their families by reflecting on their childhoods and authoritatively reporting back on how normal LGBT families are and how exceptionally same-sex couples parent.

In addition to deploying members of the Outspoken Generation as part of larger public education efforts, the Council also found a way to use the numerous stories collected through the program to support courtroom battles for marriage equality. In the spring of 2013, as the U.S. Supreme Court prepared for hearings on the constitutionality of California's Prop 8 and DOMA's

federal definition of marriage, governmental organizations, nongovern-
mental agencies, and individual parties submitted more than 150 "friends
of the court" briefs for consideration in one or both of the cases. On March 1,
the Council, in collaboration with other LGBT family advocates (including
COLAGE and the California-based Our Family Coalition), filed what they
dubbed the "Voices of Children" brief. While this was not the Council's first
foray into amicus brief territory—in 2010, the organization joined Garden
State Equality in submitting a brief to the New Jersey Supreme Court in support of the plaintiffs who were challenging the state's exclusionary marriage
laws—this earlier brief relied entirely on the expertise of pediatricians, psychiatrists, and social scientists to demonstrate the harmful effects of marriage
inequality on children. In distinction, the "Voices of Children" brief compiled
direct quotes from young people, either from the testimonies they delivered
before their state legislatures or from interviews they did with the Council or
Our Family Coalition. These children, the Council argued, were "uniquely
qualified to speak about how their families look, feel, and function and how
the availability—or unavailability—of marriage as an option for their parents
colors their daily lives" (Brief of Family Equality Council 2013, 2–3). Significantly, while McKinley, Kasey, and Sam, along with Zach and Ella, all make
an appearance in the brief, Evann's testimony is never mentioned. Her case for
same-sex marriage rights was based on a progressive call for equality and as
such was out of step with the more affectively charged argument developed by
the Council's legal counsel.

The "Voices of Children" brief opened by debunking the assumption that
LGBT lives have nothing to do with parenthood, reproduction, or other child-
centric family matters. Responding to conservative attempts to justify discriminatory laws on the basis of marriage's kinship with procreation and child
rearing, the Council pointed out how the presumed childlessness of same-sex
couples ignores and, in effect, endangers the approximately quarter of a million children growing up in LGBT families (Brief of Family Equality Council
2013, 8). The brief cited the work of demographer Gary J. Gates to establish
the prevalence of "same-sex-parented" households in the United States but did
so without addressing the race and class disparities that his research identifies
within this larger population. As such, the Council's efforts to make a case for
marriage rights on behalf of an imagined and unmarked two-parent LGBT
family end up showcasing the voices of children with concerns that reflect a
racially and economically privileged upbringing.

The first section of the brief performed the rhetorical move skillfully executed by Zach on the floor of the Iowa House: the Council constructed the
LGBT family as both typical and exceptional. Even as the brief emphasized
the ways in which same-sex couples share the same values as other "American" parents—these "moms and dads are raising their children to love their

country, stand up for their friends, treat others the way they would like to be treated, and tell the truth" (12–13)—the Council also highlighted the ways in which these children's everyday lives meet and often surpass white middle-class familial norms. The testimonies collected in the brief are peppered with references to the children's various extracurricular activities (including sports, bands and choirs, academic decathlons, and community service projects) and to their parents' active involvement in their lives inside and outside of school (as coaches, classroom volunteers, parent-teacher association leaders, and dedicated spectators who never miss a single concert or competition). While the supportiveness attributed to these parents, which likely requires a flexible work schedule and a sufficient amount of disposable income, is primarily a marker of class privilege, the Council presented these anecdotes as evidence of the exceptional parenting skills of the same-sex couples who are raising happy, healthy, and well (if not better) adjusted children.[25]

In the second part, however, the brief took on a very different tone and zeroed in on the vulnerabilities characterizing the lives of children growing up in LGBT-headed households. Far from reflecting an "internally inconsistent" position (as Chief Justice Roberts suggested during the Prop 8 hearings), the construction of the LGBT family as simultaneously the safest and most dangerous place to raise a child was an effect of arguing that children need protection not from homosexuality but from state-sponsored forms of homophobia. Bans on same-sex marriage, the Council argued, harm LGBT families by stigmatizing parents and children alike. According to the brief, the sense of inferiority and illegitimacy experienced on account of having unmarried parents left some children feeling scared and insecure about the stability of their families and others enraged over the injustice of being unrecognizable to their own governments (23–31). To make matters worse, the Council explained, these psychological burdens were exacerbated by the material effects of marriage inequality: same-sex couples carried "a heavier tax burden" than their straight counterparts because they could not "file joint federal tax returns or maximize dependency exemptions, child tax credits, children and dependent care credits, and education deductions" (30). While the Council did mention how the illegibility of same-sex relationships rendered some households ineligible for social safety net programs like Medicaid, Supplemental Security Income, and Temporary Assistance for Needy Families (30–31), the primary goal of the "Voices of Children" brief was to secure "recognition, respect, and protection" for middle-class LGBT families via access to the institution of marriage (37).

On the Outspoken Generation website, the Council touts its amicus brief as "key to victory" in the Supreme Court's decision to overturn the section of DOMA that defined marriage, for federal purposes, as between one man and one woman (Family Equality Council, "Outspoken Generation," n.d.).

While there is no way of knowing exactly how much weight the brief held for the justices who joined the majority opinion, there is evidence that childrens' voices may have played a role in the court's landmark decision. Because the DOMA case dealt with a lawsuit against the U.S. government over its "differential treatment" of same-sex marriages—in 2010, eighty-one-year-old Edith Windsor sued to recoup the $363,053 she paid in estate taxes after inheriting property from her deceased wife—the oral arguments focused exclusively on whether the Fifth Amendment prevented federal law from "injuring" a class of citizens that the state of New York sought to protect.[26]

In contrast, the Prop 8 hearing, which asked whether California's ban on marriage violated the Fourteenth Amendment's guarantee of equal protection, explored the interests compelling a state's definition of marriage and, in doing so, took up the question of procreation and child rearing. While the defense of Prop 8 rested on the symbolic importance of promoting heterosexual marriage as the ideal familial formation, proponents of marriage equality emphasized the state's obligation to protect the actual children living with same-sex couples. During the oral arguments, as the Prop 8 defenders called into question the research demonstrating the fitness of lesbian and gay parents, Justice Anthony Kennedy reminded the court of the approximately 40,000 children being raised by same-sex couples in California and asked, "The voice of those children is important in this case, don't you think?" Three months later, when the court announced its opinions in these cases, the interests of children growing up in LGBT families were once again on the table. Although the court never issued a decision on the constitutionality of Prop 8,[27] the ruling in favor of Windsor, a ruling ostensibly about property, inheritance, and federal tax codes, concluded with a discussion of the "personhood and dignity" of lesbian and gay couples and their children (*United States v. Windsor* 2013, 26). The majority opinion, authored by Justice Kennedy, took DOMA to task for imposing a federal "stigma" upon locally authorized same-sex marriages and, in the process, "humiliat[ing]" and "financial[ly] harm[ing]" children growing up in LGBT-headed households (21, 23–24). Thanks to the "voices of children," the court was able to cast a decision that was technically in favor of a rich, old, white lady trying to avoid estate taxes as a ruling in the name of protecting innocent children.

The COGs

The rhetorical effectiveness of deploying children's voices did not go unnoticed by opponents of marriage equality in the United States. Shortly after the Prop 8 hearings, an article titled "Justice Kennedy's 40,000 Children" appeared in *Public Discourse*, the Witherspoon Institute's online journal. (The Witherspoon Institute is a Princeton-based conservative think tank founded in 2003 by two of the men who would later form NOM.) In this article, Robert Oscar López, then a tenured English professor at California State University, Northridge, and cofounder of the largely web-based International Children's Rights Institute, cautioned the court against assuming that all children raised by same-sex couples had "desires and concerns . . . identical to and uncritical of the decisions made by [their] parents" (2013b). López identifies as a COG (his shorthand for "children of gays") and has written extensively about the horrors of being raised by a lesbian mother in the 1970s and 1980s. Claiming to speak on behalf of the countless adults who "were raised by parents in same-sex part-nerships" and "are terrified of speaking publicly about their feelings," López implored the court to take into account the voices of children who have been "brushed aside in the so-called 'social science research' on same-sex parenting." In direct response to the Outspoken Generation's efforts to craft a celebra-tory image of LGBT families, López insisted on the inadequacy of same-sex parenting: "Having a mom and a dad is a precious value in its own right and not something that can be overridden, even if a gay couple has lots of money, can send a kid to the best schools, and raises the kid to be an Eagle Scout." While it may be tempting to dismiss a homophobic diatribe like this as unwor-thy of further examination, a closer look at how conservative forces wielded the newly politicized position of the child from an LGBT-headed household yields new insights into the limits and possibilities of the marriage and family equality movement.

Over the past few years, whenever I mention the work of López, I am often asked if I know who is paying him. While there is no concrete evidence avail-able to prove NOM hired him as an "outreach coordinator" to fulfill their plans of mobilizing grown children to speak out against their lesbian and gay parents, it is hard to believe that he is not tied to the organization in some way. Despite his vehement denial of any formal affiliations with antigay or right-wing groups, journalists have been speculating about his ties to NOM for several years now (Rose 2012; Hawkins 2013). He began contributing to the Witherspoon Institute's online journal in August 2012, when he published an autobiographical account of the gender and sexual confusion he experienced "growing up with two moms" and the miraculous ascent he made from out of the "gay underworld" and into a happy and healthy heterosexual marriage (López 2012).

Strikingly, his first *Public Discourse* article appeared online shortly after Mark Regnerus, author of the Witherspoon-funded and widely discredited "New Family Structures Study," reached out to López to thank him for pub-licly supporting his controversial research on the negative outcomes associated with "same-sex parenting."[28] The alliance between Regnerus and López, when considered in relation to the confidential NOM documents that revealed plans to locate both "experts" on and "victims" of lesbian and gay parenting, seems to more than coincidentally advance the organization's official strategy for thwarting marriage equality efforts. Additionally, finding a Latino-identified spokesperson would have served the interests of what NOM referred to in those 2009 planning documents as "The Latino Project," an information campaign designed to turn opposition to gay marriage into "a key badge of Latino identity" and a symbol of "rebellion [against] conformist assimilation to the bad side of 'Anglo' culture" (2009, 16–17). Although López has written elsewhere about the ways in which he negotiates his Filipino and Puerto Rican heritage, he described himself in his debut article for the Witherspoon Institute as a "Latino intellectual." Regardless of the precise nature of his relationship with NOM, a figure like López aligned with the organization's plans to rally the Latino communities it perceived as steeped in traditional family values and uniformly opposed to homosexual lifestyles.[29]

Following the Supreme Court's 2013 ruling against DOMA's federal definition of marriage, López joined forces with three other adult COGs to defend the rights of individual states to limit marriage to a union between one man and one woman. Together, they filed amicus briefs in several marriage cases heard in both state supreme courts and federal circuit courts. López's fellow amici included Dawn Stefanowicz, author of the self-published memoir *Out from Under: The Impact of Homosexual Parenting* (Stefanowicz 2007); Katy Faust, a Christian blogger who has been fighting marriage equality at AsktheBigot.com since September 2012; and B. N. Klein (a.k.a. Rivka Edelman), a former adjunct literature professor and the coeditor with López of the self-published collection *Jephthah's Daughters: Innocent Casualties in the War for Family 'Equality'* (López and Edelman 2015).

By March 2015, the "quartet of truth," as they were affectionately known among right-wing circles (Ford 2015), had teamed up with two additional COGs: Heather Barwick, a "former gay-marriage advocate turned children's rights activist," and Denise Shick, a Christian advocate who self-published her memoir, *My Daddy's Secret* (Shick and Gramckow 2008), and who has been ministering to other families impacted by "transsexualism" for over a decade. In anticipation of the Supreme Court's hearing on the constitutionality of state-level bans on and refusals to recognize same-sex marriages, the six COGs, working in pairs, filed three amicus briefs in defense of traditional marriage. Substituting anecdotal evidence for legal reasoning or factual analysis, the briefs offered no opinions on the questions of due process or equal protection and did not engage with any of the leading scholarship on parenting and sexual orientation; instead, amici called upon their personal histories to fabricate cautionary tales about the perils of raising children in "homosexual" or "transsexual" households.

Faust and Barwick filed what is arguably the tamest of the three briefs. In an open letter to Justice Kennedy, which appeared in *Public Discourse* shortly before they filed their brief, Faust echoed López's earlier plea and begged the court to take seriously the adult children brave enough to "stand against the bluster of the gay lobby" and to occupy the supposedly "impossible" position of "lov[ing] [their] gay parent(s) and oppos[ing] gay marriage" (Faust 2015). In the brief she filed with Barwick, Faust presented their childhood experiences as a corrective to the testimonies collected by Family Equality Council for its "Voices of Children" brief. Recalling the feeling of wanting to please their parents as they were growing up, they sympathized with the children who have spoken out in favor of marriage equality and who, at such a young age, cannot fully comprehend the traumatic nature of their lives. Faust and Barwick, who believe so ferociously in the life-making power of heterosexual marriage that they remain skeptical of the idea of infertility (Brief of Barwick and Faust 2015, 33–34), organized their defense of man-woman marriage around their belief in a child's "natural right" to a relationship with their two birth parents (2). While they admit that their lesbian mothers and their mothers' partners provided them with loving homes throughout their youths (1), they have come to realize, after building their own families and seeing their husbands interact with their children, just how traumatized and "emotionally malnourished" they were (19). As Faust and Barwick see it, if the U.S. government cares about the health and well-being of children, then the law should only incentivize family structures that afford children the "dual-gender influence" of their biological parents (2).

While Faust and Barwick's brief is organized around an unmarked but unmistakable investment in conservative Christian ideology, López and Klein distanced their critiques of LGBT family life from religious concerns and framed their brief as a "scholarly" intervention into debates on parenting (Brief of López and Klein 2015, 4). They argued that decisions in favor of marriage equality legitimate the actions of LGBT-identified adults who use their children as "political tool[s]" (32), treating them like "piece[s] of property" (32), and heartlessly denying them their "inalienable right to their [biological] mother and father" (24). Compared to Faust and Barwick, López and Klein were far more damning in their critique of Family Equality Council: they saw the "overly sweet testimonials" collected in the "Voices of Children" brief as "red flags" that reveal how "small children under the power of their parents" have no choice but to "champion the cause" of marriage equality (29–30). López, who worked with black queer studies scholar Cathy Cohen as a Yale undergraduate (López 2013c), pushed even further: he likened his childhood to the experiences of enslaved Africans in the Americas, speculating that he has endured "many of the same traumas as a result of feeling 'owned' by the gay community" (10). This rhetorical maneuver, especially when read alongside López's interpretation of the family equality movement as an "international gay war on black people" (López 2013a), seems in line with the racially divisive strategies endorsed by NOM. Along with the planning documents discussed previously, NOM was also forced to disclose its 2008–9 board update, which contained plans for the "Not a Civil Right Project." The goal of this proposed initiative was to "drive a wedge between gays and blacks—two key democratic constituencies"—by "fanning the hostility raised in the wake of Prop 8."[30] As a close ally of López, Klein appears to have contributed to these efforts by accusing homosexuals of acquiring their children through racist and sexist means—referring, in their collective brief, to the use of donors and surrogates as "reproductive prostitution" (25) and writing elsewhere about adoption as a form of "human trafficking" designed to "strip poor and minority women" of their parental rights (Edelman 2015). That said, their brief's attack on marriage equality activism hinged primarily on their denouncement of the coercive power LGBT-identified parents allegedly wield over young COGs.

Similar accusations of coercion, coupled with reports of abuse, structure the argument against LGBT parenting advanced in the third and final brief. In an attempt to expose how "sanitized [and] laudatory" images of exceptional LGBT families obscure the actual toxicity of "gay" and "transgender" lifestyles, Stefanowicz and Shick described the diseased and dysfunctional homes in which they were raised and recounted, in great detail, the sexual and physical violence they suffered at the hands of their "unstable" fathers (Brief of Stefanowicz and Shick 2015, 35–36). Both women attribute their fathers' abusive behaviors to the misogyny at the heart of their gender and sexual "confusion"—Stefanowicz blaming her father's desire for other men, Shick blaming her father's desire to be the woman she was becoming. Additionally, Stefanowicz points to the medical dangers associated with homosexual parenting: she claimed that her father's promiscuous lifestyle infected her home and that blood tests later in life confirmed that she had been "exposed to pathogens" as a child (10). Together, Stefanowicz and Shick offered their stories as a rebuttal to the "happy gay family pictures" circulated by "LGBT activists" and "the transgender lobby" (9, 22). They attempted to revive nearly every existing homophobic and transphobic fear as they implored the court to resist the regime of "political correctness" and to protect "the Nation and its coming generations" (2–3). Speaking not only as children's rights activists but also from the newly politicized position of the child from an LGBT family, Stefanowicz and Shick defended traditional man-woman marriage out of what they described as a selfless concern for the well-being of innocent children beholden to the perverse whims of their parents. They joined the other amici in urging the court not to fall for the stories that LGBT activists have coerced out of the children they own and control.

Indoctrinations

In the end, López and his fellow COGs were unable to prevent the arrival of marriage equality. On June 26, 2015, in a 5–4 split decision, the U.S. Supreme Court declared marriage "a fundamental right inherent in the liberty of a person" (*Obergefell v. Hodges* 2015, 4).[31] The majority opinion, authored by Justice Kennedy, interpreted the Constitution as protecting the "dignity" of same-sex couples aspiring to the "love, fidelity, devotion, sacrifice, and family" embodied in marital unions (28). While it may be tempting to simply dismiss the amici given their failure to interfere with the LGBT rights agenda, I think there is much to be gained by dwelling on their briefs and in sharpening our understanding of right-wing attacks on trans and queer lives. A closer look at these documents reveals the ways in which the arguments advanced across the briefs dovetail with Marxist feminist analyses of marriage and the modern family and with the concerns queer scholars and activists have raised regarding the freedom to marry movement.

Take, for example, the claim that, within the realm of family equality activism, children circulate as a form of property. Same-sex couples, the COGs asserted, acquire children through "unnatural" means and then use them as "props . . . to prove that gay families [are] just like heterosexual ones" (Brief of López and Klein 2015, 27). Within the context of their amicus briefs, the willingness to treat "children like traded commodities" is supposed to serve as evidence that LGBT-identified adults are unfit for parenthood (Brief of Stefanowicz and Shick 2015, 14). In contrast, I am struck by how this attempt to paint same-sex couples and LGBT rights activists as monstrous figures exposes not the particular perversity of LGBT families but rather the property logics organizing family life under capitalism. In many ways, I agree with amici in their assessment of the family equality movement's attempt to secure parental recognition through marriage rights: such a gesture does amount to asking the state to acknowledge a couple's private ownership over a specific child while doing very little to ensure that the child's basic needs are met. The Supreme Court's legalization of same-sex marriage may help legitimate family ties for LGBT-identified adults who parent or plan to parent in pairs and for whom marriage is possible and desirable, but it does so through a legal institution designed to preserve white supremacy and patriarchal property rights by identifying rightful heirs and assigning responsibility for their care. Within this discursive framework, the child exists as not just the inheritor to but also an extension of paternal property.

In the context of the United States, the marital family form has figured centrally in the ongoing projects of colonization, the policing of national borders, and the management of racialized and sexualized populations. To borrow the words of Chief Justice Roberts, marriage serves a "vital need" for capitalist states (*Obergefell v. Hodges* [Roberts dissenting] 2015, 4). When the court announced its ruling in favor of nationwide marriage equality, Roberts, in a move unprecedented in his ten years in office, read a summary of his dissent from the bench and expressed his dismay over the majority's disregard for the "historic definition" of marriage, a definition derived out of a concern "for the good of children and society" (2, 5). Notably, in spite of his efforts to establish marriage as a prepolitical institution that naturally arose out of a need to procreate, Roberts's dissent also acknowledged the state's reliance on marriage as a political tool designed to control the intimate lives of its citizenry. Specifically, he cited James Q. Wilson, the political scientist known for his racist and classist "broken windows" theory of policing, to describe marriage as "a socially arranged solution for the problem of getting people to stay together and care for [their] children" (5).[32] Roberts's citational practice calls attention to the continuities that Christina Hanhardt (2016) has traced between order maintenance policing and state-sponsored efforts to regulate social and sexual norms, especially among the most racially and economically vulnerable populations.[33] When pressed to defend the merits of traditional man-woman marriage, the COGs and the chief justice end up laying bare the ways in which marriage has little to do with love and everything to do with law and order.

This is exactly why marriage equality works for capital and the state. Although the House Judiciary Committee justified the passage of DOMA in 1996 by claiming that same-sex marriage would place a drain on precious government resources, the Congressional Budget Office's 2004 report on the potential economic impact of marriage equality concluded that the extension of marital benefits to lesbian and gay couples would not cost the federal government any additional money. In fact, the report found that recognizing same-sex marriages would, on net, likely "improve the budget's bottom line to a small extent" (1). While forcing the government to extend benefits to same-sex partners would increase outlays for Social Security and for the Federal Employees Health Benefits program (5), it would simultaneously reduce spending for Supplemental Security Income, Medicaid, and Medicare because marriage could render LGBT-identified recipients of public assistance (a disproportionate number of whom are raising children) ineligible once their spouse's income and assets figure into eligibility determinations (8–9). Thus the legalization of same-sex marriage can be read, as I do in the following chapter, as working in tandem with other state-administered marriage promotion initiatives designed to privatize the costs of social reproduction.

In the majority opinion for the 2015 ruling in favor of marriage equality, Justice Kennedy returned to the questions of liberty and personhood on which he left off in the *Windsor* decision and, in doing so, masked the economic function of marital relations with the language of dignity. The court offered marriage as a corrective to the state's "long history" of legally and medically

stigmatizing homosexuality and its "imposition of [a] disability on gays and
lesbians [that has] serve[d] to disrespect and subordinate them" (*Obergefell v.
Hodges* 2015, 22). For lesbian and gay parents, Kennedy suggested, access to
marriage bestows upon them an institutionalized form of respect and, in welcoming them into the folds of "normal" familial life, enables them to ensure
emotional and economic security for their children. In practice, however, the
court's attempt to heal past "dignitary wounds" by offering relationship recognition does not necessarily improve the material lives of parents struggling to
pay their rent, feed their children, or cover their family's medical bills (which
is a particularly pressing concern for families dealing with actual illnesses or
disabilities). Consequently, when López and the COGs insisted that "a lack of
'marriage equality' is not the primary struggle [children in LGBT families] are
facing" (Brief of Barwick and Faust 2015, 32), they joined a chorus of critically
queer voices who have made the same argument about the freedom to marry
movement. For scholars and activists working within an expansive economic
justice framework, however, the list of children's basic needs does not start and
end with access to one's biological mother and father. Things like food, shelter, health care, gun control, and public education seem far more important.
As Terry Boggis suggested on my cruise and as the "queer kids of queer parents" argued in their blog post, if the goal were really to keep families intact,
then "children's rights activists" like the COGs and LGBT family advocates
like Family Equality Council would be working to end war, abolish prisons,
stop deportations, strengthen labor movements, and expand protections for
all workers, regardless of their citizenship statuses.

Further, while López and his collaborators have no interest in denatural-
izing the marital family or disrupting a fiscally and culturally conservative
family values agenda, their accusations about the LGBT community's use
and abuse of children resonate, in many ways, with the queer cultural studies analyses I develop across this book. For instance, López and Klein raise a
number of questions about the political economy of LGBT family building and what they call the "commercialization of 'baby-making'" (Brief of
López and Klein 2015, 25). I am not persuaded by their conclusion that donor
and surrogacy arrangements are always exploitative and inherently misogynistic, but I appreciate the ways in which their brief highlights the eugenic ramifications of "designer baby" industries, the racism and classism of the U.S. foster
care system, and the transnational circuits of reproductive labor and material
on which the American family currently depends. For the purposes of this
chapter, however, I want to linger on the amici's collective claim that LGBT-
identified parents exert an oppressive amount of "physical, financial, and even
emotional power" over their children (Brief of López and Klein 2015, 9).

Consider Faust and Barwick's concern for how children raised in LGBT
households are bullied into becoming "flag-bearers of their parents' lifestyle[s]"

(Brief of Barwick and Faust 2015, 30). Tasked with the work of standing up for their families, children must suppress their true emotions and perform happy and healthy at every turn. As far as Faust and Barwick are concerned, all children raised by same-sex couples have had to withstand some sort of "familial carnage" as their families can only come into being through one of four traumatic methods (20)—death, divorce, "abandonment," or "third-party reproduction" (32). Children raised "under the rainbow" are then forced to live, in silence, with the pain of being denied one or both of their biological parents (29). Now, I remain unconvinced that the LGBT family is any more or less traumatic than other domestic settings—even without recourse to psychoanalytic theorizations of the family as a site of personal psychic trauma, it is still possible to recognize what Juana María Rodríguez describes as the "emotional and political consequences of the complex bonds we seek to create" and the "heartache, stresses, and loss associated with different forms of familial formations" (2014, 49)—but the COGs do raise legitimate questions about the ethics of placing children at the center of the marriage movement and asking them to participate in their own rhetorical deployment. While I am not interested in denying agency to young people and am excited by the ways in which the recognition of the child as a desiring political subject might destabilize the law's age-based definitions of consent,[34] I do think it is possible and necessary to read the desires expressed in the Family Equality Council's "Voices of Children" brief as circumscribed by the LGBT movement's investment in privatized domestic life and a rights-based notion of legal equality. That said, I do not find anything particularly alarming or even unique about parents influencing the ways in which their children see the world and envision their futures. Childhood, as Rodríguez observes, does resemble enslavement in the sense that no child, not even the ones being raised by their married biological parents, consents to their condition (55). Families are, by design, coercive institutions: the modern nation-state banks on the family's function as an ideological apparatus.[35] Is the "indoctrination" of children into LGBT rights activism any different, in form, from raising kids to be good citizens, good capitalists, or good Christians?

What we might find concerning are the limits of a political movement dependent upon the unwavering confidence and happiness of children growing up in LGBT families. What other reactions are unheard, what family dynamics are obscured, and what political possibilities are foreclosed? For example, younger children whose parents come out after they are born may feel confused or frustrated and will likely have many questions—about small things, such as what to tell their friends about their families, and big things, like how love and desire work. Similarly, children whose parents' gender identities change over the course of their lifetimes may want to talk at length about bodies and body parts, about the meanings we are told to attach to them, and about the meanings we might want to attach to them instead. Ensnared, like all parents, in a perpetual cycle of negotiation and confrontation with their children, many queer and trans parents engage in the day-to-day work of trying to develop innovative and age-appropriate vocabularies for talking about genitals, gender performances, and bodily self-determination and for encouraging self-exploration and experimentation as lifelong, open-ended processes. Rather than providing parents with a singular script for narrating their family life (as the Family Equality Council tried to do on my R Family cruise), a queer family politics might instead showcase the affective and intellectual labor taking place within LGBT families and insist on its value for anyone raising children, regardless of their precise family configuration.

This is not, however, to ignore or detract from the anger and anxiety children can experience growing up in nonheteronormative households. Even in planned families headed by same-sex couples, children might feel a sense of loss when it comes to wondering about donors, surrogates, and birth parents and might find themselves longing for the married mom and dad still so prominent in children's storybooks and television programs. Children, as Kathryn Bond Stockton (2009) argues, may have a propensity for queerness, but they also have the capacity to become ruthless enforcers of gender rules and sexual regulations. The tendency within family equality circles can be to downplay the significance of these kinds of feelings, dismissing them as reasonable reactions to the pervasiveness of heterosexism, and to counter those feelings by instilling a sense of pride in the face of shame and adversity. Yet by demanding a certain degree of antinormativity on the part of their children, parenting activists obscure the ways in which they too are tempted by the lure of normativity. The fight for marriage rights and family recognition may be motivated by the material desire for less uncertainty and less vulnerability, but as my detailed account of the freedom to marry movement suggests, it is also about wanting access to the comforts and pleasures that can be derived from social acceptance via marital relations and reproductive citizenship. A queer approach to LGBT family advocacy might try to sit with these contradictions, validating the normative longings of parents and children alike while also reaching toward what Janet Jakobsen calls "perverse happiness"—a kind of happiness that can account for the grief and losses that accompany nonconformity and that will risk unhappiness in the name of experimenting with new forms of intimacy and relationality.[36]

On the flipside, I also read the COGs' briefs as putting a very different kind of pressure on the family equality movement. Stefanowicz and Shick, for example, express a similar concern about the emotionally coercive nature of LGBT families, but they fixate on the ways in which gay, lesbian, and transsexual parents corrupt their children's understanding of gender and sexuality by forcing them to participate in erotic subcultures. While I have no interest in trying to recuperate the troubling childhood stories Stefanowicz and Shick share in their brief—tales of being made to watch porn, attend orgies, and "cruise" with their parents—I am willing to concede that, yes, children growing up with LGBT-identified parents will likely be exposed to queer communities and queer cultural productions and that, yes, there is good reason to believe these experiences will prove formative to their children's affective development.

It is true that LGBT family advocates and the justices who ruled in their favor have relied heavily on research indicating that a parent's sexual orientation does not matter when it comes to parenting outcomes. But Judith Stacey and Timothy Biblarz's meta-analysis of the social science findings on lesbian, gay, and bisexual parenting conducted over the course of the 1980s and 1990s finds that "significant differences" *do* exist in the data. According to their analysis, young adults raised by lesbian mothers, when compared to those raised by straight mothers, appear more open to a broader range of sexual possibilities, with a significantly greater proportion reporting "having had a homoerotic relationship" or "having thought they might experience homoerotic attraction" (2001, 170–171). In other words, there might be some credence to Stefanowicz's indictment of LGBT-identified parents as "'familial role model[s]' for sodomy" (Brief of Stefanowicz and Shick 2015, 36). What if organizations like the Family Equality Council, rather than emphasizing parents' efforts to teach their children to "tell the truth, love their country, and be good neighbors" (Family Equality Council, "Outspoken Generation," n.d.), celebrated the capacity of LGBT families for cultivating a wide range of gender identities and sexual proclivities for people of all ages? What would it look like for a queer family movement to relish in the perverse potential of all children and to assert that a world with more erotic variety would be a better place to live?

Intergenerational Solidarity?

In the world of marriage-centric LGBT family advocacy, it often seems as if queerness and childhood never coincide. Efforts to dispel false notions about the unfitness of LGBT-identified parents rarely challenge the heteropatriarchal standards informing evaluations of parental outcomes and have, as this chapter demonstrates, frequently depended upon the visibility of children who have turned out happy, healthy, and heterosexual in spite of their unusual familial lives. Family Equality Council, for example, has long encouraged parents to counter myths about their families by citing "published studies" proving that "children raised by gay or lesbian parents are no more likely to grow up gay or lesbian than any other children" (Family Pride Coalition n.d., 15). Notably, as Stacey and Biblarz argue, this defensive stance requires parents, activists, and researchers to disregard every credible theory of sexual development—including psychoanalytic, biologically determinist, and social constructionist perspectives—all of which would suggest that the children of lesbian, gay, or bisexual parents would manifest "a somewhat higher incidence of homoerotic desire, behavior, and identity" (2001, 163).[37] Unlike the COGs and, more broadly, the Religious Right who are attuned to the myriad social and cultural factors that might influence sexual identity acquisition, LGBT parenting activists adopt a rather conservative and potentially dangerous stance in their refusal to theorize desire formation or even think critically about sexuality. Instead, sexual identity is imagined as a core of the self, an essential truth that remains unknown to us during our childhoods but becomes available for discovery once we reach an appropriate age. Within this discursive context, it is possible for advocates to concede that some of the children growing up in LGBT families may turn out to have been "born that way," but this outcome would have absolutely nothing to do with the genetics or the lifestyles of the parents in question. Yet even as organizations like Family Equality Council admit to the statistical existence of LGBT children with LGBT parents, these perverse familial formations seem to have no place within family equality activism. The voices of "second gen" queerspawn are assumed to offer little to the project of securing parental rights for LGBT parents.

When LGBT youth do come into view within family equality activism, they often appear as the "next generation of LGBT parents" (Brief of Family Equality Council 2013, 35). In order to assuage persisting anxieties about queerness's capacity for breeding queerness, advocates maintain a strategic distance between LGBT youth and LGBT parents by establishing young LGBT-identified people as the future producers (as opposed to the current products) of LGBT family life. The Family Equality Council's "Voices of Children" brief is an excellent example of this strategy in action. At the end of the document, the Council dedicated a few pages to the ways in which marriage inequality endangered LGBT-identified adolescents and young adults (who are coded as "youth" mature enough to be worrying about their prospects for adulthood and thus held apart from the "children" of LGBT families worried about their parents' relationship status). In other words, the brief's concern lies not with the present-day and presumably straight family lives of LGBT youth but rather with their familial desires for the future. The testimonies featured at the end of the brief constructed lesbian and gay youth as collectively aspiring toward a healthy, middle-class adulthood in which they will fall in love, plan a wedding, and start building a family of their own. Consequently, marriage inequality was interpreted as having a profoundly negative impact on the emotional satisfaction and overall well-being of LGBT youth. According to the Council, the government's stigmatization of same-sex relationships left "these young people to question their own dignity and self-worth," and the foreclosure of a marital future "exacerbate[d] feelings of hopelessness . . . and perpetual 'different-ness'" (3, 33).

Although the Council made no mention of the spate of suicides a few years earlier that had sparked public concern for the safety and mental health of LGBT youth (McKinley 2010; Graves 2010), the specter of the troubled and potentially suicidal LGBT teen—a figure most often embodied by white, non-disabled, and nontrans gay boys in news media coverage—haunted the brief and bolstered its attempt to document the devastating effects of heterosexist policies on children. Framed as an antidote to systemic forms of homophobia, the legalization of same-sex marriage promised to alleviate the fear and despair plaguing LGBT youth. For the select teens who are yearning for normative familial futures, marriage equality may in fact make the mantra "It gets better" more meaningful and even more believable.[38] And unlike proposals for antibullying campaigns and harsher hate crimes legislation, calls for marriage equality refrained from explicitly hinging the well-being of LGBT teens on the expansion of policing and punishment systems. That said, the Council's argument vis-à-vis LGBT youth depended, in large part, on the regulatory function the institution of marriage performs for the state. Echoing the conservative case Andrew Sullivan made for marriage rights almost twenty-five years earlier, the brief posited marriage equality as serving the broader interests of society by ushering LGBT youth toward long-term monogamous commitments and respectable modes of adult citizenship. Denying people access to marriage, the Council argued, risks "discourag[ing] them from aspiring to full participation in civic life" (Brief of Family Equality Council 2013, 33). In contrast, the legalization of same-sex marriage would serve an educative purpose by providing LGBT youth with a "gateway to adult responsibilities, including childbearing, childrearing, and the inculcating of civic virtues in the next generation" (35).[39] Put another way, marriage equality advances governmental interests by channeling the potentially unruly desires of adolescents into social formations amenable to the demands of capital and the reproduction of U.S. national culture.

Generally speaking, however, the LGBT family movement has not prioritized the needs of LGBT youth. This tradition has continued even as Family Equality Council has retooled its rights-based agenda in the wake of marriage equality. Following the Supreme Court's declaration of marriage as a fundamental right for all U.S. citizens, the Council ramped up its efforts to secure expanded joint and second-parent adoption rights for same-sex couples and to combat the expansion of discriminatory anti-LGBT foster and adoption policies. One of the most urgent concerns for family equality activists today is the slew of "religious freedom" acts that have been passed or proposed by state legislatures in the lead-up to and, with even more vigor, after the legalization of same-sex marriage. Emboldened by the Hobby Lobby decision (which opened space for private corporations to claim religious exemption from federal laws [*Burwell v. Hobby Lobby Stores* 2014]), conservative proponents of traditional family values are fighting to protect the rights of businesses to deny services to LGBT-identified people and, specifically, of foster and adoption agencies to refuse to work with LGBT-identified prospective parents.[40] Family Equality Council is working with other family advocacy organizations to push back against state and federal laws that would allow publicly funded child welfare service providers to discriminate against prospective parents on the basis of their gender identity or sexual orientation. Some LGBT rights groups—the Council included—have expressed concerns over how these acts will impact the emotional and physical well-being of LGBT youth in foster care and may expose them to agency-mandated "religious education" programs and other forms of "conversion therapy." Overall, though, the Council's advocacy efforts have focused primarily on the rights of LGBT adults who wish to build families by fostering to adopt.

Fostering Queerness

Take, for example, the Council's endorsement of the Every Child Deserves a Family Act (ECDFA). First introduced in 2009, the ECDFA was conceived as analogous to the Multiethnic Placement Act of 1994, which prohibited federally funded adoption and foster care agencies from discriminating against prospective parents and children in care on the basis of race and ethnicity.[41] In a similar fashion, the ECDFA proposes to prohibit federally funded adoption and foster care agencies from discriminating against prospective parents and children in care on the basis of sexual orientation, gender identity, and marital status (the latter applying to adults looking to foster or adopt). This bill has been reintroduced into Congress multiple times, most recently right before the Supreme Court legalized same-sex marriage in 2015 and then again two years later in 2017. In its attempt to redress the homophobia and transphobia that pervades the U.S. family welfare system, the ECDFA has prompted a conversation about national family policy that brings LGBT parents into close proximity with LGBT youth. Media coverage of these legislative efforts has drawn attention to initiatives already under way in New York and California: city and state officials have been working on a local level since the early 2000s to improve services for LGBT youth in care and more recently to expand parental recruitment efforts to attract not just LGBT-affirming adults but, specifically, LGBT-identified adults (Gay 2013; Nichols 2016). While organizations like the Human Rights Campaign have applauded the ECDFA for recognizing LGBT parents as "good match[es]" for LGBT youth (Kahn 2013),

Family Equality Council's official literature on the proposed bill makes no mention of nonheteronormative or gender-nonconforming youth.

Instead, the Council's formal endorsement of the ECDFA echoes the arguments advanced by Rosie O'Donnell a decade earlier. The organization emphasizes the ways in which ending discrimination against LGBT adults offers a simple answer to the alleged "shortage" of "forever homes" for children in foster care. For instance, in May 2015, when the Council announced the reintroduction of the ECDFA back into Congress, then executive director Gabriel Blau provided a mathematical justification for passing this legislation: "There are *five* times more prospective LGBTQ parents than there are youth in foster care awaiting homes. And LGBTQ adults are three times as likely to adopt a foster child. Let's get these youth in loving homes" (Family Equality Council 2015b, emphasis in original). According to the Council's calculations, the passage of the ECDFA would increase the prospective parent pool by an estimated two million people and would thus provide local agencies with the means to care for the more than four hundred thousand children perceived to be without homes. As such, the bill promises to yield an annual savings, at the state and federal levels, of somewhere between three and six billion dollars (Family Equality Council, "ECDF Act Facts," n.d.). By sounding alarm bells over a "crisis" in the foster care system without considering the history of child and family welfare in the United States (which I discuss in the previous chapter), the Council is able to frame the problem as an "accounting" issue and then offer "diversification," via antidiscrimination law, as the practical solution. Cost-benefit analyses obscure the racist and classist logics governing the ECDFA and mask the ways in which this legislation serves the state's broader interest in privatizing the affective and monetary costs of social reproduction.

Even as the Council acknowledges the overrepresentation of nonwhite children in the system—their "fact sheet" on the ECDFA mentions that more than 50 percent of the children in foster care are of color and that nearly a quarter of the children available for adoption are black (Family Equality Council, "ECDF Act Facts," n.d.)—the organization makes no attempt to account for the racial disparities that characterize the state's mass removal of children from their family homes and its accelerated processes for terminating parental rights. In the absence of an analysis of how the U.S. family welfare system disrupts and forcibly restructures the lives of poor families of color, the Council is able to get behind the ECDFA's goals of decreasing the time children in care wait for permanent placements and increasing the number of qualified adoptive parents (by including LGBT-identified adults). Family equality advocates thus invite the state to mobilize the labor of respectable LGBT adults in support of population control efforts. In doing so, they encourage middle-class LGBT family-building practices that capitalize on the vulnerabilities of poor families, including families headed by LGBT-identified adults. Women with adequate cultural and economic capital may no longer worry about maintaining custody of their children after coming out, but poor lesbian mothers and queer parents who do not conform to white supremacist gender, sexual, and relational norms remain in jeopardy of losing their children to the punitive child welfare system. Despite its purported mission of protecting all loving families, the Council's calls for legal equality and domestic rights for aspiring LGBT parents unwittingly intensifies coercive state efforts to dismantle racially, sexually, and economically marginalized families.

In this light, I once again find a kernel of truth in the arguments advanced by the COGs. Shortly before submitting their brief to the Supreme Court, B. N. Klein contributed an article to the *Federalist* under her pseudonym in which she accuses "gay couples" of acquiring children by "tear[ing] apart other people's families using the oppressive force of the state and its legal apparatuses" (Edelman 2015). While her critique of the U.S. government stems directly from her attempt to conjure images of a predatory form of queerness, I want to dwell on the predatory nature of the state to further illuminate the ways in which children circulate as property within U.S. family law. To talk about parental rights, as I explain earlier, is to talk about an adult's right to have or, more accurately, possess a child. Within the realm of the foster care system, the property logics organizing family-related public policy become readily apparent: if a parent is perceived to be abusing or neglecting their children (i.e., not properly cultivating their property), then the state can remove those children from their home (i.e., seize the parent's property); if the parent is later deemed categorically unfit and family reunification declared an impossibility, then the state can terminate the parental rights of biological parents and put the children in question up for adoption (i.e., attempt to transfer ownership of the child to more responsible property owners). Moreover, the state not only governs family life according to capitalist logics but also charges the family with the work of reproducing allegiance to those logics. As such, in pushing for foster and adoption rights, the Council offers up prospective LGBT parents as doing more than saving "unwanted" children and even more than saving the government money. Rather, the adoptive LGBT family is held out as protecting national interests by raising the next generation of respectable capitalist subjects who will aspire to their own futures of property ownership.

By way of conclusion and in the hopes of reimagining the relationship between LGBT family politics and LGBT youth, I want to return to the provision of the ECDFA that Family Equality Council tends to sidestep—namely, the bill's proposed prohibition of discrimination against children in care on the basis of gender identity or sexual orientation. Over the past twenty years, amid a widening public interest in enhancing the lives of LGBT adolescents, activists, researchers, and policymakers have begun to pay more attention to the overrepresentation and uneven treatment of "LGBTQ youth" in the foster care system (with the Q signaling "questioning" more often than "queer" within these advocacy contexts).[42] In fact, the federal government's Department of Health and Human Services took up this issue under the Obama presidency and in 2010 awarded a multimillion-dollar grant to the Los Angeles LGBT Center for conducting research on and developing programs for LGBTQ youth in foster care.[43] Studies have consistently shown that LGBTQ-identified adolescents of color endure hostility and harassment from peers, foster parents, and case managers while often dealing with rejection from their families of origin. As a result, they are often subject to multiple placements and are more likely to run away, which, given the pervasive criminalization of queerness (especially nonwhite and gender-nonconforming kinds of queerness), increases their chances of becoming entangled with the juvenile justice system. For children who remain under the "protective" care of the state, the conflation of racial and sexual difference with deviance frequently means being labeled "hard to place" and often leads to aging out of the system without having established sustainable relationships with supportive adults. A number of policy recommendations have emerged out of these reports: in addition to calling for sensitivity and competency trainings for social workers and prospective parents, advocates have also encouraged local agencies to develop strategies for recruiting and retaining a racially diverse pool of LGBT-identified adults who would presumably be kinder and more understanding caregivers (Richter et al. 2006; Wilber, Reyes, and Marksamer 2006).

Given the persisting fear of predacious homosexuals out to convert innocent young people—and given the short-lived nature of state-level efforts during the 1970s to place openly gay youth with openly gay foster parents[44]—I must admit that, when I first heard about such initiatives, I was rather delighted by the admission that young queers might actually need other older queers. In practice, however, the action plans put forth by cities like New York and Los Angeles often envision outreach efforts targeting LGBT communities as part of larger multicultural initiatives designed to attract a "rainbow" of "LGBT-affirming" parents. This is not a coordinated and state-funded effort to manufacture families capable of nurturing erotic variety and nourishing gender nonconformity. Far from resulting in the availability of state funds for cultivating radically and regeneratively perverse households, the child welfare system's interest lies in placing LGBTQ youth with parents who will foster a particular kind of happy and healthy queerness. Homophobia and transphobia, neatly cordoned off from the issue of racial discrimination, may be a widespread social problem, but the solution can be found within the privacy of a proper family home: by affirming the child's gender or sexual identity, foster parents can raise proud, productive, and maybe even reproductive

LGBT citizens who can thrive in the face of adversity and eventually take full advantage of the newly achieved marriage equality. State-sponsored attempts to recruit LGBT-affirming parents who just happen to be L, G, B, or T are best understood as strategies for incorporating more families into the privatizing project of rehabilitating potentially dysfunctional forms of racialized gender and sexual nonconformity. The ECDFA can thus be interpreted, first and foremost, as an effort to make sure queerness will, now and in the future, work for capital and the state.

Still, I remain intrigued by the appearance of LGBT parents alongside LGBT youth within the context of national family policy debates. As such, I suggest reading the proposed legislation as an invitation to think in new directions. What would it look like for the LGBT family movement to move beyond its exclusive focus on parents and to consider instead the familial lives of LGBT people regardless of age? What would happen if activists adopted what Dean Spade (2011) describes as a "trickle-up" approach to social justice and prioritized the needs and desires of LGBTQ youth in care, one of the populations that is most vulnerable to state violence and most in need of social services? For starters, a more transformative family movement could join in calling for nonreformist reforms that, while moving toward the abolition of the current child welfare system and the building of alternative community-based infrastructures, would make the immediate everyday lives of youth in care more livable. In addition to backing research and policy recommendations based on the expertise of LGBTQ adolescents who have experience with the child welfare system, activists could also advocate for resources dedicated to helping children in care develop supportive and sustainable relationships (Mountz 2011). This might take the form of programs designed to engage, when possible, children and their families of origin in mediated, meaningful, and restorative conversations about gender and sexual identity, or this might entail organized efforts to connect youth in care to groups and organizations, like FIERCE in New York City,[45] that are run by and for young queer and trans people of color and that are working to produce the next generation of social and economic justice movement leaders.

At the heart of this alternative model of LGBT family politics would be an investment in forging intergenerational alliances—that is, what would happen if LGBT family advocates set aside their narrow focus on a privatized notion of domesticity in which parents take responsibility only for the children who legally belong to them?[46] A queer family movement might instead make a commitment to nurturing young trans and queer lives—not by relocating youth to more "affirming" families, but by helping them cultivate stable and diverse networks of material and emotional support. These creative forms of relationality, based on alternative ways of being and belonging, hold out the promise of inciting disruptive desire formations and cultivating ethical visions at odds with capital's individualizing logics. Within this "willfully idealistic" context (Muñoz 2009, 96), older queers could join youth in care in resisting the assumption that all they really need is a familial home and insisting instead on just how deeply the survival of younger queers—and the future of racial, sexual, and economic justice—depends not on the promise of marriage and reproductive futurity but on the development of far broader communities of care in the right here and right now.

4

Vitality

• •

The Family Business of
Health Promotion and
Wealth Management

What exactly did LGBT families win when "love won"? The legalization of same-sex marriage, according to the family equality movement, promised to enhance the physical, emotional, and financial well-being of families by enabling same-sex couples to more efficiently manage their property relations and parenting obligations. While the preceding chapters have offered analyses of how the logics driving identitarian rights-based activism—and the freedom to marry movement in particular—advance the interests of the capitalist nation-state and prioritize the needs of the most privileged LGBT communities, my task in this chapter, now that we have arrived on the other side of marriage equality, is to think more concretely about how access to marriage is and is not improving the health and economic security of queer and trans parents and the children they are raising. My aim is to begin tracing the newly configured contours of U.S. racial and sexual politics and to start accounting for the political and economic function of same-sex marriage within the context of the United States. To begin, I turn my attention to what I believe are some of the first attempts to gather empirical data regarding the effects of marriage equality on the financial health of LGBT families.

In the summer of 2016, one year after the *Obergefell* ruling, two of the largest U.S.-based financial services institutions published reports based on recent surveys of LGBT Americans on the state of their financial lives. Both Wells Fargo and Prudential set out to identify the most pressing financial planning needs of the LGBT community in the wake of marriage equality. Although both reports highlighted the ways in which LGBT households now share many of the same financial concerns as their straight counterparts—a fact the reports attribute to the availability of marriage and the growing number of LGBT-identified adults raising children or planning families—the survey data also suggested that same-sex couples face unique barriers in their efforts to achieve economic security and are therefore in need of financial products and solutions tailored to their distinct situations.

Wells Fargo (2016), for instance, found that, while there was "a great deal of optimism" about the potentially positive impact that marriage equality would have on personal financial futures, only one-third of those surveyed reported "having a full understanding of [the] financial benefits or potential downsides of marriage." The legalization of same-sex marriage may have ushered in a feeling of safety and security for some households, but that newfound sense of comfort was not necessarily grounded in material reality or evidenced by any tangible effects. According to the company's LGBT segment manager, the confusion over the economic implications of marriage "signal[ed] a real need, and desire, for more education" and as such represented an opportunity for Wells Fargo to support the LGBT community by providing guidance in "making sound financial decisions." Prudential drew similar conclusions regarding the demand for LGBT-focused advisory services, but their findings depicted the LGBT community as far less confident about its economic well-being. The *LGBT Financial Experience* report found that, even though marriage equality had standardizing effects on tax and estate planning and made sharing employer-based health care plans easier, same-sex couples and LGBT families remained incredibly "uneasy" about their "ability to attain true financial security" (Prudential 2016, 2). LGBT-headed households are not only struggling, like their straight counterparts, in the face of a "poor job market" and a "stagnant economy" but also enduring the compounding effects of persisting wage inequities and the pervasiveness of homophobic housing and employment practices (4). To address these economic vulnerabilities, the report concludes, LGBT Americans are in desperate need of both expanded nondiscrimination protections and greater access to LGBT-specific financial expertise. In their collective efforts to generate new consumer demands, Wells Fargo and Prudential effectively outlined the limits of marriage equality.

Now, while I appreciate the ways in which these marketing reports call into question the central tenets of the freedom to marry movement and threaten to unsettle the very foundations of LGBT rights projects, I am certainly not endorsing financial services as the answer to the economic injustices endemic to neoliberal forms of capitalism. I am also not suggesting that we should treat these surveys as serious social scientific research or that we should accept their findings as representative data on queer precarity after *Obergefell*. Rather, I begin with these reports as a way of opening up a larger conversation about how "the rhetoric of financial protection" has, as David Eng astutely notes, come to function as "moral justification for increased access to (legal) rights and recognition" (2010, 99). It is important to clarify that the 2016 reports from Wells Fargo and Prudential were not indicative of a new or sudden interest in the financial lives of LGBT families. Prudential had released an earlier version of the *LGBT Financial Experience* in 2012, and Wells Fargo had been conducting annual marriage-focused surveys each spring since the *Windsor* decision.[1] This very recent past of LGBT marketing outreach must also be situated within the longer history of gay-specific financial products, which stretches back to the inception of the financial services industry during the late twentieth century. What the 2016 reports mark is a shift in the needs being identified and the services being sold. The initial emergence of a lesbian and gay niche within the finance industry was predicated on a desire for financial guidance in the absence of marriage rights, whereas now, financial services institutions are offering private consumer solutions to the problems and complexities associated with marriage equality. In this chapter, the first of my two goals is to examine how financial logics became entangled with the rhetoric of LGBT equality and to untangle the ways in which financialization has served as a desexualizing and domesticating force with respect to LGBT rights organizing. Paying particular attention to the interplay between family-building practices and financial planning strategies, I consider how discourses of risk management increasingly organize the everyday lives of LGBT families and the advocacy work of the family equality movement.

This historical analysis provides further insight into how "a political movement of resistance and redistribution has been reconfigured and transformed into an interest group and niche market . . . in which gays and lesbians are liberated precisely by proving that they can be proper U.S. citizen-subjects of the capitalist nation-state" (Eng 2010, 30). Severed from any sort of demands for racial or economic justice, rights-based projects have been routed through calls for financial security and have, in many ways, lent themselves to alliances with the banking industry. In this light, the family equality movement can be understood as working to remove the legal barriers that might prevent LGBT-identified parents from more efficiently assuming responsibility for their children and more effectively preparing for the possibility of future medical or financial emergencies. The promise of marriage equality was less about guaranteeing more access to basic necessities and actual resources and was more focused on maximizing a couple's capacity to manage their household finances and to accumulate economic property. For the wealthiest of LGBT families, as

I will demonstrate, the freedom to marry is often experienced as the freedom to work with financial planners and to take strategic advantage of marriage as a wealth preservation technique.

My second goal in this chapter is thus to document the uneven effects of marriage equality on different LGBT populations and to unpack the ways in which the financial mechanisms used to consolidate private family wealth end up causing harm to racially, sexually, and economically marginalized families. Despite the distorted image of LGBT parents as predominantly white and at least comfortably middle class, recent census data reveal that two-parent LGBT homes are twice as likely as their straight counterparts to report incomes near the poverty threshold (Gates 2013, 5) and that households headed by same-sex couples are significantly more likely to receive public assistance (Badgett, Durso, and Schneebaum 2013, 21). Researchers attribute these differences to the prevalence of queers of color raising children and to the statistical tendency for these couples to consist of younger women. Under Obama, as part of a larger LGBT health promotion initiative, the Department of Health and Human Services (HHS) took historic (if inadequate) steps to address the widespread problem of LGBT poverty.[2] While his administration advanced a rather progressive LGBT family politics agenda that, especially in the case of health care reform, seemed to depart from the logics of marriage and family equality, HHS did, following *Obergefell*, start trying to incorporate same-sex couples into marriage promotion efforts that, as feminist critics have documented, were designed to minimize the state's economic obligations to the poor. This chapter concludes by showing how the proposed development of LGBT-inclusive "healthy marriage and relationship education" programs signals the federal government's investment in deploying same-sex marriage as a tool for national wealth management and a method of racialized sexual and social control.

From DINKS to Families

The invention of gay-specific financial services during the late 1970s and early 1980s occurred at a moment when many gay-owned businesses were doing quite well and as national advertisers were beginning to take an interest in what appeared to be a vibrant gay market. More specifically, however, the origins of this product can be traced back to the establishment of a single New York City–based firm. In 1981, the "financial and political visionary" Robert Casaletto founded Christopher Street Financial as "the first investment and financial services firm committed to serving the gay, lesbian, and supportive community" (Christopher Street Financial, "History," n.d.). What started out as a one-man operation, with Casaletto managing $1 million for fewer than a dozen NYC-based clients, grew, over the course of a decade, into a small but successful firm handling over $30 million for more than a thousand clients from across the country (Tuller 1988, 3). With the launch of his firm, Casaletto set out to fulfill—and, perhaps more accurately, to generate—a demand among wealthy gay men for specialized financial services. He founded Christopher Street with a particular gay subject in mind: a childless gay man who, freed from the burden of suburban homeownership and the need to save for a child's college education, was struggling to figure out how to most efficiently build his wealth and manage his disposable income (Fatsis 1991). This niche, Casaletto insisted, deserved access to qualified financial counselors who could offer advice tailored to the needs of this specific "lifestyle."³ By situating the history of Christopher Street with respect to the AIDS crisis, the "gay marketing moment," and the broader U.S.-based financial industry, it is possible to apprehend how the expansion of gay-oriented financial products facilitated and was facilitated by a domesticated lesbian and gay rights agenda.

By the early 1990s, Casaletto had moved his operation from his apartment to an office on Wall Street and was projecting an annual revenue of nearly $1 million (Fatsis 1991). While many gay-owned bars, bathhouses, and other businesses were obliterated by the deadly toll the AIDS epidemic was taking on the gay community, individuals and companies offering gay-specific lifestyle products and professional services—such as law firms, health clubs, travel agencies, real estate brokers, medical care providers, and, most relevantly here, financial services programs—were thriving in the face of and, in many ways, because of the crisis (Tuller 1988; Sender 2004). This is not to say Christopher Street did not feel the effects of the disease. During the late 1980s, the firm lost four staff members and an average of one client per week to AIDS-related complications (Fatsis 1991). For Casaletto, the epidemic only further clarified the vital importance of developing financial products for the gay market.

In many ways, his firm participated in the marketization of HIV/AIDS. In addition to helping men who were HIV positive or living with AIDS devise strategies for accessing cash, preserving capital, and planning their estates, Christopher Street offered prophylactic financial advice for clients who saw themselves at risk of contracting the virus, encouraging them to keep open lines of credit, to secure disability coverage from their employers, and to supplement their company-based insurance with private health care plans (Davis 1993). While Casaletto's relatively small-scale enterprise was hardly as insidious as the vampiric endeavors of viatical industries and drug companies during this period, his firm was similar in that it was profiting from the epidemic by selling private consumer solutions to what was, in fact, a public health crisis. The firm's efforts to consolidate personal wealth via participation in global financial markets may have been beneficial to clients on an individual level, but such practices ultimately diverted resources away from collective responses to the epidemic and, in effect, exacerbated the vulnerabilities of people without access to medical care or other basic necessities (let alone investment capital). In short, the lifesaving work in which Christopher Street engaged at the height of the AIDS crisis had less to do with saving actual lives and was more about the management of life savings.

Still, Casaletto saw his firm as a community organization taking part in the fight against the epidemic. While he was careful to distance Christopher Street from radical direct action groups like Queer Nation, he actively forged alliances with other AIDS and LGBT organizations: in addition to managing investment accounts for the Gay and Lesbian Alliance against Defamation, the firm regularly contributed to Gay Men's Health Crisis and the Lambda Legal Defense Fund and, on occasion, ran advertising "tributes" to publicize the work of those organizations (Fatsis 1991). Casaletto was also involved in the founding of what would later become the Empire State Pride Agenda, an organization that would eventually play an instrumental role in the freedom to marry movement in New York State (Christopher Street Financial, "History," n.d.). In addition to fostering explicit connections to activist circles, Christopher Street also engaged in the subtler work of changing the public's perception of homosexuality.

It was during this period, across the 1980s and into the 1990s, that broad-based coalitional movements were fracturing into balkanized identity-based projects and that lesbian and gay agendas were being rerouted through a politics of recognition and respectability (Duggan 2003). By increasing the visibility of a professional class of gay men and distancing them from any hint of perversity or promiscuity—for instance, by the early 1990s, Christopher Street had stopped advertising in lesbian and gay publications that included sexually explicit material (Fatsis 1991)—the firm was helping to consolidate a nascent form of homonormativity. In 1987, when the *New York Times* ran a piece about how the AIDS crisis instigated a "significant change in the mores" of Fire Island and gay culture as a whole, Christopher Street figured prominently (Gutis 1987). The article opened with the firm's managing partner reflecting on the new preference among gay men for evening tea parties (instead of all-night dancing) and closed with him highlighting how weekends on the island provided important networking opportunities for gay professionals and with Casaletto adding that this is what makes their vacations "tax-deductible." The final line of the piece was a quote from Casaletto: "We may not be Republicans," he joked, "but we can think like them" (Gutis 1987). A few years later, in a story on financial counseling services for people living with AIDS, a vice president from Christopher Street told the Associated Press that the firm was "consistently amazed at the amount of liquid assets gay men and women have that are uninvested" (Davis 1993). Contributing to the larger project of resignifying same-sex desires and relations on the other side of the AIDS crisis, Christopher Street offered up a gay subject who would deploy his risk management skills not to sustain a debauched lifestyle but to enhance his financial profile. Such efforts produced a distorted image of the gay community as wielding a disproportionate degree of purchasing and, by extension, political power.[4] As a result, a myth of gay affluence took hold and, to this day, continues to obscure the precarious and impoverished conditions under which the majority of LGBTQ people in the United States lived and continue to live.[5]

During the early 1990s, mainstream corporations and advertising experts, relying on largely unrepresentative survey data, identified gay men and, to a lesser extent, lesbians as a niche market filled with lucrative potential. In the process, they launched what Amy Gluckman and Betsy Reed termed the "gay marketing moment" (1997).[6] Although the AIDS crisis had initially discouraged companies from pursuing "pink dollars" out of a fear of associating themselves with a particularly perverse form of death, the sheer breadth of AIDS activism—along with the use of consumer boycotts by lesbian and gay activists[7]—demonstrated to business leaders that a critical mass of politicized lesbians and gay men were looking to make a statement with their money (Sender 2004, 40). In his oft-cited *Untold Millions: Positioning Your Business for the Gay and Lesbian Consumer Revolution*, marketing consultant Grant Lukenbill emphasized the enormous "buying power" and "commercial influence" of lesbian and gay communities (1995, 3). Acknowledging that earlier studies had produced a skewed view of the community, he stressed instead the fact that lesbians and gay men "are everywhere" and as such cut across all other consumer segments (53). Moreover, Lukenbill reasoned, the unwavering loyalty lesbian and gay customers have historically shown toward allied brands suggests that businesses would be foolish not to invest resources into courting this emerging niche market. As mainstream corporations ramped up their outreach efforts, both lifestyle products, like travel and tourism services (as I discussed in chapter 2), and needs-based products, like financial services, proved to be huge growth areas (Sender 2004, 100).[8]

In some cases, banking institutions tried to attract lesbian and gay customers by publicizing gay-friendly hiring policies and engaging in corporate forms of activism. American Express was the first major company to target this consumer segment. After its 1993 survey of underserved markets identified lesbians and gay men as a key niche for financial advising, American Express started recruiting openly gay financial planners and sponsoring gay pride events across the country (Gallagher 1998; Weissman 1999). In other cases, investment firms tried to tap the market by developing gay-specific financial products. Following the modest success of the Myers Pride Value Fund—a "socially conscious" mutual fund that invested exclusively in companies deemed "gay friendly" based on their domestic partner benefits packages, their adoption of antidiscrimination employment policies, or their financial support of AIDS activism and other gay causes—similar products were made available at major

U.S.-based financial institutions, such as Merrill Lynch's Principled Values Portfolio, Smith and Barney's Concert Social Awareness Fund, and Prudential Services's Lambda Strategies Stock Portfolio (Abelson 1996; Gallagher 1998).

This politicization of investment practices—or what M. V. Lee Badgett calls "investor activism" (2001, 248–252)—facilitated the financialization of the lesbian and gay movement. As a form of activism, socially conscious banking and investing may have some bearing on corporate policies, but ultimately, it is the company's owners and shareholders (not its workers or the larger community) who stand to profit from efforts of this kind (Chasin 2000, 242–243). Within this context, identitarian political attachments are severed from any sort of ethical obligation to build solidarities with labor movements or economic justice projects, and the realm of what counts as righteous political action is redefined to include one's enthusiastic participation in the world of finance. In effect, gay pride became a vehicle for encouraging individuals to invest more widely and aggressively and to understand their personal financial security as contingent on the health of the global financial market—a market that has been built upon colonial legacies and modes of primitive accumulation and that continues to depend on the chronic economic insecurities of the most marginalized populations in the United States and across the globe.

Over the course of the 1990s, in an effort to usher potential lesbian and gay investors into the financial marketplace, mainstream banking institutions and smaller planning firms followed the lead of Christopher Street Financial and began offering services tailored to the needs of same-sex couples. Major financial firms, like American Express, started developing domestic partner planning services and advertising their expertise in handling lesbian and gay financial matters (Weissman 1999). Calling attention to the ways in which heterosexist and marriage-centric family law and financial policy rendered lesbian and gay couples susceptible—not only to excessive penalties with respect to income and estate taxes, but also to interference from families of origin who might refuse to recognize same-sex partners—financial planners promised to help clients deploy an array of legal and financial mechanisms to secure their relationships and protect their shared assets. Specifically, lesbian and gay couples could work with planners to draw up domestic partnership agreements, to establish joint tenancy with survivorship rights on any shared property, and to determine how large of a life insurance policy they would need to cover any anticipated estate taxes. In addition to providing a practical solution to a particular problem, the development of gay-specific financial services was also a way of teaching same-sex couples to imagine their futures in financial terms and according to risk management logics.

In fact, outreach to lesbian and gay investors during this period can be understood as part of a wider initiative among financial institutions to tap underserved markets. Because the finance industry and financial power players stood to profit from the incorporation of small long-term investors into the global market, financial institutions had a vested interest in courting not just the whitest and wealthiest of clients but a diverse range of middle-net investors. Targeted marketing efforts thus served the pedagogical function of instructing people in how to conceptualize the task of saving and managing money in the age of finance capital. Such lessons were, as Randy Martin argues, reinforced by a growing field of financial self-help literature (2002, 91–93),[9] a small subsection of which addressed the needs of lesbians and gay men.

Take, for example, the books written by the gay-identified financial planner Peter M. Berkery Jr. during the late 1990s: *Personal Financial Planning for Gays and Lesbians: Our Guide to Prudent Decision Making* (1996), which was endorsed by the Human Rights Campaign, and *Gay Finances in a Straight World: A Comprehensive Financial Planning Handbook* (1998), which Berkery cowrote with his life partner and which was published in association with the *Advocate*. Additionally, in 1998, at a moment when marketing experts were zeroing in on the internet as a key venue for reaching gay consumers (Sender 2004, 111–113), the Gay Financial Network launched at gfn.com and provided users with articles on the art of financial planning and access to an online brokerage service (Robaton 1999; Weissman 1999). The proliferation of print and online resources was meant not to eliminate but rather to accentuate the need for consulting financial professionals: the Gay Financial Network featured an extensive list of referrals for gay-friendly insurance agents, financial planners, and real estate brokers, and Berkery cautioned his readers against mistaking his book for "a how-to-guide for do-it-yourselfers" that could substitute for "competent professional service" (1996, 3). In other words, these resources doubled as advertisements for gay-oriented financial services.

Like Casaletto, Berkery saw his financial planning work as a way of serving the lesbian and gay community and contributing to the fight for equal rights and relationship recognition. In the introduction to *Personal Financial Planning for Gays and Lesbians*, he clarifies that, while his book serves the pragmatic purpose of helping same-sex couples navigate a financial landscape organized around the interests of the heterosexual family, he is also making "an important political statement": specifically, he sets out to document the various financial injustices lesbians and gay men face when trying to save, invest, pay taxes, buy homes, and build families while living in the United States (1996, vi). In a distinctly neoliberal reworking of the concept of economic justice, Berkery's concern does not lie with those left most vulnerable under the new global financial order, and his vision for lesbian and gay equality does not involve the downward distribution of wealth or other resources.

Organizing his call for rights and recognition around an imagined nondisabled same-sex couple adhering to white middle-class relational norms and enjoying a great deal of racial and financial privilege, Berkery believed that what lesbians and gay men needed most was unfettered access to the same financial mechanisms and loopholes as their heterosexual counterparts. Until then, industry professionals would be there to help lesbians and gay men more efficiently manage their wealth and assume control over their economic futures. By tailoring their services to couples and domestic partners or, as Berkery did, to lesbian and gay "families" and "households," the financial industry rendered the unfamiliar needs of lesbians and gay men familial and, as such, more palatable. The dying or deadly queer subject who was blamed and berated for his failure to curtail his risky sexual desires was supplanted by the financially savvy and future-oriented same-sex couple who adopts risk management practices as a way of nurturing their long-term relationships and growing their joint net worth. In short, the development of gay-specific financial services had a desexualizing and, more specifically, domesticating effect on the discursive construction of same-sex relationality at the turn of the twenty-first century.

Building Healthy Families

When Berkery was writing about the financial needs of "families" in the mid-1990s, he was not particularly concerned about lesbian- and gay-identified parents. At this point, the financial services industry was catering to a gay (and, on occasion, lesbian) subject who, while presumed to be increasingly domesticated, was marked by a conspicuous childlessness.[10] A few years later, however, the perception of gay life began to change in the finance sector. With the "gayby boom" well under way, lesbians, as mothers, started to gain visibility as potential investors and possible financial planning clients. Both John Hancock and Wachovia (which would later become Wells Fargo) ran mainstream television ads, in 2000 and 2001, respectively, featuring white lesbian couples planning for their parental futures.[11]

Not long after, Christopher Street Financial also began to take an interest in lesbian and gay parents. When the firm's original founder Casaletto died in 1996, he left the firm in a charitable fund for the Lesbian and Gay Rights Project at the American Civil Liberties Union (ACLU). The following year, the ACLU sold the firm to Jennifer Hatch, a white lesbian "who hated her Wall Street bond sales job" and who would, over the next twenty years, revamp the company's focus (Garmhausen 2010). Under her leadership, Christopher Street moved away from its function as a brokerage firm and began branding itself as offering a "holistic" approach to long-term financial planning. Along the way, Hatch began working to reach a market made up of an increasing number of parents. As she explained in a 2012 interview, this "demographic has become hugely important for us because it's people who are raising children that recognize their need for specialized services. They have to get all their ducks in a row to protect each other and their children" (Gold 2012).

During the early 2010s, Hatch forged a formal alliance between Christopher Street and the national nonprofit Family Equality Council, an alliance that has doubled as a way of promoting her firm among LGBT families while also performing its philanthropic commitment to "giving back to the gay and lesbian community" (Christopher Street Financial, "Community Involvement," n.d.). Aside from contributing to "dozens of LGBT organizations" and providing "pro bono investment accounts" to various nonprofits, the firm also tries to "concentrate [its] corporate giving" by adopting a specific organization each year, sponsoring a fundraising event on that organization's behalf, and working to "raise consciousness about what the organization does and what it needs" (Christopher Street Financial, "Community Involvement," n.d.).[12] While it is unclear whether Christopher Street has kept up with this annual practice, the Council, along with SAGE (Advocacy and Services for LGBT Elders),[13] is listed as one of the past benefactors of this community partnership project. In 2014, the firm sponsored the Council's annual "Night at the Pier" fundraiser, which is a $500-per-plate dinner held in a high-end waterfront venue at Chelsea Piers in Manhattan. But the relationship between Christopher Street and the Council extends beyond this one well-publicized collaboration. In 2010, the firm "presented" a "movie night and pajama party" as part of the Council's Family Week programming. In 2012 and 2014, Hatch appeared in Provincetown as the facilitator of financial planning workshops respectively titled "What's So Gay about Money?" and "What Does 'I Do' Really Mean? Marriage vs. Shacking Up Post-DOMA."[14] Additionally, in 2011, when the Council, working in conjunction with Center Families (of the LGBT Community Center in New York City), launched its "Ask the Experts" website,[15] Hatch was named as the "financial expert" who would field anonymously submitted questions about how parents can most effectively "grow and protect [their family's] wealth."[16] She, along with another member of Christopher Street's planning team, still appear on the Council's website in this capacity. More recently, Hatch has allowed the Council, which is based in Boston and Washington, to use part of the firm's New York City office space free of charge (McCarthy 2015), an in-kind donation that highlights the rather intimate form corporate sponsorships can take within the nonprofit industrial complex. Pitching itself as a generous, gay-focused, and community-based organization (and masking its actual role as a for-profit life and wealth management company), Christopher Street Financial positions itself as uniquely equipped to help current and aspiring parents prepare for their financial futures. The firm's relationship with the Council sheds light on the place of financial planning services within family equality advocacy and the broader LGBT family-building industry and effectively brings into focus the financial logics that have come to guide the work of promoting the health and safety of LGBT households.

In May 2013, when Center Families hosted its first LGBT Family Building Expo, Christopher Street Financial joined Goldman Sachs, Family Equality Council, R Family Vacations (the LGBT family travel company started by Rosie O'Donnell), Growing Generations (the surrogacy agency started by Kim Bergman, who facilitated some of the workshops I attended on my cruise to Alaska), and a host of other fertility clinics, surrogacy agencies, and adoption providers in cosponsoring what would become an inaugural event.[17] The purpose of the expo, according to Center Families, was to connect prospective LGBT parents with "culturally competent resources" in order to assist them in managing the "financial, legal, medical, [and] psychological" aspects of the family-building process.[18] Held at the LGBT Community Center in the West Village, the first expo and all the subsequent ones have been all-day affairs that include free one-on-one sessions with lawyers and fertility specialists and a series of informational sessions on surrogacy, private adoptions, fostering to adopt, and artificial insemination (AI) and in vitro fertilization (IVF).

As the name of the event suggests, Center Families also stages a trade show of sorts where representatives from the sponsoring organizations are invited to set up display tables and distribute information about the LGBT family-building services they offer. On the one hand, the decision to start organizing annual expos can be read as part of a growing trend within the fertility industry in the United States.[19] On the other hand, Center Families was also building upon a longer lesbian feminist tradition of creating, collecting, and circulating information on alternative routes to parenthood. Over the course of the 1980s, an increasing number of lesbians sought advice on at-home inseminations (as a way of both resisting the masculinist authority of the medical establishment and evading the homophobic discriminatory practices of most sperm banks and fertility clinics at that time). In response, individual women and feminist health collectives began publishing how-to guides, running classes and workshops on self-insemination, and establishing grassroots insemination networks designed to connect aspiring mothers with gay men willing to donate sperm (Rivers 2013, 174–181). Today, with the expansion of legal and biomedical options not just for aspiring lesbian mothers but for prospective parents of all genders, the landscape of LGBT family building is far more complex: decisions about parenthood are being made at a moment marked by the wider availability of transnational adoptions, the development of local and global surrogacy industries, the increasing willingness of some U.S.-based child welfare agencies to work with and even recruit LGBT-identified foster parents, and the expansive and, in the United States, largely unregulated circulation of reproductive biomaterials (e.g., eggs, sperm, and embryos). Responding to these newly configured conditions of reproductive possibility, the

LGBT Family Building Expo sets out to introduce prospective parents to a range of family-building options and to empower them to make "informed and appropriate choices."[20]

By framing these informational events as "expos," Center Families packages the process of becoming a parent as a marketplace activity. The collective forms of care practiced within the self-insemination clinics of an earlier era advocated a distinctly feminist approach to health that emphasized an "active, even vigilant" relationship to bodies and reproduction and, in the process, laid the groundwork for the transformation of prospective LGBT parents into what, following Lisa Diedrich, we might call "consuming patients" (2016, 64–65). Today, people looking to have children are perceived—and are encouraged to perceive themselves—as consumers who, if they want to build secure and healthy families, must learn how to effectively navigate the medicolegal family-building industry. Severed from any attachments to racial, economic, or reproductive justice projects, an event like the expo focuses on enhancing the consumer potential of relatively privileged and able-bodied and able-minded adults living in the United States without accounting for the ways in which the expansion of LGBT family-building possibilities is premised upon expanded structural inequalities and an intensified system of stratified reproduction.[21]

More specifically, the explosion of the bioeconomy during the 1980s and 1990s must be understood with respect to the violent processes of financialization that defined the late twentieth century: the deregulation of fertility markets, coupled with a decrease in public funding for infertility research (thanks, in part, to the efforts of a religious right skeptical of assisted reproduction), instigated the rapid entrepreneurial expansion of reproductive medicine, reprogenetic technologies, and related reproductive services.[22] Additionally, the neoliberalization of a global economy founded upon histories of slavery and imperial domination has only fueled privatized domestic and international adoption practices that respond to the increasing polarization of wealth not by trying to alleviate systemic inequalities but by capitalizing on the transfer of children from less privileged to more privileged parents.[23] In short, the emergence of a global industry that finds value in the reproductive futures of a select class of LGBT adults has taken shape via a set of ideologies and institutions, operating at local, national, and transnational levels, that unevenly distribute resources, life chances, and reproductive decision-making capacities across racist, ableist, and classist lines.

To be sure, informational sessions for prospective parents do, on occasion, open space for discussing the ethics of different LGBT family-building practices. For instance, at the second expo, I witnessed conversations about the politics of transracial and transnational adoptions and about the implications of selecting reproductive biomaterial from known versus unknown donors. Generally speaking, however, these discussions do not serve as the basis for developing larger structural critiques and instead frame ethical negotiations as yet another part of the private process of choosing an individualized path to parenthood and performing cost-benefit analyses on the available options. At the same time, even as these events approach family building as involving a set of personal decisions, the expo cautions against pursuing at-home, do-it-yourself procreative practices and relying on informal donation, surrogacy, or coparenting arrangements; instead, the event stresses the importance of consulting with industry experts in order to optimize one's chances of building a legally secure, physically fit, and emotionally healthy family. Breaking from the women-centered and community-based approaches practiced by lesbian feminists a few decades before, these events are organized around a top-down style of information delivery, where professionals in the field (some of whom are LGBT-identified parents themselves) share their legal and biomedical expertise with prospective parents and, in doing so, advertise the family-building services they provide. Within this context, the work of LGBT family advocacy, when it comes to the issue of becoming a parent, is neither about demanding universal access to fertility services and reproductive health care nor about resisting the coercive state and market practices that make it impossible for so many people, especially poor women of color, to determine their own reproductive and familial futures. In contrast, advocacy efforts around LGBT family building turn on the project of empowering aspiring parents to enter the reproductive marketplace as savvy, risk-managing, and personally responsible consumers.

Given the expenses involved in becoming a parent via the mechanisms advertised at the expo, the process of planning a family often requires some level of financial planning. While there are, of course, low-cost routes to LGBT parenthood (e.g., fostering to adopt or inseminating at home with freely donated sperm), the bulk of the family-building options offered by the event's sponsoring organizations are quite expensive, ranging from tens of thousands of dollars for AI, IVF, or private domestic or transnational adoptions to over $100,000 for a gestational surrogacy arrangement involving donor eggs. Additionally, parents might spend several thousand dollars more on related reproductive medical services—including genetic testing (for biological parents and donated biomaterials), preimplantation genetic diagnosis (a screening test for detecting genetic or chromosomal disorders in embryos conceived through IVF),[24] or sperm washing (a technique designed to enable HIV-positive men to use their own biomaterials to conceive without putting their surrogate or their child in danger of contracting the virus)—in the hopes of minimizing the "risk" of disease or disability and enhancing their children's potential according to normative standards of health and abledness. Consequently, LGBT family-building resources, the expo included, often offer advice for dealing with the high costs associated with these medicolegal reproductive technologies. In addition to encountering suggestions on how to negotiate with insurance companies to secure more coverage for fertility treatments, I have also heard tips for developing savings plans, strategies for mobilizing investment accounts, the pros and cons of crowdfunding sites, and general information on fertility financing options (which, since the 2008 financial crisis, tend to be most readily available through peer-to-peer lending firms). Importantly, however, parents have also been instructed to see financial planning services as a crucial component not just of the family-building process but of everyday LGBT family life.

One of the common refrains in the specific context of the expo and in the broader world of LGBT family advocacy is the importance of understanding how to use legal and financial mechanisms to secure the health and wealth of one's family. In the absence of comprehensive parental and relationship recognition laws, LGBT families are tasked with taking personal responsibility for their own safety and security by creating a web of contracts, directives, and other agreements that ideally approximate the protections automatically afforded to married heterosexual couples raising their own biological children. Take, for example, Family Equality Council's "Protecting Your Family" resource. Prepared before the Supreme Court's rulings in favor of marriage equality, this two-page document opened by reminding LGBT people of the vulnerabilities they face in terms of their "family's ability to inherit, make medical decisions for [each other], or visit [each other] in the hospital" (Family Equality Council, "Protecting Your Family," n.d.). The rest of the document combines general financial tips for parents with specific estate planning advice for same-sex couples to create a list of "extra precautions" that LGBT-identified parents can take in an effort to make and maintain healthy families—namely, by preparing for the possibility of future medical emergencies and by preserving their familial wealth within the nuclear unit they have created.

The Council first outlines the advance health care directives that same-sex couples raising children should have in place: a living will, a health care proxy (through which partners designate each other as the person in charge of making medical decisions on their behalf), a hospital visitation directive (which authorizes all members of the family to visit either parent in the hospital), and an "authorization to consent to medical treatment of a minor child" (which ensures that both parents, regardless of their legal status, can make emergency decisions for their children). On the second page, after stressing the importance of drawing up a will that names one's partner and children as the rightful heirs to their property (and that prevents the state from determining inheritance lines according to local laws that likely privilege marital and biological ties), the Council instructs couples to draw up a parenting contract, a domestic partnership agreement, and in cases where only one parent has legal custody of their children, a "nomination of a guardian" document that, while not legally binding, can be an effective way of establishing their partner's parental (or at least guardian) status in the event of their death or incapacitation. The document then concludes with a disclaimer clarifying that parents should seek professional guidance when developing these documents. While the "Protecting Your Family" resource directs parents toward attorneys with expertise in LGBT family law, Jennifer Hatch offers up her firm as uniquely equipped to assist LGBT-identified adults in planning their families and growing their familial assets. As a life and wealth management company attuned to the needs of LGBT families, Christopher Street Financial promises to help parents not only with tax and estate planning but also with coordinating the assortment of legal and financial mechanisms on which their health and economic security seems to depend. By sponsoring events like the family-building expo and forging an alliance with Family Equality Council, Hatch has worked hard to establish financial planning experts as integral components of the LGBT family-building process.

The Taxing Effects of Marriage Equality

When Hatch assumed control of Christopher Street Financial nearly twenty years before same-sex marriage would be legalized, she followed her predecessor Casaletto's lead and continued packaging the firm as providing a crucial service for the lesbian and gay community. If the state were going to deny lesbians and gay men the right to marry their partners, then her firm would be there to assist couples in constructing the near equivalent of a marriage out of legal contracts and financial products. Posing no challenge to the relational norms organizing U.S. tax code and family law, Christopher Street offered a private consumer solution to what was understood by Hatch and many of her clients as a problem of antigay discrimination. While her firm was technically capitalizing on the insecurities created by the unavailability of same-sex marriage, Hatch offset the potentially suspect nature of her profit-making endeavor by regularly speaking out in favor of marriage equality. In interviews with investment trade publications and mainstream news media outlets, she would stress the "very practical" set of concerns underlying the desire to marry while also fleshing out the affective dimensions of this "economic issue" (Blackman 2005). Specifically, she would enumerate the various and complicated steps that same-sex couples, especially couples who were building families and raising children, had to take in order to achieve a sense of security. Her concern was not, however, with the potentially prohibitive costs associated with hiring attorneys and financial advisors;[25] she was enraged by the viciousness of denying lesbians and gay men the privilege of enjoying the mystifying effects of romantic love. Same-sex couples, Hatch would explain, had no choice but to confront the economic function of marriage and to reckon with the entanglement of their emotional lives with financial considerations. Whereas the "average straight couple [could get] a lot of their financial setup simply by saying 'I do'" (Quittner 2010), her clients were forced to engage in "terribly unromantic conversation[s]" about their futures (Wiedeman 2012). Marriage equality was thus held up as the key to ensuring the financial health and emotional happiness of same-sex couples and LGBT families.

In practice, however, same-sex marriage has not delivered on these promises. For starters, the perceived need for LGBT-specific financial planning services did not dissipate with the arrival of marriage equality. Despite the extent to which Christopher Street hinged its relevance on the absence of marriage rights, neither the *Windsor* nor the *Obergefell* decisions rendered Hatch's enterprise obsolete. In fact, the freedom to marry only incited new concerns for lesbians and gay men and generated a new set of consumer demands for the finance industry to meet. The uneven process of legalizing same-sex marriage in the United States, a process that took place across a twelve-year span, created much confusion and frustration.

Before *Windsor*, couples who were married in states where same-sex marriage was allowed were often unsure of how their marital status translated at the state and federal levels. As a result, those who could afford it often turned to financial experts for advice. In the state of New York, the Marriage Equality Act of 2011 created a boon for accounting firms and wealth management companies, Christopher Street included (Wiedeman 2012). Many newly married couples were incensed to learn that, because DOMA prevented the U.S. government from acknowledging their marriages, they would still be required to file their federal income tax returns as two single adults. Some of the firm's clients expressed an interest in joining the "Refuse to Lie" campaign, which encouraged couples to take a stand against the discriminatory law either by ignoring the rules and filing their federal returns jointly or by attaching an addendum to their returns clarifying their marital status.[26] (For instance, Evan Wolfson, who founded the national Freedom to Marry campaign and who married his partner shortly after same-sex marriage became legal in New York State, insisted his accountant send a letter to the Internal Revenue Service [IRS] along with his federal returns. He wanted to go "on record" as a married taxpayer unjustly forced to file a single return [Cloud 2013].) Despite this political outrage, Christopher Street encouraged married couples to file separately at the federal level. In doing so, the firm's advisors explained, couples not only avoided committing tax fraud but, in many cases, were likely "better off" in terms of minimizing their tax obligations (Wiedeman 2012).

Over the next few years, the Supreme Court alleviated much of this anger and uncertainty by overturning the section of DOMA prohibiting federal recognition of state-level marriages and eventually recognizing the fundamental right of same-sex couples to marry. Nevertheless, Christopher Street remained relevant. In an interview with Reuters published the same day as the *Obergefell* decision, Hatch cautioned lesbians and gay men against dropping their guard on the financial planning front: "I wish I could say marriage makes it easy, but it doesn't" (Pinsker 2015). LGBT families, for instance, should not assume their marital status has any bearing on their parental status: second-parent adoptions, Hatch explained, would remain necessary into the foreseeable future. (The major U.S.-based LGBT rights organizations were issuing similar warnings about the importance of not confusing relationship recognition for parental recognition and were recommending that every nonlegal or nonbiological parent, married or not, pursue an adoption or, if possible, a court judgment of parentage.[27]) Further, the firm's advisors would also be essential resources for couples who have a significant amount of shared assets and who are deciding to marry after having been together for a long time. Because they have likely set up trusts or charitable funds as a way of shielding themselves from estate taxes in the event of one of their deaths, they would presumably need help reassessing their wealth management plans and untangling the complex arrangements they made over the years. In other cases, couples planning to marry might not want to incorporate as a single economic unit and could benefit from Christopher Street's expertise in developing prenuptial and postnuptial agreements. Finally—and most surprisingly (given the freedom to marry movement's insistence on the universal appeal of marriage)—one of the primary dilemmas facing Hatch's clients on the other side of *Windsor* and *Obergefell* is whether to even get married at all.

To be clear, what her clients are asking is if marriage makes financial sense for them. The answer depends, in large part, on a couple's specific situation. In the case of a middle-class LGBT household, marriage has the potential to alleviate a degree of financial insecurity and to make life more affordable in the immediate present. For example, parents who, after marrying, become eligible to use tax-free dollars to cover their partners and children under employer-based health insurance plans might find that marriage helps the family's monthly budget. That said, the financial benefits of marriage are often most acutely felt by couples with a significant disparity in their individual incomes. Because U.S. tax code is organized around the interests of a heteropatriarchal family and designed to reward the breadwinning head of household for supporting his family, the legalization of same-sex marriage has enabled lesbian and gay couples who make vastly different amounts of money to enjoy the tax-savings benefits of filing jointly and bringing the higher earner into a lower income tax bracket.

For many of Hatch's clients, however, the advantages of marrying tend to be less clear-cut. Since taking over in the mid-1990s, Hatch has focused on serving the wealthiest segments of the lesbian and gay community. In an attempt to continue turning profits in the face of competition from mainstream banking institutions, Hatch began focusing exclusively on higher-net clientele. While the firm had historically served clients from across the country who were drawn to the novelty of its gay-specific focus, the majority of Christopher Street's clients are now from the New York metro area (Quittner 2010). By the early 2010s, the average client was worth a little over $1 million, and new clients were required to have at least $500,000 ready to invest (Garmhausen 2010). For the same-sex couples and LGBT families working with Hatch's firm, the answer to the question of whether to get married often requires a careful assessment of their financial profiles and a cost-benefit analysis of marriage as an economic arrangement.

Christopher Street is tasked with the work of helping clients figure out if and how to deploy same-sex marriage as a wealth management tool. Consider, for example, income tax planning. Before marriage equality, same-sex couples who shared money, property, and/or the responsibility of raising children were forced to file their federal taxes as two single people. Their actual economic lives may have been intimately intertwined, but on paper, they needed to distill that messy reality into two separate returns. Not surprisingly, many families turned to financial experts for assistance. Because there was no prescribed formula on how to proceed, advisors and accountants were able to play around with the numbers: the goal was to strategically divvy up children and other deductions to minimize a couple's tax burden. Much to the dismay of Hatch's clients, access to marriage has a limiting effect on the ability to exercise creativity in tax planning and frequently ends up being "more detrimental . . . than positive" when it comes to paying income taxes (Arden 2014). Since most of the couples working with Christopher Street consist of high earners partnered with other high earners, the shift in filing status from single to married often resulted in an increase in their total tax obligations: in addition to pushing them into a higher tax bracket and leaving them ineligible for tax credits they once enjoyed, their larger joint income threatened to trigger the 3.8 percent net investment income tax as well as the alternative minimum tax (Arden 2014).

In other words, these couples faced what their straight counterparts have long termed the "marriage penalty" (i.e., the increase in taxes owed that married couples experience when both spouses have similar incomes). Consequently, after the *Windsor* decision, when the IRS invited same-sex couples who, under DOMA, had been forced to file individual federal returns despite being married at the state level to refile their taxes for up to the past three years, many couples declined. (In fact, faced with the marriage penalty, even Wolfson stopped obsessing over the freedom to file a joint federal return. He explained to *Bloomberg Businessweek* that since *Windsor*, he now approaches the process as a "routine tax matter" and had little interest in back filing his taxes, especially since he and his husband would likely end up owing more money. Equality, he clarified, is about ensuring that lesbians and gay men have access to the same "range of choices" as their straight counterparts and are free to deploy any and all legal strategies to minimize their personal tax burdens [Cloud 2013].) In short, on a year-to-year basis, marriage tends to cost wealthy LGBT families. Yet as Hatch advises her clients, it is necessary for couples to weigh these "losses" against what they stand to "gain" by way of eventually avoiding estate taxes.

For Christopher Street's clients, the question of marriage can boil down to deciding if it is worth paying more in annual income taxes while both members of the couple are alive to ensure that when in death do they part, the surviving partner can take advantage of laws that allow for the unlimited and tax-free transfer of assets from a deceased spouse to their widow/er. Put more crudely, the legalization of same-sex marriage may have had less to do with enhancing the vitality of LGBT families and more to do with securing against lesbian and gay mortality. Since the economic benefits of being married often become most stark after marriage (i.e., after a spouse dies), it is hardly a coincidence that the two names sutured to marriage equality in the United States, Edith Windsor and Jim Obergefell, belong respectively to a widow and a widower. There is, of course, a significant difference between these two cases: Obergefell's fight to be named as the surviving spouse on his husband's death certificate only involved gaining access to $255 in monthly Social Security survivor benefits and was largely framed by his lawyers as an issue not of money but of dignity; in distinction, Windsor's lawsuit against the U.S. government, as I discussed in the previous chapter, was organized around the injustice of the federal law requiring her to pay over $300,000 in estate taxes on the inheritance her deceased wife had bequeathed to her.[28] From the perspective of wealthy same-sex couples, what marriage equality offers is access to yet another financial mechanism that can be deployed as part of a larger arsenal of wealth preservation techniques. Thus for Christopher Street's clients, the question of *whether* to marry can become an issue of *when* to marry. Younger couples might delay marriage to continue enjoying income tax savings, but older couples might feel more pressure to prioritize their estate planning needs. For example, Hatch's decision to marry her partner was motivated, in part, by the fact that they are aging: while they are not pleased about paying thousands of dollars more in income tax each year, they are more appalled by the prospect of owing estate taxes when one of them dies (Cloud 2013). Within the domain of financial planning, marriage reveals itself as a legally binding economic arrangement designed to consolidate a family's net worth and, perhaps more important, to contain that wealth within a privately designated network of care and accumulation.

During public interviews, Hatch often mentions the cost-benefit analyses that her clients perform before walking down the aisle, but she is also careful to clarify that love always wins (Hobbs 2014; Skinner 2014). The desire to be married, she claims, inevitably trumps all other concerns. Estimating that 80 to 90 percent of her clients have married (Hobbs 2014), the bulk of them now enduring a higher tax burden (Cloud 2013), Hatch explains that lesbians and gay men understand that equality is not free and that "this is the price that [they] pay" for the "other rights [they're] going to get" (Skinner 2014). This sudden willingness to pay additional income tax does not necessarily mark a break from the tax-evading practices previously described. According to Hatch, her clients find taxes bearable only when they experience a direct personal gain in exchange for their payment to the government—in this case, the state's recognition of same-sex relationships and the related but not-yet-named benefits that will presumably follow. To borrow Lisa Duggan's formulation, Hatch and her clients adopt a consumer model of citizenship: they proceed as if they are "consumers of government, expecting the best return for the price paid in taxes" (2003, 38). Rather than approaching taxation as a way for citizens to pool their resources to fund public goods and services, they approach the process as an individualized exchange in which they essentially pay the government for legal protections and social legitimation.

In sum, at the heart of most celebratory takes on same-sex marriage is what Katherine Franke describes as an "anti-tax ethos" (2015, 235)—an ethos that suppresses any sense of collective responsibility for things like education, health care, or a more robust system of social services. This mind-set, which drives Hatch's advocacy work and her firm's advisory practices, is deeply at odds with the politics of resistance and redistribution associated with the gay liberation movement—a movement led by street youth, gender-variant folks, and other poor queers of color—that is believed to have originated on the street honored in her firm's name. The symbolic appropriation of Christopher Street is helpful in bringing into focus the transformation of a broad-based movement concerned with economic justice into an assimilatory project working to create a more inclusive global marketplace. By seeking financial security in the form of legal recognition, LGBT rights advocates offer a "demobilized gay constituency" uninterested in contesting the capitalist state or challenging the idea that individuals should be personally responsible for their economic well-being (Duggan 2003, 50). In this light, the tax-evading practices of the gay elite can be understood as indicative of larger shifts taking place within LGBT politics and U.S. political culture. The use of marriage and other financial mechanisms to amass private wealth and to shield one's assets from taxation both fuels and is fueled by the sense that there is a scarcity of resources available and that families need to do what they can to protect themselves. This perpetual feeling of insecurity, coupled with a belief in the doctrine of personal responsibility, serves as the U.S. government's justification for the cutting and constriction of social welfare programs.

Promoting LGBT Family Health

In the wake of the *Windsor* and *Obergefell* decisions, wealthy same-sex couples were not the only ones left wondering whether marriage made financial sense for them. For poor and disabled LGBT-identified people who rely on the dwindling welfare state for their everyday survival needs, the sudden availability of marriage was not a cause for immediate celebration but was, in fact, the impetus for much caution and calculation.[29] In 2013, after the Supreme Court ordered the federal government to start recognizing state-level same-sex marriages, Family Equality Council joined forces with other LGBT rights organizations to produce a "fact sheet series" titled "After DOMA: What It Means for You."[30] Collectively, these documents were designed to provide same-sex couples—with or without children, but in which at least one partner was a U.S. citizen—guidance on navigating a newly configured legal landscape.

In addition to including information on filing income taxes, securing spousal benefits from the military or private employers, and sponsoring a non-citizen spouse's application for permanent resident status, the fact sheets also addressed the effects of the recent ruling on accessing Medicaid, Temporary Assistance for Needy Families (TANF), and Supplemental Security Income (SSI) for the aged, blind, and disabled. Each of these latter documents cautioned same-sex couples against getting married without fully understanding how a shift in relationship status would affect the government's assessment of their family income and how any resulting changes would impact their eligibility for these safety net programs. For many (if not most) couples, the fact sheets explain, being married is not beneficial for Medicaid, TANF, or SSI purposes; people relying on these programs were advised to consult an attorney, if possible, about their benefits before deciding to marry. Social welfare programs tend to penalize people for getting married by offering spouses fewer benefits than what they would receive as two single adults. In contrast to the claims made by the freedom to marry movement, marriage equality does not represent an unambiguous source of health security and economic stability for all LGBT-identified individuals. A consideration of exactly what marriage means for families depending on public assistance thus opens space for unsettling dominant activist narratives about rights and recognition and for identifying the limits of a marriage and family equality framework.

At first glance, Family Equality Council's circulation of the "After DOMA" fact sheets and its admission that marriage may not be universally beneficial to LGBT families appears to mark a significant break in the organization's embrace of the freedom to marry movement. In fact, prior to the *Windsor* ruling, the Council had made a very different argument about the effects marriage equality would have on access to social welfare programs. In 2011, the Council coauthored, with the Movement Advancement Project and the Center for American Progress, a two-page issue brief titled "How DOMA Harms Children" (Movement Advancement Project et al. 2011b). In addition to rehearsing what were becoming, by this point, familiar arguments in favor of same-sex marriage rights—that is, calling attention to how DOMA imposed unfair tax burdens on many LGBT families and created barriers for parents trying to access employer-based family health insurance plans—the brief also indicted the federal law for prohibiting states from recognizing nuclear LGBT families and depriving them of the public support their heterosexual counterparts received. Because families "aren't accurately counted when determining eligibility for safety net programs," the brief argued, children in need "can be unfairly denied critical economic, health care, and other assistance."[31] While this claim is likely true for two-parent families in which the parent excluded from the household eligibility calculation (due to a lack of legal ties to their partner and their children) has no income or makes very little money, a closer look at the Council's engagement with the issue of LGBT poverty reveals that the organization possessed a far more nuanced understanding of how families participate in these social programs and the ways in which access to marriage might interfere with poverty relief efforts. For starters, the issue brief was distilled from a much longer document on how "unequal treatment and social stigma" compromised the health, well-being, and economic security of LGBT-headed households (Movement Advancement Project et al. 2011a, 1).

Drawing upon the expertise of several progressive scholars and researchers (including Gary Gates and Nancy Polikoff, who I cite throughout this book), the 125-page report, titled *All Children Matter: How Legal and Social Inequalities Hurt LGBT Families*, provides a detailed account of the diverse needs of same-sex couples raising children in the United States. Pushing back against perceptions of this demographic as predominantly white and comfortably middle class, the document opens by asserting that LGBT families are "more racially and ethnically diverse than married different-sex couples raising children" and that children growing up in LGBT families are "twice as likely to live in poverty as children being raised by married heterosexual households" (1). In a section dedicated to safety net programs, the report teases out the ways in which eligibility guidelines for government assistance create "economic disincentives" that force many parents, queer or not, to choose "between accessing the important protections that come with legal relationship recognition and formal parental recognition and losing vital benefits that help families meet basic needs" (2011a, 56, 57). Although the authors never identify these "penalties" as symptomatic of the state's systematic use of the family as a vehicle

for privatizing the social costs of reproduction, they do advocate for new policies that would facilitate a more equitable distribution of the limited resources
the government sets aside for poverty alleviation. Echoing the calls of feminist
and queer organizers who championed family diversity before the marriage
equality movement took over, the body of the report recommends organizing social welfare programs around a more expansive definition of family
that focuses on "the actual interconnectedness of people (such as the extent
to which individuals share economic resources like food or housing)"[32] (52)
and then basing eligibility requirements on factors like family size and demonstrated need (as opposed to obsessing over whether parents and children
are legally bound together; 51). In the end, however, the legal and policy solutions put forth by *All Children Matter* privilege the assimilatory aim of achieving rights and recognition over the more progressive goal of destabilizing
the primacy of the marital family and expanding the availability of resources
and social services. While the executive summary of the report does include
a call for "broadening the definition of 'family'" to "accommodate the reality
of LGBT and other 21st century families," this call is limited to the realm of
safety net programs and is ultimately overshadowed by the top two demands
on the list of recommendations: comprehensive parental recognition laws and
the legalization of same-sex marriage (4).

Over the next few years, the work of LGBT family advocacy, which, at the
national level, was increasingly taking place in dialogue with senior government officials, often revolved around the issue of marriage equality. Take, for
example, the White House LGBT Conference on Families. In April 2012, as
part of a conference series designed to publicize the Obama administration's
efforts to "ensure health, dignity, security, and justice for LGBT Americans,"
Family Equality Council partnered with the White House's Office of Public
Engagement to repurpose its annual midwestern conference-vacation. The
resulting event served as an opportunity for LGBT rights advocates, family
equality proponents, and federal policy makers to exchange ideas and discuss best practices for supporting same-sex couples raising children as well as
LGBT-identified youth.[33] The mainstream movement may have been initially
frustrated by President Obama's slow start on the LGBT rights front, but
by the time this conference series launched, his administration had amassed
an unprecedented record of achievements in terms of advancing LGBT-
inclusive laws and policies. In their opening remarks at the LGBT Conference on Families, both Jennifer Chrisler, the executive director of Family
Equality Council, and Matt Nosanchuk, a senior counselor at the Department of Justice (DOJ), kicked off the event by applauding what were largely
regarded as the Obama administration's most significant actions in the service
of LGBT equality—namely, the 2009 passage of the Matthew Shepard and

James Byrd Jr. Hate Crimes Prevention Act, the 2010 repeal of the U.S. military's "Don't Ask, Don't Tell" policy, and the 2011 decision to stop defending DOMA in federal courts.

This enthusiastic celebration of the administration's agenda diverted attention from the ways in which these "achievements" might have otherwise illuminated the organization of contemporary political culture around what Chandan Reddy refers to as "freedom with violence" (2011, 2). The extension of federal hate crimes protections to include attacks targeting a victim's disability, gender identity, or sexual orientation not only advocated the expansion of a racist and repressive system of policing and punishing but actually occurred via the authorization of a national defense act that approved what was, at that time, the highest military budget in U.S. history and that appropriated funds for the continuation of ground wars in Iraq and Afghanistan and unmanned drone strikes in a number of other locations.[34] Relatedly, the removal of homophobic discriminatory barriers to military service effectively augmented an imperial force tasked with the deadly work of protecting and expanding financialized markets at home and abroad.[35] While these two legislative changes were only mentioned in passing at the LGBT Conference on Families as a way of way of demonstrating Obama's commitment to the LGBT community, the opening keynote address focused specifically on same-sex marriage rights, which were held up as the top priority for families. The first keynote speaker was Stuart Delery, the acting assistant attorney general for the DOJ's Civil Division. Just a few weeks before, he had made a name for himself within the LGBT rights community when he argued *against* the constitutionality of DOMA in a federal appeals court. In his remarks at the conference, after talking about his own experiences as a gay father, he outlined the legal arguments undergirding the U.S. government's new position on DOMA and denounced the federal law for "undermin[ing] the security of the very children it claim[ed] to protect." Over the course of his address, Delery flagged the DOJ's other efforts to advocate for American families, such as their enforcement of consumer protection laws (mainly around mortgage lending and drug manufacturing), but the audience, perhaps predictably, reserved their loudest cheers and applause for his forceful endorsement of marriage equality.

Immediately following Delery's keynote, the tone of the conference shifted as a panel of representatives from the federal government came on stage to discuss the smaller-scale administrative changes that their respective agencies and departments had enacted to support same-sex couples raising children. Together, the panelists set aside the question of marriage equality and reoriented the conversation around the subtler work of administrative law. The representative from the Department of Labor (DOL), for instance, discussed the Obama administration's efforts to ensure LGBT families could take advantage of the protections afforded through the Family and Medical Leave Act (FMLA). Since its inception, the FMLA has broadly defined the parent-child relationship to include biological children, foster or adopted children, and stepchildren as well as "a child of a person standing *in loco parentis*" (Family and Medical Leave Act 1993). In 2010, the DOL issued a clarification explicitly stating that anyone who is acting (or intending to act) as a parent, regardless of whether they are legally recognized as such, is eligible to take leave to care for a sick, newborn, or newly adopted child.[36] These new guidelines may not have done anything to alter the fact that the FMLA denied unmarried couples of all genders the right to take leave to care for one another, but the administration's clarification of the law did gesture toward a framework of family recognition in line with the more contextual and individualized approaches recommended in the *All Children Matter* report.

In a similar vein, the representative from the Department of Health and Human Services (HHS) discussed the administration's 2010 memorandum that directed all hospitals receiving funding through Medicare and Medicaid, which includes nearly all the hospitals in the United States, to respect the wishes that patients outline in advance health care directives and to honor the rights of patients to designate visitation privileges, regardless of whether visitors are legally related to them.[37] Interestingly, the memo named LGBT Americans alongside widows/ers and members of religious orders as potential beneficiaries of more flexible hospital visitation policies and, in doing so, showed how progressive approaches to family-oriented policies, when not routed through marriage-centric logics, can support the diverse networks of care on which so many lives, not just LGBT ones, depend. While these administrative efforts certainly fall short of a radical intervention—neither the clarification nor the memo resulted in an expansion or redistribution of material resources, and both were designed to enhance a family's capacity to privately handle medical emergencies—the act of insisting on the importance of developing a broader definition of family posed a challenge to the often unquestioned relational norms organizing U.S. political culture. Within the wider frame of the conference series and of mainstream LGBT rights organizing, however, the representatives from DOL and HHS were not heard as offering alternative models for designing family law and public policy writ large. Instead, these administrative fixes were appreciated for the relief they provided LGBT families on their march toward equality—that is, as measures that would cease to be relevant once same-sex couples could fulfill their marital desires and form proper nuclear families.

Although the keynote address and the panel presentations on LGBT families turned almost entirely on a politics not of redistribution but of recognition, there was a slight deviation from the prevailing family equality advocacy script during the HHS representative's remarks. After highlighting his department's efforts to improve hospital visitation and medical decision-making policies, he directed the audience's attention to what HHS and the Obama administration as a whole believed would enhance the health and security of same-sex couples raising children: the passage of the Patient Protection and Affordable Care Act (ACA). The framing of the ACA as a major victory for LGBT families was consistent with the administration's ongoing outreach efforts to LGBT communities, which had, from the beginning, emphasized the importance of addressing LGBT health disparities and promoting LGBT health across the country.[38] In fact, the inaugural event in the White House LGBT Conference Series focused on the theme of health and featured a keynote address by then HHS secretary Kathleen Sebelius on the department's most noteworthy accomplishments in this area.[39] In addition to integrating sexual orientation– and gender identity–specific questions into national health surveys as a way of better assessing the health challenges facing LGBT-identified individuals, her department was also investing in the development of LGBT health-related resources and had already awarded funding to SAGE for establishing the National Resource Center on LGBT Aging[40] and to Fenway Health for starting a National LGBT Health Education Center designed to support the training of more culturally competent health care providers.[41] She also drew attention to the administration's reinvestment in HIV/AIDS research and domestic prevention efforts and applauded the president's decision to lift the travel ban on HIV-positive visitors, denouncing the "outdated and misguided policy" for having "broke[n] apart families, hurt our economy, and [gone] against our fundamental values." (Keeping in mind the administration's simultaneous expansion and intensification of detention and deportation efforts, this rhetorical embrace of open borders and a more compassionate immigration system begs a deeper analysis of the entanglement of sexual freedoms with racialized violences.) The majority of the secretary's address, however, focused on how the ACA would improve LGBT lives.

According to Sebelius, when Obama took office, the U.S. health care system "wasn't working for a lot of Americans" and "was especially broken for LGBT Americans." She opened her address by highlighting the alarming number of LGBT-identified people who lack access to health care, but in a significant departure from the norms of mainstream LGBT politics, she did not attribute this problem to marriage inequality. Whereas LGBT rights organizations often cited the inability of couples to share insurance coverage or access family health care plans as an argument in favor of same-sex marriage rights, Sebelius took as her starting point the fact that many LGBT-identified people, regardless of their relationship status, do not have jobs with health benefits. "Given the discrimination they sometimes faced in the workplace, LGBT Americans often had a harder time getting access to employment-based coverage," she explained, "and many childless LGBT adults with low incomes fell through the cracks in our health insurance market, unable to afford private insurance but unable to qualify for Medicaid either." By lowering the costs of insurance plans and expanding the availability of culturally competent health care, the ACA, from the perspective of the Obama administration, promised to make great strides in alleviating some of these vulnerabilities and enhancing the health and well-being of LGBT communities.

In reality, the ACA failed to deliver on its lofty promises, a failure due in no small part to the persistent conservative forces working against the perceived socialist underpinnings of what became disaffectionately known as Obamacare. Moreover, the creation of a system organized around individual mandates, federal tax subsidies, and state-based insurance exchanges was unable to achieve universal access to care as a "coverage gap" continued to leave many working people and families without affordable health care options. Further, from the perspective of LGBT communities, ACA-related efforts to expand access to gender-affirming care for transgender and gender-nonconforming people have been slow and uneven at best, and the new patient protection provisions have done little to increase access to fertility treatments, advanced reproductive technologies, and other alternative family-building options. That said, the White House's break from the mainstream movement's narrow conception of LGBT politics is noteworthy. Moving beyond a singular focus on identity-based rights, the Obama administration insisted that access to health care be understood as a top priority for the LGBT movement.[42] At the LGBT Conference on Families, however, the HHS representative's discussion of the ACA did not frame health care as an economic justice issue for LGBT families; instead, his presentation highlighted the development of a new tool on the federal government's website that enabled LGBT families to specifically search for plans that cover same-sex domestic partners when comparison shopping for insurance options. Ultimately, the Obama administration's investment in providing quality affordable health care for LGBT communities was buried under the resounding theme of family recognition, thus allowing the fact of LGBT poverty to remain outside the frame of family equality advocacy.

LGBT Poverty and Same-Sex Marriage Promotion

The White House LGBT Conference on Families only addressed issues of poverty when the focus shifted from LGBT parents to LGBT youth. While several of the speakers tasked with discussing youth issues zeroed in on the president and the first lady's centering of LGBT students in their antibullying initiatives, a representative from HHS's Administration for Children and Families (ACF) directed attention to the work his agency was doing on behalf of "at-risk" LGBT-identified and queer or questioning youth. He delivered a keynote address and a panel presentation that outlined the ACF's strategies for expanding support services for LGBTQ youth in foster care and runaway and homeless LGBTQ youth. The conference's refusal to talk about social welfare programs except in relation to the needs of young people was indicative of a common trend within U.S.-based LGBT politics: as a sympathetic subject, the LGBTQ-identified teenager could, if not marked as excessively racially or sexually perverse, be absolved of responsibility for their personal situation and deemed deserving of public assistance.[43] This is not, however, to suggest that HHS was unaware of or ignoring the widespread problem of LGBT poverty. In fact, the White House conference series dedicated an entire event to the issue of housing and homelessness. Additionally, two years later, the ACF commissioned a report titled *Human Services for Low-Income and At-Risk LGBT Populations: An Assessment of the Knowledge Base and Research Needs* (Burwick et al. 2014). In a move suggesting a crack (if only slight) in the enduring myth of gay affluence, the ACF set out to learn more about the socioeconomic situation of LGBT populations and to devise strategies for tailoring human services to meet their distinct needs, focusing specifically on the child welfare system,[44] income assistance and self-sufficiency programs for adults, and support services for runaway and homeless youth, with an emphasis on sexual health education initiatives.

In addition to demonstrating how racial marginalization exacerbates trends in LGBT poverty and underlining the particular precarity of trans people and nontrans women (especially bisexual women), the report also identified LGBT-headed households with children as facing disproportionate risks to their economic well-being: in comparison to their married heterosexual counterparts, these families were more likely to rely on Medicaid, to receive cash assistance (via programs like TANF), and to depend on the Supplemental Nutrition Assistance Program (SNAP, formerly known as the Food Stamp Program; 28). Given the severity of LGBT poverty in the United States, the authors feared that, despite the high levels of participation in safety net programs by LGBT populations, homophobic and transphobic discriminatory barriers were preventing even greater numbers of LGBT-identified adults from accessing human services. Writing during the period between *Windsor* and *Obergefell* (and citing findings from the *All Children Matter* report), the authors called for further research on how exclusionary marriage laws in some states might have been negatively impacting the ability of LGBT households to receive assistance (30–32). They also recognized a need for more information on how "marriage penalties" might have been stopping some low-income couples from marrying even if they lived in a marriage equality state. Here, writing after *Obergefell* and driven by a different set of political and intellectual concerns, I want to ask a separate yet related question about the relationship between marriage and the social problem of LGBT poverty. What happens when the federal government finally has access to same-sex marriage as a tool for social and sexual control? Or, more specifically, how might marriage enable the state to deploy social welfare programs in imposing white supremacist relational norms upon LGBT populations and embedding queer bodies and desires within privatized networks of care?

In the age of marriage equality, LGBT communities have become potential targets for federally funded programs designed to promote marital family norms. For the past two decades, marriage promotion efforts have figured centrally in the reorganization—or, more accurately, the decimation—of the Keynesian welfare state. Thanks to President Bill Clinton's inclusion of marriage promotion funding within the Welfare Reform Act of 1996 and President George W. Bush's subsequent expansion of grant programs for "healthy marriage" and "responsible fatherhood" initiatives, federal money has been made readily available for developing relationship education programs. Many of these programs were designed to encourage marriage and discourage divorce among low-income populations, with special initiatives targeting "Hispanic," "American Indian," and "African American" families. Underlying these efforts was a belief that poor people—specifically, poor women of color and especially single black mothers—are to blame for their financial situations because they lack "family values," sexual mores, and the skills needed to create "stable" homes with the fathers of their children. According to these racist and (hetero)sexist logics, marriage is the obvious solution to the problem of economic inequality.

The Welfare Reform Act opens by asserting that marriage is "the foundation of a successful society" and that the "promotion of responsible fatherhood and motherhood is integral to successful child rearing and the well-being of children" (Personal Responsibility 1996). In doing so, the act tried to pass itself off as a law designed to strengthen families. What the legislation actually did was drastically decrease the availability of support for families living in the United States. Specifically, the law replaced the federally administered Aid to Families with Dependent Children program (AFDC, which guaranteed cash assistance to anyone eligible) with the TANF block grant system (which provides states with limited funds for welfare programs while simultaneously enforcing harsher eligibility standards and work requirements). Despite cutting support for struggling parents and children, the act was celebrated by its proponents as a profamily initiative. Supporters pointed to the law's marriage promotion provisions as evidence of how reform efforts would repair a welfare system that had historically discouraged marriage and worked against family preservation by denying benefits to two-parent households and disqualifying women who were living with different-sex partners.

In practice, however, welfare reform has sent conflicting messages about marriage. On the one hand, TANF-funded programs encourage marriage and, in some states, have even offered cash bonuses to women who marry the fathers of their children. On the other hand, as I explained earlier, the system also discourages marriage by lowering benefits for recipients who marry their partners. Officially, this policy maneuver reflects the belief that marriage automatically improves a person's economic situation and alleviates their financial need. Unofficially, the state's seemingly contradictory practices—promoting *and* penalizing marriage—can be understood as another way the U.S. government privatizes the work of social reproduction. The government aims to save money by offloading the financial burden of caring for poor women and children onto individual men. In this light, the ideological function of marriage promotion programs becomes quite clear. To maximize the cost savings of welfare reform, the state needs to instill in low-income couples an appreciation for marriage so great that it will override concerns about the economic disadvantages of marital life.

Perhaps unsurprisingly then, just four months after the *Obergefell* decision, the federal government began devising plans for promoting same-sex marriage. In October 2015, ACF launched a research project that I understand as directly related to its recent investigation into the reliance of LGBT-identified people on safety net programs. The agency hired an outside research firm to "provide an assessment of the current state of the healthy marriage and relationship education (HMRE) practice field" and to "identify and promote promising approaches for serving same-sex couples and lesbian, gay, and bisexual individuals—whether adult or youth—who may become involved in same-sex relationships" (Office of Planning, Research and Evaluation 2015). In June 2016, the agency posted a story about its efforts to support healthy marriages and relationships for LGBT populations on its *Family Room* blog. ACF introduced the initiative by explaining that LGBT parents and same-sex couples face "stressors," like "higher rates of poverty" and "poorer health outcomes," that "undermine their efforts to form strong, nurturing families" (Chamberlain 2016). This initial framing of the project suggests at first that HHS was acknowledging the negative impact that economic insecurity, especially when experienced with and exacerbated by homophobia and transphobia, can have on romantic and familial relationships. In its entirety, however, the blog post presents the development of LGBT-inclusive HMRE programs as advancing ACF's mission to "support *all* vulnerable children and families to achieve health, wellbeing, and economic self-sufficiency" (Chamberlain 2016, emphasis in original). In doing so, HHS admits that it was looking to update its privatizing strategies by presenting marriage as a cure (or at least a treatment) for poverty.[45] Save for a letter from the Family Equality Council—which applauded ACF's efforts to support LGBT families and, somewhat unexpectedly, implored officials to prioritize trans inclusivity when implementing new HMRE programming[46]—the major U.S.-based LGBT rights organizations, in their continued sidestepping of poverty-related issues, paid little attention to this recent development.

For the past two decades, antiracist feminist scholars and activists have pushed back against welfare reform.[47] In addition to calling for the restoration and expansion of programs that provide people with material resources and immediate relief, they have also challenged the faulty assumptions on which marriage promotion initiatives are based. Specifically, critics point to research on the structural factors creating economic insecurities in the United States—namely, a substandard public education system, the absence of living wage employment opportunities, the adoption of increasingly punitive immigration policies, the lack of affordable housing and health care options, and the pervasiveness of institutionalized racism, ableism, and (hetero)sexism. Getting married, they argue, solves none of these larger problems. As such, they have questioned the ethics of welfare policies that cut funding from cash assistance programs that provide direct help to struggling families and, instead, spend that money on developing relationship education programs (for which there is currently no social scientific evidence indicating they are effective in combatting poverty[48]). This is not to discount the ways in which access to free support services designed to teach communication, conflict resolution, and financial literacy skills might enhance the collective well-being of families, especially if offered via a community-based voluntary system and made available to a wide array of household forms. (In the face of limited public resources and a lack of living wage jobs, a familiarity with basic budgeting techniques is probably an invaluable survival skill.) As a poverty relief program, however, HMRE initiatives address neither systemic injustices nor the pressing needs of individual families. Within this context, there is a particularly cruel irony in the federal government's decision to deliver money management lessons in lieu of actual cash assistance.

Shortly after taking office, the Obama administration made an attempt to address some of the critiques waged against his predecessors' marriage promotion policies. In 2010, the president proposed a budget for the following fiscal year that eliminated funding for the promotion of marriage and instead allocated $500 million of TANF money for a new Fatherhood, Marriage, and Families Innovation Fund. If approved, this federally administered grants program would have supported state-level "responsible fatherhood" initiatives that focused specifically on providing job training and other educational opportunities, "reentry" assistance for formerly incarcerated men, and support services for men dealing with substance abuse or mental health issues. While Obama's attempt to increase the availability of material resources for fathers fell short in terms of addressing the concerns of feminist critics enraged by the organization of safety net programs around white middle-class patriarchal norms,[49] marriage promotion proponents were appalled by what they perceived as the president's devaluing of the marital family form and, in response, mobilized what had become at this point a well-oiled conservative marriage movement machine (Heath 2012, 192). As a result, the Obama administration revised its original plans, and the 2011 budget earmarked $150 million for the Healthy Marriage Promotion and Responsible Fatherhood initiative (which split the allocated money evenly between marriage promotion efforts and responsible fatherhood programs). For the next six years, even as HHS tried to signal its investment in promoting healthy relationships and long-term partnerships (as opposed to fixating on marital relations alone), marriage remained rhetorically central when it came to relationship education, and the two-parent family continued to function as the national ideal.

Given the Obama administration's commitment to LGBT health promotion and its investment in broadening the scope of relationship education, it is hardly surprising that, following the *Obergefell* decision, HHS started working on how to fold same-sex intimacies into its HMRE programming. While the plan to adapt marriage promotion techniques for a domesticated homosexual lifestyle would have likely upset a good portion of the right-wing marriage movement—lest we forget that the welfare reformers who blamed single mothers for failing to marry were also the most vociferous opponents of same-sex couples seeking the right to marry (Smith 2001; Cahill 2005)—other marriage promotion enthusiasts have since revised their positions on marriage equality and have expressed appreciation for the freedom to marry movement's advancement of a promarriage agenda.[50] As such, the HHS's seemingly progressive recognition of LGBT families in the area of HMRE programming is best understood as a continuation of morally and fiscally conservative marriage promotion policies.

In a similar fashion, the Obama administration's efforts to develop more LGBT-inclusive sexual health education programs for at-risk youth also advanced a rather conservative agenda via ostensibly progressive means. For the past two decades, federally funded sexual health education programs in the United States have largely functioned as an extension of government-sponsored marriage promotion projects.[51] While the federal government first started supporting abstinence-only-until-marriage programs under President Ronald Reagan—in 1981, the Adolescent Family Life Act (AFLA) designated funds for youth programs promoting "chastity" and "self-discipline"[52]—it was during the Clinton presidency that the amount of funding allotted for abstinence education initiatives grew exponentially. The opening of the Welfare Reform Act of 1996 follows its declaration of marriage as the "foundation of a successful society" with a frantic account of how a supposed increase in "out-of-wedlock pregnancies" and a rising rate of "nonmarital teen pregnancy" had led to an epidemic of single mothers dependent on the AFDC program and draining the government of its scarce resources (Personal Responsibility

1996). In an effort to solve the allegedly costly problem of teenage pregnancies by discouraging all adolescent sexual activity, the law amended Title V of the Social Security Act and, in doing so, allocated $50 million annually for abstinence education projects.

To be eligible for this funding, a program was required to meet a detailed set of criteria, which included teaching that "a mutually faithful monogamous relationship in the context of marriage is the expected standard of human sexual activity" and that "sexual activity outside the context of marriage is likely to have harmful psychological and physical effects." Thinly veiling the economic logics driving these curricular demands, the law's provisions for abstinence education attempted to cast moralizing lessons on the "importance of attaining self-sufficiency before engaging in sexual activity" as promoting the health and well-being of adolescents. Within these federally endorsed programs, homosexuality was, at best, never mentioned and, at worst, stigmatized as a shameful (if not deadly) lifestyle. Under Bush, additional abstinence funding was made available through the Healthy Marriage Initiative, which allotted money for abstinence education and marriage promotion programs for high school students, and the Community-Based Abstinence Education grants program, which required grantees to teach youth to avoid "any type of genital contact or sexual stimulation between two persons, including, but not limited to, sexual intercourse" while denying funding to programs that provided participants with positive information about contraception (SIECUS n.d.). Sexual health educators, feminist and queer critics, and antiracist youth advocates have waged a number of critiques against these initiatives. In addition to raising concerns about the heterosexism and sex negativity of abstinence education, they have also pointed to studies documenting the inefficacy of these programs in achieving their stated goals and to evidence indicating the potentially dangerous effects of these curricular initiatives.[53] Aware of these critiques (and on the heels of a congressional hearing on the need to rethink sexual health education),[54] Obama stepped into office and promptly eliminated AFLA and Title V funding for abstinence education. In 2009, he approved a budget for the following fiscal year that reallocated the money to establish the Teen Pregnancy Prevention (TPP) program, which funded local efforts that targeted at-risk youth and that, while still extolling the virtues of abstinence, provided detailed information on contraceptive use.[55]

The president's bold budgetary move sparked a serious backlash from right-wing proponents of abstinence education and marriage promotion. Consequently, during Obama's first year in office, as congressional representatives engaged in a bitter battle over the terms and conditions of health care reform, the issue of sex ed emerged as a kind of bargaining chip. As a result, the passage of the ACA led to the formation of the Adolescent Pregnancy

Prevention (APP) program, which reinstated Title V funding for abstinence education projects (Stewart 2012). Although the negotiations surrounding health care reform forced the Obama administration to backtrack on its anti-abstinence stance, the passage of the ACA did stipulate that federally funded abstinence education projects were required to adopt "evidence-based" and "medically accurate" curricular strategies. Additionally, the APP allocated a significant portion of Title V funding for a new Personal Responsibility Education Program (PREP), which provided states with grant money for projects that educated young people on both abstinence and contraception as a way of preventing pregnancy and the spread of HIV and other sexually transmitted infections (STIs).

Following suit with the administration's ongoing LGBT health promotion efforts, the first PREP funding opportunity announcement, released in August 2010, named "sexual minorities" among the at-risk youth that grantees could identify as their target populations and encouraged grantees, regardless of their intended targets, to consider the needs of LGBTQ youth when developing sexual health education programming. Earlier that year, in a letter to the president and congressional leaders, sexuality education advocates and major LGBT rights organizations (including Family Equality Council) had applauded the administration's defunding of abstinence initiatives, but they also expressed concern about how the TPP's myopic focus on pregnancy prevention threatened to alienate LGBTQ youth, diverted attention away from the issue of STIs and HIV/AIDS, and thus fell short in its stated aim of promoting healthy relationships for all young people.[56] The Obama administration's subsequent decision to prioritize LGBTQ youth in its call for PREP grant proposals may have been in response to these critiques and may have been facilitated by the program's official goals of preventing both pregnancies and the transmission of STIs and HIV.

That said, the push for more LGBT-affirming sexual health education must also be understood in relation to the growing body of research that was identifying LGBTQ youth as at higher risk for unintentionally becoming pregnant or causing unwanted pregnancies.[57] In other words, LGBTQ youth were gaining visibility within health promotion projects as reproductive subjects—the source of their "at-riskness" stemming not only from their nonprocreative sexual activity but also from their procreative potentiality. Such a realization did not, however, require a more substantive discussion about the complexity of erotic desire and identity formation and was instead easily folded into a broader narrative about the unruly nature of adolescence and the inherent riskiness of teen sexuality.[58] Under Obama, federally funded sexual health education programs sought to rehabilitate at-risk youth not just by providing lessons in risk reduction (executed via preaching abstinence and/or teaching contraception) but also by promoting monogamy, stable partnerships, and properly reproductive futures.

While it remains to be seen whether the legalization of same-sex marriage will eventually lead to the development of abstinence-only-until-marriage curricula for LGBTQ youth, the call for more LGBT-inclusive policies within PREP-funded programs has potentially facilitated the imposition of relational norms on queer and trans youth, albeit in slightly subtler ways.[59] Recipients of PREP grants were required to deliver educational programs that supplemented information about sexual health with lessons in what the HHS described as "adult preparation" subjects, including financial literacy, healthy relationship skills, and educational and career success. As such, PREP-funded initiatives were tasked with encouraging all youth, regardless of their gender identities or sexual orientations, to strive for economic self-sufficiency and to value sexual activity in the context of monogamous couplehood. More than simply affirming young LGBTQ lives, the Obama administration was arguably funding projects designed to channel same-sex adolescent desires toward marital and even parental futures. If properly rehabilitated, the queer and trans youth who are imagined to be at risk today might grow into risk-managing adults looking to plan weddings, hire financial advisors, and attend family-building expos. In attempting to relocate a population that has historically been marked for death over to the side of life, the state set out not simply to make queer and trans youth live but to make them live according to homonormative standards of citizenship—as properly desiring and personally responsible subjects committed to long-term partners and embedded in privatized networks of affective care and economic accountability.

Conclusion

•••••••••••••••••••••

Toward a Queer Family Politics

In this book, I have provided a detailed analysis of LGBT family politics in the United States. By tracing and contextualizing the recent history of family equality advocacy, I have elaborated upon the discursive limits and material effects of a rights-based project organized around the interests of an imagined two-parent LGBT-headed household. My hope has been to sharpen our understanding of the familial methods of social control currently at work and, in doing so, to lay the analytic groundwork needed for building broader and more just grassroots movements. To this end, I approached the rise and recent successes of family equality advocacy as conditioned by and constitutive of the neoliberal reconfiguration of U.S. racial and sexual politics. Rather than blaming LGBT-identified parents and their children for dulling the critical and sexual edge of queerness, I mapped the convergence of social, political, and economic forces that has enabled domesticated same-sex relations to be put to work for global capital, white supremacy, and U.S. nationalism.

It would thus be a mistake for scholars or activists to assume that a more transformative approach to queer organizing must necessarily distance itself from procreation and child rearing and excise any familial language from its vision for the future. In contrast, this book is far more interested in aligning with and cultivating a queer politics willing to engage in the work of resignifying and strategically deploying the family. To call upon the alternative genealogies of family-centric activism I highlighted in chapter 1—and to make queer demands for racial, sexual, and economic justice in the name of the family—opens possibilities for strengthening cross-movement alliances and waging intersectional critiquesagainst the white middle-class relational norms governing the distribution of wealth, resources, and other life chances. Despite all the trouble our various families have likely caused us and all the trouble we have tried to cause this category, family remains a meaningful concept, even for many of the crankiest queers I know, myself included. Building on these affective (if ambivalent) attachments, a queer family politics insists on the value of queer social formations at their most intimate levels and imagines strategies for maximizing the perversely reproductive potential residing within queer ways of life.

In many ways, to organize around the needs of families is to pose a significant challenge to the individualizing logics driving social movements in the early twenty-first century. Rather than lobbying the state on behalf of singular subjects in search of the symbolic protections afforded by identity-based rights, a queer approach to family politics takes relationality as its starting point and as such is premised not on a belief in autonomy but on lived experiences of interdependence. If organized around a more intentional refusal of the (neo)liberal fantasy of individualism, parent-centered activism can be forged in connection with other movements—such as queer elder organizing[1] and disability justice activism—that are working to secure the discursive space, material resources, and built environments needed to support the various networks of care that make our day-to-day lives possible. A queer family politics provides a framework for interrogating the ageism and ableism structuring LGBT rights organizing and family equality advocacy and, in doing so, opens space for reconceptualizing familiar issues and identifying new avenues for coalition building.

Take, for example, the ongoing "transgender bathroom" debates. Revolving primarily around bathroom access in public high schools and on university campuses, the debates often hinge on whether schools should permit transgender-identified students to use the bathroom corresponding to their gender identity or require them to use the bathroom that aligns with the sex designator on their birth certificate. (Notably, the narrow focus on school bathrooms limits the discussion of trans lives to a sympathetic and relatively privileged subject and effectively obscures the other sex-segregated sites of administrative violence that a disproportionate number of trans and gender-nonconforming people are forced to navigate, including prisons, juvenile detention centers, and homeless shelter systems.) The major U.S.-based LGBT organizations frame the bathroom question as an issue of individual rights for subjects assumed to identify as either transgender boys/men or transgender girls/women: the trans subject at the heart of this debate is always assumed to have transitioned from one gender to the other and thus poses no ideological challenge to the sex/gender binary system or to the idea of sex-segregated bathrooms. Alternatively, a queer family politics follows the lead of critical trans activists, who have long insisted that bathrooms can serve as a rallying point for building solidarities among people impacted by sex-segregated restrooms—such as parents with young children; disabled folks, elderly people, and others requiring assistance to use the facilities; and anyone who does not conform to white, middle-class, and able-bodied/able-minded standards of femininity and masculinity.[2] The goal of such coordinated efforts would be to demand more all-gender bathrooms and more spacious single-stall options as a way of transforming the architectural structures that naturalize normative conceptions of gender and sexual difference and that threaten to interfere with our intimate and interdependent lives. Parenthood, as a subject position, can be a productive place from which to politicize the otherwise depoliticized family bathroom, to lay bare the subversive ways in which these spaces are already being used, and to interrogate the ethics of mediating access to public space via sex-segregated bathrooms. In addition to striving to create material environments more accommodating to a wide range of familial configurations, however, a queer family politics also advocates for the development of public programs and community-based structures designed to subsidize or in some way support the various relational forms that perform the affective and reproductive labor on which society depends.

As queer feminists like Nancy Polikoff, Terry Boggis, Paula Ettelbrick, and others have consistently argued, one of the primary goals of family-centric queer organizing is to provide immediate relief for the families and communities enduring the greatest violences at the hands of the capitalist state. While this kind of work prioritizes supporting community-based survival networks and mass mobilizations led by poor families, undocumented immigrants, people who are or have been incarcerated, and other highly vulnerable populations, the project of trying to make more lives more livable is further served by putting pressure on administrative governing bodies and strategically making policy-oriented demands. Heeding Dean Spade's call for a reconceptualization of the role law reform might play within queer and trans politics, we can begin to appreciate activist projects striving to intervene on the "legal and administrative systems of domination" that control the lives of racially, sexually, and economically marginalized populations (2011, 13). Such an approach breaks from the mainstream movement's obsession with securing a formal "pronouncement of equality from various government institutions" (28) and focuses instead on the distributive functions of the law that determine "who lives, for how long, and under what conditions" (26). Given the ways in which the family—as a set of gender, sexual, and relational norms—continues to govern which intimate social relations are deemed deserving of state recognition and granted access to the limited pool of public resources, one way of trying to reduce the harm caused by an increasingly militarized and rapidly shrinking welfare state is to fight even harder for more contextual and individualized frameworks for recognizing familial relations.

When reaching toward an abolitionist future where prisons, imperialism, border control, and private property no longer exist, activists demanding a reorganization of public policies around broader definitions of family can emphasize the ways in which such efforts serve the interests of all communities marginalized by the tyranny of marital family norms—which, as this book has shown, includes poor, trans, queer, disabled, nonwhite, indigenous, and/or immigrant populations. A queer family politics insists on defining family not according to blood or legal ties but in ways that privilege self-determination and mutual dependence. In addition to unhinging familial recognition from marital status, such efforts can challenge the assumption that family life must be organized around monogamous couplehood or even around erotic attachments at all. With a definition of family like this in place, eligibility for public assistance programs like Medicaid, TANF, or SSI would, as the *All Children Matter* report that I discussed in chapter 4 explains, turn not on the question of conjugality but instead on family size and demonstrated need. Within the realm of immigration law, as organizers working at the nexus of queer and migration politics have argued, the adoption of a more capacious understanding of family would disrupt the heteronormativity of border control practices and open space for family reunification policies willing to recognize the contingent networks of kinship and friendship in which many immigrants, particularly queer and trans immigrants, live.[3] In short, rather than eschewing the family as a repressively normative institution at odds with an ethical commitment to a redistributive politics, it is possible to mobilize the family as a way of demanding recognition differently—that is, as a way of moving beyond identitarian calls for recognition in the form of consumer or political rights and toward broad-based calls for recognition in the form of material support for the interpersonal connections on which our collective survival depends.

Central to this kind of movement, I want to suggest, is an insistence on the value of caretaking networks, even and especially in their most perverse forms. While the immediate goal of developing broader frameworks for familial recognition may be to provide more families with material support and a sense of security, one of the unintended effects of moving closer to the deregulation of sex, gender, and intimacy is the enhancement of family settings that might be conducive to what Eve Sedgwick would call "gay generation" or what I want to think of as a proliferation of perversity (1991, 26).[4] With respect to the social networks that support the labor of child rearing, I am very willing to entertain the ways in which the relationships between and the sexual identities of parental figures *do* indeed matter and *can* affect the erotic and relational futures of children. In her critical exploration of queer kinship and perverse domesticity, Juana María Rodríguez reflects on the role families play in teaching children the "social rules and significance that govern touch, eye contact, movement through space, and all other manner of seemingly mundane corporeal action" (2014, 29). In doing so, she reminds us of the formative (and potentially transformative) nature of kinship relations: the intimate and often seemingly ordinary gestures of parenting, while surely not the sole force at work, play a vital role in the shaping of social and sexual subjects. With the generative function of familial scenes in mind, parenthood seems not, as some might fear, to signal the end of queerness but instead to mark its new beginnings.

Rather than turning away from the realms of procreation and child rearing, what if we approach reproductive life as a potential site for "queer world-making"?[5] In other words, the struggle to access material support for families in all their diversity can double as the struggle toward a future filled with more erotic variety and greater gender variance. To be clear, I have no desire to turn all children into homosexuals, nor am I under any illusion that such an unimaginative project is even possible; in distinction, I invoke Gayle Rubin's language of erotic variety as a way of pushing past "a simple hetero-homo opposition" and reaching for "sexual diversity" in terms of conduct, practices, and living or inanimate objects of desire (Rubin 2011, 284, 292). Similarly, a call for greater gender variance should not be misread as a demand for more transgender children. In contrast, I am invested in interrogating the practice of implanting medicalized notions of transness in increasingly younger bodies and effectively subjecting them to the same coercive systems of gender regulation forced upon nontrans children. How might we instead imagine more creative ways of encouraging gender nonconformity and bodily self-determination among children? A queer family politics can and must do better when it comes to doing sex, gender, and sexuality.

Moving beyond the rhetoric of affirmation that tends to dominate progressive discussions about LGBT youth—within this narrative framework, young people discover their gender and sexual identities at an appropriate age and are then "accepted" by open-minded parental figures who guide them in developing a sense of pride[6]—we might instead consider prioritizing the intentional cultivation of perversity among children. Parents and organizers might invest in collaboratively developing parenting approaches and domestic styles designed to nurture erotic curiosity and to foster open-ended experiences of bodily exploration and identity formation. Put another way, a queer family politics would not just acknowledge the perverse effects of destabilizing familial norms but actually insist on the value of gender variance and sexual variety. But—and this point is crucial—gender and sexual diversity alone are not enough.

There is nothing inherently transgressive or transformative about queerness or gender nonconformity. Consequently, it is necessary to devise strategies for putting perversity to work in "resisting the construction of the world in terms most suited to the prevailing economic system" (Jakobsen 2012, 32). In her essay "Perverse Justice," Janet Jakobsen explores the radical potential of "queer relationality" in producing subjectivities not easily reconciled with neoliberal discourses of individualism and personal responsibility (34). Her interest in "queer sex" focuses her attention on lives organized outside the bounds of traditional family life—namely, public sex cultures, lesbian networks of ex-lovers, and the "buddy system" developed in response to the AIDS crisis— but we can also consider the ways in which nonnormative parenting arrangements might generate perverse ways of inhabiting the world and building collective networks of interdependency. The strengthening of a queerer and more diverse array of families with children—families that might do gender differently, that might span multiple generations or multiple households, and that might provide models for single parenting, polyamorous parenting relationships, or coparenting agreements among exes or friends—could potentially interrupt the reproduction of privatized family desires. A queer family politics approaches the work of raising children as a potential site for radical intervention, for instilling an anticapitalist ethical vision in the next generation, and for inciting perverse desires and embodiments that could lay the affective groundwork for assembling intimate socialities at odds with the forms of subjectivity and relationality on which neoliberal capitalism and U.S. imperial interests depend.

This is not, however, to suggest that parents should have complete access to or could even exercise total control over their children's intimate lives. Rather, I am committed to protecting what Judith Levine names as the "sexual-intellectual autonomy" of young people and to finding ways for parents and other adults to provide children, from a very young age, with the emotional space, physical privacy, and age-appropriate knowledge needed to explore their own bodies and desires (2002, 111). To this end—and in line with chapter 3's exploration of a queer family politics invested in forging intergenerational solidarities—family advocates might work to support youth-led sexual health education efforts and to zero in on those initiatives that are effectively designed to breed perversity among young people. As part of the larger struggle for universal access to mental health support, reproductive health services, and nonhomophobic and gender-confirming health care, community organizers have been working to supply youth, especially racially, sexually, and economically marginalized youth, with sex-positive information about sex and social justice.

Two projects of this kind come immediately to mind: the Fierce Youth Reclaiming and Empowering (FYRE) program of SPARK Reproductive

Justice Now, which aims to "amplify" the power and leadership of "lesbian, gay, bi, trans, same gender loving and questioning young people of color" living in the U.S. South,[7] and the Native Youth Sexual Health Network (NYSHN), which is an organization "by and for Indigenous youth that works across issues of sexual and reproductive health, rights, and justice throughout the United States and Canada."[8] Both of these projects have organized innovative sexual health education initiatives: FYRE published the resource zine *Fire: Sparking the Flames in Each Other* about "sex, sexuality, dating and relationships, how to be an ally, safety, and more!" (2010, 1), and NYSHN regularly runs "Sexy Health Carnivals" as a way of combatting fear and shame among Native youth and educating them about STIs, birth control, sexual violence, and queer issues and Two-Spirit roles.[9] In addition to offering lessons in safety and harm reduction (for young people engaging in sex work, casual sexual encounters, or long-term partnerships) and in techniques of pleasure (while keeping in mind questions of dis/ability and access needs), these initiatives encourage young people to understand their intimate lives as embedded within larger structures of power and to approach the issue of sexual health as bound up with assertions of Native sovereignty, calls for environmental justice, and resistance against racism and state violence. Given their insistence on the entanglement of one's personal happiness and emotional satisfaction with broader cultural, political, and economic forces, both FYRE and NYSHN frame bodily and sexual self-determination as achieved not by individuals but in the context of supportive friendship circles and community formations. A queer family politics would strive to support, secure resources for, or by some means work in solidarity with these kinds of youth-led initiatives as a way of opening up new ways of being, practicing kinship, and creating community.

What I find particularly exciting about young people helping one another to build stronger and more creative networks of love and care is the fact that they are offering lessons in intimacy that interrupt the work of federally funded projects tasked, as I explained in the last chapter, with delivering "relationship education" to vulnerable youth populations. By talking about desire and dating in historicized and contextualized ways, sexual health education projects, like those led by FYRE and NYSHN, provide children and teenagers with a more expansive vocabulary for describing their various social connections and with alternative models for valuing and giving meaning to their different relationships. Unlike the formulaic and narrowly conceived LGBT family life script that, as I discussed in chapter 2, I was prescribed aboard my R Family cruise, the sex ed initiatives I see as central to a queer family politics encourage young people to develop individualized narratives for mapping their past and present intimate lives. Within this framework, social and sexual futures are seen as open-ended and as always in process.

Such initiatives neither begin with the presumption that sexual activity is, at every age, best contained within a committed partnership nor operate under the assumption that all youth are longing for an adult life organized around marriage, parenthood, and homeownership. Instead, they insist on the value of erotic experimentation as a way of exploring attractions, expressing and experimenting with gender, and enjoying the embodied and emotional pleasures of sex and intimacy. Pushing back against the heteronormative romance narrative, a sex-positive and queerly inflected sexual health education project would actively refuse the mandate that, each time we take a new lover, we need to downplay (if not downright erase) our previous partners. In distinction, a queer family politics would teach youth—and empower youth to teach each other—the "long [queer] history of loving and living differently" and invite them to inhabit alternative geographies and temporalities of desire and commitment (Rodríguez 2014, 53). Parent-focused organizing might work in solidarity with youth-led community initiatives to disrupt what, following Spade, we might think of as the scarcity model of love and romance. While prevalent beliefs about romantic partnership and long-term monogamy turn on an understanding of affection as a limited resource—as if each of us "only has a certain amount of attention or attraction or love or interest, and if any of it goes to someone besides [our] partner, [our] partner must lose out"[10]—a queerer style of "relationship education" insists that we are capable of generating an unlimited degree of love and care that we can extend to our primary partners, to our other partners, to former and potential lovers, and no less importantly, to the friends who play an equally substantial role in sustaining us. In short, a queer family politics strives to pervert the next generation by encouraging young people to call into question the idea that a privatized version of family life could ever really fulfill all our erotic and nonerotic desires.

To destabilize the primacy of the nuclear family is to challenge the white supremacist capitalist logics governing our psychic and affective lives and, in the process, to resist neoliberalism's attempted annihilation of collectivity and mutual responsibility. The work of encouraging young people to imagine family in more flexible and contextual ways—and to expect their networks of love and support to shift over the course of their lifetimes—has the potential not only to incite more opportunities for erotic exploration but also to inspire a reconceptualization of ethical obligations. In this light, sexual health education initiatives might serve as a key site for intervening on how young people think about the material aspects of their intimate lives—namely, how they might organize their economic interdependencies and approach the practices of saving and spending money. As unsexy as this might sound, a queer family politics might find value in pairing lessons in sex positivity with a radical style of financial literacy instruction. To be clear, I am neither proposing the incorporation of disciplinary lectures on the importance of savings plans and debt avoidance nor calling for seminars on cultivating investment portfolios or risk management skills. But what a queer family project might do is facilitate the forms of knowledge production and exchange already taking place among economically vulnerable communities. Organizers might look for ways to back or develop community-based programs where the young and the old can teach each other strategies for managing their money otherwise—for collectively pooling and distributing their resources; for assembling cooperative caretaking arrangements for children, sick people, disabled folks, and aging family members; and for maintaining shared emergency funds for handling medical or housing crises within local communities. Such efforts support the development of practical skills for navigating a capitalist landscape in the name of erotic and ethical attachments that exceed the marital family form and according to a set of principles that refuses to be bound by capital's privatizing logics and thus values collective sustenance over individual accumulation.

By way of conclusion, I have illuminated how a queer approach to family-centered organizing could potentially enliven coalitional movements for racial, sexual, and economic justice.[11] The work of challenging white, abled, and middle-class relational norms might allow for a more equitable availability of wealth and resources, but this redistribution of life chances still takes place according to the terms of capital and in line with the multicultural settler state's exploitative modes of domination. If, however, we insist on the fact of relationality, in all its perversity, and on our mutual interdependencies, which defy the normative rules of kinship, then our organizing efforts might hold out more transformative possibilities. To actively cultivate creative and expansive modes of family life may prove an effective strategy for dislodging marital family norms and for unsettling the very foundations of racial capitalism and the imperial sexual and social order. To this end, the queer family project of trying to transform our material and discursive conditions must aim not just to sustain but, crucially, to spawn and strengthen more perverse ways of being, belonging, and building families.

Acknowledgments

As I close this book about families, I'd like to acknowledge my own immediate one. I am very lucky to have been born into a wonderful network of love, care, and humor. My parents, Kathie and Kevin Montegary, have been an unwavering source of support for my decidedly "uncool" pursuits for as long as I can remember. I'm not sure I will ever have the words to adequately thank them. My sisters by chance, Katie and Nicole, are my friends by choice, and I couldn't live (let alone write) without them. Their respective partners, Tony Sessa and Pat Cucci, have been solid additions to the mix. My aunts, uncles, and cousins never cease to amaze me with their seemingly limitless generosity and kindness, and my grandmother, Jackie Tabacsko (a.k.a. Nanny Scoop), is simply the best. Finally, a shout-out to the smallest members of my family, who regularly remind me just how unruly childhood can and should be: Talia, Anthony, and Rosalie Arecchi; Krissy, Ellie, and Joey Tabacsko; and last but certainly not least, my kid best friend Mila Robcis.

At the University of California, Davis, I had the pleasure of completing my PhD in the cultural studies program. Working with Caren Kaplan as a graduate student was a true honor. She taught me a lot about the practicalities of being an interdisciplinary scholar, but perhaps more important, she taught me what it means to be a mentor. Over the years, as Caren was honing my feminist capacities for materialist critique, Juana María Rodríguez was pushing me to think about desire in wilder and more utopian ways. I like to think that *Familiar Perversions* brings together Caren's and Juana's competing visions for a queer cultural studies and, in doing so, reveals their ostensibly divergent approaches to be quite complementary of one another. During my early years at Davis, Gayatri Gopinath was also a key advisor. Additionally, I learned a great deal from Omnia El Shakry, Nicole Fleetwood, Elizabeth Freeman, Laura Grindstaff, Luz Mena, Rhacel Parreñas, Eric Smoodin, and Carolyn Thomas. It was also at this time when I first met Deborah Cohler and Inderpal Grewal, who have remained important mentors in my life. My sincerest thanks to what was then the Consortium for Women and Research for providing me with the funding to conduct ethnographic research aboard Rosie O'Donnell's gay family cruise. I may not have realized it at the time, but that trip sparked an interest in LGBT family politics that would become the genesis for this book.

I am proud to be a part of a broader community of Davis cult studs engaged in transformative work in and out of the academy. I want to thank the friends I made in grad school who played a formative role in my life (and who continue to be the reason I attend conferences): Toby Beauchamp, Tallie Ben Daniel, Santiago Castellanos, Cyn Degnan, Sandy Gómez, Cathy Hannabach, Tristan Josephson, Nick Mitchell, Christina Owens, Magalí Rabasa, and Kara Thompson. Many thanks to Toby and Tallie for their careful readings of parts of this manuscript and to Cathy and the Ideas on Fire team for working their index magic on this project. Extra appreciation to Tristan, who has refused to allow the three thousand miles currently separating us to interfere with our friendship. He is a model teacher, a righteous scholar, and an award-winning friend. I am also thankful for the wider circle of friends—both old and new—who have been there for me over the past few years: Lezlie Frye, Julie Garren, Adam Hale, Bret Hanlon, Eli Kim, Judy Massis-Sanchez, Micah Mitrosky, Kryst Muroya, Yasmine Orangi, Maile Thiesen, Emily Thuma, and Talya Zemach-Bersin. Em deserves special recognition for the time and thought she has dedicated to my manuscript. Her advice and insights have been invaluable.

At Stony Brook University, I have once again found myself surrounded by an inspiring community of thinkers and teachers. My colleagues in what is now the Department of Women's, Gender, and Sexuality Studies are nothing short of spectacular. The junior faculty with whom I started, Kadji Amin, Melissa Forbis, and Nancy Hiemstra, are among the most excellent people I know, and our senior colleagues, Mary Jo Bona, Ritch Calvin, Lisa Diedrich, Victoria Hesford, and Teri Tiso have been astoundingly generous (and hilarious) with their mentorship. A special thanks to Lisa and my other official mentor, Pamela Block, for taking their titles seriously and providing me with guidance and encouragement at every turn. I am also grateful for the number of people at Stony Brook who have become my friends, who have shown support for queer and feminist scholarship, or who I have come to know through what, against all odds, continues to be a vibrant humanities presence on campus: Tim August, Nerissa Balce, Lena Burgos-Lafuente, Daniela Flesler, Michele Friedner, Sohl Lee, Shirley Lim, Sara Lipton, Kristina Lucenko, Celia Marshik, Andrew Newman, Elizabeth Newman, Anne O'Byrne, Adrián Pérez-Melgosa, Joseph Pierce, Donna Rilling, Jeffrey Santa Ana, Susan Scheckel,

Katherine Sugg, Chris Tanaka, Nancy Tomes, and Kathleen Wilson. As a Faculty Fellow at the Humanities Institute at Stony Brook, I spent a semester immersed in this rich intellectual community while completing the research for this book. Thank you to the Offices of the President and the Provost for funding such an opportunity.

The students I have worked with here at Stony Brook and on other campuses inspire me as a writer and a teacher. A special thanks to the undergraduates who took my special topics course, Sex, Politics, Families, in springs 2015 and 2016. Our classroom conversations pushed my thinking in new directions and, in the process, made this a stronger book. I am also indebted to Rachel Corbman for graciously sharing her "herstorical" expertise and for making me want to become both a better lesbian and a more rigorous historian.

Many thanks to Leslie Mitchner, my editor at Rutgers University Press, who saw the potential in this project at a very early stage and whose persistent enthusiasm helped me stay the course. I am also thankful to Kim Guinta, Alissa Zarro, Bethany Luckenbach, and the rest of the Rutgers team for shepherding this project through the final stages. I am super grateful that the press secured such an outstanding reviewer for my manuscript. Christina Hanhardt's incredibly generative feedback reflected her careful engagement with my writing as well as her investment in the work of mentoring. She went above and beyond her role as reviewer and took the time to meet with me in person to discuss my revision plans. I know that I cannot properly thank her for her labor, but I can at least promise to pay it forward when I get the chance.

Finally, this book would not have been possible without Benjamin D'Harlingue and Abigail Boggs. Ben read every word of this book, often more than once. He knew what it was about long before I did, even though he kept trying to tell me. He regularly crawled inside my head, cleared things up, and then cracked me up before sending me back to work. In many ways, Abbie is the reason this book was written. I am referring, in part, to the fact that she is the one who first pointed me toward O'Donnell's cruises and persuaded me to take up questions of parenting, but more than that, she has been my person—an endless and essential source of emotional and intellectual support. I take full responsibility for the shortcomings of this book, but I will gladly share any of its successes with these two.

My deepest thanks are reserved for Yael Kropsky, who witnessed my writing process and somehow still manages to like me. Her patience, encouragement, and refusal to take academia all that seriously mean the world to me. I don't know how she did it, but she gave me the space I needed while always being right there. Becoming familiar with Yael over the past five years has not only brought me more happiness and laughter than I knew possible but also broadened the horizons of what I want from life in the most wonderfully perverse ways. These days, she is pretty much my favorite.

Notes

Introduction

1   During the late 1990s, as the acronym LGBT was becoming increasingly common, the language of "LGBT families" started circulating in the scholarly literature about the merits of lesbian, gay, and bisexual parenting. In 1998, the national nonprofit organization Gay and Lesbian Parents Coalition International changed its name to Family Pride Coalition and, shortly after, started officially focusing on "LGBT family issues." The term "LGBT families" became increasingly popular in the lesbian and gay press over the course of the 2000s and, by the end of the decade, was crossing over into mainstream media publications.

2   In the spring of 2014, Chevy, Nabisco, and Coca-Cola launched television ad campaigns designed to capitalize on the popularity of pro-LGBT family positions while also tapping into a niche within a niche market (Merevick 2014). These much-talked-about commercials followed an almost identical formula: a montage tribute to the "wholesome" diversity of American families featuring a few shots of same-sex partners and their children alongside footage of (presumably hetero-sexual) extended families, interracial couples, and single parents.

3   This sentence requires unpacking. First, I would like to comment on my use of the word "queer" here and throughout this book. On occasion, as in this sentence, I use the term to signal sexual subjects or activist projects that exceed the parameters of lesbian, gay, bisexual, and/or transgender. More often, however, I use the term to describe a theoretical and methodological approach that analyzes the mutually constitutive relationship between gender and sexual norms, racial and ethnic hierar-chies, class divisions and capitalist structures, and dominant standards of health and dis/ability. Second, I want to clarify this particular sentence. On the one hand, my reference to dying queers is a way of marking the tragically overwhelming number of lives that were lost to AIDS-related complications across the 1980s and into the 1990s. On the other hand, my allusion to "dying in the streets" is meant to recall the innovative strategies deployed by AIDS activists during this period, such as the "die ins" where activists from the AIDS Coalition to Unleash Power (ACT UP) protested the lack of FDA-approved drugs by lying in the streets holding make-shift tombstones above their heads. By juxtaposing a collective political action organized

around death alongside private family-centered, life-making consumer activities, this sentence is intended to flag the shift that has taken place within LGBT (political) culture over the past few decades and that I explore in great detail in the chapters that follow.

4 I am referring specifically to the body of work that emerged around Lee Edelman's critique of assimilatory LGBT rights projects in *No Future* (2004). Reviving what has come to be known as the antisocial thesis, Edelman follows Leo Bersani (1995) in locating the efficacy of queerness, which he understands as representing an unwaveringly nonprocreative force, in its inherent incompatibility with civic life and the social order. The only ethical way of figuring queer, according to this logic, is via a refusal of relationality and a rejection of the lure of reproductivity and the very idea of futurity. Responses to Edelman's polemical denouncement of lesbian and gay respectability politics have, generally speaking, taken two different forms. Some queer studies scholars have embraced his call for political negativity (albeit without necessarily embracing the psychoanalytic underpinnings of his original thesis). Jack Halberstam exemplifies such a perspective in his work on the "queer art of failure" (2011) and in his theorization of queer temporalities as residing intentionally and aggressively outside the temporal frames of birth, marriage, reproduction, inheritance, and normative family life (2005). In contrast, other scholars, especially queer of color critics, have taken issue with the uncritical and racially privileged romanticization of negativity undergirding calls for an abandonment of the future. José Esteban Muñoz (2009), most notably, answers the antisocial thesis by drawing on a well-established tradition of critical idealism to put forth a vision of queerness as a collective longing and struggle for a different and better future to come. What strikes me about these calls for a queer politics that is resistant to uncritical attachments to reproductive forms of futurity is the way in which the figure of the LGBTQ-identified parent haunts the conversation without ever making an actual appearance. Parenthood serves as the constitutive outside for the queer subcultural formations emerging out of a politics of negativity, and the queer social worlds conjured up via a politics of utopianism make room for queer and trans youth of color without asking after the work of parenting and raising children. One of my goals in this book is to ask what we might gain if we center parenting in our critical analyses. What can be learned through a closer examination of the place of parents and parenthood within mainstream LGBT rights organizing? And what queer political possibilities become available if we refuse to distance our projects from parenting relationships and other intergenerational networks of care?

5 There are two notable exceptions to this trend in the field of queer studies. I return to the work of these scholars later and throughout this book, but here I want to note the ways in which their critiques of mainstream U.S.-based LGBT politics stand out in their explicit engagement with questions of parenthood. In *The Feeling of Kinship*, David Eng (2010) contextualizes the development of a pragmatic rights-based lesbian and gay agenda with respect to the historical construction of intimacy as the property of white settler subjects and, in doing so, brings into focus the racialized forms of labor that undergird the fantasy of privacy and that make possible legal demands for same-sex relationship recognition. Turning his attention to the late-capitalist practice of transnational adoption from Asia, he considers the role that white lesbian and gay couples from the United States are playing in the emergence of what he calls "the new global family" (97). He shows how, for these couples, access to full and robust citizenship depends on their status as parents

and as such on their exploitation of the psychic and affective labor of Asian girl children. In *Sexual Futures, Queer Gestures, and Other Latina Longings*, Juana María Rodríguez (2014) also takes up the question of queer adoption practices and racialized forms of trauma. But in pushing back against what she sees as Eng's exceptionalization of these practices, she situates transracial and transnational adoption in relation to the psychic harms enacted by all forms of domestic life and the structural violences that all families must endure under neoliberalism. More broadly, her work builds on Muñoz's theorization of queerness as collectivity to provide a model for conceptualizing domesticity—and parenting in particular—as a mode of queer sociality. Taking as her starting point the erotic pleasures and possibilities of racialized female subjects, her decidedly feminist approach to exploring the politics of queer relationalities draws her into the world of kinship and opens space for entertaining the family's potential as a vehicle for moving us closer to "another kind of sexual future" (1).

6 For an overview of the psychological and sociological research on gay and lesbian parenting since the early 1980s, visit the online research portal of Columbia Law School's "What We Know" Project dedicated to the question "What does the scholarly research say about the wellbeing of children with gay or lesbian parents?" The project staff, under the leadership of director Nathaniel Frank and principal investigator Katherine Franke, has compiled a list of (and links to) the seventy-nine most credible, relevant, and useful studies on gay and lesbian parenting in order to illustrate the "overwhelming scholarly consensus, based on over three decades of peer-reviewed research, that having a gay or lesbian parent does not harm children" (http://whatweknow.law.columbia.edu/topics/lgbt-equality/what-does-the-scholarly -research-say-about-the-wellbeing-of-children-with-gay-or-lesbian-parents/).

7 See, for example, Ellen Lewin's *Lesbian Mothers* (1993) and *Gay Fatherhood* (2009), Mignon Moore's *Invisible Families* (2011), Aaron Goodfellow's *Gay Fathers, Their Children, and the Making of Kinship* (2015), and Joshua Gamson's *Modern Families* (2015).

8 I am very grateful for the historical foundation that Daniel Rivers's *Radical Relations* (2013) has laid for contemporary studies of LGBT family politics. Drawing upon extensive archival research and oral history interviews, he tells the story of lesbian and gay parenting in the United States since World War II, and he illuminates the different paths through which lesbian- and gay-identified adults became parents and the different ways they contested, negotiated, and reimagined queerness's antagonistic relationship to the family. In his celebratory account of the shifting focus of lesbian and gay activism during the latter half of the twentieth century, Rivers casts parents and children as heroically pushing domestic rights and family advocacy to the fore of LGBT political projects. The narrative he crafts, while complex and highly detailed, neither interrogates the broader social context nor asks after the ramifications of this shift in activist focus; as such, his work invites further scholarly analysis of this important history. Additionally, I have learned a great deal from several collections on queer family politics that offer historical snapshots of different periods by featuring critically reflective essays by LGBTQ-identified parents and their children, including editors Noelle Howey and Ellen Samuels's *Out of the Ordinary* (2000), editors Mary Bernstein and Renate Reimann's *Queer Families, Queer Politics* (2001), and editor Rachel Epstein's *Who's Your Daddy?* (2009).

9 This book is, first and foremost, inspired by Nancy Polikoff's extensive career as a lawyer, legal advocate, and critical legal studies scholar. Her book *Beyond*

(Straight and Gay) Marriage (2008) has been instrumental in shaping my vision for a queer family politics. Other excellent examples of critical legal scholarship on LGBT family politics include Kimberly Richman's analysis of judicial decisions concerning the rights of lesbian and gay parents in *Courting Change* (2009) and Stewart (Stu) Marvel's recent work on queer kinship and assisted reproductive technologies (2015). Further, my critiques of public policy and the law have been sharpened thanks to work emerging out of the field of political theory, such as Valerie Lehr's *Queer Family Values* (1999) and Anna Marie Smith's smart analyses of welfare reform and sexual regulation (2001, 2007, 2009).

10 In their preface to the thirty-fifth anniversary edition of *Policing the Crisis* (2013), Stuart Hall, Chas Critcher, Tony Jefferson, John Clarke, and Brian Roberts reflect on the ethnographic impulses that drove the work of the Centre for Contemporary Cultural Studies at the University of Birmingham. While they shared the traditional ethnographer's desire to develop "a detailed empirical knowledge of a particular 'social world,'" their method for apprehending the structural configurations surrounding concrete events, practices, and relationships was not via interviews but by "wading through mounds of newspapers," "reading masses of secondary material," and "living and working in the 'social world'" in question (xi–xii). In their attempt to "emulate the ethnographic imagination," they "move[d] beyond the focus on the here and now of everyday 'interactions and practices' by locating them in the histories taking place behind all our backs" (xi). *Familiar Perversions* follows in the methodological footsteps of the Birmingham school and engages in a similarly ethnographic study of LGBT family politics in the United States.

11 In *Cultural Studies in the Future Tense*, Lawrence Grossberg returns to what he views as the foundational texts of the field to historically ground his vision for cultural studies as a "radically contextual and conjuncturalist practice" (2010, 3). Specifically, he turns to *Policing the Crisis*—as well as to several other essays in which Hall clarifies their political and intellectual goals in that project—to show how a figure like the mugger and an event like a mugging serve as the starting point for studying the convergence of historical, economic, and political forces that can make such a figure and such an event possible in that particular moment (26). As Hall explains in "Cultural Composition" (1998b), a cultural studies project approaches "race and crime" as "a prism for a much larger social crisis" (quoted in Grossberg 2010, 20): "I have never worked on race and ethnicity as a kind of subcategory," he writes in "Aspirations and Attitude" (1998a). "I have always worked on the whole social formation which is racialized" (quoted in Grossberg 2010, 21). In a similar vein, *Familiar Perversions* takes the figure of the LGBT family and the practice of family equality advocacy as a starting point for figuring out the precise historical conjuncture and the specific forms of power that have made this figure possible and this practice (relatively) successful. The task of a queer cultural studies project, as I see it, is not to merely apply the contextual moves of cultural studies to cultural practices and productions that might be described as queer (i.e., practices and productions obviously connected to LGBTQ-identified individuals or communities). Rather, to modify the project of cultural studies with the language of queer is to signal a methodological investment in analyzing the racialization and sexualization of the whole social formation.

12 Here I am referencing Inderpal Grewal and Caren Kaplan's field-(trans)forming collection *Scattered Hegemonies* (1994). My work is indebted to the body of

work that has grown out of their call for historicized modes of analysis that can acknowledge how feminist—and, as they later add, queer (Grewal and Kaplan 2001)—practices of resistance are always forged in relation to the nation-state and embedded within global economic structures. This book builds on their vision for a transnational feminist cultural studies that, by deploying feminist (and, I will add, queer) theory to bridge the conceptual divides between Marxist and poststructuralist thought, can develop a nuanced theory of power capable of accounting for political-economic conditions without reproducing the masculinism and economic determinism of classically leftist critiques (Kaplan and Grewal 1994).

13 See, for example, Lisa Duggan's *The Twilight of Equality?* (2003), Roderick Ferguson's *Aberrations in Black* (2004), Jasbir Puar's *Terrorist Assemblages* (2007), David Eng's *The Feeling of Kinship* (2010), Chandan Reddy's *Freedom with Violence* (2011), and Christina Hanhardt's *Safe Space* (2013). With the exception of Duggan's slim volume (which strikes an intentionally polemical tone), this body of work models a mode of queer analysis that seeks not just to evaluate Leftist strategies and queer activist ideologies but to contextualize the development of those strategies and ideologies within the broader field of political economy and cultural politics. *Familiar Perversions* is indebted to this brilliant scholarship and engages in a similar study of LGBT and queer political culture. Additionally, while this book departs in style and method from more activist-focused critiques of U.S.-based LGBT rights organizing, I am very much inspired by the political visions put forth in Dean Spade's *Normal Life* (2011); Joey Mogul, Andrea Ritchie, and Kay Whitlock's *Queer Injustices* (2011); and Ryan Conrad's edited collection *Against Equality* (2014).

14 I would like to thank Christina Hanhardt for helping me clarify what I am trying to do in this book and why this kind of analytical work is important. I am referring broadly to the extremely generous and thoughtful feedback she offered on my manuscript, but I also want to mark this specific sentence as inspired by the way she describes her own methodological approach in her introduction to *Safe Space* (2013, 27–28).

15 Starting in the 1950s and 1960s, the U.S. family welfare system began using the term "special needs" to refer to a range of children who the state believed would be difficult to place with foster parents. This category includes older children, children of color, sets of siblings, and children who are ill or who have cognitive or physical disabilities. For more on LGBT adoption practices and the figure of the "hard-to-place" child, see Briggs (2012) and Romesburg (2014). In chapter 2, I offer a more sustained analysis of where the practice of fostering to adopt figures into family equality advocacy.

16 According to Gates's most recent estimates, "States with the highest proportions of same-sex couples raising biological, adopted, or step children include Mississippi (26%), Wyoming (25%), Alaska (23%), Idaho (22%), and Montana (22%)" (2013, 1).

17 For more on queer aspirations to normative citizenship in the United States, see Brandzel (2016). In *Against Citizenship*, Brandzel outlines a critique of citizenship as a "violent exclusionary operation" that "relies upon and reproduces a multi-pronged, gatekeeping apparatus that works to create, retain, and imbue citizenship with meaning at the direct expense of the noncitizen" (5).

18 Jasbir Puar first coined the term "homonationalism" in her 2006 essay "Mapping US Homonormativities" and then developed the concept in her 2007 book *Terrorist Assemblages*. A few years later, in response to some of the ways in which scholars have taken up the term, she clarified the meaning of the concept and offered what

I find to be her most helpful discussion of homonationalism. In her 2013 essay "Homonationalism as Assemblage," she stresses that we must not reduce homonationalism to an identity or a position or act as though certain activities or practices can be named as such and then accusatorily attributed to specific organizations or nation-states (25). Rather, homonationalism functions as an analytic for apprehending a newly configured field of power and for tracking the uneven and unpredictable shifts taking place within the structures of modernity. To think of homonationalism as an assemblage allows us to understand the successes and consequences of LGBT rights movements in relation to "a convergence of geopolitical and historical forces, neoliberal interests in capitalist accumulation both cultural and material, biopolitical state practices of population control, and affective investments in discourses of freedom, liberation, and rights" (2013, 39).

19 See, for example, Scott Lauria Morgensen's theorization of "settler homonationalism" and his analysis of how the ongoing colonization of the Americas conditions U.S.-based lesbian and gay politics in *Spaces between Us* (2011) or the critical examination of both the subtle and the spectacular "death-making" projects that, under late capitalism, engulf entire populations marked as racially and sexually abject in the collection *Queer Necropolitics* (2014).

20 For more on sexual violence and U.S. settler colonialism, see Smith (2005) and Deer (2015). See Hartman (1997, ch. 3) for a detailed study of rape and sexual exploitation as modes of terror and subjection within the context of slavery in the United States, and see Morgan (2004) for a historical analysis of how the management of enslaved women's reproductive capacities figured into the organization of slave labor.

21 See Goeman and Denetdale (2009) and Barker (2017) for excellent examples of how Native feminist scholars have brought critical gender and sexuality studies perspectives to bear on theorizing colonization in North America.

22 For more on how Western kinship norms facilitated the assault on Native governance and self-determination, see Rifkin (2011).

23 Black feminist thinkers have written extensively about the social construction of black masculinity and femininity and the production of blackness as an always already sexually deviant formation. See, for example, Davis (1983), Lorde (1984), Carby (1987), Spillers (1987), and Collins (2000).

24 See Hunter (2017) for a detailed history of how African Americans reworked Christian marriage traditions and practiced flexible forms of family and kinship under slavery.

25 For more on the history of antimiscegenation laws in the United States, see Koshy (2004) and Pascoe (2009).

26 See Franke (2015) and Hunter (2017) for rich historical accounts of the coercive and repressive effects of civil marriage rights on African Americans following the abolition of slavery.

27 For a sustained discussion of how the racialization of indigeneity serves the interests of the colonizing state and the institutions of settler colonialism, see Kauanui (2008a), O'Brien (2010), and Byrd (2011).

28 See Deloria and Wilkins (2011) for an analysis of how the Dawes Act mobilized property ownership as a civilizing force. For more on the heteropatriarchal logics organizing this legislation, see Brandzel (2016, 75). For an incisive analysis of the disability imagery undergirding the assessment of Native "competency," see Samuels (2014, 164–165).

29   For more on the gender and sexual politics of Indian boarding schools, see Lomawaima (1993) or Smith (2005).

30   In the first chapter of *Entry Denied* (2002), Eithne Luibhéid provides a succinct historical overview of the gendered and sexualized dimensions of U.S. immigration policy that brings into focus the privatizing function of the family within the context of this legal realm.

31   See Lowe (1996) for an analysis of Asian exclusion laws and of the ramifications of this history for Asian American culture and identity.

32   For more on the shifting borders of whiteness during this period, see Omi and Winant (1994) and Jacobson (1998). See also Carter (2007) for an astute analysis of the ways in which (hetero)sexualized discourses of "normality" structured this remapping of whiteness.

33   For more on the pathologization of Chinese intimacies within U.S. immigration policies, see Shah (2001, 2011) and Cho (2013).

34   See Ann Laura Stoler's edited volume *Haunted by Empire* (2006) for a collection of essays that offer a comparative analysis of the "intimate" side of U.S. state power in different imperial settings. For more on how U.S. colonial interventions impacted Native Hawaiian practices of gender, kinship, and sexuality, see Merry (2000) and Kauanui (2008b). For more on the racial and sexual politics of "decency" in Puerto Rico and on the United States' imposition of marital norms via colonial rule, see Findlay (1999, esp. ch. 4) and Briggs (2002). For a queer studies analysis of U.S. imperial practices of "racial-sexual governance" in the Philippines, see Mendoza (2015).

35   The invention of the modern family depended upon the liberal fantasy of separate public and private spheres: the feminized realm of reproduction and family life was cordoned off from the masculinist space of paid work and political process, and the birthing, raising of, and caring for citizen-workers was figured not as a productive form of labor but as the natural and desirable culmination of adult life. For an elaboration on feminist critiques of marriage, the family, and the ideology of separate spheres in the context of the United States, see Coontz (1992), Cott (2002), and Davidson and Hatcher (2002).

36   For more on the intersections among sexology, scientific racism, and settler colonialism in the United States, see Duggan (1993), Carter (1997), Ordover (2003), and Morgensen (2011, esp. ch. 1).

37   For more on city life and sexual politics in the United States during this period, see Peiss (1986) and Meyerowitz (1988).

38   See Terry (1999, esp. 100–103) for more on the treatment of "sexual maladjustment" during the early twentieth century. For more on the twentieth-century history of eugenics, white supremacy, and heteronormativity in the United States, see Bederman (1995), Ordover (2003), Kline (2005), Carter (2007), and Lovett (2007).

39   A special thanks to Benjamin D'Harlingue for providing me with this formulation.

40   See, for example, Barbara Ehrenreich and Deirdre English's discussion of the figural child in *For Her Own Good* (2005). Reflecting on the exertion of masculinist professional authority over the feminized realm of reproductive labor, they argue that the child of the twentieth century is valued not just as an heir but as "a means of *control* over society's not-so-distant future" (210, emphasis in original). Judith Stacey contextualizes this rhetorical shift with respect to the rise of industrial capitalism and companionate marriage in *In the Name of the Family* (1996), pointing to the ways

in which nineteenth-century discourses of maternal love and care disrupted legal constructions of children as patriarchal property (40).

41 Here I have in mind Freud's theorizations of perversity and sexual development as specifically articulated in *Three Essays on the Theory of Sexuality* (2000). For a thoughtful overview of this text and its relation to more recent queer studies investigations into childhood sexuality, see Kelleher (2004).

42 Feminist scholars have traced this gendered division of labor back to the rise of the "cult of domesticity" during the mid–nineteenth century. As Anne McClintock (1995) and Ann Laura Stoler (1995) have convincingly argued, the production of white middle-class womanhood as the frontline of defense against disorder and disease depended upon the construction of the working classes and racialized colonial subjects as inherently unhealthy populations.

43 See Freedman (1987) for a great overview of the invention of the "sexual psychopath" and an incisive analysis of the gendered dimensions of early sex offender laws.

44 For more on the policing of homosexuality in U.S. cities during this period, see Chauncey (1994), Mumford (1997), Boyd (2003), and Hurewitz (2007).

45 For instance, Nayan Shah examines the policing of same-sex sex practices among Chinese and South Asian men in California during the early twentieth century and documents the ways in which authorities unevenly prosecuted older immigrant workers who engaged in consensual sex with younger white U.S. citizens (2011, ch. 4).

46 For an excellent analysis of how state-sponsored efforts to "contain" the threat of Communism shaped discourses of American familialism and motherhood during the Cold War, see May (1988).

47 See Canaday (2009, ch. 5 and 6) for a historical account of how Cold War–fueled fears of homosexuality shaped U.S. military policy and immigration law during the postwar era.

Chapter 1 Anxiety

1 I was in Provincetown for Family Week 2015 and attended several official events, including the "State of the Movement" address and the very popular "Teen Panel" (where children growing up in LGBT families reflect on their experiences). Although this chapter has little to do with the twentieth anniversary of Family Week in particular, my participation observation research gave me access to detailed event schedules, clarified my understanding of the tone and style of the annual celebration, and thus informs my reading of the place of LGBT-identified parents in P'town.

2 *The Fosters* is a family drama television series about an interracial black-white lesbian couple living in San Diego, California, and raising a houseful of children, including the white woman's biological son from a previous heterosexual marriage and four children they adopted through the state's foster care system (including a set of Latino twins and a white genderqueer child). The show began airing on the ABC Family network, now known as Freeform, in 2013.

3 While this cautious form of celebration structured the entire "State of the Movement" address, I am quoting here from the official "Message from the Executive Director of Family Equality Council," which was printed in the 2015 Family Week program brochure and is contained in my personal files.

4 In *Provincetown*, Karen Krahulik (2005) describes the town's efforts to establish itself as a "colonial outpost" during the early twentieth century. Although the creation of "New England" as a mythic time and place began several decades earlier in response to the influx of non–Western European immigrants to northeastern cities, Provincetown's "colonial" campaign followed the same pattern of glossing over histories of theft and genocidal violence against indigenous peoples to capture an imagined period in U.S. history where racial, ethnic, and class tensions did not yet exist (36–37). We might also think about the building of the Pilgrim Monument (and its commemoration of the Mayflower's first landing) as an extension of the nineteenth-century practice of what Jean O'Brien calls "firsting" (2010, esp. ch. 1). Through a meticulous analysis of local New England histories from 1820 to 1880, O'Brien shows how Anglo-Americans claimed Indian land by crafting origin stories that cast Indians as prefatory to their own legitimate histories and to the modern social order.

5 For more on the history of race, ethnicity, and sexuality and the rise of the tourism industry in Provincetown, see Krahulik (2005) and Faiman-Silva (2004).

6 In 1999, the Provincetown Business Guild, which worked to promote P'town as an LGBT travel destination, published a guidebook that reminded potential tourists that "ever since the Pilgrims first landed here, this fishing village on the tip of Cape Cod, Massachusetts, has been providing the perfect oasis for people in need of escape" (quoted in Krahulik 2005, 45).

7 Here, I am building on Jasbir Puar's critique of the modern queer subject's entanglement with U.S. exceptionalism (2007, 22–23) and Andrea Smith's and Scott Lauria Morgensen's clarifications of the relevance of Puar's analysis for Native studies (Smith 2010, 49; Morgensen 2011, 2–3).

8 See, for example, Hay's "The Homosexual and History" (1996). For more on the homosexual emancipation movement's fascination with "sexual primitivity" and with the berdache in particular, see Morgensen (2011, ch. 2).

9 For more on the history of the Daughters of Bilitis, see Gallo (2006). See also Hanhardt (2013) for a brief discussion of Phyllis Lyon, Del Martin, and Barbara Denning's involvement in cross-race organizing against police violence in San Francisco during the late 1960s (67–68).

10 In *Crime against Nature*, Minnie Bruce Pratt (2013) offers a moving autobiographical account, in the form of lyrical narrative poetry, of losing custody of her children after being identified as a lesbian in the 1970s. The most recent edition of this collection includes an afterword by Pratt that situates her experience with respect to twenty-first-century struggles for family self-determination and, in the process, offers an inspiring vision for a queer family politics.

11 For more on the history of the Lesbian Mothers' National Defense Fund, see the documentary *Mom's Apple Pie: The Heart of the Lesbian Mothers' Custody Movement* (2006).

12 See Goeman and Denetdale (2009) and Tuck and Yang (2012) for more on the incommensurability of redistributive feminist social justice projects and the sovereignty of Native land and people. See also Rifkin (2013) for an analysis of how non-Native activist projects ostensibly forged in opposition to the (settler) state are best understood as "emerg[ing] out of the ongoing work of settler occupation" (323).

13 For a moving and thoughtful portrayal of lesbian family-building practices during this period, see the documentary *Choosing Children: Launching the Lesbian Baby Boom* (1985).

14   Christina Hanhardt (2013) offers a brief yet insightful account of how the social sci-
     ence research of racial liberals during the 1960s laid the groundwork for the cultur-
     ally coded racisms that would underpin welfare reform during the 1990s. She writes,
     "Considered collectively, this research [which sought to fight against segregation
     and discrimination] tended to pose narrowly predictive relationships between
     structure and psychosocial effects and were imbued with moralistic notions of what
     counted as a good community, highlighting the problems of failed nuclear families
     and sexual and gender nonconformity" (46).

15   Black feminist thinkers have waged detailed critiques against Senator Daniel
     Patrick Moynihan's *The Negro Family: The Case for National Action* (1965) and
     against the broader suggestion that racial equality can only be achieved once black
     men assumed their roles as patriarchal heads of heterosexual family households.
     See, for example, Toni Cade Bambara's edited collection *The Black Woman* (1970),
     Hortense Spillers's "Mama's Baby, Papa's Maybe" (1987), and Patricia Hill Collins's
     Black Feminist Thought (1990).

16   See Mink (1998, ch. 2) for a succinct history of U.S. welfare policy and a
     detailed analysis of the moralism undergirding this legislative history. See also
     Piven and Cloward (1993) for a historical account of the regulatory function of
     poverty relief programs in the United States. For more on the racial and gender
     politics of welfare programs (specifically in relation to black citizenship), see
     Roberts (1996).

17   It is worth noting here that Kevin Mumford's rereading of *The Moynihan Report*
     reveals that this policy-forming document turns less on a concern about "domineer-
     ing African American mothers" and more on the "problem of diminished black
     manhood" (2012, 57). As such, he concludes that the report and its afterlife are
     shaped by often unacknowledged anxieties over homosexuality and, in doing so,
     illuminates the sexual politics organizing coercive efforts to normalize black social
     relations during the mid- to late twentieth century.

18   The full text of the vice president's address can be found at http://www.vice
     presidentdanquayle.com/speeches_StandingFirm_CCC_1.html.

19   For more on the figure of the "welfare queen," see Lubiano (1992).

20   Alexandra Chasin reflects on the effects of these funding trends on "gay-related
     causes" during the 1990s in her book *Selling Out*: "The smaller, more local,
     more grassroots organizations, and those working for radical social change, are
     surely among the least favored by funders. As a result, market-related funding
     mechanisms—while providing increased visibility for the larger national service-
     oriented organizations—can contribute to the invisibility and/or the de-resourcing
     of less mainstream organizations" (2000, 202).

21   These numbers, from the American Bar Association's family law section, were
     based on the assumption that 10 percent of the population identifies as gay or
     lesbian and on rough estimates that one-fourth of gay men and one-third of
     lesbians are parenting children (Griffin 1992; Pressley and Andrews 1992). Today,
     Family Equality Council estimates that there are about three million parents who
     are lesbian, gay, bisexual, transgender, or queer raising approximately six million
     children, suggesting that these initial numbers were a bit inflated ("About
     Us" n.d.).

22   Even as the Democratic Party's pledge to lift the military's ban on homosexuality
     arguably expanded "employment opportunities" for the working-class lesbians and
     gay men who were more likely to enlist in the armed forces, the proposed expansion

of U.S. imperial power ultimately served the financial interests of the gay moneyed elite. Moreover, the sudden visibility of lesbian and gay servicemembers helped to symbolically transform the diseased or otherwise pathological homosexual into a strong, healthy, and patriotic citizen worthy of legal protections (Montegary 2015b).

23   I return to the racial and sexual politics of the Welfare Reform Act of 1996 in chapter 4.

24   For more on queer (counter)publics, see Berlant and Warner (1998). In their canonical discussion of the "radical aspirations of queer culture building" (548), they emphasize the ways in which "making a queer world has required the development of kinds of intimacy that bear no necessary relation to domestic space, to kinship, to the couple form, to property, or to the nation" (558).

25   One of the most widely covered lesbian custody cases in the 1990s was the Virginia-based battle between Sharon Bottoms and her mother. Although there was nothing unusual about a mother challenging the right of her lesbian daughter to raise a child, news media outlets, intoxicated by the newfound visibility of lesbian and gay parents, seized on this dispute as if Bottoms's case was out of the ordinary. In 1995, in spite of the widespread support for Bottoms expressed in major U.S. newspapers, the Virginia Supreme Court awarded custody to her mother and prohibited her from visiting her son if her same-sex partner was present (Polikoff 1999, 45).

26   Between 1996 and 2003, Family Week attendance saw an almost 20 percent increase each year (Howey 2003). As I mention at the start of the chapter, more than five hundred families registered for the twentieth anniversary of the annual event (Family Equality Council 2015a).

27   Here I have in mind Gayle Rubin's discussion of kinship and the "acquisition of our sexual and gender programming," where she draws on the work of Carole Vance to think through the social and psychic dimensions of desire formation (2011, 283).

28   Dan Cherubin, who identifies as gay and has a lesbian-identified mother, coined the term to describe LGBT-identified children with LGBT-identified parents. He started the group Second Generation in the early 1990s and was featured in a *New York Times* article in 1998. In this article, lesbian and gay parenting experts and activists weigh in on the possibility of gayness breeding more gayness. While all the parties interviewed acknowledged that this does, in fact, happen and emphasized how supportive lesbian and gay parents could be during their children's coming-out processes, the voices assembled in the article are quite forceful in their assertion that sexual identity is an essential part of each person and that parents have zero effect on the kinds of sexual subjects their children become (Kirby 1998). Shortly after the article appeared, Cherubin partnered up with COLAGE. Today, the language of "second generation" is still used among COLAGErs, and the COLAGE website includes information about the term for parents and children, but the organization no longer houses a separate Second Gen program (COLAGE, "Second Gen FAQ," n.d.).

29   For an incisive critique of the impact of professionalization and service-provision models on progressive social movements in the United States, see Spade (2011), 174–180. See also Barbara Smith's commentary on the "501(c)(3)-ing of the movement" in the interview she did for the collection *Homo Economics* (1997, 203–205) as well as INCITE! Women of Color against Violence's collection of essays on the "non-profit industrial complex" titled *The Revolution Will Not Be Funded* (2007).

30 For instance, one commenter accused the town's tourism office and chamber of commerce of trying to "CHANGE [Provincetown] to make it the way they want [it] to be." Kids, he argues, "are honestly not wanted in a WILD GAY PARTY TOWN": "Who the heck wants MORE STROLLERS on the sidewalk, KIDS making noise in nice restaurants, who wants to tuck in [a] bulge, put on a shirt, watch your language, [and] be appropriate in front of the kids[?]" (Sowers 2008; comments available in author's personal files).

Chapter 2 Visibility

1 For an overview of how the tourism industry worked to penetrate the lesbian and gay travel market, see Hughes (2006). See Puar (2002b) for a transnational feminist critique of lesbian, gay, and queer tourist practices and economies.

2 While I do not have access to R Family Vacations's financial records and have been unable to determine how this venture has affected O'Donnell's personal wealth, I understand this performance of celebrity charity work as suturing her brand as "queen of nice" to her new commitment to the cause of lesbian and gay parenting.

3 Although cruises have been criticized for being "elitist, expensive ventures," travel experts consider the cruise to be one of the "best travel values," offering "room, board, and entertainment for one, often relatively inexpensive, fixed price" (Puar 2002b, 944n6). The cost of a cabin on R Family's inaugural journey started at $999 per adult for an inside cabin (Salvato 2004), thus making O'Donnell's vacation package within reach for a wide range of middle-class families.

4 The businesses catering to newly emerging lesbian and gay communities during the early twentieth century were often owned by straight-identified business owners who were participating in what M. V. Lee Badgett describes as "an early form of 'niche marketing'" (2001, 104–105).

5 In his article "Tourism and the Military," Adam Weaver explains how the threat of terrorism has shaped the travel industry in the early twenty-first century. Terrorist attacks, not only the events of September 11 in the United States, but also other attacks on mass transit facilities and landmark luxury hotels around the world, had created a sense of "global and national insecurity" (2011, 680). During this period, the cruise industry bolstered the perceived safety of cruise ships by adopting increasingly militarized security measures, including navigation, surveillance, and even weapons technologies (680–681).

6 In 1999, at the annual Gay and Lesbian World Travel Expo, tourism promoters were already talking about the possibility of running cruises for lesbians and gay men with children (Puar 2002a, 105). Two years later, the Third Annual Gay and Lesbian Tourism Conference included a panel titled "Lesbian and Gay Family Market" (Puar 2002b, 944n8).

7 See Chasin (2000) for a sustained analysis of the relationship between the emergence of a lesbian and gay niche market and the rise of the lesbian and gay civil rights movement. For a materialist account of the transformation of sexual identities under late capitalism, see Hennessy (2000).

8 In *Selling Out*, Alexandra Chasin (2000) documents the ways in which lesbians and gay men conflate consumption with political action. For instance, some people choose to use credit card companies that donate a fraction of their profits to LGBT-focused organizations, whereas others view any purchase of pride-related paraphernalia, whether from an LGBT rights group or from a private outlet selling such

products, as an activist gesture (133–142). In other cases, as I discuss in chapter 4, people purposefully invest their assets in LGBT-friendly companies and try to build socially conscious financial portfolios.

9 For more on the gendered and racialized dimensions of consumer citizenship in "transnational America," see Grewal (2005).

10 Here I am referring to the historic Supreme Court decision *Lawrence and Garner v. Texas* (2003). As David Eng argues, the decision effectively desexualized homosexuality within the political-legal realm by ignoring the interracial "love triangle" at the heart of the case and insisting on an analogous relationship between same-sex couplings and heterosexual marriage (2010, 42). "The case," Eng argues, "deemphasizes acts (one night of sodomy) while inscribing a normative vision of acceptable queer identity and lifestyle (twenty years of intimacy, domesticity, coupledom, and consumption)" (43).

11 In her analysis of the marketization of lesbian and gay social movements, Chasin calls attention to the ways in which advertising "appeal[s] to gays on the basis of their identifications as Americans" and "promise[s] that full inclusion in the national community of Americans is available through personal consumption" (2000, 101). Her analysis of the function of nationalism within lesbian and gay niche marketing, as Jasbir Puar (2006) demonstrates, is particularly helpful in contextualizing lesbian and gay tourist consumption after September 11, 2001. The history of Americanization through consumer practices, which can be traced to the case of nonwhite ethnic immigrants seeking national belonging through consumption in the early twentieth century (Chasin 2000, 105–107), helps make sense of the collusion between gay tourism and U.S. patriotism during the early days of the war on terror. In an October 2001 newsletter, Community Marketing Inc. urged lesbians and gay men to recognize the therapeutic value of tourism for themselves and the nation (Puar 2006, 78). At a moment when mobility and consumption signaled an unwavering commitment to the American way of life, lesbian and gay subjects, provided their practices remained within the properly gendered and aspirationally white parameters of consumer citizenship, could "embrace as well as be embraced by the nation" (78). The lesbian and gay tourist was no longer just a consumer par excellence (a consumer whose desires threaten a level of unacceptable excess) but a U.S. patriot par excellence (a citizen whose desires align with the interests of the nation-state).

12 For more on the parallels between family welfare policies and systems of policing and incarceration, see Tina Lee's ethnographic analysis of the child welfare system in New York City in *Catching a Case* (2016).

13 Over the past four decades, the federal government has taken steps to incentivize the adoption of "special needs" children. Don Romesburg provides a brief overview of these efforts in his essay on queer transracial families: "In 1980, Congress codified the Adoption Assistance and Child Welfare Act, which established a federal foster-adoption subsidy. 'Special needs' was defined as a condition, 'such as . . . ethnic background, age, or membership in a minority or sibling group, or . . . medical conditions or physical, mental, or emotional handicaps.' . . . In 1996, a $6,000 special-needs adoption credit was also added to the tax code. In 2001, Congress added another $4,000" (2014, 13, the first two ellipses from the original).

14 According to Laura Briggs, over the course of the 1980s, lesbians and gay men looking to adopt were pushed to consider "hard-to-place children," a category that

includes black children, older children, "crack bab[ies]," "terminal AIDS bab[ies]," and children with other "special needs" (2012, 256). By the late 1990s, she argues, white middle-class lesbians and gay men had become the "safety valve" for a child welfare system overburdened by its own practices of forcibly removing children from their biological mothers (242). According to researchers at the Williams and Urban Institutes, based on information culled from surveys and census data collected between 2000 and 2004, lesbian and gay parents are raising "nearly three percent of the half million children in all forms of family foster care (both kin and non-kin)" and 6 percent of the more than 230,000 children placed with nonrelative caregivers (Gates et al. 2007, 15). However, contrary to Briggs's suggestion that lesbians and gay men might be fostering a disproportionate number of "hard-to-place" children, this study found few statistically significant differences between the characteristics of foster children living with same-sex couples and those living in other family settings. That said, "while not statistically significant, the portion of foster children with a disability [was] highest among those in same-sex couple households (32 percent). In particular, female couples appear[ed] to be more likely to be fostering a child with a disability" (16).

15 For a critical reflection on the "free baby market" and the racial politics of adoption and reproduction more broadly, see Williams (1997). See also Romesburg (2014) and Rodríguez (2014, 41–51) for analyses of queer family formation and transracial and transnational adoption.

16 According to Gates et al.'s analysis of lesbian and gay families formed through adoption and living in the United States during this period, "Among adopted children of same-sex couples, 14% [were] foreign born, twice the rate among children of different-sex married couples (7%) and higher than that of children with single parents. One in five adopted children being raised by a different-sex unmarried couple [was] foreign born, a higher proportion than among adopted children in any other family type. Almost one quarter of children adopted by female same-sex couples [were] foreign born" (2007, 12).

17 For more on the Cayman Island incident, see Puar (2002a, 101–102) and Waitt and Markwell (2006, 148–150).

18 According to what Cynthia Enloe calls the "tourism formula for development," developing nations are instructed to build their capacity for tourism: to remove trade barriers for tourism developers, to create desirable investment climates for tourism corporations, and to commodify (and, ultimately, exoticize) cultural formations for tourists (1989, 31). For an insightful analysis of the sexual politics of neocolonial relations with respect to the Bahamian tourism industry in particular, see Alexander (2005).

19 In his autoethnographic account of transracial adoption, Romesburg calls into question what he perceives as Eng's characterization of lesbian and gay parents as "passive dupes of homonormativity" (2014, 20). In contrast, he proposes strategies for doing queer transracial family in ways that challenge discourses of "colorblindness" and the privatized consumer model of family life.

20 This formulation of the lesbian and gay family is indebted to Caren Kaplan's discussion of the modern tourist's role in creating the borders and boundaries that the figure appears to traverse. She writes, "The tourist confirms and legitimates the social reality of constructions such as 'First' and 'Third' Worlds, 'development' and 'underdevelopment,' or 'metropolitan' and 'rural.' Created out of increasing leisure time in industrialized nations and driven by a need to ascertain identity and location in a

world that undermines the certainty of those categories, the tourist acts as an agent of modernity" (1996, 58).

21 R Family Vacations was not maintaining detailed demographic data on its clientele at this time. As Kaminsky explained to me a few days later, the company much preferred to invest its limited resources elsewhere. Consequently, rather than offer precise statistical information concerning the identities of the passengers, I reflect on the trends I observed over the course of my week on the ship.

22 Here I am referring to the "Open Letter from Barack Obama to the LGBT Community," which he released as one of the Democratic presidential candidates in February 2008. A copy of this letter is available via the *Bilerico Report* at http://bilerico.lgbtqnation.com/2008/02/open_letter_from_barack_obama_to_the_lgb .php.

23 In July 2008, after Senator John McCain told the *New York Times* that he did not "believe in gay adoption," the executive director of Family Equality Council sent letters to both McCain and Obama asking how their administrations would support the diverse array of family forms in the United States. Obama replied with a detailed letter addressed directly to the executive director in which he outlined how his platform sought to support people raising children and promised to be "a president that [would stand] up for American families—all of them." The Council archived Obama's letter on the *Family Room* blog at http://www.familyequality .org/equal_family_blog/2008/08/05/601/sen_obama_responds_to_jennifer _chrislers_questions_on_family_policy.

24 I was not particularly surprised to hear such claims, but not simply because I had faith in the capacity of queer sexual cultures to permeate an O'Donnell-branded family vacation. One year earlier, when I mentioned R Family Vacations while giving a talk on tourism and activism at New York University, an undergraduate came up to me afterward to tell me about a friend who had spent a week working as talent on one of the company's cruises and had been delighted to discover a wild night life and ample cruising opportunities aboard the ship.

25 This continues to be the trend within LGBT travel. In the *20th Annual Survey on LGBT Tourism & Hospitality*, Community Marketing Inc. (2015) reported that lesbians and gay men are taking regular advantage of LGBT-inclusive options from mainstream outlets: the majority of cruise goers are opting for general population departures over charter or group cruises, and parents are increasingly reporting a preference for "child-friendly" over "LGBT-friendly" destinations.

26 It is telling that the executive director of this national nonprofit was on the cruise herself and taking almost complete responsibility for administering the educational programming. While the Council's corporate ties point to the ways in which family equality efforts have been swept up in the nonprofitization of social movements, it is worth noting that this organization remains on the periphery of the mainstream LGBT rights industry, operating with a much smaller budget and devoid of many of the resources enjoyed by larger organizations.

27 Here I am quoting from the flyer circulated aboard the *Norwegian Star* titled "R Family Cruise July 2009: Family Equality Council Programming." This flyer is in my personal files.

28 While the Council continued to reference studies concluding that the sexual orientation of parents has absolutely no bearing on parental outcomes, I heard, over the course of the week, several references to the ways in which lesbians and gay men might actually make better parents than heterosexual adults: for example,

gay fathers are more emotionally responsive and thus more nurturing than straight fathers; children raised by lesbians have been shown to do better academically and to have fewer behavior problems; and because lesbians and gay men have endured the pain of discrimination, they tend to be more open about their feelings, thus encouraging more communication and promoting better psychological health.

29 I am once again referencing the "Family Equality Council Programming" flyer cited previously.

30 The Donor Sibling Registry (DSR), which began as a Yahoo group created by a single mother and her donor-conceived son based in the United States, has since grown into a 501(c)(3) charity organization with its own database-driven website (https://donorsiblingregistry.com). The DSR's official mission is to "assist individuals conceived as a result of sperm, egg or embryo donation who are seeking to make mutually desired contact with others with whom they share genetic ties." Waging a critique against what they perceive as the donor conception industry's failure to acknowledge the "humanity" of the people created using the "products" they sell, the DSR seeks to intervene in larger public debates by advocating for the "rights of the donor-conceived" and insisting that all people have the "fundamental right to information about their biological origins and identities."

31 While I am directly quoting from the same "Family Equality Council Programming" flyer referenced previously, this turn of phrase was repeated throughout the workshops over the course of the week and was (and continues to be today) a staple line in the Council's print and online publicity materials.

32 Writing in the late 1990s (and seemingly in anticipation of Web 2.0), Anagnost identified the increasingly popular "family web page" as the latest technological development, following family photography and the personal camcorder, in what Berlant describes as "middle-class familial theatricality in late capitalism" (Berlant 1997, 142, quoted in Anagnost 2000, 398). The feverish archiving of family life that Anagnost observes among adoptive parents and that Chrisler encourages among lesbian and gay parents must not be reduced to the anxious product of nonbiological or nonnormative parenting relationships. Rather, as Anagnost argues, explicit efforts to consolidate one's family status simply bring into focus the often unmarked labor involved in producing "an intensified aura of sentiment surrounding family life" and constructing the domestic sphere as a haven from the "impersonal" nature of the marketplace (391, 411).

33 The Council's investment in lesbian and gay parents being open with their communities and willing to reveal the details of how their families were formed stretches back at least a decade. In a 1998 article for the lesbian and gay periodical *In the Family*, Tim Fisher, the co-founder of Family Week and the president of GLPCI at the time, encouraged parents to be "in-your-face" in their daily lives—that is, "coming out—not angrily, combatively, or defensively, but patiently, confidently, armed with information and resources, and above all, honestly and pro-actively."

34 For more on Family Pride Coalition's organizing efforts during this period, see Hernandez (2006).

35 In *Radical Relations*, Daniel Rivers refers to children from LGBT families as "bridge workers" as a way of signaling the labor they perform in mediating the relationship "between their families and mainstream heterosexual society" (2013, 153).

36 For more on her vision for a queer family politics, see Boggis (2001, 2012, 2013).

37 While it is not within the scope of this chapter to elaborate on the gender, sexual, and disability politics of genetic selection and deselection, I want to point to Alison

Kafer's brilliant discussion of the ethics of reprogenetic technologies in relation to feminist, queer, and crip positionalities (2013, ch. 3).

Chapter 3   Equality

1   The WordPress blog featuring their single post "Resist the Gay Marriage Agenda!" is still live at https://queerkidssaynomarriage.wordpress.com, but their essay is also anthologized in Ryan Conrad's collection *Against Equality* (2010). In the later printed version, Kaufman and Miles reflect on their original post and attenuate their initial critique. While Miles acknowledges the ways in which their calls for "solidarity" inadvertently positioned queer communities as isolated from other identity groups or community formations, Kaufman expresses discomfort with the prescriptive tone they struck when distinguishing between "help[ful]" and "hurt[ful]" organizing strategies. Both authors also speak to the fact that they had not fully understood or appreciated just how meaningful marriage and state valida-tion can be for some couples.

2   See, for example, the other work featured in Conrad's edited collection (2010). For more scholarly analyses of the limits of same-sex marriage activism, see Warner (1999), Butler (2002), Brandzel (2005), Willse and Spade (2005), and Kandaswamy (2008).

3   After the highest court in New York ruled in favor of Braschi, New York's Divi-sion of Housing and Community Renewal issued new regulations governing rent-controlled and rent-stabilized apartments and included in the list of those entitled to succession rights those "who can prove emotional and financial com-mitment and interdependence with the tenant" (quoted in Polikoff 2008, 57). The ACLU's Lesbian and Gay Rights Project represented Braschi, but the victory was understood as the result of coalitional work and the coordinated effort of a variety of organizations who submitted amicus briefs identifying all the nontraditional families harmed by rent laws organized around marriage-based definitions of family. Activists working to support family diversity celebrated the ruling as a huge step toward redefining family in public policy and disentangling social and economic benefits from marriage (55–57).

4   I have borrowed from Robert McRuer's succinct summary of the Kowalski incident (2006, 4). For more on the case of Sharon Kowalski and her partner Karen Thomp-son, see Thompson and Andrzejewski (1988) and Charles (2003). For incisive analyses of how this case might complicate queer critiques of family and domestic life, see Hunter (1995) and McRuer (2006).

5   In the "Family Bill of Rights," Lambda Legal argued that, because families in the United States are "formed in many ways, through blood, marriage, and adoption, as well as by choice, commitment, and association," family is best defined "not by reliance on fictitious legal distinctions" but by "pattern[s] of conduct, agreement, or action which evidences their intention of creating long-term, emotionally commit-ted relationships" (quoted in Polikoff 2008, 60).

6   Given this book's investment in documenting the use of marriage as a tool of racial and imperial domination, it is important to acknowledge the particular settler colo-nial context in which this early marriage case took shape. In the Barnard Center for Research on Women's educational video titled "Marriage Is a Colonial Imposition," J. Kēhaulani Kauanui provides an analysis of the paradoxes structuring the bid for same-sex marriage in Hawaii during the early 1990s. She explains that

the non–Native Hawaiian plaintiffs involved in the case—and the non–Native Hawaiian LGBT community more broadly—frequently invoked a version of Native Hawaiian culture that they used as a way of naturalizing same-sex sexualities in Hawaii and constructing the fiftieth state as the "natural" place to start legalizing same-sex marriage in the United States. This search for legitimacy *via* the state stood in opposition to and effectively undermined Hawaiian nationalist efforts to challenge the legitimacy *of* the state—a colonial state that, as Kauanui reminds us, has historically imposed marital norms upon Native Hawaiians and pulverized Kanaka Maoli notions of gender, sexuality, and kinship. (The video in question is available at https://www.youtube.com/watch?v=u6ySbk35Y-k.)

7   On August 30, 1996, two weeks before the trial in Hawaii was set to begin, the GLPCI issued a press release inviting news outlets to reprint an op-ed by Dr. April Martin, the organization's executive vice president and the psychologist who wrote *The Lesbian and Gay Parenting Handbook* (1993). In addition to pushing back against the invisibility of lesbian and gay families and asserting the fitness of same-sex couples for parenthood, she also highlighted the ways in which homophobic marriage laws unfairly disadvantage the children of lesbians and gay men. Outlining her specifically middle-class concerns, Martin explained that, rather than saving for her children's future education, she and her partner spent "many thousands of dollars" on additional health insurance (since they were denied access to standard family plans) and "side-door legal documents" (in the hopes of legitimating their connections to each other and their children). This op-ed is on file with the author.

8   Here the House report references E. L. Pattullo's article "Straight Talk about Gays," which appeared in *Commentary* magazine in December 1992.

9   Wolfson regularly cited the U.S. General Accounting Office's 1997 report, which had found 1,049 federal statutory provisions related to marital status. This number was updated in 2004, when a follow-up report identified 1,138 such provisions (U.S. General Accounting Office 2004).

10 For more on how private foundation funding has systematically squelched radical social movements, see INCITE! Women of Color against Violence (2007).

11 See McCreery (2008) for a brief overview of how Lambda Legal and the Human Rights Campaign invoked the symbolic figure of the endangered child when advocating for same-sex marriage during this period.

12 In April 2001, Gay and Lesbian Advocates and Defenders (GLAD) filed a lawsuit against the Massachusetts Department of Public Health on behalf of seven couples, four of whom were raising children, over the state's refusal to issue them marriage licenses. Mary Bonauto, the attorney who served as lead counsel for the plaintiffs (and who would later successfully argue against DOMA before the U.S. Supreme Court in 2015), contended that the ban on same-sex marriage violated the state's due process and equal protection laws by denying these couples and their children the protections marriage would afford. Two and a half years later, in November 2003, the Massachusetts Supreme Judicial Court decided in favor of the plaintiffs, ruling that the state was unlawfully interfering with the fundamental liberties of these families: "Excluding same-sex couples from civil marriage will not make children of opposite-sex marriages more secure, but it does prevent children of same-sex couples from enjoying the immeasurable advantages [associated with marriage]" (*Goodridge v. Department of Public Health* 2003, 335). In February 2004, the court rejected the legislature's proposal for a civil union law and ordered the state

to grant same-sex couples access to marriage. For a detailed account of how GLAD approached this case, see Bonauto (2005).

13 Just a few months after securing same-sex marriage in Massachusetts, GLAD sued the Connecticut Department of Public Health on behalf of eight couples, six of whom were raising children, over the state's discriminatory marriage laws and once again argued for the right to marry in the name of protecting families. In October 2008, the Supreme Court of Connecticut overturned the lower court's ruling against the plaintiffs (which had, in 2006, interpreted the state's newly passed civil union law as an adequate substitute for marriage) and granted same-sex couples marriage rights. The court expressed its concern for the "especially deleterious effect" marriage bans have on children growing up in LGBT families and agreed with the plaintiffs that the right to marry would help these children "feel secure in knowing that their parents' relationships are as valid and as valued as the marital relationships of their friends' parents" (*Kerrigan v. Commissioner of Public Health* 2008). Five months earlier, the California Supreme Court had also issued a ruling in favor of marriage equality that took into account the interests of children growing up in LGBT-headed households: "A stable two-parent family relationship, supported by the state's official recognition and protection, is equally as important for the numerous children in California who are being raised by same-sex couples as for those children being raised by opposite-sex couples (whether they are biological parents or adoptive parents)" (*In re Marriage Cases* 2008, 77–78). Shortly after California legalized same-sex marriages in 2008, voters passed a state constitutional amendment that rendered the court's findings irrelevant and effectively reinstated marriage inequality.

14 Freedom to Marry and its allies only released information about the Marriage Research Consortium after the U.S. Supreme Court ruled in favor of marriage equality in June 2015 (Zepatos and Hatalsky 2015; Ball 2015).

15 In *Baker v. Vermont* (1999), the Vermont Supreme Court ruled that lesbians and gay men were entitled to the same benefits and protections afforded to heterosexuals through marriage but left it up to the legislature to determine precisely how the state would amend its legal code to satisfy the ruling.

16 Jetter, an award-winning journalist, and Orleck, a tenured historian at Dartmouth, are the coeditors (with their colleague Diana Taylor) of the collection *The Politics of Motherhood: Activist Voices from Left to Right* (1997).

17 Freedom to Marry has archived this ad at http://freemarry.3cdn.net/59487178d70dd6ff64_tsm6bja96.PDF.

18 Video of Sam's testimony is available on Protect Maine Equality's YouTube channel at https://www.youtube.com/watch?v=pT1Bd8MXyqo.

19 The commercial featuring Sam is also available on Protect Maine Equality's YouTube channel at https://www.youtube.com/watch?v=y8YYJKIbSJE.

20 The commercial featuring Peter is available on Mass Equality's YouTube channel at https://www.youtube.com/watch?v=CQBfrImBYBA.

21 For incisive critiques of Edelman's failure to mark the figural child at the center of the political realm as always already white, see Muñoz (2009, 94–96) and Rodríguez (2014, 35–36).

22 The full text of Zach's op-ed was republished in his book, *My Two Moms* (2012, 196–198).

23 Video of Zach's testimony is available on the Iowa House Democrats' YouTube channel at https://www.youtube.com/watch?v=FSQQK2Vuf9Q.

24 This is how Zach describes himself at the 2012 Straight Talk conference held in New York City and hosted by dot429 (a networking community for LGBT professionals and allies). Video of his remarks is available through *Gay Parent* magazine's YouTube channel at https://www.youtube.com/watch?v=Nm17s0XNBvQ.

25 Citing articles from the *American Journal of Orthopsychiatry* and the *Journal of Family Psychology*, the brief notes that "several studies have even suggested that children raised by LGBT families are better adjusted psychologically than their peers" (21).

26 For a concise overview of the case and access to official court records (including recordings and transcripts of the oral arguments as well as the majority and dissenting opinions), see the entry for *United States v. Windsor* in the Oyez Project at https://www.oyez.org/cases/2012/12-307.

27 After the U.S. District Court for the Northern District of California ruled Prop 8 unconstitutional in 2009, both then governor Arnold Schwarzenegger and his successor, Jerry Brown, refused to appeal the decision to the U.S. Supreme Court. The original sponsors of the ballot initiative, ProtectMarriage.com, stepped in to defend Prop 8 and took over as plaintiffs in the appeal case. Ultimately, the Supreme Court determined that the petitioners lacked appellate standing, which led to the dissolution of the stay on the district court's ruling and the legalization of same-sex marriages in California (*Hollingsworth v. Perry* 2013).

28 Mark Regnerus (2012) had attempted to prove the dangers of LGBT family life by comparing the experiences of people whose biological mothers and fathers stayed married for their entire childhoods with people whose parents divorced and one of them entered a same-sex romantic partnership for some period of time. In addition to claiming to find children with parents who engaged in same-sex relationships less likely to identify as "entirely heterosexual," he also argued that homosexual parenting was associated with negative outcomes in the areas of drug use, criminal activity, and mental health issues. Shortly after Regnerus went public with his findings, scholars called into question the peer-review process that surrounded the publication of this study, and the American Sociological Association expressed "serious concerns" about his methodology.

29 See Hardisty and Gluckman for a brief history of the Right's efforts, since at least the early 1990s, to mobilize Latino and African American communities for antihomosexual purposes (1997, 219–220).

30 I have a copy of this document saved in my personal files.

31 For a concise overview of the case and access to official court records (including recordings and transcripts of the oral arguments as well as the majority and dissenting opinions), see the entry for *Obergefell v. Hodges* in the Oyez Project at https://www.oyez.org/cases/2014/14-556.

32 In his dissent, Roberts is quoting from Wilson's *The Marriage Problem: How Our Culture Has Weakened Families* (2002). See Kelling and Wilson (1982) for their theorization of "broken windows" and "neighborhood safety."

33 In her queer reading of "broken windows" theory and the enforcement of NYC-based "quality of life" laws during the late twentieth century, Christina Hanhardt maps the ways in which gay identity begins to operate "in opposition to *disorder*" and "gay safety" comes to require the targeted policing of unruly intimacies, nonnormative social behaviors, improper gender expressions, and the wide range of other so-called deviances associated with racialized poverty (2016, 58).

34 Writing in response to the marriage movement's symbolic invocation of figural children (but before its mobilization of actual children's voices), Patrick McCreery (2008) made a somewhat related argument about the political potential of allowing the children of same-sex couples to speak on their own behalf. Frustrated by the deployment of child-protectionist sentiments and by what he saw as "a fundamental and wholly normative shift in gay-rights rhetoric" (187), he longed for a form of same-sex marriage activism that would transform popular and political understandings of the family. According to McCreery, this would only be possible if activists rejected a "normative vision of family," accepted the complicated erotic and intimate lives of adults, and treated children "as autonomous individuals who must have a space to develop as intellectual, moral, and sexual people" (202). To this end, activists would need to create opportunities for children to talk about their experiences growing up in lesbian and gay families.

35 I am gesturing toward Louis Althusser's theorization of the family as an ideological state apparatus, a mechanism for reproducing the "relations of production" by instilling the ruling ideology into children during their most vulnerable years (1971, 145–147).

36 In her essay "The Economics of Fear, the Politics of Hope, and the Perversity of Happiness," Jakobsen draws upon Sara Ahmed's theorization of the cultural mandate to be happy in order to posit a "perverse happiness" that "break[s] the bargain that holds sexuality and economics to modern morality, the very bargain that also keeps sex and economics tied to each other in the form of normative familial relations that are simultaneously sexual and economic" (2009, 225).

37 Judith Stacey and Timothy Biblarz demonstrate how researchers, in their quest to affirm the fitness of lesbian, gay, and bisexual parents, have downplayed the significance of the differences their data reveal and, in doing so, have ignored the ways in which the sexual orientation of parents might actually matter when it comes to desire formation. Stacey and Biblarz are particularly struck by the fact that none of the studies they examined even attempted to theorize about the "implausib[ility]" of their outcomes: "It is difficult to conceive of a credible theory of sexual development that would not expect the adult children of lesbigay parents to display a somewhat higher incidence of homoerotic desire, behavior, and identity than children of heterosexual parents. For example, biological determinist theory should predict at least some difference in an inherited predisposition to same-sex desire; a social constructionist theory would expect lesbigay parents to provide an environment in which children would feel freer to explore and affirm such desires; psychoanalytic theory might hypothesize that the absence of a male parent would weaken a daughter's need to relinquish her pre-oedipal desire for her mother or that the absence of a female parent would foster a son's pre-oedipal love for his father that no fear of castration or oedipal crisis would interrupt" (2001, 163).

38 I am referring to Dan Savage's widely acclaimed It Gets Better Project (http://www .itgetsbetter.org/). This project, which began with the video Savage and his partner made in response to what appeared to be a surge in teen suicides in the fall of 2010, seeks to comfort LGBT youth dealing with bullying and harassment by reminding them it will "get better" as they get older. Queer scholars and activists have since taken Savage's project to task for its lack of an intersectional analysis, its valuing of white gay boy lives over other forms of queerness, and its failure to account for the various social and economic factors that might impact a person's capacity to survive

(let alone thrive) in the face of structural modes of oppression. See, for example, Nyong'o (2010) and Puar (2010).

39   Here the Council is strategically appropriating language from the amicus brief submitted in defense of traditional marriage by Helen M. Alvaré, a law professor at George Mason University and senior fellow at the Witherspoon Institute.

40   On June 11, 2015, just two weeks before the Supreme Court issued its ruling in favor of marriage equality, Michigan passed a religious freedom act enabling private adoption and foster care agencies to refuse to provide adoption services that would conflict with their religious beliefs. Virginia, North Dakota, and South Dakota have since passed similar "conscience clause" laws allowing child welfare providers to discriminate against LGBTQ-identified prospective parents and children in care based on their moral objections, and Alabama has passed a narrower "religious liberty" law that applies only to service providers that do not receive federal funding (Day and Gingold 2017). More recently, in June 2017, the Texas governor signed a bill allowing child welfare agencies to withhold services to LGBTQ youth and to exclude LGBTQ adults as prospective foster parents (Thompson 2017).

41   The Multiethnic Placement Act (MEPA) effectively undid the race-matching policies that had been governing public adoption practices for decades and that had been advocated for by the National Association of Black Social Workers during the 1970s. Holding up transracial adoption as the obvious solution to a child welfare system overburdened with children of color, MEPA was passed in the name of preventing "reverse racism" against white adoptive parents and, in the process, putting an end to the "placement delays" supposedly caused by race-matching efforts. For more on the racist neoliberal logics informing the passage of MEPA, see Roberts (2002, 165–169) and Jennings (2006).

42   See, for example, Mallon (1998); Sullivan, Sommer, and Moff (2001); Laver and Khoury (2008); Wilson et al. (2014).

43   The Children's Bureau of the Administration for Children and Families awarded the Los Angeles LGBT Center a Permanency Innovations Initiative (PII) grant and facilitated the creation of the "Recognize. Intervene. Support. Empower." (RISE) initiative. According to the Center's PII grantee profile, the purpose of this initiative was to "expand durable adult connections, strengthen emotionally permanent adult connections, and achieve legal permanency (family reunification, adoption, or legal guardianship) for LGBTQ+ children and youth in foster care" (https://www.acf.hhs.gov/sites/default/files/cb/rise_grantee _profile.pdf). For more on this initiative, see the RISE website at https:// lalgbtcenter.org/rise and the PII-funded report titled *Sexual and Gender Minority Youth in Foster Care* (Wilson et al. 2014).

44   In *Radical Relations*, Daniel Rivers documents the efforts on behalf of a few city agencies during this period to place gay teens in foster care with gay couples, noting that such programs were small scale and quickly shut down following public outrage. He writes, "In 1973, the director of the Department of Children and Family Services of Illinois admitted that the office had been quietly placing children with 'homosexual tendencies' with gay foster parents. The New Jersey Department of Human Services formally announced the opening of such a program in 1979. Bruce Voeller [the activist who cofounded what would become the National LGBTQ Task Force] mentioned in a [1979] newspaper interview that he knew of two dozen of these cases that were 'quietly negotiated' by the adoption agencies and gay couples" (2013, 182–183).

45 For firsthand accounts of FIERCE's organizing efforts against "quality of life" laws in New York City, see Rosado (2008) and Mananzala (2012). See also Hanhardt (2013, ch. 5) for a historicized ethnographic analysis of the organization's strategies for surviving and resisting the neoliberal city.

46 In *Queer Family Values* (1999), Valerie Lehr's chapter, "Who Are 'Our' Children?," pursues a related line of inquiry regarding the "intergenerational interdependence" between gay and lesbian adults and gay and lesbian youth.

Chapter 4   Vitality

1 Wells Fargo is also known for establishing the Accredited Domestic Partnership Advisor program. In 2009, the bank teamed up with the College for Financial Planning to develop a certification program to educate financial advisors on the specific needs of domestic partners and same-sex couples in particular. This program was discontinued after the *Obergefell* ruling supposedly "rendered the majority of the program content no longer relevant" (http://www.cffpinfo.com/adpa/).

2 For a detailed analysis of the precarious economic conditions facing a disproportionate number of LGBTQ-identified people in the United States, see DeFilippis (2016).

3 In 1984, Casaletto placed an advertisement in the *New York Times* featuring the large, bolded phrase "Gay Money, Straight Advice." The ad opens by asserting that financial counselors should be "someone you can trust" and "someone with whom you can discuss your lifestyle." Then after highlighting some of the unique concerns facing gay investors (i.e., what kind of life insurance policy to take out, whether to include a partner's name on shared investments), the ad encourages investors to reflect on the quality of advice they are currently receiving and closes with the threatening reminder that they might be "dealing with a company that practices anti-gay discrimination in lending or hiring." I have a copy of this ad in my personal files.

4 The perception of the gay community as an influential consumer group undermined activist efforts by galvanizing resistance against "special rights" for homosexuals during this period. See Hardisty and Gluckman (1997) for an account of how right-wing forces mobilized this "economic caricature" of lesbians and gay men to undercut claims that these populations were deserving of legal and financial protections.

5 See Weiss and Hollibaugh (2015) for an analysis of the damaging effects that this myth has had on LGBTQ culture and politics.

6 For more on the misrepresentation of lesbian and gay populations in marketing research, see Bronski (1984), Badgett (1997), Schulman (1998), and Chasin (2000).

7 For a brief history of lesbian and gay consumer activism, see Badgett (2001, 231–237).

8 In *Pedagogies of Crossing*, M. Jacqui Alexander calls attention to how the "gay marketing moment" of the early 1990s resulted in the paradoxical juxtaposition of "advertisements for gay travel options" and "agencies offering cash in exchange for life insurance policies" within lesbian and gay publications: as the finance and tourism industries targeted this new niche market, "the provisions or supplies necessary for the journey of people living with AIDS [were] advertised on the same pages as those presumed to be able-bodied travelers" (2005, 74).

9 There is an expanding body of scholarship on the role of financial literacy education in (re)producing the logics, subjects, and affective orientations needed to sustain

the global finance market. See, for example, Langley (2008), Joseph (2013), Arthur (2014), and Marron (2014).

10 This is not, however, to suggest that marketing experts were oblivious to the existence of lesbian and gay parents. In fact, Lukenbill opens *Untold Millions* with a reference to lesbian motherhood: "The time is nearing when lesbian mothers will promote bleach and fabric softener on national television" (1995, 1). Additionally, he includes information on parental status with his detailed demographic data on lesbian and gay consumers, claiming that 27 percent of gay men and 67 percent of lesbians are parents (97). While he stops short of identifying a separate lesbian and gay family market requiring niche marketing techniques, he does stress the importance of developing general ad campaigns with a wider and gayer appeal since "there are many products related to parenting that are relevant to this segment of gay/lesbian parents" (97). In her critique of the marketization of lesbian and gay politics, Alexandra Chasin points to Lukenbill's construction of lesbians as mothers as evidence of the ways in which the rhetoric emerging around gay consumption during the 1990s reinforced traditional gender ideologies: "If, indeed, women will still be the figures of domestic consumption and unpaid housework," she writes, "then Lukenbill's [consumer] 'revolution' will not apply to gender roles" (2000, 129).

11 John Hancock's commercial featured a white lesbian couple going through U.S. customs with their newly adopted Chinese baby. (In his work on queer diasporas and the "racialization of intimacy," David Eng uses this commercial as his entry point for examining the "historical conditions and contradictions" that have made "the new global family" possible as a valid social formation and for exploring the "increased outsourcing of not just domestic, but reproductive labor to the global south" [2010, 95].) Wachovia's commercial, which aired a year later, starred a lesbian couple walking down the beach talking about their future children, grandchildren, and great-grandchildren.

12 Hatch is also involved in lesbian and gay advocacy outside of her position at Christopher Street Financial. Most recently, in March 2016, Hatch was named board president of the newly formed Rockland County Pride Center in Nyack, New York, where she and her wife have lived for the past twenty years. Incidentally, Rosie O'Donnell, also a Nyack resident, played an instrumental role in establishing the Pride Center when she donated $150,000 to the cause (Brum 2016).

13 Founded in 1978 and based in New York City, SAGE is the oldest and largest organization focusing on improving the lives of LGBT elders. According to their website, the organization "offers supportive services and consumer resources to LGBT older adults and their caregivers," "advocates for public policy changes that address the needs of LGBT older people," and "provides education and technical assistance for aging providers and LGBT organizations." For more on SAGE, visit http://www.sageusa.org/. In October 2016, at their annual awards gala, SAGE honored Jennifer Hatch for her work as cochair of the organization's Leadership Committee and for Christopher Street Financial's broader commitment to the organization and other LGBT community programs (Taliaferro 2016).

14 According to the Family Week schedules I found archived online (and now have in my personal files), Hatch's workshops were included as part of the "Parent Café" series, which featured daily sessions run by two invited speakers who would address different LGBT family issues and then facilitate a discussion among the parents in attendance. In 2012, Hatch was paired with Terry Boggis, whose impressive record

of queer family activism I discussed in chapter 2 and who was, for the purposes of this event, tasked with talking about "The Role of Our Exes in Our Families." I mention this scheduling decision because I am struck by how clearly the juxtaposition of the current president of a gay wealth management firm alongside a founding member of Queers for Economic Justice brings into focus the tensions and contradictions structuring the domain of LGBT family politics in the United States.

15 The Council's official announcement launching the new web page described the "Ask the Expert" tool as providing a space where users can submit questions about family building, legal protections, financial planning, and creating safer schools "in an anonymous, dear-Abby style" (Family Equality Council 2011).

16 Here I am referencing the archived version of the "Ask the Experts" web page from January 1, 2011, which is available at https://web.archive.org/web/20110101232617/http://ask.familyequality.org/.

17 While I did attend the second annual LGBT Family Building Expo in 2013 (which included a lunchtime panel presentation by members of Family Equality Council's Outspoken Generation, the youth-centered initiative I discussed in the previous chapter), I was not present for the inaugural event. I am relying here on publicity materials for the first expo that I accessed online via Facebook and the Internet Archive: Wayback Machine. See the following footnotes for relevant URLs.

18 Here I am referencing both the event registration page on the LGBT Community Center's website (which is archived at https://web.archive.org/web/20130430095923/https://mycenter.gaycenter.org/lgbtfamilyexpo) and the "Save the Date" announcement posted on Center Families' Facebook page (https://www.facebook.com/events/604443686250766/).

19 In January 2013, the founder of Fertility PlanIt, a digital media platform designed to connect aspiring parents with family-building experts, organized what was described in a press release as the "first, largest and highest quality consumer expo of its kind in the USA" (24-7 Press Release 2012). Held in Los Angeles, the Fertility PlanIt Show was a weekend-long event involving two full days of informational sessions (which focused largely on assisted reproductive technologies) and an exhibit hall where fertility specialists and other reproductive professionals would distribute information about their services. The event included a panel dedicated exclusively to LGBT family-building practices, which featured a presentation by Bergman of Growing Generations (the surrogacy agency that would, three months later, serve as the lead sponsor of Center Families' LGBT Family Building Expo). Fertility PlanIt organized a follow-up show in New York City in September 2013, where Jennifer Hatch appeared on a panel dedicated to financial planning and family building, and another one in Los Angeles in April 2014, which included three informational panels sponsored by Family Equality Council. Similar kinds of family-building expos have cropped up in the years following Fertility PlanIt's initial foray into the field, including the UK-based Fertility Show (https://www.fertilityshow.co.uk/) and the American Fertility Expo (http://www.americanfertilityexpo.com/).

20 I am borrowing language from the program schedule for the first LGBT Family Building Expo. At the session titled "Navigating Family Building Options: What Do You Need to Know?," attendees could expect to "be challenged to think about their own decision making, with the goal of helping them to make informed and appropriate choices." The original schedule is archived at https://web.archive.org/web/20130420042929/http://mycenter.gaycenter.org/lgbtfamilyexpo/programs.

21 Here I follow Faye Ginsburg and Rayna Rapp in taking up Shellee Colen's (1995) concept of "stratified reproduction" to describe "the power relations by which some categories of people are empowered to nurture and reproduce, while others are disempowered" (1995, 3). For an excellent exploration of the ways in which queer intimacies and reproductive futures are embedded in these broader structures of power, see Mamo and Alston-Stepnitz (2015).

22 For more on the relationship between financialization and the bioeconomy, see Rose (2007) and Cooper (2008).

23 There is an extensive body of work on the political-economy of transracial and transnational adoptions. See, for example, Perry (1998), Dorow (2006), Trenka (2009), Eng (2010), and Briggs (2012).

24 For more on the politics of race, class, gender, and disability surrounding preimplantation genetic diagnosis (PGD), see Roberts (2009). In this essay, Dorothy Roberts explores the relationship between genetic selection technologies and eugenical population control strategies. Both practices, she argues, "reinforce biological explanations for social problems and place reproductive responsibility on women, thus privatizing remedies for illness and social inequity" (785). She then considers the ways in which PGD might be deployed as a population control mechanism and coercively encouraged (if not explicitly mandated) as the prerequisite for responsible parenthood. In this new version of a reproductive dystopia, "the biological definition of race is stronger than ever, validated by genetic science and cemented in popular culture by race-based biotechnologies. The state has disclaimed all responsibility for supporting its citizens, placing the duty of ensuring public welfare in all women's self-regulation of genetic risk. The medical model of disability is embedded in a neoliberal health policy that relies on widespread use of genetic technologies to disqualify citizens from claiming public support and to avoid the need for social change" (799).

25 In 2011, parents could expect to pay between several hundred and several thousand dollars in professional service fees if they wanted to draw up all the documents recommended by Family Equality Council and Christopher Street Financial. For a list of the average costs of specific documents, see Movement Advancement Project et al. (2011a, 120–121).

26 The "Refuse to Lie" campaign was spearheaded by Nadine Smith of Equality Florida and Kate Kendall of the National Center for Lesbian Rights. For more on their campaign, see Smith (2012).

27 On the day of the *Obergefell* ruling, the American Civil Liberties Union, Freedom to Marry, Gay and Lesbian Advocates and Defenders, the Human Rights Campaign, Lambda Legal, and the National Center for Lesbian Rights launched the website Marriage Equality Facts at https://marriageequalityfacts.org/. In addition to including information on income taxes, spousal benefits, retirement accounts, and wedding planning, the site also features a page dedicated to frequently asked questions concerning "Parent-Child Relationships" (https://marriageequalityfacts .org/topic/parentage/).

28 I should clarify that, technically speaking, Windsor was no longer a widow when she died in September 2017. In October 2016, she married her new partner, Judith Kasen, a vice president at Wells Fargo Advisors (Bernstein 2016). It seems somewhat fitting that Windsor ended up with a wife presumably immersed in the business of estate planning.

29　The legalization of same-sex marriage reinvigorated organizing to secure "marriage equality for people with disabilities" and sparked mainstream media and lesbian and gay press coverage of such efforts. See, for example, Davis (2015), Evans (2015), and Sprayberry (2015).

30　The "After DOMA" fact sheets are available on Family Equality Council's website at http://www.familyequality.org/get_informed/advocacy/after_doma/. The Council worked with the following organizations to produce these documents: the American Civil Liberties Union, the Center for American Progress, Freedom to Marry, Gay and Lesbian Advocates and Defenders, the Human Rights Campaign, Immigration Equality, Lambda Legal, the National Center for Lesbian Rights, the National Gay and Lesbian Task Force (now known as the National LGBTQ Task Force), and OutServe-SLDN.

31　In the "Voices of Children" amicus brief (which was submitted to the Supreme Court in 2013 and which I discussed at length in the previous chapter), the Council made its sole reference to the fact of LGBT poverty when it cites the "How DOMA Harms Children" document and advances this same argument: "Same-sex headed families are not accurately counted when determining eligibility for safety-net programs such as Medicaid or Children's Health Insurance Program (CHIP), which provide free or low-cost health insurance to low-income children; Supplemental Security Income (SSI), which provides assistance to children who are blind or disabled; and Temporary Assistance for Needy Families (TANF), which provides monetary assistance to help with food, clothing, housing, and other basic needs. This inaccurate counting of same-sex headed families can unfairly deny children with same-sex parents assistance that would be granted to children with married, opposite-sex parents" (30–31).

32　The *All Children Matter* report points to the definitions of family used by public housing programs and the Supplemental Nutrition Assistance Program (SNAP) as alternative models for organizing the distribution of public assistance benefits. According to the 2003 Public Housing Occupancy Guidebook, the Department of Housing and Urban Development defines family as "two or more persons related by blood, marriage, adoption, or other operation of law (such as guardianship or a custody order), or two or more persons who are not so related but will live together in a stable relationship and share resources" (Movement Advancement Project et al. 2011a, 60). Within the context of SNAP, eligibility is "based on household size and economic resources, yet a household can include a person or group of people living together who buy food and make meals together. There is no requirement that applicants be related legally or by blood" (59).

33　The six conferences were held between February and May 2012 and, in addition to addressing families, covered the themes of health, housing and homelessness, safe schools and communities, HIV/AIDS, and aging. For more on the White House LGBT Conferences, visit https://obamawhitehouse.archives.gov/lgbt/white-house-conferences. Video of the keynote addresses and panel presentations from the Families conference is available at https://www.youtube.com/watch?v=_OSiY5hPqHE.

34　For a detailed analysis of the entanglement of military spending with hate crimes legislation, see the introduction to Chandan Reddy's *Freedom with Violence* (2011). See also Hanhardt (2013, ch. 4) for a historical account of how hate crime laws gained prominence within lesbian and gay political agendas in the United States.

35 I have written elsewhere on the militarization of the LGBT rights movement and on how U.S.-led practices of war sustain global finance capital (Montegary 2015a, 2015b).

36 The full text of the DOL's clarification (known officially as the Wage and Hour Division's "Administrator's Interpretation No. 2010-3") is available at https://www .dol.gov/Whd/opinion/adminIntrprtn/FMLA/2010/FMLAAI2010_3.htm.

37 The full text of the president's memo is available at https://obamawhitehouse .archives.gov/the-press-office/presidential-memorandum-hospital-visitation.

38 For an overview of the major disparities in LGBT health—and a sense of how the Obama administration was conceptualizing the issue—see the section dedicated to LGBT health from the *Healthy People 2020* report (2010) and the Institute of Medicine's *The Health of Lesbian, Gay, Bisexual, and Transgender People* (2011).

39 Video of the White House LGBT Conference on Health, which was held at Thomas Jefferson University in Philadelphia, is available via Jefferson Digital Commons at http://jdc.jefferson.edu/lgbt_white_house_summit/. The transcript of Sebelius's keynote address has been archived at https://web.archive.org/web/ 20121002030633/http://www.hhs.gov/secretary/about/speeches/sp20120216.html.

40 According to their website, the National Resource Center on LGBT Aging, which is led by SAGE in collaboration with other organizations from across the country, "provides training, technical assistance, and educational resources to aging provid- ers, LGBT organizations and LGBT older adults." For more on the resource center, visit http://www.lgbtagingcenter.org/.

41 Although Sebelius did not mention this particular example by name in her keynote address, the Obama administration often pointed to this initiative as evidence of their LGBT health promotion efforts. The National LGBT Health Education Center is a part of the Fenway Institute, the research, training, and health policy division of Fenway Health (which began in the early 1970s as a community-based clinic serving Boston-area lesbians and gay men and has, over the past forty years, grown into a leading LGBT health and HIV research organization). According to their website, the Education Center "provides educational programs, resources, and consultation to health care organizations with the goal of optimizing quality, cost- effective health care for lesbian, gay, bisexual, and transgender (LGBT) people." For more on the center, visit http://fenwayhealth.org/the-fenway-institute/education/ the-national-lgbt-health-education-center/.

42 To be clear, scholars, activists, and researchers engaged in critical trans and queer politics and committed to advancing racial, economic, and disability justice have consistently regarded access to quality health care as a central concern and have pressured local, state, and federal government officials to adopt more progressive approaches to providing care and coverage. For a detailed analysis of why access to health care must be a top priority in the fight for queer economic justice, see Red- man (2010). See also Redman (2011) for a brief overview of the limits and possibili- ties of the ACA from a sexual-economic justice perspective.

43 Amber Hollibaugh made this point during a roundtable session titled "Deadly Denial: The Unacknowledged Epidemic of Queer Poverty" at the After Marriage: The Future of LGBTQ Politics and Scholarship conference hosted by the Center for LGBTQ Studies (CLAGS) in October 2016. She argued that U.S.-based LGBT rights organizations are only willing to grapple with the realities of LGBT poverty and homelessness in relation to young people who have not yet been shamed for their economic situation. Similarly, she critiqued mainstream activists for limiting

any discussions of sex work to the plight of "innocent" LGBT youth without ever asking after the needs of queer and trans adults who work in sex trades.

44 As I discussed in the previous chapter, the Department of Health and Human Services had taken an interest in the well-being of LGBTQ youth in foster care a few years earlier, awarding a large grant to the Los Angeles LGBT Center for the RISE initiative.

45 This is not to suggest that the state was previously unaware of the usefulness of being able to hold same-sex partners accountable to their familial responsibilities. See, for example, Anna Marie Smith's (2009) insightful analysis of family law, same-sex parenting, and the postwelfare state. In 2005, the California Supreme Court issued three decisions in favor of recognizing lesbian nonbiological mothers as legitimate parents with enforceable obligations to their children. While many activists celebrated these rulings as a major victory for same-sex families and the LGBT community, Smith cautioned against such a response, arguing that these decisions were actually about expanding state power and enhancing privatizing poverty laws. She explains that the case at the center of these decisions involved a lesbian mother who had a child via donor insemination when she was still with her ex-partner but who was now raising the child alone and applying for TANF benefits. In deciding on her ex's status as a parent, the court was ruling on whether the state could forcibly recover child support payments from someone who was involved in planning a child's conception but had no legal or biological ties to that child. As such, the decision to recognize this same-sex assisted-reproduction family as legitimate was largely motivated by the government's interest in preventing donor-conceived children from becoming recipients of public assistance.

46 In a letter to the Office of Management and Budget dated March 9, 2016, Family Equality Council commended HHS for the "steps they have taken to ensure that healthy marriage programs are able to better serve the LGBT community" and recommended they "include consideration of transgender individuals in the data collection and program administration processes." This letter is available online at http://www.familyequality.org/_asset/xmx1jc/Family-Equality-Council-ACF -Data-Collection-Comment.pdf.

47 For more on the racial and sexual politics of the Welfare Reform Act of 1996, see Roberts (1997), Mink (1998), Albelda and Withorn (2002), and Smith (2007). Several antiracist feminist scholars have outlined the ways in which marriage promotion policies serve the interests of the capitalist state and do virtually nothing to address the underlying factors contributing to poverty. See, for example, Coontz and Folbre (2002), Silag (2003), Onwuachi-Willig (2005), Hardisty (2008b), and Heath (2012).

48 For a detailed critique of the Right's use of questionable social science research to justify the use of marriage promotion as a cure for poverty, see Hardisty (2008a). For more on the 2010 government-funded study that found state-sponsored marriage promotion programs to be ineffective in improving relationships or keeping couples married, see Heath (2012, 189–191).

49 Nancy Polikoff raised similar concerns regarding Obama's marriage promotion and fatherhood responsibility rhetoric on her blog *Beyond (Straight and Gay) Marriage*. Responding to a speech the president delivered in February 2013, she explained that, unlike the LGBT family advocates who were celebrating the support he expressed for "all kinds of parents," including "gay or straight parents," she remained deeply concerned by how the emphasis he places on fathers and marital

relations effectively "blam[es] violence on single mothers and offer[s] marriage as the solution" (2013).

50 See, for example, David Blankenhorn's 2012 op-ed "How My View on Gay Marriage Changed" in the *New York Times*. Blankenhorn, a well-known leader of the marriage movement and the founder of the Institute for American Values, explains his decision to stop "fighting gay marriage" and, instead, to "help build new coalitions bringing together gays who want to strengthen marriage with straight people who want to do the same."

51 See SIECUS (n.d.) for a brief but instructive overview of the history of abstinence education in the United States. For an incisive historical and social analysis of sex ed debates since the 1960s and the development of a U.S.-based "Christian evangelical sexuality industry," see Irvine (2002).

52 See Irvine (2002, ch. 4) for a detailed analysis of the cultural and political context surrounding the passage of AFLA.

53 The organizations SIECUS and Advocates for Youth have waged powerful critiques of the limits and dangers of abstinence education in their advocacy work in support of more comprehensive approaches to sexual health education. For feminist and sex-positive scholarly critiques of abstinence-only education, see Levine (2002), Dreger (2015), and Josephson (2016, ch. 3).

54 Two government studies found abstinence-only education to be ineffective in achieving its stated goals of delaying sexual activity and preventing unwanted pregnancies. In 2004, Representative Henry Waxman, a Republican from California, released a report titled *The Content of Federally Funded Abstinence-Only Education Programs* that found abstinence-only-until-marriage curricula to contain medical inaccuracies, to perpetuate heteropatriarchal gender stereotypes, and to deploy fear-mongering and shame-inducing techniques (U.S. House of Representatives 2004). Two years later, in 2006, the U.S. Government Accountability Office released a report called *Abstinence Education: Efforts to Assess the Accuracy and Effectiveness of Federally Funded Programs*, which also highlighted concerns about the scientific accuracy of educational materials used by Title V or CBAE grantees. In April 2008, the House Committee on Oversight and Government Reform held a hearing on the effectiveness of abstinence-only education where representatives from the Institute of Medicine and the American Public Health Association testified that there is no evidence base to support federal funding of such programs (Boonstra 2008).

55 For a brief overview of the TPP program, see Office of Adolescent Health (2014).

56 A copy of this letter is available on Family Equality Council's website at https://www.familyequality.org/_asset/vyxt4r/FY10AppropsThankYou-FINALwsigs-clean.pdf.

57 Although lesbian feminist and LGBT family activists have long been citing anecdotal evidence about the fact that queer teenagers often end up accidentally pregnant (Hollibaugh and Moraga 2000, 83; Boggis 2001, 177), the body of scholarly research on this topic is relatively new. In its 2011 report on LGBT health disparities, the Institute of Medicine drew attention to the work of Elizabeth M. Saewyc and her colleagues (1999, 2008), who identified lesbian, gay, and bisexual adolescents as more likely to have had heterosexual intercourse and more likely to have been pregnant (153–154). In 2014, HHS's report on low-income and at-risk LGBT populations also highlighted Saewyc's work in raising concerns about the relatively higher rates of pregnancy among LGB-identified teens (64). More recent

studies on pregnancy and parenting among LGBTQ youth include Fletcher (2012) and Tornello, Riskind, and Patterson (2014).

58 For a brief overview of the historical construction of adolescence as an intrinsically dangerous period in specific relation to discourses of sexual health education, see Levine (2002, xxix–xxx). For an astute take of the production of teenagers as a chronically endangered population, see Elman (2014). In this book-length analysis of late twentieth century public policy, popular culture, and science journalism in the United States, Julie Passanante Elman shows "how representations of adolescence, sexuality, and disability, as sites of development, management, and investment, helped to naturalize a culture of rehabilitation as coterminous with good citizenship not just for those deemed disabled—but for all of us" (9).

59 See Zief, Shapiro, and Strong (2013) for an overview of the PREP initiative and for information on local programs implemented by PREP grantees.

Conclusion

1 For more on the needs of queer elders and the kinds of organizing efforts under way, see Hollibaugh (2012).

2 For an excellent overview of the politics of bathroom access, see director Tara Mateik's documentary, *Toilet Training* (2003). See also Alison Kafer's discussion of her work with People in Search of Safe and Accessible Restrooms (PISSAR) in *Feminist, Queer, Crip* (2013, 154–157).

3 For more on the coalitional possibilities linking queer and migration politics, see DasGupta (2012) and Chávez (2013). In her analysis of queer immigration manifestos—including the Audre Lorde Project's "No One Is Illegal" manifesto (2006), Queers for Economic Justice's "Queers and Immigration: A Vision Statement" (2007), and the Horizontal Alliances of Very (or Vaguely or Voraciously) Organized Queers (HAVOQ) piece "Undoing Borders: A Queer Manifesto" (2011)—Chávez tracks the strategies activists have used to resist the "family values" rhetoric that dominates LGBT and immigrant rights work and to put forth a vision of "queer migration politics" committed to "uphold[ing] all people's right to construct families as they desire" (33–35).

4 In her essay "How to Bring Your Kids Up Gay," Sedgwick tries to imagine a world in which scientists might positively describe a particular hormonal balance or endocrine environment as a "gay-producing circumstance," and she insists on the need for "a strong, explicit, *erotically invested* affirmation of many people's felt desire or need that there be gay people in the immediate world" (1991, 26, emphasis in original).

5 My use of the language "queer world-making" is a nod to Lauren Berlant and Michael Warner's (1998) canonical discussion of queer counterpublics and, perhaps more immediately, to José Esteban Muñoz's (2009) invocation of this framework in his theorizations of utopian longings and queer political imaginations.

6 See Jacobs (2014) for an interesting exploration of queer reproductive futures and a commentary on the rhetoric of affirmation (via the popular television show *Glee*).

7 For more about SPARK Reproductive Justice Now, visit http://www.sparkrj.org/. For more on the FYRE program in particular, visit http://www.sparkrj.org/fierce -youth-reclaiming-empowering/.

8 For more about the Native Youth Sexual Health Network, visit http://www .nativeyouthsexualhealth.com/.

9 I had the opportunity to see a staging of the brilliant Sexy Health Carnival at the 2015 Critical Ethnic Studies Association conference in Toronto. For more on this initiative, visit http://www.nativeyouthsexualhealth.com/sexyhealthcarnivalinformation.pdf.

10 I am quoting from Spade's undated essay "For Lovers and Fighters," which is available at https://web.archive.org/web/20171007124928/http://www.makezine.enoughenough.org/newpoly2.htm.

11 I would like to clarify that my vision for a queer family politics, while willfully optimistic, is not wholly naive. The material complexities of and the ongoing negotiations involved in progressive coalitional movements are not lost on me. As Amber Hollibaugh, Janet Jakobsen, and Catherine Sameh (2009) have documented, organizers face very real challenges when attempting to pursue cross-issue work: they struggle with the "difficulty of keeping a radical, sex-positive politics alive" in their activist projects, and they must contend with the "perils" that accompany the "promise" of maintaining a wide view of social justice in a climate marked by limited funding opportunities and evermore urgent community needs (4). Yet in the spirt of "desiring change"—that is, of asking what happens to our "methods of making social change" when we "infuse all of our activities with queerly comprehended perceptions of desire and gender" (4)—I close *Familiar Perversions* by highlighting exciting coalitional work already under way and gesturing toward new avenues, emphases, and configurations through which we might advance a queer family politics.

References

Abelson, Reed. 1996. "Welcome Mat Is Out for Gay Investors." *New York Times*, September 1.

Albelda, Randy, and Ann Withorn, eds. 2002. *Lost Ground: Welfare Reform, Poverty, and Beyond*. Cambridge, Mass.: South End.

Alexander, M. Jacqui. 1994. "Not Just (Any) Body Can Be a Citizen: The Politics of Law, Sexuality, and Postcoloniality in Trinidad and Tobago and the Bahamas." *Feminist Review* 48:5–23.

———. 2005. *Pedagogies of Crossing: Mediations on Feminism, Sexual Politics, Memory, and the Sacred*. Durham: Duke University Press.

All Aboard! Rosie's Family Cruise. 2006. Directed by Shari Cookson. New York: HBO Documentary Films.

Alterio, Julie Moran. 2004. "Cruising into a New Era." *Journal News*, February 18.

Althusser, Louis. 1971. "Ideology and Ideological State Apparatuses." In *Lenin and Philosophy, and Other Essays*, translated by Ben Brewster, 127–188. London: New Left Books.

Anagnost, Ann. 2000. "Scenes of Misrecognition: Maternal Citizenship in the Age of Transnational Adoption." *positions: east asia cultures critique* 8 (2): 389–421.

Arden, Dale. 2014. "Married Gay Couples Find Equality Taxing." *Wall Street Journal*, March 21. https://www.wsj.com/articles/married-gay-couples-find-equality-taxing -1395408545.

Arthur, Chris. 2014. "Financial Literacy Education as Public Pedagogy for the Capitalist Debt Economy." *Topia*, no. 30/31 (Fall 2013–Spring 2014): 147–163. https://topia .journals.yorku.ca/index.php/topia/article/view/38425.

Badgett, M. V. Lee. 1997. "Beyond Biased Samples: Challenging the Myths on the Economic Status of Lesbians and Gay Men." In *Homo Economics: Capitalism, Community, and Lesbian and Gay Life*, edited by Amy Gluckman and Betsy Reed, 65–71. New York: Routledge.

———. 2001. *Money, Myths, and Change: The Economic Lives of Lesbians and Gay Men*. Chicago: University of Chicago Press.

Badgett, M. V. Lee, Laura E. Durso, and Alyssa Schneebaum. 2013. *New Patterns of Poverty in the Lesbian, Gay, and Bisexual Community*. Los Angeles: Williams Institute, June. http:// williamsinstitute.law.ucla.edu/wp-content/uploads/LGB-Poverty-Update-Jun-2013.pdf.

Baehr v. Miike. 1996. First Circuit Court No. 91-1394. State of Hawaii.

Baker v. Vermont. 1999. 744 A.2d 864. State of Vermont.

Ball, Molly. 2015. "How Gay Marriage Became a Constitutional Right." *Atlantic*, July 1. http://www.theatlantic.com/politics/archive/2015/07/gay-marriage-supreme-court-politics-activism/397052/.

Bambara, Toni Cade, ed. 1970. *The Black Woman: An Anthology.* New York: Washington Square.

Barker, Joanne, ed. 2017. *Critically Sovereign: Indigenous Gender, Sexuality, and Feminist Studies.* Durham: Duke University Press.

Baynton, Douglas C. 2001. "Disability and the Justification of Inequality in American History." In *The New Disability History: American Perspectives*, edited by Paul K. Longmore and Lauri Umansky, 33–57. New York: New York University Press.

Bederman, Gail. 1995. *Manliness and Civilization: A Cultural History of Gender and Race in the United States, 1880–1917.* Chicago: University of Chicago Press.

Bellantoni, Christina. 2009. "Gay Parents Invited to Easter Egg Roll under New Policy." *Washington Times*, April 8. http://www.washingtontimes.com/news/2009/apr/08/gay-parents-invited-to-easter-egg-roll-under-new-p/.

Berkery, Peter M., Jr. 1996. *Personal Financial Planning for Gays & Lesbians: Our Guide to Prudent Decision Making.* Chicago: Irwin.

Berkery, Peter M., Jr., and Gregory A. Diggins. 1998. *Gay Finances in a Straight World: A Comprehensive Financial Planning Handbook.* New York: Palgrave Macmillan.

Berlant, Lauren. 1997. *The Queen of America Goes to Washington City: Essays on Sex and Citizenship.* Durham: Duke University Press.

Berlant, Lauren, and Michael Warner. 1998. "Sex in Public." *Critical Inquiry* 24 (2): 547–566.

Bernstein, Fred. 2007. "For Gay Parents, a Big Week in the Sun." *New York Times*, July 22. http://www.nytimes.com/2007/07/22/travel/22journeys.html.

Bernstein, Jacob. 2016. "The Remarriage of Edie Windsor, a Gay Marriage Pioneer." *New York Times*, September 30. https://www.nytimes.com/2016/09/30/fashion/weddings/edie-windsor-lgbt-activist-marriage.html.

Bernstein, Mary, and Renate Reimann, eds. 2001. *Queer Families, Queer Politics: Challenging Culture and the State.* New York: Columbia University Press.

Bersani, Leo. 1995. *Homos.* Cambridge, Mass.: Harvard University Press.

Bérubé, Allan. 1990. *Coming Out under Fire: The History of Gay Men and Women in World War Two.* New York: Free Press.

Beyond Marriage. 2006. *Beyond Same-Sex Marriage: A New Strategic Vision for All Our Families and Relationships.* BeyondMarriage.org, July 26. https://web.archive.org/web/20060807081028/http://www.beyondmarriage.org/.

Blackman, Andrew. 2005. "Family Finances: For Unmarried Partners, Planning Is Key." *Wall Street Journal*, September 18.

Blankenhorn, David. 2012. "How My View on Gay Marriage Changed." *New York Times*, June 22. http://www.nytimes.com/2012/06/23/opinion/how-my-view-on-gay-marriage-changed.html.

Boggis, Terry. 2001. "Affording Our Families: Class Issues in Family Formation." In *Queer Families, Queer Politics: Challenging Culture and the State*, edited by Mary Bernstein and Renate Reimann, 175–181. New York: Columbia University Press.

———. 2012. "Still Coming Ashore: The LGBT Community and the Many Meanings of Family." Special issue, *A New Queer Agenda*. Edited by Joseph N. DeFilippis, Lisa Duggan, Kenyon Farrow, and Richard Kim. *Scholar and Feminist Online* 10 (1/2). http://sfonline.barnard.edu/a-new-queer-agenda/still-coming-ashore-the-lgbt-community-and-the-many-meanings-of-family/.

————. 2013. "Queer Family Liberation: What's Next?" *Huffington Post*, June 10. http://
www.huffingtonpost.com/terry-boggis/queer-family-liberation-whats-next_b_3413274
.html.

Bolcer, Julie. 2011. "Zach Wahls, Rick Perry Videos Top YouTube for 2011." *Advocate*, December 20. http://www.advocate.com/news/daily-news/2011/12/20/zach-wahls-rick-perry
-videos-top-youtube-2011.

Boluda, Anna, dir. 2005. *Queer Spawn*. https://vimeo.com/20349933.

Bonauto, Mary L. 2005. "*Goodridge* in Context." *Harvard Civil Rights-Civil Liberties Law
Review* 40 (1): 1–70.

Boonstra, Heather D. 2008. "Congress Examines the Evidence on Abstinence-Only Education Programs." *Guttmacher Policy Review* 11 (2): 19–20. https://www.guttmacher.org/
gpr/2008/05/congress-examines-evidence-abstinence-only-education-programs.

Bowers v. Hardwick. 1986. 478 U.S. 186. No. 85-140. Supreme Court.

Boyd, Nan. 2003. *Wide-Open Town: A History of Queer San Francisco to 1965*. Berkeley: University of California Press.

Bragg, Mary Ann. 2008. "Park Officials Target Sex in Dunes." *Cape Cod Times*, June 13.
https://web.archive.org/web/20080614094206/http://www.capecodonline.com/apps/
pbcs.dll/article?AID=/20080613/NEWS/806130324.

Brandzel, Amy L. 2005. "Queering Citizenship? Same-Sex Marriage and the State." *GLQ: A
Journal of Lesbian and Gay Studies* 11 (2): 171–204.

————. 2016. *Against Citizenship: The Violence of the Normative*. Urbana: University of Illinois Press.

Brief of Dawn Stefanowicz and Denise Shick. *Obergefell v. Hodges*. 2015. 576 U.S. ___. Nos.
14-556, 14-562, 14-571, 14-574. Supreme Court.

Brief of Family Equality Council, COLAGE, Our Family Coalition, Gay, Lesbian, and
Straight Education Network, the Center on Children and Families, the Child Rights
Project, and Sarah Gogin. 2013. *Hollingsworth v. Perry*. No. 12-144, *United States v.
Windsor*. No. 12-307. Supreme Court.

Brief of Heather Barwick and Katy Faust. *Obergefell v. Hodges*. 2015. 576 U.S. ___. Nos. 14-
556, 14-562, 14-571, 14-574. Supreme Court.

Brief of Robert Oscar López and B. N. Klein. *Obergefell v. Hodges*. 2015. 576 U.S. ___. Nos.
14-556, 14-562, 14-571, 14-574. Supreme Court.

Briggs, Laura. 2002. *Reproducing Empire: Race, Sex, Science, and US Imperialism in Puerto
Rico*. Berkeley: University of California Press.

————. 2012. *Somebody's Children: The Politics of Transracial and Transnational Adoption*.
Durham: Duke University Press.

Bronski, Michael. 1984. *Culture Clash: The Making of Gay Sensibility*. Boston: South End
Press.

Brown, Wendy. 2006. "American Nightmare: Neoliberalism, Neoconservatism, and De-
Democratization." *Political Theory* 34 (6): 690–714.

Brum, Robert. 2016. "Rosie O'Donnell Gives Rockland Pride Center a Big Lift." *Lohud: The
Journal News*, March 4. http://www.lohud.com/story/news/local/rockland/2016/03/
04/rosie-odonnell-gives-rockland-pride-center-big-lift/81260544/.

Brunner, Jeryl. 2005. "R Family: We Are Family." *Passport Magazine*, February. https://
web.archive.org/web/20070505085601/http://www.passportmagazine.com/29/
RFamilyVacation.php.

Burwell v. Hobby Lobby Stores. 2014. 573 U.S. ___. No. 13-354. Supreme Court.

Burwick, Andrew, Gary Gates, Scott Baumgartner, and Daniel Friend. 2014. *Human Services
for Low-Income and At-Risk LGBT Populations: An Assessment of the Knowledge Base*

and Research Needs. Washington, D.C.: Office of Planning, Research, and Evaluation (Administration for Children and Families); Princeton: Mathematica Policy Research; Los Angeles: The Williams Institute, December.

Butler, Judith. 2002. "Is Kinship Always Already Heterosexual?" *differences: A Journal of Feminist Cultural Studies* 13 (1): 14–44.

Byrd, Jodi. 2011. *The Transit of Empire: Indigenous Critiques of Colonialism*. Minneapolis: University of Minnesota Press.

Cahill, Sean. 2005. "Welfare Moms and the Two Grooms: The Concurrent Promotion and Restriction of Marriage in US Public Policy." *Sexualities* 8 (2): 169–187.

Canaday, Margot. 2009. *The Straight State: Sexuality and Citizenship in Twentieth-Century America*. Princeton: Princeton University Press.

Carby, Hazel V. 1987. *Reconstructing Womanhood: The Emergence of the Afro-American Woman Novelist*. New York: Oxford University Press.

Carter, Julian. 1997. "Normality, Whiteness, Authorship: Evolutionary Sexology and the Primitive Pervert." In *Science and Homosexualities*, edited by Vernon A. Rosario, 155–176. New York: Routledge.

———. 2007. *The Heart of Whiteness: Normal Sexuality and Race in America, 1880–1940*. Durham: Duke University Press.

Cayleff, Susan E. 2007. Review of *The Courage to Connect: Sexuality, Citizenship, and Community in Provincetown*, by Sandra L. Faiman-Silva. *Journal of the History of Sexuality* 16 (1): 114–120.

Chamberlain, Seth. 2016. "Supporting Healthy Marriage and Relationships for LGBT Populations." *The Family Room* (blog). Administration for Children and Families, June 16. http://www.acf.hhs.gov/blog/2016/06/supporting-healthy-marriage-and-relationships-for-lgbt-populations.

Chanoff, Debra, and Kim Klausner, dirs. 1985. *Choosing Children: Launching the Lesbian Baby Boom*. Newburgh, N.Y.: New Day Films.

Charles, Casey. 2003. *The Sharon Kowalski Case: Lesbian and Gay Rights on Trial*. Lawrence: University of Kansas Press.

Chasin, Alexandra. 2000. *Selling Out: The Gay and Lesbian Movement Goes to Market*. New York: Palgrave Macmillan.

Chauncey, George. 1994. *Gay New York: Gender, Urban Culture, and the Making of the Gay Male World 1890–1940*. New York: Basic Books.

Chávez, Karma R. 2013. *Queer Migration Politics: Activist Rhetoric and Coalitional Possibilities*. Urbana: University of Illinois Press.

Chira, Susan. 1993. "Gay Parents Become Increasingly Visible." *New York Times*, September 30. http://www.nytimes.com/1993/09/30/us/gay-parents-become-increasingly-visible.html.

Cho, Yu-Fang. 2013. *Uncoupling American Empire: Cultural Politics of Deviance and Unequal Difference, 1890–1910*. Albany: State University of New York Press.

Christopher Street Financial. n.d. "Community Involvement." http://www.christopherstreet.com/community-involvement.

———. n.d. "History." http://www.christopherstreet.com/history.

Churchill, David S. 2008. "Transnationalism and Homophile Political Culture in the Postwar Decades." *GLQ: A Journal of Lesbian and Gay Studies* 15 (1): 31–66.

Clark, Danae. 1991. "Commodity Lesbianism." *Camera Obscura* 9 (1/2): 181–201.

Cloud, John. 2013. "My Big Gay Tax Return." *Bloomberg Businessweek*, September 26. http://www.bloomberg.com/news/articles/2013-09-26/gay-couples-tax-returns-to-refile-jointly-or-not.

Cohen, Cathy J. 1997. "Punks, Bulldaggers, and Welfare Queens: The Radical Potential of Queer Politics?" *GLQ: A Journal of Lesbian and Gay Studies* 3 (4): 437–465.

COLAGE. n.d. "Second Gen FAQ: For LGBTQ Folks with LGBTQ Parents." http://www.colage.org/resources/second-gen-faq/.

———. n.d. "Tips for Making Family Week More Affordable." http://www.colage.org/wp-content/uploads/2012/12/TipsforMakingFamilyWeekMoreAffordable-41.pdf.

Colen, Shellee. 1995. "'Like a Mother to Them': Stratified Reproduction and West Indian Childcare Workers and Employers in New York." In *Conceiving the New World Order: The Global Politics of Reproduction*, edited by Faye D. Ginsburg and Rayna Rapp, 78–102. Berkeley: University of California Press.

Collins, Patricia Hill. 2000. *Black Feminist Thought: Knowledge, Consciousness, and the Politics of Empowerment*. 2nd ed. New York: Routledge.

Colman, David. 2005. "Rich Gay, Poor Gay." *New York Times*, September 4.

Community Marketing. 2010. *15th Annual Gay and Lesbian Tourism Report*. San Francisco: Community Marketing.

———. 2015. *20th Annual Survey on LGBT Tourism & Hospitality: U.S. Overview Report*. San Francisco: Community Marketing.

Conrad, Ryan, ed. 2010. *Against Equality: Queer Critiques of Gay Marriage*. Lewiston, Maine: Against Equality Publishing Collective.

———, ed. 2014. *Against Equality: Queer Revolution, Not Mere Inclusion*. Oakland, Calif.: AK Press.

Coontz, Stephanie. 1992. *The Way We Never Were: American Families and the Nostalgia Trap*. New York: Basic Books.

Coontz, Stephanie, and Nancy Folbre. 2002. "Marriage, Poverty, and Public Policy." *American Prospect*, March 21. http://prospect.org/article/marriage-poverty-and-public-policy.

Cooper, Melinda. 2008. *Life as Surplus: Biotechnology and Capitalism in the Neoliberal Era*. Seattle: University of Washington Press.

Cott, Nancy F. 2002. *Public Vows: A History of Marriage and the Nation*. Cambridge, Mass.: Harvard University Press.

Cowen, Deborah, and Emily Gilbert. 2008. "Citizenship in the 'Homeland': Families at War." In *War, Citizenship, Territory*, edited by Deborah Cowen and Emily Gilbert, 261–279. New York: Routledge.

Cravens, Hamilton. 1993. "Child Saving in Modern America 1870s–1990s." In *Children at Risk in America: History, Concepts, and Public Policy*, edited by Roberta Wollons, 3–31. Albany: State University of New York Press.

DasGupta, Debanuj. 2012. "Queering Immigration: Perspectives on Cross-Movement Organizing." Special issue, *A New Queer Agenda*. Edited by Joseph N. DeFilippis, Lisa Duggan, Kenyon Farrow, and Richard Kim. *Scholar and Feminist Online* 10 (1/2). http://sfonline.barnard.edu/a-new-queer-agenda/queering-immigration-perspectives-on-cross-movement-organizing.

Davidson, Cathy N., and Jessamyn Hatcher, eds. 2002. *No More Separate Spheres! A Next Wave American Studies Reader*. Durham: Duke University Press.

Davis, Amanda. 1993. "Financial Counseling for AIDS Sufferers." Associated Press, October 26.

Davis, Angela Y. 1983. *Women, Race and Class*. New York: Vintage Books.

Davis, Jordan Gwendolyn. 2015. "Why, No Matter What, I Still Can't Marry My Girlfriend." *Advocate*, June 29. https://www.advocate.com/commentary/2015/06/29/op-ed-why-no-matter-what-i-still-cant-marry-my-girlfriend.

Day, Shelbi, and Arielle Gingold. 2017. "Religious Exemptions for Child Welfare Agencies: A License to Discriminate against LGBTQ Parents and Children." *The Family Room* (blog), May 20. http://www.familyequality.org/equal_family_blog/2017/05/20/2170/ religious_exemptions_for_child_welfare_agencies_a_license_to_discriminate_against _lgbtq_parents_and_children.

Dean, Tim. 2006. "The Antisocial Homosexual." *PMLA* 121 (3): 826–828.

Deer, Sarah. 2015. *The Beginning and End of Rape: Confronting Sexual Violence in Native America*. Minneapolis: University of Minnesota Press.

DeFilippis, Joseph Nicholas. 2016. "'What about the Rest of Us?': An Overview of LGBT Poverty Issues and a Call to Action." *Journal of Progressive Human Services* 27 (3): 143–174.

de Haan, Linda, and Stern Nijland. 2000. *King and King*. Berkeley, Calif.: Tricycle.

Deloria, Vine, Jr., and David E. Wilkins. 2011. *The Legal Universe: Observations on the Foundations of American Law*. Golden, Colo.: Fulcrum.

D'Emilio, John. 1983. *Sexual Politics, Sexual Communities: The Making of a Homosexual Minority in the United States, 1940–1970*. Chicago: University of Chicago Press.

———. 1993. "Capitalism and Gay Identity." In *The Lesbian and Gay Studies Reader*, edited by Henry Abelove, Michèle Aina Barale, and David M. Halperin, 467–476. New York: Routledge.

Democracy Now! 2009. "Testimony of 12-Year-Old with Two Moms Moves Some Vermont Legislators to Support Gay Marriage Bill." April 8. http://www.democracynow.org/ 2009/4/8/testimony_of_12_year_old_with.

Desroches, Steve. 2006. "The Future of Tourism in Provincetown." *Provincetown Journal*, August 26. http://provincetownjournal.com/provincetown/entry/the-future-of-tourism -in-provincetown/.

Dickinson, Bob, and Andy Vladimir. 2008. *Selling the Sea: An Inside Look at the Cruise Industry*. 2nd ed. Hoboken, N.J.: John Wiley & Sons.

Diedrich, Lisa. 2016. *Indirect Action: Schizophrenia, Epilepsy, AIDS, and the Course of Health Activism*. Minneapolis: University of Minnesota Press.

Dorow, Sara K. 2006. *Transnational Adoption: A Cultural Economy of Race, Gender, and Kinship*. New York: New York University Press.

Dreger, Alice. 2015. "What I Learned When I Attended My Son's 'Abstinence-Based' Sex Ed Class." *Guardian*, April 21. https://www.theguardian.com/education/2015/apr/21/what-i -learned-sex-ed-class-absintence.

Duberman, Martin. 1993. *Stonewall*. New York: Dutton.

Duggan, Lisa. 1993. "The Trials of Alice Mitchell: Sensationalism, Sexology, and the Lesbian Subject in Turn-of-the-Century America." *Signs: Journal of Women in Culture and Society* 18 (4): 791–814.

———. 2003. *The Twilight of Equality? Neoliberalism, Cultural Politics, and the Attack on Democracy*. Boston: Beacon.

Edelman, Lee. 2004. *No Future: Queer Theory and the Death Drive*. Durham: Duke University Press.

Edelman, Rivka. 2015. "LGBT Demands for Other People's Children Are Misogynistic." *Federalist*, February 3. http://thefederalist.com/2015/02/03/lbgt-demands-for-other -peoples-children-are-misogynistic/.

Ehrenreich, Barbara, and Deirdre English. 2005. *For Her Own Good: Two Centuries of the Experts' Advice to Women*. New York: Anchor Books.

Elman, Julie Passanante. 2014. *Chronic Youth: Disability, Sexuality, and U.S. Media Cultures of Rehabilitation*. New York: New York University Press.

Eng, David L. 2010. *The Feeling of Kinship: Queer Liberalism and the Racialization of Intimacy*. Durham: Duke University Press.

Enloe, Cynthia. 1989. *Bananas, Beaches, and Bases: Making Feminist Sense of International Politics.* Berkeley: University of California Press.

Epstein, Rachel. 2005. "Queer Parenting in the New Millennium: Resisting Normal." *Canadian Women's Studies* 24 (2/3): 7–14.

———. 2009. *Who's Your Daddy? And Other Writings on Queer Parenting.* Toronto: Sumach.

Ettelbrick, Paula L. 1998. "Since When Is Marriage a Path to Liberation?" In *Families in the U.S.: Kinship and Domestic Politics,* edited by Karen V. Hansen and Anita Ilta Garey, 481–485. Philadelphia: Temple University Press.

Evans, Dominick. 2015. "Some People with Disabilities ARE Prevented from Getting Married and Here's Why." DominickEvans.com, June 27. http://www.dominickevans.com/2015/06/some-people-with-disabilities-are-prevented-from-getting-married-and-heres-why/.

Faiman-Silva, Sandra. 2004. *The Courage to Connect: Sexuality, Citizenship, and Community in Provincetown.* Urbana: University of Illinois Press.

Family Equality Council. 2008. "Sen. Obama Responds to Jennifer Chrisler's Questions on Family Policy." *The Family Room* (blog), August 5. https://www.familyequality.org/equal_family_blog/2008/08/05/601/sen_obama_responds_to_jennifer_chrislers_questions_on_family_policy.

———. 2009a. "Iowa Supreme Court Upholds Marriage Equality!" *The Family Room* (blog), April 3. http://www.familyequality.org/equal_family_blog/2009/04/03/767/iowa_supreme_court_upholds_marriage_equality.

———. 2009b. "Tickets for White House Egg Roll." *The Family Room* (blog), March 25. https://www.familyequality.org/equal_family_blog/2009/03/25/763/tickets_for_white_house_egg_roll_2009.

———. 2011. "Announcing the Launch of Family Equality Council's Ask the Experts Page!" *The Family Room* (blog), January 28. http://www.familyequality.org/equal_family_blog/2011/01/28/998/announcing_the_launch_of_family_equality_councils_ask_the_experts_page.

———. 2015a. "Family Equality Council Kicks Off 20th Anniversary of Family Week in Provincetown July 25." July 20. http://www.familyequality.org/news__media/2015/07/20/1986/family_equality_council_kicks_off_20th_anniversary_of_family_week_in_provincetown_july_25.

———. 2015b. "Family Equality Council to Launch National Foster Care Month Campaign, Spotlighting the Urgent Need to Pass the Every Child Deserves a Family Act." May 3. http://www.familyequality.org/news__media/2015/05/03/1922/family_equality_council_to_launch_national_foster_care_month_campaign_spotlighting_the_urgent_need_to_pass_the_every_child_deserves_a_family_act.

———. n.d. "About Us." https://www.familyequality.org/about_us/about_us/.

———. n.d. "ECDF Act Facts: What Is the Every Child Deserves a Family Act?" http://www.familyequality.org/get_informed/advocacy/adoption_and_foster/ecdf_facts/.

———. n.d. "Family Week." http://www.familyequality.org/get_involved/events/annual_events/family_week/.

———. n.d. "Family Week FAQs." http://www.familyequality.org/get_involved/events/annual_events/family_week/family_week_faqs/.

———. n.d. "The Outspoken Generation." http://www.familyequality.org/get_involved/outspoken/.

———. n.d. "Protecting Your Family." http://www.familyequality.org/_asset/lmkovk/Tools-for-Parents.pdf.

Family and Medical Leave Act. 1993. Pub. L. No. 103-3, 107 Stat. 6 (29 U.S. Code 2601 *et seq.*).

Family Pride Coalition. n.d. "OUTSpoken Families: Family Pride's Speakers Bureau: Speakers Toolkit." http://www.familyequality.org/_asset/h26fmj/speakerstoolkit.pdf.

Fatsis, Stefan. 1991. "Brokerage Firm Catering to Gay Community Struggles with AIDS Crisis." Associated Press, December 1.

Faust, Katy. 2015. "Dear Justice Kennedy: An Open Letter from the Child of a Loving Gay Parent." *Public Discourse*, February 2. http://www.thepublicdiscourse.com/2015/02/14370/.

Ferguson, Kathy E., and Phyllis Turnbull. 1999. *Oh, Say, Can You See: The Semiotics of the Military in Hawai'i*. Minneapolis: University of Minnesota Press.

Ferguson, Roderick A. 2004. *Aberrations in Black: Toward a Queer of Color Critique*. Minneapolis: University of Minnesota Press.

———. 2006. "Race-ing Homonormativity: Citizenship, Sociology, and Gay Identity." In *Black Queer Studies: A Critical Anthology*, edited by E. Patrick Johnson and Mae G. Henderson, 52–67. Durham: Duke University Press.

Fierce Youth Reclaiming and Empowering (FYRE). 2010. *Fire: Sparking the Flames in Each Other*. Atlanta, Ga.: SPARK Reproductive Justice Now.

Findlay, Eileen J. Suárez. 1999. *Imposing Decency: The Politics of Sexuality and Race in Puerto Rico, 1870–1920*. Durham: Duke University Press.

Fisher, Tim. 1998. "In Your Face: A Family with Two Dads." *In the Family: The Magazine for Queer People and their Loved Ones* 4 (1): 17.

Fleischer, David. 2010. *The Prop 8 Report: What Defeat in California Can Teach Us about Winning Future Ballot Measures on Same-Sex Marriage*. LGBT Mentoring Project. http://prop8report.lgbtmentoring.org/.

Fletcher, Rachel. March 2012. *Invisible Needs: A Report on LGBTQ Youth Pregnancy and Parenting Experiences*. Minneapolis: Rainbow Health Initiative. http://www.rainbowhealth.org/files/1113/6070/9174/Invisible_Needs_A_Report_on_LGBTQ_Youth_Pregnancy_and_Parenting_Experiences.pdf.

Ford, Zack. 2015. "The Full Story of the 'Poster Children' Conservatives Are Using to Oppose Gay Marriage." *Think Progress*, February 4. http://thinkprogress.org/lgbt/2015/02/04/3618907/four-kids-gay-parent-oppose-equality/.

Foucault, Michel. 1990. *The History of Sexuality, Volume 1: An Introduction*. Translated by Robert Hurley. New York: Vintage Books.

Franke, Katherine. 2015. *Wedlocked: The Perils of Marriage Equality*. New York: New York University Press.

Freedman, Estelle. 1987. "'Uncontrolled Desires': The Response to the Sexual Psychopath, 1920–60." *Journal of American History* 74 (1): 83–106.

Freedom to Marry. 2010. *Moving Marriage Forward: Building Majority Support for Marriage*. http://freemarry.3cdn.net/1809cf9c79a249a415_ztm6blgzo.pdf.

Freud, Sigmund. 2000. *Three Essays on the Theory of Sexuality*. Translated by James Strachey. New York: Basic Books.

Gallagher, John. 1995. "Gay . . . with Children." *Advocate*, May 30.

———. 1998. "Many Happy Returns: Financial Companies See a Future with Gay Investors." *Advocate*, April 28.

Gallo, Marcia M. 2006. *Different Daughters: A History of the Daughters of Bilitis and the Rise of the Lesbian Rights Movement*. New York: Avalon.

Gamson, Joshua. 2015. *Modern Families: Stories of Extraordinary Journeys to Kinship*. New York: New York University Press.

Garafoli, Joe. 2015. "S.F. Foundation Supported Gay Marriage Long before It Was Cool." *San Francisco Chronicle*, June 28. http://www.sfchronicle.com/bayarea/article/S-F-foundation-supported-gay-marriage-long-6354668.php.

Garmhausen, Steve. 2010. "Advisor Spotlight: How a Former JPMorgan Bond Saleswoman Transformed an Iconic Advisory into a Business." *RIABiz*, October 25. http://www.riabiz.com/a/2989001/advisorspotlighthowaformerjpmorganbondsaleswomantransformed aniconicadvisoryintoabusiness.

Gates, Gary J. 2013. *LGBT Parenting in the United States*. Los Angeles: Williams Institute. http://williamsinstitute.law.ucla.edu/wp-content/uploads/LGBT-Parenting.pdf.

Gates, Gary J., M. V. Lee Badgett, Jennifer Ehrle Macomber, and Kate Chambers. 2007. *Adoption and Foster Care by Gay and Lesbian Parents in the United States*. Los Angeles: Williams Institute; Washington, D.C.: Urban Institute. https://williamsinstitute.law.ucla.edu/wp-content/uploads/Gates-Badgett-Macomber-Chambers-Final-Adoption-Report -Mar-2007.pdf.

Gates, Gary J., and Adam P. Romero. 2009. "Parenting by Gay Men and Lesbians: Beyond the Current Research." In *Marriage and Family: Perspectives and Complexities*, edited by H. Elizabeth Peters and Claire M. Kamp Dush, 227–243. New York: Columbia University Press.

Gay, Mara. 2013. "City Seeking to Diversify Foster System." *Wall Street Journal*, June 2. http://www.wsj.com/articles/SB10001424127887324563004578521604208702758.

Gay and Lesbian Parents Coalition International (GLPCI). 1992. "An Open Letter to President Bush." *Dallas Voice*, September 18.

Gilomen, Jen, dir. 2005. *In My Shoes*. COLAGE Youth Leadership and Action Program. http://www.colage.org/resources/in-my-shoes/.

Ginsburg, Faye D., and Rayna Rapp. 1995. *Conceiving the New World Order: The Global Politics of Reproduction*. Berkeley: University of California Press.

Gluckman, Amy, and Betsy Reed. 1997. "The Gay Marketing Moment." In *Homo Economics: Capitalism, Community, and Lesbian and Gay Life*, edited by Amy Gluckman and Betsy Reed, 3–9. New York: Routledge.

Goeman, Mishuana R., and Jennifer Nez Denetdale, eds. 2009. Special issue, *Native Feminisms: Legacies, Interventions, and Indigenous Sovereignties. Wicazo Sa Review* 24 (2).

Gold, Liz. 2012. "Wealth Management Firm Meets Needs of LGBT Clients." *Accounting Web*, December 11. http://www.accountingweb.com/tax/individuals/wealth -management-firm-meets-needs-of-lgbt-clients.

Goleman, Daniel. 1992. "Studies Find No Disadvantage in Growing Up in a Gay Home." *New York Times*, December 2. http://www.nytimes.com/1992/12/02/health/studies-find -no-disadvantage-in-growing-up-in-a-gay-home.html.

Goodfellow, Aaron. 2015. *Gay Fathers, Their Children, and the Making of Kinship*. New York: Fordham University Press.

Goodridge v. Department of Public Health. 2003. 798 N.E. 2d 941. State of Massachusetts.

Graves, Lucia. 2010. "Gay Teen Suicides Pervasive, a 'Hidden Problem': Expert." *Huffington Post*, October 22. http://www.huffingtonpost.com/2010/10/22/gay-teen-suicides-a -hidden-problem_n_772707.html.

Grewal, Inderpal. 2005. *Transnational America: Feminisms, Diasporas, Neoliberalisms*. Durham: Duke University Press.

———. 2006. "'Security Moms' in the Early Twenty-First-Century United States: The Gender of Security in Neoliberalism." *Women's Studies Quarterly* 34 (1/2): 25–39.

Grewal, Inderpal, and Caren Kaplan, eds. 1994. *Scattered Hegemonies: Postmodernity and Transnational Feminist Practices*. Minneapolis: University of Minnesota Press.

———. 2001. "Global Identities: Theorizing Transnational Studies of Sexuality." *GLQ: A Journal of Lesbian and Gay Studies* 7 (4): 663–679.

Griffin, Jean Latz. 1992. "The Gay Baby Boom." *Chicago Tribune*, September 3. http://articles
.chicagotribune.com/1992-09-03/features/9203200303_1_gay-rights-movement-lesbian
-parents-coalition-international-couples.

Gross, Jane. 1991. "New Challenges of Youth: Growing Up in a Gay Home." *New York Times*,
February 11.

Grossberg, Lawrence. 2010. *Cultural Studies in the Future Tense*. Durham: Duke University
Press.

Gutis, Philip S. 1987. "Fire Island Pines in Age of AIDS." *New York Times*, June 8.

Haider-Markel, Donald P. 1997. *From Bullhorns to PACs: Lesbian and Gay Politics, Interest
Groups, and Policy*. Ann Arbor: University of Michigan Press.

Halberstam, J. Jack. 2005. *In a Queer Time and Place: Transgender Bodies, Subcultural Lives*.
New York: New York University Press.

———. 2011. *The Queer Art of Failure*. Durham: Duke University Press.

Hall, Stuart. 1998a. "Aspiration and Attitude: Reflections on Black Britons in the Nineties."
New Formations (33): 38–46.

———. 1998b. "Cultural Composition: Stuart Hall on Ethnicity and the Discursive Turn."
Journal of Composition and Theory 18 (2): 171–196.

Hall, Stuart, Chas Critcher, Tony Jefferson, John Clarke, and Brian Roberts. 2013. *Policing
the Crisis: Mugging, the State, and Law & Order*. New York: Palgrave Macmillan.

Hanhardt, Christina B. 2013. *Safe Space: Gay Neighborhood History and the Politics of Violence*. Durham: Duke University Press.

———. 2016. "Broken Windows at Blue's: A Queer History of Gentrification and Policing."
In *Policing the Planet: Why the Policing Crisis Led to Black Lives Matter*, edited by Jordan T. Camp and Christina Heatherton, 41–61. New York: Verso.

Hardisty, Jean. 2008a. "Marriage as a Cure for Poverty? Social Science through a 'Family
Values' Lens." Political Research Associates and the Women of Color Resource Center.
http://www.publiceye.org/jeans_report/marriage-promotion-part-2.pdf.

———. 2008b. "Pushed to the Altar: The Right Wing Roots of Marriage Promotion."
Policy Research Associates and the Women of Color Resource Center. http://www
.politicalresearch.org/2008/04/01/pushed-to-the-altar-the-right-wing-roots-of-marriage
-promotion/#sthash.GCx34G7H.dpbs.

Hardisty, Jean, and Amy Gluckman. 1997. "The Hoax of 'Special Rights': The Right Wing's
Attack on Gay Men and Lesbians." In *Homo Economics: Capitalism, Community, and
Lesbian and Gay Life*, edited by Amy Gluckman and Betsy Reed, 209–222. New York:
Routledge.

Haritaworn, Jin, Adi Kuntsman, and Silvia Posocco, eds. 2014. *Queer Necropolitics*. New
York: Routledge.

Hartman, Saidiya V. 1997. *Scenes of Subjection: Terror, Slavery, and Self-Making in
Nineteenth-Century America*. New York: Oxford University Press.

Hawkins, Beth. 2013. "Same-Sex Marriage Opponent Robert Oscar Lopez Calls Himself a
'Children's Activist.'" *MinnPost*, March 18. https://www.minnpost.com/politics-policy/
2013/03/same-sex-marriage-opponent-robert-oscar-lopez-calls-himself-childrens-activi.

Hay, Harry. 1996. "The Homosexual and History . . . an Invitation to Further Study." In
Radically Gay: Gay Liberation in the Words of Its Founder, edited by Will Roscoe, 94–119.
Boston: Beacon.

Heath, Melanie. 2012. *One Marriage under God: The Campaign to Promote Marriage in
America*. New York: New York University Press.

Hennessy, Rosemary. 2000. *Profit and Pleasure: Sexual Identities in Late Capitalism*. New
York: Routledge.

Hernandez, Greg. 2006. "It's All about Our Children." *Advocate*, April 10. http://www
.advocate.com/politics/commentary/2006/04/10/its-all-about-our-children.

Hobbs, John. 2014. "Should We or Shouldn't We?" *Instinct*, March 28. http://
instinctmagazine.com/article/should-we-or-shouldn%E2%80%99t-we.

Hollibaugh, Amber. 2012. "2, 4, 6, 8: Who Says That Your Grandmother's Straight?" Special
issue, *A New Queer Agenda*. Edited by Joseph N. DeFilippis, Lisa Duggan, Kenyon Farrow, and Richard Kim. *Scholar and Feminist Online* 10 (1/2). http://sfonline.barnard
.edu/a-new-queer-agenda/2-4-6-8-who-says-that-your-grandmothers-straight/.

Hollibaugh, Amber, Janet Jakobsen, and Catherine Sameh. 2011. *Desiring Change*. New
Feminist Solutions 6. New York: Barnard Center for Research on Women. http://bcrw
.barnard.edu/publications/desiring-change/.

Hollibaugh, Amber, and Cherríe Moraga. 2000. "What We're Rolling around in Bed With."
In *My Dangerous Desires: A Queer Girl Dreaming Her Way Home*, 62–63, 72–84. Durham: Duke University Press.

Hollibaugh, Amber, and Margot Weiss. 2015. "Queer Precarity and the Myth of Gay Affluence." *New Labor Forum* 24 (3): 18–27.

Hollingsworth v. Perry. 2013. 570 U.S. ___. No. 12-144. Supreme Court.

Howey, Noelle. 2003. "Generations of Pride." *Advocate*, June 10, 40–41.

Howey, Noelle, and Ellen Samuels, eds. 2000. *Out of the Ordinary: Essays on Growing Up
with Gay, Lesbian, and Transgender Parents*. New York: St. Martin's.

Hughes, Howard L. 2006. *Pink Tourism: Holidays of Gay Men and Lesbians*. Cambridge,
Mass.: CAB International.

Hunter, Nan D. 1995. "Sexual Dissent and the Family: The Sharon Kowalski Case." In *Sex
Wars: Sexual Dissent and Political Culture*, edited by Lisa Duggan and Nan D. Hunter,
101–105. New York: Routledge.

Hunter, Tera W. 2017. *Bound in Wedlock: Slave and Free Black Marriage in the Nineteenth
Century*. Cambridge, Mass.: Harvard University Press.

Hurewitz, Daniel. 2007. *Bohemian Los Angeles and the Making of Modern Politics*. Berkeley:
University of California Press.

Hurwitz, Darrin. 2013. "In Maine, the National Organization for Marriage Fights for Its
Own Survival as Marriage Equality Reigns." *Huffington Post*, April 17. http://www
.huffingtonpost.com/darrin-hurwitz/in-maine-the-national-organization-for-marriage
-fights-for-its-own-survival-as-marriage-equality-reigns_b_3094925.html.

INCITE! Women of Color against Violence. 2007. *The Revolution Will Not Be Funded:
Beyond the Non-profit Industrial Complex*. Cambridge, Mass.: South End.

In re Marriage Cases. 2008. 43 Cal. 4th 757. State of California.

Institute of Medicine. 2011. *The Health of Lesbian, Gay, Bisexual, and Transgender People: Building
a Foundation for Better Understanding*. Washington, D.C.: National Academies Press.

Irvine, Janice M. 2002. *Talk about Sex: The Battles over Sex Education in the United States*.
Berkeley: University of California Press.

Jacobs, Jason. 2014. "Raising Gays: On *Glee*, Queer Kids, and the Limits of the Family."
GLQ: A Journal of Lesbian and Gay Studies 20 (3): 319–352.

Jacobson, Matthew Frye. 1998. *Whiteness of a Different Color: European Immigrants and the
Alchemy of Race*. Cambridge, Mass.: Harvard University Press.

Jakobsen, Janet R. 2009. "The Economics of Fear, the Politics of Hope, and the Perversity of
Happiness." *Women & Performance: A Journal of Feminist Theory* 19 (2): 219–226.

——. 2012. "Perverse Justice." *GLQ: A Journal of Lesbian and Gay Studies* 18 (1): 19–45.

Jennings, Patricia K. 2006. "The Trouble with the Multiethnic Placement Act: An Empirical
Look at Transracial Adoption." *Sociological Perspectives* 49 (4): 559–581.

Jetter, Alexis, Annelise Orleck, and Diana Taylor. 1997. *The Politics of Motherhood: Activist Voices from Left to Right*. Hanover, N.H.: Dartmouth College Press.

Johnson, David K. 2004. *The Lavender Scare: The Cold War Persecution of Gays and Lesbians in the Federal Government*. Chicago: University of Chicago Press.

Jordan, Katy. 2008. "Sex Acts on Provincetown Beaches Prompt Outrage." *Boston Herald*, July 8. http://www.bostonherald.com/news_opinion/local_coverage/2008/07/sex_acts _provincetown_beaches_prompt_outrage.

Joseph, Miranda. 2013. "Gender, Entrepreneurial Subjectivity, and Pathologies of Personal Finance." *Social Politics: International Studies in Gender, State & Society* 20 (2): 242–273.

Josephson, Jyl J. 2016. *Rethinking Sexual Citizenship*. Albany: State University of New York Press.

Kafer, Alison. 2013. *Feminist, Queer, Crip*. Indianapolis: Indiana University Press.

Kahn, Ellen. 2013. "Every Child Deserves a Family Act Reintroduced." *Human Rights Campaign*, May 17. http://www.hrc.org/blog/entry/every-child-deserves-a-family-act -reintroduced.

Kaminer, Ariel. 2008. "A High-Seas Show with Gay Family Values." *New York Times*, July 19. http://www.nytimes.com/2008/07/19/arts/19rosie.html.

Kandaswamy, Priya. 2008. "State Austerity and the Racial Politics of Same-Sex Marriage in the US." *Sexualities* 11 (6): 706–725.

Kaplan, Amy. 1998. "Manifest Domesticity." *American Literature* 70 (3): 581–606.

Kaplan, Caren. 1996. *Questions of Travel: Postmodern Discourses of Displacement*. Durham: Duke University Press.

Kaplan, Caren, and Inderpal Grewal. 1994. "Transnational Feminist Cultural Studies: Beyond the Marxism/Poststructuralism/Feminism Divides." *positions: east asia cultures critique* 2 (2): 430–445.

Kauanui, J. Kēhaulani. 2008a. *Hawaiian Blood: Colonialism and the Politics of Sovereignty and Indigeneity*. Durham: Duke University Press.

———. 2008b. "Native Hawaiian Decolonization and the Politics of Gender." *American Quarterly* 60 (2): 281–287.

Kaufman, M. J., and Katie Miles. 2009. "Resist the Gay Marriage Agenda!" *Queer Kids of Queer Parents against Gay Marriage!*, October 9. https://queerkidssaynomarriage .wordpress.com/.

Kelleher, Paul. 2004. "How to Do Things with Perversion: Psychoanalysis and the 'Child in Danger.'" In *Curiouser: On the Queerness of Children*, edited by Steven Bruhm and Natasha Hurley, 151–171. Minneapolis: University of Minnesota Press.

Kelling, George L., and James Q. Wilson. 1982. "Broken Windows: The Police and Neighborhood Safety." *Atlantic*, March. http://www.theatlantic.com/magazine/archive/1982/ 03/broken-windows/304465/.

Kerrigan v. Commissioner of Public Health. 2007. 89 Conn. 135, 957 A.2d 407. State of Connecticut.

Kirby, David. 1998. "The Second Generation." *New York Times*, June 7. http://www.nytimes .com/1998/06/07/nyregion/the-second-generation.html.

Kiritsy, Laura. 2002. "Week in P'town Fills an Important Need for GLBT Families." *Edge Media Network*, August 15. http://boston.edgemedianetwork.com/news///69235.

Klein, Ross A. 2017. "Representation without Taxation." In *Cruise Ship Tourism*, 2nd ed., edited by Ross Dowling and Clare Weeden, 57–71. Cambridge, Mass.: CAB International.

Kline, Wendy. 2005. *Building a Better Race: Gender, Sexuality, and Eugenics from the Turn of the Century to the Baby Boom*. Berkeley: University of California Press.

Koshy, Susan. 2004. *Sexual Naturalization: Asian Americans and Miscegenation*. Palo Alto, Calif.: Stanford University Press.

Krahulik, Karen C. 2005. *Provincetown: From Pilgrim Landing to Gay Resort*. New York: New York University Press.

Laine, Jody, Shan Ottey, and Shad Reinstein, dirs. 2006. *Mom's Apple Pie: The Heart of the Lesbian Mothers' Custody Movement*. San Francisco: Frameline.

Lambda Legal. n.d. "Plaintiff Couples in Lambda Legal's Iowa Marriage Lawsuit: *Varnum v. Brien*." http://www.lambdalegal.org/publications/fs_plaintiff-couples-in-varnum.

Langley, Paul. 2008. *The Everyday Life of Global Finance: Saving and Borrowing in Anglo-America*. New York: Oxford University Press.

Largent, Mark A. 2011. *Breeding Contempt: The History of Coerced Sterilization in the United States*. Piscataway, N.J.: Rutgers University Press.

Laver, Mimi, and Andrea Khoury. 2008. *Opening Doors for LGBTQ Youth in Foster Care: A Guide for Lawyers and Judges*. Washington, D.C.: American Bar Association.

Lee, Felicia R. 2006. "On HBO, Rosie O'Donnell's Cruise for Gay Families." *New York Times*, April 3. http://www.nytimes.com/2006/04/03/arts/television/on-hbo-rosie-odonnells-cruise-for-gay-families.html.

Lee, Tina. 2016. *Catching a Case: Inequality and Fear in New York City's Child Welfare System*. New Brunswick, N.J.: Rutgers University Press.

Lehr, Valerie. 1999. *Queer Family Values: Debunking the Myth of the Nuclear Family*. Philadelphia: Temple University Press.

Levine, Judith. 2002. *Harmful to Minors: The Perils of Protecting Children from Sex*. New York: Thunder's Month.

Lewin, Ellen. 1993. *Lesbian Mothers: Accounts of Gender in American Culture*. Ithaca, N.Y.: Cornell University Press.

———. 2009. *Gay Fatherhood: Narratives of Family and Citizenship in America*. Chicago: University of Chicago Press.

Lomawaima, K. Tsianina. 1993. "Domesticity in the Federal Indian Schools: The Power of Authority over Mind and Body." *American Ethnologist* 20 (2): 227–240.

López, Robert Oscar. 2012. "Growing Up with Two Moms: The Untold Children's View." *Public Discourse*, August 6. http://www.thepublicdiscourse.com/2012/08/6065/.

———. 2013a. "The International Gay War on Black People." *American Thinker*, August 18. http://www.americanthinker.com/articles/2013/08/the_international_gay_war_on_black_people.html.

———. 2013b. "Justice Kennedy's 40,000 Children." *Public Discourse*, May 2. http://www.thepublicdiscourse.com/2013/05/10034/.

———. 2013c. "The Late Great Left." *American Thinker*, September 13. https://www.americanthinker.com/articles/2013/09/the_late_great_left.html.

López, Robert Oscar, and Rivka Edelman. 2015. *Jephthah's Daughters: Innocent Casualties in the War for Family "Equality."* Los Angeles: CreateSpace.

Lorde, Audre. 1984. *Sister Outsider: Essays and Speeches by Audre Lorde*. Trumansburg, N.Y.: Crossing.

Lovett, Laura L. 2007. *Conceiving the Future: Pronatalism, Reproduction, and the Family in the United States, 1890–1938*. Chapel Hill: University of North Carolina Press.

Lowe, Lisa. 1996. *Immigrant Acts: On Asian American Cultural Politics*. Durham: Duke University Press.

Lubiano, Wahneema. 1992. "Black Ladies, Welfare Queens, and State Minstrels: Ideological War by Narrative Means." In *Race-ing Justice, En-gendering Power: Essays on Anita*

Hill, Clarence Thomas, and the Construction of Social Reality, edited by Toni Morrison, 323–363. New York: Pantheon.

Luibhéid, Eithne. 2002. *Entry Denied: Controlling Sexuality at the Border*. Minneapolis: University of Minnesota Press.

Lukenbill, Grant. 1995. *Untold Millions: Positioning Your Business for the Gay and Lesbian Consumer Solution*. New York: HarperCollins.

Lyle, Amaani. 2014. "AMPA Dinner Honors Gay, Lesbian Military Families." *American Forces Press Service*, May 18. http://www.defense.gov/news/newsarticle.aspx?id= 122281.

Lynch, Stefan. 2000. "I Remember Reaching for Michael's Hand." In *Out of the Ordinary: Essays on Growing Up with Gay, Lesbian, and Transgender Parents*, edited by Noelle Howey and Ellen Samuels, 63–71. New York: St. Martin's.

MacCannell, Dean. 1999. *The Tourist: A New Theory of the Leisure Class*. Berkeley: University of California Press.

Majors, Steve. 2012. "Family Equality Council Empowers 'the Outspoken Generation.'" Family Equality Council, April 6. http://www.familyequality.org/news__media/2012/ 04/06/1217/family_equality_council_empowers_the_outspoken_generation/.

Mallon, Gerald P. 1998. *We Don't Exactly Get the Welcome Wagon: The Experiences of Gay and Lesbian Adolescents in Child Welfare Systems*. New York: Columbia University Press.

Mamo, Laura, and Eli Alston-Stepnitz. 2015. "Queer Intimacies and Structural Inequalities: New Directions in Stratified Reproduction." *Journal of Family Issues* 36 (4): 519–540.

Mananzala, Rickke. 2012. "The FIERCE Fight for Power and the Preservation of Public Space in the West Village." Special issue, *A New Queer Agenda*. Edited by Joseph N. DeFilippis, Lisa Duggan, Kenyon Farrow, and Richard Kim. *Scholar and Feminist Online* 10 (1/2). http://sfonline.barnard.edu/a-new-queer-agenda/the-fierce-fight-for-power -and-the-preservation-of-public-space-in-the-west-village/.

Marron, Donncha. 2014. "'Informed, Educated, and More Confident': Financial Capability and the Problematization of Personal Finance Consumption." *Consumption Markets & Culture* 17 (5): 491–511.

Martin, April. 1993. *The Lesbian and Gay Parenting Handbook: Creating and Raising Our Families*. New York: HarperCollins.

Martin, Randy. 2002. *Financialization of Daily Life*. Philadelphia: Temple University Press.

Marvel, Stewart Donnell. 2015. "Tracking Queer Kinships: Assisted Reproduction, Family Law and the Infertility Trap." PhD thesis, Osgoode Digital Commons.

Mateik, Tara, dir. 2003. *Toilet Training*. New York: Sylvia Rivera Law Project. https://vimeo .com/85470055.

May, Elaine Tyler. 1988. *Homeward Bound: American Families in the Cold War Era*. New York: Basic Books.

McCarthy, Ed. 2015. "Winning Over Clients and Employees with Values-Based Investing." *Enterprising Investor* (blog), CFA Institute, September 15. https://blogs.cfainstitute.org/ investor/2015/09/15/the-values-proposition/.

McClintock, Anne. 1995. *Imperial Leather: Race, Gender, and Sexuality in the Colonial Contest*. New York: Routledge.

McCreery, Patrick. 2008. "Save Our Children/Let Us Marry: Gay Activists Appropriate the Rhetoric of Child Protectionism." *Radical History Review* 100:186–207.

McKinley, Jesse. 2010. "Suicides Put Light on Pressures of Gay Teenagers." *New York Times*, October 3. http://www.nytimes.com/2010/10/04/us/04suicide.html.

McRuer, Robert. 2006. *Crip Theory: Cultural Signs of Queerness and Disability*. New York: New York University Press.

Meeker, Martin. 2001. "Behind the Mask of Respectability: Reconsidering the Mattachine Society and Male Homophile Practice, 1950s and 1960s." *Journal of the History of Sexuality* 10 (1): 78–116.

Mendoza, Victor Román. 2015. *Metroimperial Intimacies: Fantasy, Racial-Sexual Governance, and the Philippines in US Imperialism, 1899–1913*. Durham: Duke University Press.

Merevick, Tony. 2014. "Big Brands' New Face Is LGBT Families." *BuzzFeed*, April 10. http://www.buzzfeed.com/tonymerevick/big-brands-new-face-is-lgbt-families.

Merry, Sally Engle. 2000. *Colonizing Hawai'i: The Cultural Power of Law*. Princeton: Princeton University Press.

Mersmann, Andrew. February 2004. "Gregg Kaminsky: R Family Vacations." *Passport Magazine*. https://web.archive.org/web/20070927134348/http://www.passportmagazine.com/21/rfamily.shtml.

Meyerowitz, Joanne J. 1988. *Women Adrift: Independent Wage Earners in Chicago, 1880–1930*. Chicago: University of Chicago Press.

Mink, Gwendolyn. 1998. *Welfare's End*. Ithaca, N.Y.: Cornell University Press.

Mogul, Joey L., Andrea J. Ritchie, and Kay Whitlock. 2011. *Queer (In)Justice: The Criminalization of LGBT People in the United States*. Boston: Beacon.

Montegary, Liz. 2011. *Queer Mobilizations: The Transnational Circuits of U.S. Lesbian and Gay Politics*. Ann Arbor: University of Michigan Press.

———. 2015a. "An Army of Debt: Financial Readiness and the Military Family." *Cultural Studies* 29 (5/6): 652–668.

———. 2015b. "Militarizing US Homonormativities: The Making of 'Ready, Willing, and Able' Gay Citizens." *Signs: Journal of Women in Culture and Society* 40 (4): 891–915.

Moore, Mignon R. 2011. *Invisible Families: Gay Identities, Relationships, and Motherhood among Black Women*. Berkeley: University of California Press.

Moraga, Cherríe. 1997. *Waiting in the Wings: Portrait of a Queer Motherhood*. Ithaca, N.Y.: Firebrand Books.

Morgan, Jennifer L. 2004. *Laboring Women: Reproduction and Gender in New World Slavery*. Philadelphia: University of Pennsylvania Press.

Morgensen, Scott Lauria. 2011. *Spaces between Us: Queer Settler Colonialism and Indigenous Decolonization*. Minneapolis: University of Minnesota Press.

Mountz, Sarah. 2011. "Revolving Doors: LGBTQ Youth at the Interface of the Child Welfare and Juvenile Justice Systems." *LGBTQ Policy Journal*. http://www.villagecounselingcenter.net/Revolving_Doors_-_LGBTQ_Youth_at_the_Interface_of_the_Child_Welfare_and_Juvenile_Justice_Systems.pdf.

Movement Advancement Project, Family Equality Council, and Center for American Progress. 2011a. *All Children Matter: How Legal and Social Inequalities Hurt LGBT Families*. October. http://www.lgbtmap.org/policy-and-issue-analysis/all-children-matter-full-report.

———. 2011b. "Issue Brief: How DOMA Harms Children." November. http://www.lgbtmap.org/policy-and-issue-analysis/issue-brief-how-doma-harms-children.

Moynihan, Daniel Patrick. 1965. *The Negro Family: The Case for National Action*. Washington, D.C.: Office of Planning and Research, U.S. Department of Labor.

Mulvihill, Geoff, and Katie Zezima. 2013. "Some N.J. Gay Couples Plan Weddings, Others Still Denied Marriage Licenses." Associated Press, October 20. http://www.lgbtqnation.com/2013/10/some-n-j-gay-couples-plan-weddings-others-still-denied-marriage-licenses/.

Mumford, Kevin J. 1997. *Interzones: Black/White Sex Districts in Chicago and New York in the Early Twentieth Century*. New York: Columbia University Press.

———. 2012. "Untangling Pathology: The Moynihan Report and Homosexual Damage, 1965–75." *Journal of Policy History* 24 (1): 53–73.

Muñoz, José Esteban. 2009. *Cruising Utopia: The Then and There of Queer Futurity*. New York: New York University Press.

National Organization for Marriage. 2009. *National Strategy for Winning the Marriage Battle*, August 11. Washington, D.C.: National Organization for Marriage.

———. n.d. "Board Update 2008–2009." Deposition Exhibit 25. *National Organization for Marriage, Inc. v. McKee*. Civil No. 09-538-B.H. U.S. District Court, Maine.

New York Times. 1992. "The 1992 Campaign: Excerpts from Interview with President Bush on First Term and Future." June 25. http://www.nytimes.com/1992/06/25/us/1992-campaign-excerpts-interview-with-president-bush-first-term-future.html.

Nichols, James Michael. 2016. "This Incredible Place Helps LGBT Foster Kids When There's Nowhere Else to Turn." *Huffington Post*, January 1. http://www.huffingtonpost.com/entry/this-incredible-place-helps-lgbt-foster-kids-when-theres-nowhere-else-to-turn_us _56817433e4b0b958f659f7c5.

Nyong'o, Tavia. 2010. "School Daze." *Bully Bloggers*, September 30. https://bullybloggers.wordpress.com/2010/09/30/school-daze/.

Oakes, Bob, and Lisa Tobin. 2010. "Provincetown High School Closes Its Doors—for Now." WBUR, June 11. http://www.wbur.org/2010/06/11/provincetown-high-school.

Obergefell v. Hodges. 2015. 576 U.S. ___. Nos. 14-556, 14-562, 14-571, and 14-574. Supreme Court.

O'Brien, Jean M. 2010. *Firsting and Lasting: Writing Indians Out of Existence in New England*. Minneapolis: University of Minnesota Press.

Office of Adolescent Health. 2014. *HHS Office of Adolescent's Teen Pregnancy Prevention Program*. Department of Health and Human Services, September. https://www.hhs.gov/ash/oah/sites/default/files/tpp-overview-brochure.pdf.

Office of Disease Prevention and Health Promotion. 2010. "Healthy People 2020." Department of Health and Human Services. https://www.healthypeople.gov/.

Office of Planning, Research and Evaluation. 2015. "Same-Sex Relationships: Updates to Healthy Marriage and Relationship Programming (SUHMRE), 2015–18." Administration for Children and Families (Department of Health and Human Services). https://www.acf.hhs.gov/opre/same-sex-relationships-updates-to-healthy-marriage-and-relationship-education-programming-suhmre-2015-2016.

O'Leary, Josh. 2010. "One Family's Journey to Marriage Equality in Iowa." *The Family Room* (blog), January 6. http://www.familyequality.org/equal_family_blog/2010/01/06/890/one_familys_journey_to_marriage_equality_in_iowa.

Omi, Michael, and Howard Winant. 1994. *Racial Formation in the United States: From the 1960s to the 1990s*. New York: Routledge.

Onwuachi-Willig, Angela. 2005. "The Return of the Ring: Welfare Reform's Marriage Cure as the Revival of Post-Bellum Control." *California Law Review* 93 (6): 1647–1696.

Ordover, Nancy. 2003. *American Eugenics: Race, Queer Anatomy, and the Science of Nationalism*. Minneapolis: University of Minnesota Press.

Palevsky, Stacey. 2010. "Family Values Redefined: Children of Same-Sex Parents Enter the Battle for Marriage Equality." *JWeekly*, March 4. http://www.jweekly.com/article/full/41529/family-values-redefined-children-of-same-sex-parents-enter-the-battle-for-m/.

Pascoe, Peggy. 2009. *What Comes Naturally: Miscegenation Law and the Making of Race in America*. New York: Oxford University Press.

Pattullo, E. L. 1992. "Straight Talk about Gays." *Commentary*, December 1. https://www.commentarymagazine.com/articles/straight-talk-about-gays/.

Pattullo, Polly. 2010. "Sailing into the Sunset: The Cruise-Ship Industry." In *Tourists and Tourism: A Reader*, 2nd. ed., edited by Sharon Bohn Gmelch, 399–418. Long Grove, Ill.: Waveland.

Pease, Donald E. 2014. "Exceptionalism." In *Keywords for American Cultural Studies*, edited by Bruce Burgett and Glenn Hendler. New York: New York University Press. http://keywords.nyupress.org/american-cultural-studies/essay/exceptionalism/.

Peiss, Kathy. 1986. *Cheap Amusements: Working Women and Leisure in the Turn-of-the-Century New York*. Philadelphia: Temple University Press.

Perry, Twila L. 1998. "Transracial and International Adoption: Mothers, Hierarchy, Race, and Feminist Legal Theory." *Yale Journal of Law and Feminism* 10 (1): 101–164.

Personal Responsibility and Work Opportunity Reconciliation Act. 1996. Pub. L. No. 104-193, 110 Stat. 2105–2355 (42 U.S. Code 1305).

Pinsker, Beth. 2015. "Same-Sex Couples Face the Music: First Comes Love, Then Taxes." Reuters, June 26. http://www.reuters.com/article/us-usa-court-gaymarriage-estate-idUSKBN0P62K520150626.

Piven, Frances Fox, and Richard A. Cloward. 1993. *Regulating the Poor: The Functions of Public Welfare*. New York: Vintage Books.

PlanetOut. 2006. "Q and A with Rosie and Kelli on 'All Aboard! Rosie's Family Cruise.'" https://web.archive.org/web/20071014182017/http://planetout.com/entertainment/news/?sernum=1227.

Polikoff, Nancy D. 1999. "The Limits of Visibility: Queer Parenting under Fire: A History of Legal Battles." *Gay Community News* 24 (3/4): 38–48.

———. 2008. *Beyond (Straight and Gay) Marriage: Valuing All Families under the Law*. Boston: Beacon.

———. 2013. "Rhetoric Matters . . . and This Is What's Wrong with Obama's." *Beyond (Straight and Gay) Marriage* (blog), February 22. http://beyondstraightandgaymarriage.blogspot.com/2013/02/rhetoric-mattersand-this-is-whats-wrong.html.

Pratt, Minnie Bruce. 2013. *Crime against Nature*. Berkeley, Calif.: Sinister Wisdom.

Pressley, Sue, and Nancy Andrews. 1992. "For Gay Couples, the Nursery Becomes the New Frontier." *Washington Post*, December 20. https://www.washingtonpost.com/archive/politics/1992/12/20/for-gay-couples-the-nursery-becomes-the-new-frontier/3dfdf84d-0fa3-4f72-90d1-f5222b5b6e2a/?utm_term=.47380707bbe5.

Prudential. 2016. *The LGBT Financial Experience, 2016–2017*. http://corporate.prudential.com/media/managed/PrudentialLGBT2016-2017.pdf.

Puar, Jasbir K. 2002a. "Circuits of Queer Mobility: Tourism, Travel, and Globalization." *GLQ: A Journal of Lesbian and Gay Studies* 8 (1/2): 101–137.

———. 2002b. "A Transnational Feminist Critique of Queer Tourism." *Antipode* 34 (5): 935–946.

———. "Mapping US Homonormativities." *Gender, Place, and Culture* 13 (1): 67–88.

———. 2007. *Terrorist Assemblages: Homonationalism in Queer Times*. Durham: Duke University Press.

———. 2010. "In the Wake of It Gets Better." *Guardian*, November 16. http://www.theguardian.com/commentisfree/cifamerica/2010/nov/16/wake-it-gets-better-campaign.

———. 2013. "Homonationalism as Assemblage: Viral Travels, Affective Sexualities." *Jindal Global Law Review* 4 (2): 23–43.

Quittner, Jeremy. 2010. "Wealth Matters." *Advocate*, April.

Reddy, Chandan. 2011. *Freedom with Violence: Race, Sexuality, and the US State*. Durham: Duke University Press.

Redman, Laura F. 2010. "Outing the Invisible Poor: Why Economic Justice and Access to Health Care Is an LGBT Issue." *Georgetown Journal on Poverty Law and Policy* 17 (3): 451–459.

————. 2011. "Afterword: Outing the Invisible Poor; Why Economic Justice and Access to Health Care Is an LGBT Issue." Special issue, *A New Queer Agenda*. Edited by Joseph N. DeFilippis, Lisa Duggan, Kenyon Farrow, and Richard Kim. *Scholar and Feminist Online* 10 (1/2). http://sfonline.barnard.edu/a-new-queer-agenda/outing-the-invisible-poor -why-economic-justice-and-access-to-health-care-is-an-lgbt-issue/.

Regnerus, Mark. 2012. "New Family Structures Study." http://www.familystructurestudies .com/.

Richman, Kimberly. 2009. *Courting Change: Queer Parents, Judges, and the Transformation of American Family Law*. New York: New York University Press.

Richter, Ronald, Alison Harte, Linda Diaz, Kimberly Forte, Ronnie Fuchs, Susan Hazeldean, Selena Higgins, Michael Katch, Liz Roberts, Karey Scheyd, Joan Siegel, Traci Shina- barger, and Mirian Young. 2006. *Proposed Strategic Plan to Improve Services to LGBTQQ Youth at the New York City Administration for Children's Services*. Administration for Children's Services, February. http://www1.nyc.gov/assets/acs/pdf/lgbtq/acs_lgbtqq _strategic_plan_2006.pdf.

Rifkin, Mark. 2011. *When Did Indians Become Straight? Kinship, the History of Sexuality, and Native Sovereignty*. New York: Oxford University Press.

————. 2013. "Settler Common Sense." *Settler Colonial Studies* 3 (3/4): 322–340.

Rivers, Daniel Winunwe. 2013. *Radical Relations: Lesbian Mothers, Gay Fathers, and Their Children in the United States since World War II*. Chapel Hill: University of North Carolina Press.

Robaton, Anna. 1999. "Gay, Lesbian Investors a Much-Ignored Market." *Investment News*, October 11.

Roberts, Dorothy E. 1996. "Welfare and the Problem of Black Citizenship." *Yale Law Journal* 105:1563–1602.

————. 1997. *Killing the Black Body: Race, Reproduction, and the Meaning of Liberty*. New York: Vintage Books.

————. 2002. *Shattered Bonds: The Color of Child Welfare*. New York: Basic Civitas Books.

————. 2009. "Race, Gender, and Genetic Technologies: A New Reproductive Dystopia?" *Signs: Journal of Women in Culture and Society* 34 (4): 783–804.

Rodríguez, Juana María. 2014. *Sexual Futures, Queer Gestures, and Other Latina Longings*. New York: New York University Press.

Romesburg, Don. 2014. "Where She Comes From: Locating Queer Transracial Adoption." *QED: A Journal in GLBTQ Worldmaking* 1 (3): 1–29.

Rosado, Justin Anton. 2008. "Corroding Our Quality of Life." In *That's Revolting! Queer Strategies for Resisting Assimilation*, edited by Mattilda Bernstein Sycamore, 317–328. Berkeley, Calif.: Soft Skull.

Rose, Nikolas. 2007. *The Politics of Life Itself: Biomedicine, Power, and Subjectivity in the Twenty-First Century*. Princeton: Princeton University Press.

Rose, Scott. 2012. "NOM, Regnerus and Robert Oscar Lopez." New Civil Rights Movement, August 9. http://www.thenewcivilrightsmovement.com/1-nom-regnerus-and-robert -oscar-lopez/politics/2012/08/09/45882.

Rubin, Gayle S. (Interview by Judith Butler). 2011. "Sexual Traffic." In *Deviations: A Gayle Rubin Reader*, 276–309. Durham: Duke University Press.

Saewyc, Elizabeth M., Linda H. Bearinger, Robert Wm. Blum, and Michael D. Resnick. 1999. "Sexual Intercourse, Abuse, and Pregnancy among Adolescent Women: Does Sexual Orientation Make a Difference?" *Family Planning Perspectives* 31 (3): 127–131.

Saewyc, Elizabeth M., Colleen S. Poon, Yuko Homma, and Carol L. Skay. 2008. "Stigma Management? The Links between Enacted Stigma and Teen Pregnancy Trends among

Gay, Lesbian, and Bisexual Students in British Columbia." *Canadian Journal of Human Sexuality* 17 (3): 123–139.

Salvato, Ed. 2004. "R Family Vacations Plies Uncharted Gay Waters." *PlanetOut*. https://web.archive.org/web/20041230165853/http://www.planetout.com/travel/article.html?sernum=9101.

Samuels, Ellen. 2014. *Fantasies of Identification: Disability, Gender, Race*. New York: New York University Press.

Schulman, Sarah. 1998. "The Making of a Market Niche." *Harvard Gay and Lesbian Review* 5 (1): 17–20.

Sears, James T. 2006. *Behind the Mask of the Mattachine: The Hal Call Chronicles and the Early Movement for Homosexual Emancipation*. New York: Harrington Park.

Sedgwick, Eve. 1991. "How to Bring Your Kids Up Gay." *Social Text* 29 (1991): 18–27.

Sender, Katherine. 2004. *Business, Not Politics: The Making of the Gay Market*. New York: Columbia University Press.

Shah, Nayan. 2001. *Contagious Divides: Epidemics and Race in San Francisco's Chinatown*. Berkeley: University of California Press.

———. 2011. *Stranger Intimacy: Contesting Race, Sexuality, and the Law in the North American West*. Berkeley: University of California Press.

Shapiro, Lila. 2015. "How a New England Beach Town Changed the Course of Gay History." *Huffington Post*, August 3. http://www.huffingtonpost.com/entry/provincetown-family-week-gay-rights_us_55bf755de4b06363d5a2a77f.

Sheller, Mimi. 2004. "Demobilizing and Remobilizing Caribbean Paradise." In *Tourism Mobilities: Places to Play, Places in Play*, edited by Mimi Sheller and John Urry, 13–21. New York: Routledge.

Shick, Denise, and Jerry Gramckow. 2008. *My Daddy's Secret*. Maitland, Fla.: Xulon.

Shonkwiler, Alison. 2008. "The Selfish-Enough Father: Gay Adoption and the Late-Capitalist Family." *GLQ: A Journal of Lesbian and Gay Studies* 14 (4): 537–567.

SIECUS (Sexuality Information and Education Council of the United States). n.d. "A History of Federal Funding for Abstinence-Only-Until-Marriage Programs." http://www.siecus.org/index.cfm?fuseaction=page.viewpage&pageid=1340&nodeid=1.

Silag, Phoebe G. 2003. "To Have, to Hold, to Receive Public Assistance: TANF Marriage-Promotion Policies." *Journal of Gender, Race, and Justice* 7:413–438.

Skinner, Liz. 2014. "As Gay Rights Expand, So Does the Need for Advice." *Investment News*, June 30.

Smith, Andrea. 2005. *Conquest: Sexual Violence and American Indian Genocide*. Cambridge, Mass.: South End.

———. 2010. "Queer Theory and Native Studies: The Heteronormativity of Settler Colonialism." *GLQ: A Journal of Lesbian and Gay Studies* 16 (1/2): 41–68.

Smith, Anna Marie. 2001. "The Politicization of Marriage in Contemporary American Public Policy: The Defense of Marriage Act and the Personal Responsibility Act." *Citizenship Studies* 5 (3): 303–320.

———. 2007. *Welfare Reform and Sexual Regulation*. New York: Cambridge University Press.

———. 2009. "Reproductive Technology, Family Law, and the Postwelfare State: The California Same-Sex Parents' Rights 'Victories' of 2005." *Signs: Journal of Women in Culture and Society* 34 (4): 827–850.

Smith, Barbara. 1997. "Where Has Gay Liberation Gone? An Interview with Barbara Smith." In *Homo Economics: Capitalism, Community, and Lesbian and Gay Life*, edited by Amy Gluckman and Betsy Reed, 195–207. New York: Routledge.

Smith, Nadine. 2012. "Gay Married Couples Are Refusing to Lie." *Huffington Post*, February 7. http://www.huffingtonpost.com/nadine-smith/gay-couples-taxes-refuse-to-lie_b_1254807.html.

Somerville, Siobhan B. 2000. *Queering the Color Line: Race and the Invention of Homosexuality in American Culture*. Durham: Duke University Press.

Sowers, Pru. 2008. "Shop Owners Grouse about Family Week." *Provincetown Banner*, August 9. http://capecod.wickedlocal.com/x1005608948/Shop-owners-grouse-about-Family-Week.

Spade, Dean. 2011. *Normal Life: Administrative Violence, Critical Trans Politics, and the Limits of the Law*. Brooklyn: South End.

Spillers, Hortense J. 1987. "Mama's Baby, Papa's Maybe: An American Grammar Book." *Diacritics* 17 (2): 64–81.

Sprayberry, Trisha Lynn. 2015. "Love Wins! What's Next for Marriage Equality?" *Huffington Post*, June 29. http://www.huffingtonpost.com/trisha-lynn-sprayberry/love-wins-whats_b_7679884.html.

Stacey, Judith. 1996. *In the Name of the Family: Rethinking Family Values in the Postmodern Age*. Boston: Beacon.

Stacey, Judith, and Timothy Biblarz. 2001. "(How) Does the Sexual Orientation of Parents Matter?" *American Sociological Review* 66 (2): 159–183.

Stefanowicz, Dawn. 2007. *Out from Under: The Impact of Homosexual Parenting*. Enumclaw, Wash.: Annotation.

Stein, Marc. 2000. *City of Sisterly and Brotherly Loves: Lesbian and Gay Philadelphia, 1945–72*. Chicago: University of Chicago Press.

Stewart, Katherine. 2012. "How Obama's Healthcare Reform Boosted Abstinence-Only Sex Education." *Guardian*, August 12. https://www.theguardian.com/commentisfree/2012/aug/15/obama-healthcare-reform-boosted-abstinence-only-sex-education.

Stockton, Kathryn Bond. 2009. *The Queer Child, or Growing Sideways in the Twentieth Century*. Durham: Duke University Press.

Stockwell, Anne. 2006. "Ro, Ro, Ro Their Boat." *Advocate*, March 28.

Stoddard, Thomas B. 1989. "Gay Adults Should Not Be Denied the Benefits of Marriage." *Minneapolis Star-Tribune*, March 7.

———. 1998. "Why Gay People Should Seek the Right to Marry." *Families in the U.S.: Kinship and Domestic Politics*, edited by Karen V. Hansen and Anita Ilta Garey, 475–479. Philadelphia: Temple University Press.

Stoler, Ann Laura. 1995. *Race and the Education of Desire: Foucault's History of Sexuality and the Colonial Order of Things*. Durham: Duke University Press.

Sullivan, Andrew. 1989. "Here Comes the Groom: A (Conservative) Case for Gay Marriage." *New Republic*, August 28. https://newrepublic.com/article/79054/here-comes-the-groom.

Sullivan, Colleen, Susan Sommer, and Jason Moff. 2001. *Youth in the Margins: A Report on the Unmet Needs of Lesbian, Gay, Bisexual, and Transgender Adolescents in Foster Care*. Lambda Legal Defense and Education Fund. http://www.lambdalegal.org/publications/youth-in-the-margins.

Sundquist, Karen. 1995. "The Family: Resources for Parents and Kids." *In the Family* 1 (2): 26.

Taliaferro, Lanning. 2016. "Nyack Businesswoman to Receive Award from LGBT Senior Group." *Nyack Patch*, October 6. http://patch.com/new-york/nyack/nyack-businesswoman-receive-award-lgbt-senior-group.

Taormino, Tristan. 2000. "My Father's Eyes." In *Out of the Ordinary: Essays on Growing Up with Gay, Lesbian, and Transgender Parents*, edited by Noelle Howey and Ellen Samuels, 15–23. New York: St. Martin's.

Terry, Jennifer. 1999. *An American Obsession: Science, Medicine, and Homosexuality in Modern Society*. Chicago: University of Chicago Press.

Terry, William C. 2017. "Flags of Convenience and the Global Cruise Labour Market." In *Cruise Ship Tourism*, 2nd ed., edited by Ross Dowling and Clare Weeden, 72–85. Cambridge, Mass.: CAB International.

Thompson, Annabel. 2017. "TX Governor Signs Bill Allowing Providers to Deny LGBTQ Youth Child Welfare Services." *ThinkProgress*, June 16. https://thinkprogress.org/texas -governor-signs-religious-freedom-lgbtq-youth-discrimination-bill-749cf6b94ec0.

Thompson, Karen, and Julie Andrzejewski. 1988. *Why Can't Sharon Kowalski Come Home?* San Francisco: Aunt Lute Books.

Tornello, Samantha L., Rachel G. Riskind, and Charlotte J. Patterson. 2014. "Sexual Orientation and Sexual and Reproductive Health among Adolescent Young Women in the United States." *Journal of Adolescent Health* 54 (2): 160–168.

Trenka, Jane Jeong. 2009. "Transnational Adoption and the 'Financialization of Everything.'" *Conducive Magazine*, August/September.

Tuck, Eve, and K. Wayne Yang. 2012. "Decolonization Is Not a Metaphor." *Decolonization: Indigeneity, Education & Society* 1 (1): 1–40.

Tuller, David. 1988. "Some Gay Businesses Suffer, Others Thrive in Era of AIDS." *Newsday*, New York ed., May 2.

24-7 Press Release. 2012. "Fertility Planit Launches First Consumer Tradeshow of Its Kind in USA!" August 24. http://www.24-7pressrelease.com/press-release/fertility-planit-launches -first-consumer-tradeshow-of-its-kind-in-usa-to-be-held-january-2013-at-hyatt-century-plaza -in-la-top-sponsors-include-ferring-cryobank-and-las-top-fertility-doctors-299708.php.

United States v. Windsor. 2013. 570 U.S. ___. No. 12-307. Supreme Court.

U.S. Congress. 1996. *Defense of Marriage Act: Report*. House Committee on the Judiciary. 104th Cong., 2nd sess., July 9. H.R. Rep. 104-664. https://www.gpo.gov/fdsys/pkg/ CRPT-104hrpt664/html/CRPT-104hrpt664.htm.

U.S. Congressional Budget Office. 2004. *The Potential Budgetary Impact of Recognizing Same-Sex Marriages*, June 21. https://www.cbo.gov/sites/default/files/108th-congress -2003-2004/reports/06-21-samesexmarriage.pdf.

U.S. General Accounting Office. 1997. GAO/OGC-97-16. *Defense of Marriage Act*, January 31. http://www.gao.gov/assets/230/223674.pdf.

———. 2004. GAO-04-353R. Defense of Marriage Act—Update to Prior Report, January 24. http://www.gao.gov/assets/100/92441.pdf.

U.S. Government Accountability Office. 2006. *Abstinence Education: Efforts to Assess the Accuracy and Effectiveness of Federally Funded Programs*. Report to Congressional Requesters, October. https://www.gao.gov/assets/260/252287.pdf.

U.S. House of Representatives. 2004. *The Content of Federally Funded Abstinence-Only Education Programs*. Committee on Government Reform—Minority Staff, December. http://spot.colorado.edu/~tooley/HenryWaxman.pdf.

Vaid, Urvashi. 1995. *Virtual Equality: The Mainstreaming of Gay and Lesbian Liberation*. New York: Anchor.

Varnum v. Brien. 2009. 763 N.W.2d 862. State of Iowa.

Wahls, Zach (with Bruce Littlefield). 2012. *My Two Moms: Lessons of Love, Strength, and What Makes a Family*. New York: Gotham Books.

Waitt, Gordon, and Kevin Markwell. 2006. *Gay Tourism: Culture and Context*. Binghamton, N.Y.: Haworth.

Warner, Michael. 1999. *The Trouble with Normal: Sex, Politics, and the Ethics of Queer Life*. New York: Free Press.

Weaver, Adam. 2011. "Tourism and the Military: Pleasure and the War Economy." *Annals of Tourism Research* 38 (2): 672–689.

Weekly Observer. 1992. "If We Don't Protect Our Families, Who Will?" October 7.

Weissman, Rachel X. 1999. "Gay Market Power." *Advertising Age*, June 1. http://adage.com/article/american-demographics/gay-market-power/43097/.

Wells Fargo. 2016. "LGBT Americans Optimistic about Planning for the Future, Says Wells Fargo Survey." July 13. https://www.wellsfargo.com/about/press/2016/lgbt-americans -optimistic_0712/.

Weston, Kath. 1991. *Families We Choose: Lesbians, Gays, Kinship.* New York: Columbia University Press.

Wetherbe, Jamie. 2008. "Attracting 'Out' Travelers." *Travel Age West*, May 12.

White, Martha C. 2014. "Sign of the Times: Greeting Cards for Kids with Gay Moms." *Today*, May 6. https://www.today.com/parents/sign-times-greeting-cards-kids-gay-moms -2D79619955.

Wiedeman, Reeves. 2012. "Tax Day." *New Yorker*, April 23. http://www.newyorker.com/magazine/2012/04/23/tax-day.

Wilber, Shannan, Carolyn Reyes, and Jody Marksamer. 2006. *The Model Standards Project: Creating Inclusive Systems for LGBT Youth in Out-of-Home Care.* Legal Services for Children; National Center for Lesbian Rights, June. http://www.nclrights.org/wp-content/uploads/2013/07/Model_Standards_Project_article.pdf.

Wildman, Sarah. 2010a. "Children Speak for Same-Sex Marriage." *New York Times*, January 20. http://www.nytimes.com/2010/01/21/fashion/21kids.html.

———. 2010b. "Gay Marriage's Biggest Supporters: Children of Gay Parents." *Politics Daily*, August 12. https://web.archive.org/web/20100815083845/http://www.politicsdaily.com/2010/08/12/gay-marriages-biggest-supporters-children-of-gay-parents.

Williams, Jeannie. 2002. "Rosie, Coy on TV, 'Comes Out' on Stage." *USA Today*, February 27. https://usatoday30.usatoday.com/life/enter/tv/2002/2002-02-27-rosie .htm.

Williams, Patricia J. 1997. "Spare Parts, Family Values, Old Children, Cheap." In *Critical Race Feminism: A Reader*, edited by Adrien Katherine Wing, 151–158. New York: New York University Press.

Willse, Craig, and Dean Spade. 2005. "Freedom in a Regulatory State? *Lawrence*, Marriage and Biopolitics." *Widener Law Review* 11:309–329.

Wilson, Bianca D. M., Khush Cooper, Angeliki Kastanis, and Sheila Nezhad. 2014. *Sexual and Gender Minority Youth in Foster Care: Assessing Disproportionality and Disparities in Los Angeles.* Los Angeles: Williams Institute.

Wilson, James Q. 2002. *The Marriage Problem: How Our Culture Has Weakened Families.* New York: HarperCollins.

Wong, Curtis M. 2014. "Hallmark Releases Gay Father's Day Ecard." *Huffington Post*, June 12. https://www.huffingtonpost.com/2014/06/12/hallmark-gay-fathers-day-_n _5489213.html.

Woog, Dan. 1999. *Friends and Family: True Stories of Gay America's Straight Allies.* Los Angeles: Alyson Books.

Yu, Wendy. 2000. "Profs Fight in Vt. Civil Union Debate." *Dartmouth*, April 6. http://www .thedartmouth.com/article/2000/04/profs-fight-in-vt-civil-union-debate/.

Zepatos, Thalia, and Lanae Erickson Hatalsky. 2015. "The Marriage Movement's Secret Weapon: Radical Cooperation." *Huffington Post*, June 26. http://www.huffingtonpost .com/thalia-zepatos/the-marriage-movements-se_b_7665696.html.

Zief, Susan, Rachel Shapiro, and Debra Strong. 2013. *The Personal Responsibility Education Program (PREP): Launching a Nationwide Adolescent Pregnancy Prevention Effort.* Princeton: Mathematica Policy Research; Washington, D.C.: Office of Planning, Research, and Evaluation (Administration for Children and Families). https://www.acf.hhs.gov/sites/default/files/opre/prep_eval_design_survey_report_102213.pdf.

Zinn, Howard, and Anthony Arnove. 2009. *Voices of a People's History of the United States.* 2nd ed. New York: Seven Stories.

Index

ableism, 4, 12, 15, 17–18, 150, 169, 175. *See also* eugenics

Adolescent Family Life Act (AFLA), 170–171, 216n52

Adolescent Pregnancy Prevention (APP) program, 171–172

adoption, 50, 163, 199n13, 203n5, 213n32; Adoption and Safe Families Act (ASFA), 74–75; Adoption Assistance and Child Welfare Act, 199n13; adoption law, 24, 41, 46, 51, 66, 72, 81, 132, 208n40; bans on lesbian and gay adoption, 24, 41, 46, 51, 66, 72, 132, 208n40; fostering to adopt, 65, 132, 149, 151, 191n15; LGBT families and, 6–7, 25, 35, 43, 64, 67, 81, 85, 102, 131, 133–134, 149, 201n23, 202n32, 205n13, 208n43, 208n44; racialized, 65, 73–76, 78, 87, 95, 110, 123, 150, 188n5, 191n15, 194n2, 199nn13–14, 200nn15–16, 200n19, 208n41, 210n11, 212n23; second-parent, 131, 155

Affordable Care Act (ACA), 164–165, 171–172, 214n42

Ahmed, Sara, 56, 207n36

Aid to Families with Dependent Children (AFDC), 167, 170. *See also* Temporary Assistance for Needy Families (TANF)

Alexander, M. Jacqui, 78, 200n18, 209n8

Alyson Adventures, 84

American Civil Liberties Union (ACLU), 212n27, 213n30; Lesbian and Gay Rights Project, 147, 203n3

American Express, 144–145

Anagnost, Ann, 64, 66, 202n32

antidiscrimination law, 50, 74, 81, 133, 139, 144

antimiscegenation law, 12, 192n25

assimilation, 4, 6, 12–13, 31, 41, 48–49, 85, 121, 158, 161, 188n4

Atheneum Society, 34–35

Atlantis Events, 66, 69–70, 76

Badgett, M. V. Lee, 69, 71, 141, 145, 198, 209n6

Baehr v. Miike, 105–106

Bahamas, 67, 76–79, 200n18

Baker v. Vermont, 205n15

BarbouRoske, McKinley, 110–111, 117

Barwick, Heather, 121–122, 126–127

berdache, 34, 195n8

Bergman, Kim, 86–88, 149, 211n19

Berkery, Peter M., Jr., 146–147

Berlant, Lauren, 64–65, 89, 197n24, 202n32, 217n5

Bersani, Leo, 188n4

Bérubé, Allan, 21, 33

Biblarz, Timothy, 129, 207n37

biopolitics, 9–10, 191n18

Blankenhorn, David, 216n50

Blau, Gabriel, 133

Boggis, Terry, 94–96, 126, 176, 202n36, 210n14, 216n57

Bonauto, Mary, 204n12

Bottoms, Sharon, 51, 197n25

About the Author

LIZ MONTEGARY is an assistant professor in the Department of Women's, Gender, and Sexuality Studies at Stony Brook University. She is the coeditor of *Mobile Desires: The Politics and Erotics of Mobility Justice*.